TERRITORIAL GOVERNANCE AND ENVIRONMENTAL PROTECTION

VOLUME 1: URBAN SPRAWL AND SUSTAINABLE URBANIZATION

RUŞEN KELEŞ

CAPPADOCIA
UNIVERSITY

2022

Cappadocia University Press: 49
Politics Book Series: 12
ISBN: 978-605-4448-29-6

© August 2022

Territorial Governance and Environmental Protection
Volume 1: Urban Sprawl and Sustainable Urbanization
Ruşen Keleş

© Copyright, 2022, CAPPADOCIA UNIVERSITY PRESS
Certificate No: 43348

Series Editor: Halil Burak Sakal
Book Editors: Hikmet Kuran & Berk İlke Dündar
Preparation: Sümeyra Demiralp
Cover Design: Nazile Arda Çakır
Page Design: ademşenel.com
Printing and Binding: Bizim Buro (Certificate No: 42488)

Keleş, R. (2022). *Territorial Governance and Environmental Protection: Volume 1: Urban Sprawl and Sustainable Urbanization*. Eds. Hikmet Kuran and Berk İlke Dündar. Nevşehir: Cappadocia University Press.
525 p, 13,5 x 21 cm.
ISBN: 978-605-4448-29-6
Keywords: 1. Environmental politics, 2. Urbanization, 3. Governance, 4. Urban sprawl, 5. Turkey.

CAPPADOCIA
UNIVERSITY

50420 Mustafapaşa, Ürgüp, Nevşehir
yayinevi@kapadokya.edu.tr
kapadokyayayinlari.kapadokya.edu.tr
0(384) 353 5009
www.kapadokya.edu.tr

TERRITORIAL GOVERNANCE AND ENVIRONMENTAL PROTECTION

VOLUME 1: URBAN SPRAWL AND SUSTAINABLE URBANIZATION

RUŞEN KELEŞ

CAPPADOCIA
UNIVERSITY

2022

Contents

PART II

SUSTAINABLE URBANIZATION

Foreword

We are very happy to be presenting this collection of articles penned by Prof. Dr. Ruşen Keleş, who we are proud to have on the staff of Cappadocia University. The fact that the author has never before published articles in English on the topics of urban, environment and local government increases the importance of this book.

The book, published by Cappadocia University Press, is a compilation of papers presented by Professor Keleş at international conferences, symposia and panels attended between 1993 and 2021, and is presented in two volumes (entitled *Urban Sprawl and Sustainable Urbanization and Writings on Urban and Environment*), with texts on urban, environmental and local government, being the author's areas of expertise.

We believe this publication will serve as a rich resource for academicians and students working in the aforementioned academic fields given the many theoretical and practical reviews it makes of several key topics. I would like to thank all of our colleagues, especially Prof. Dr. Ruşen Keleş, for contributing to the preparation and publication of this collection of works.

Prof. Dr. Hasan Ali Karasar
Rector, Cappadocia University

Editors' Note

Territorial Governance and Environmental Protection is a compilation of papers by Prof. Dr. Ruşen Keleş presented and/or published at several international conferences, symposiums and panels between 1993 and 2021. The two volumes include substantial texts on Urban, Environmental and Local Government – areas in which Prof. Dr. Ruşen Keleş is considered an epochal figure. The papers have been categorized into main themes and placed under subheadings selected by us, and all of the papers in these two volumes are presented in their original presented/published versions. Considering the relative dearth of literature on urban, environmental and local government published in English, we humbly believe that these volumes can fill a noteworthy void and be of considerable benefit to researchers, academicians, students and authorities alike. We would like to thank Cappadocia University Press for their thorough efforts leading up to the publication of these works.

Editors
Hikmet Kuran and Berk İlke Dündar
Cappadocia, May, 2022.

Introductory Remarks

This book, entitled Territorial Governance and Environmental Protection in the Light of Legal and Ethical Considerations, is a collection of my writings from over the last 30 years. Some of the articles have already been published in international journals, while others have been presented at international meetings convened all over the world, including World Habitat Conferences. The book also contains the papers and reports submitted to the Congress of Local and Regional Authorities of the Council of Europe, in my capacity as a member of the Group of Independent Experts in charge of monitoring the implementation of the European Charter of Local Self-Government in the 1993–2021 period.

I believe that the topics dealt with in all these articles and papers can contribute to a better understanding of some of the socio-political and administrative issues that are still being debated extensively in our everyday life. At the same time, they may serve as a useful source for public servants and students concerned with such topics as territorial governance, sustainable development and legal and ethical rules in Public Administration.

I would like to take this opportunity to thank my close colleagues in the Cappadocia University Department of Local

Government, Urbanization and Environment who kindly gave their support to the publication of these two volumes. Dr. Hikmet Kuran, Berk İlke Dündar and Sümeyra Demiralp must be particularly mentioned in this respect. I must also mention our distinguished Rector, Prof. Dr. Hasan Ali Karasar, and express my gratitude for his kind suggestion that these volumes be published for inclusion among the Cappadocia University publications.

Prof. Dr. Ruşen Keleş
May 2022, Mustafapaşa, Ürgüp
Nevşehir

PART I

URBAN SPRAWL

Urban Sprawl and Its Implications for Sustainable Development[*]

Introduction: Planned Growth

Rural to urban migration and urban sprawl have been the most important phenomena fur sustainable use of natural resources, and particularly for fertile agricultural land. During the process of urbanization several interrelated changes take place in the use of landed property. Businesses expand or decline according to the general macro-economic conditions. Buildings vacated by one occupant may be adopted for use by new occupants, or they may be demolished, and replaced by different structures.

It is the function of the land market to bring about the adjustment necessitated by the urban growth or decline of urban activities and populations. If the urban growth brings an increase in demand for residential accommodation (houses, dwellings), housing prices rise in the short run. If the price rise is sufficiently great, construction firms will be able to earn huge amount of profits. This of course would encourage an increase in the supply of houses as vacant land is

---

[*]   International Conference on New Perspectives in Eco-Technology and Eco-Economy 10-12 May 2010, Yıldız Technical University Auditorium, Beşiktaş, İstanbul.

converted to residential use and certain sites are redeveloped for residential use.

Urban growth takes place either in a planned manner or spontaneously. The choice of urban areas as local or regional administrative centers through political decisions as in the cases of Ankara, Brasilia, Canberra or Islamabad, that can promote the growth of the favored urban areas.

Elimination of Inequalities requires planned intervention. Because growth does not affect all urban areas equally. While some area will be increasing faster than the others, some may be declining. Urban growth and structure are affected by changes in the economic base of an urban area, such as basic industries, exports, etc. Normally, urban growth proceeds centrifugally (horizontally) along major transport routes. This leaves the core of the city as the oldest part of the urban area. Growth of an urban area is not a continuous process. There are ups and downs in this process. It is consisted of a succession of jumps which may be related to the indivisibility of certain basic investments in infrastructure that is essential for growth (Goodall, 1972, pp. 185/187).

Expansion of cities occurs in two opposing directions: Vertically and horizontally. The cost factor, in other words, economic rationality is determining the extent of both under normal conditions.

Patterns of Unplanned Growth

Sometimes, particularly in societies and times where planning instrument is not regarded as the guiding principle, physical growth takes the form of urban sprawl. Infilling takes place where the areas previously by-passed in the urban expansion of an urban area normally depends on a) the size of the urban area, b) the rate of growth, c) the proportion of demand channeled into suburban preferences and finally d) the density of new development (Lean, 1969, pp. 147-165). The patterns of urban expansion are the direct outcome of haphazard growth. Expansion is the initial improvement of vacant land. This is usually confined to residential and industrial uses.

A major feature of outward expansion under the price mechanism is that there is a tendency towards discontinuity. This is the sprawl or haphazard development, which means unplanned growth or urban diffusion. This phenomenon is also called as leapfrog sprawl which means that areas of underdeveloped land separate new developments from each other and from the continuously built-up area. Dormitory settlements are examples of sprawl. Its economic and non-material cost will certainly be on the shoulders of the inhabitants of the settlement ultimately.

Ribbon development occurs when land on either side of a main road is converted into urban use, in other words, from mainly agricultural uses to urban uses. This is also called conversion which would constitute a potential threat, if not appropriately controlled, to sustainable agriculture. Low density continuous development is another major form of sprawl.

Potential urban development is really a threat to the existence of agriculture in the rural-urban fringe. Because, much underdeveloped land in the periphery may be taken out of farming and allowed to lie idle until such time as it

is developed for speculative purposes. Such land derives
its value from expectations of development. As a result,
successful farming becomes increasingly difficult. Sprawl
is largely determined by the scattering of manufacturing
plants away from areas already too crowded into districts
with good transport facilities. This is also called *spatial diffusion process.*

Economic Limits to Urban Sprawl

For an urban area as a whole, outward expansion would be
undertaken up to the point where the marginal net benefit
from the last unit of suburban development is equal to the
marginal net benefit from the last unit of redevelopment
and modification within the built-up area. Each new development is the outward expansion of an urban area and
it needs to be served by transport routes and utility lines
(Goodall, 1972. pp. 190-193).

The role of the developer in the building process is also
important. Main parties in this process are a) the original
landowner, b) a developer, and c) the consumer of the completed property. The building process is an evolutionary sequence of stages and decisions by all these actors. The first
stage is called the stage of urban interest. The second stage
is more complicated: When land is actively considered for
development, landowners or institutions offer land for sale,
and developers and builders advertise for development. In
the third stage land is programmed for development, and
will be purchased by the developer or builder (contractor).
The fourth stage follows the approval of the detailed plans
of the developer by the local planning authority. In the final

stage a consumer buys a completed house and the land is passed into its new use, namely residence.

Criticisms of Urban Sprawl

First of all, it is believed that sprawled or discontinued urban development, as opposed to compact development is more costly and less efficient than a mere compact form of urban expansion. Ribbon development can lead to congestion of radial routes and consequently to higher transport costs. Perhaps this is one of the main reasons behind the suggested guiding principles of the European institutions favoring compact development. Secondly, where new development at the periphery occurs, this means that it bypasses large areas of usable lands in outward expansion. As a result, urban area may grow unnecessarily large.

Then, transport, utility and local public services may all become less efficient and less economic. (Goodall, *op. cit,* pp.198-199). Thirdly, the prime farmland, market gardens and dairy farms may be lost. This is at the same time the loss of the possibility of urban agriculture. In other words, a greater agricultural output is sacrified in case the better lands are used for urban development instead of farming. Fourthly, the sprawl is further criticisized because it paves the way for land speculation. Sprawl which is often accompanied with land speculation is regarded as unproductive, absorbing of capital, manpower and entrepreneurial skills. A final point to be made in this connection is that urban sprawl is regarded as unaesthetic and unattractive, an aimless overspill into the countryside incompatible with ecological considerations.

The Role of the Planner

Since the sprawl represents a net disadvantage for the urban area and the nation as a whole, the planner must seek to redress the balance in favor of the public interest. The basic role of the planner in this process is to locate growing urban population and economic activities appropriately. The planner has a crucial role to play in certain important issues: Firstly, he has to decide which lands will be developed. Secondly, the purpose for which the land will be developed has to be determined by the planner. Finally, the timing of development will be decided by him, taking into consideration the needs of the present and future generations.

To exclude non-conforming uses is also within the responsibilities of the planner. The presence of a green belt will increase the pressure for more intensive use and compact development within the built-up area as well as the demand for building land beyond the green belt. (Goodall, *op. cit*, p. 301).

Its Impact on Sustainable Urban Development in Turkey

Urban sprawl as a phenomenon accelerated by an unplanned urban development is one of the major causes of unsustainable patterns of urbanization. Urban development that does not care for the principles of sustainability and the protection of natural resources, like farmland, paves the ways for the destruction of fertile agricultural land, green and open spaces. Especially in rapidly industrializing regions, agricultural land is often expropriated for industry with no regard at all to the concerns for productivity and sustainability. An agriculturally viable belt of land surrounding agglomerations along the Mersin-Adana-Osmaniye axis in the Mediterranean Region has been totally appropriated for urban development purposes and for industry, even though it would have been possible to locate these installations on less fertile agricultural land somewhere else and still operate them efficiently (Keleş, 2006, pp. 32).

It has been estimated that approximately 150 thousands hectares of the best quality agricultural land has been converted into non-agricultural uses in these areas during the two decades between 1975 and 1995 ((Keleş, 2000, pp. 113-128). Relatedly, Turkey's experiences show that squatting was an activity of genuine self-help and mutual aid during 1945 and 1965, while a partial commercialization and co-modification began to establish itself in the process of squatter formation thereafter.

Policies based on the approaches disregarding the vital role of the fertile agricultural land cannot be reconciled with the strategic imperatives of sustainable development which includes reviving growth, changing its quality, meeting essential needs of human beings, ensuring a sustainable level of population, conserving and enhancing the resource base, and merging environmental and economic considerations in decision-making. Therefore, care should be taken to ensure that the necessary change in the content of growth is made in such a way that as to make it less material-and energy- intensive and more equitable in its impact, taking into consideration the fact that sustainable development involves more than growth (Ruşen Keleş, "Sustainable Urbanization and its Policy Implications," *op. cit.,* p.30).

Land degradation has become a worldwide problem. Nearly 2 billion hectares of cropland, pastures and forests have been degraded over the past 50 years. This causes economic instability and political unrest in the areas affected all over the world. The impacts fall disproportionately on poor segments of the societies in the developing world. Efforts are badly needed to be linked to measures fostering broad economic and social change to overcome the conditions that have resulted in degradation.

Conclusions

Haphazard development taking place in the outskirts of metropolitan settlements is a kind of costly as well as unsustainable form of development. It does not comply with the principle of sustainable development defined as "the kind of development that meets the needs of the present generation without compromising the ability of future generations to meet their own needs." Both intra and intergenerational equity considerations are extremely important in his respect. This principles require that the needs of present and future generations be taken into consideration, limits be placed upon the use and exploitation of natural resources, and an integration of all aspects of environment and development must be ensured.

Sustainable urban development requires an integrated and multi-disciplinary approach, combining aspects of land use planning, pollution control, transport planning, environmental impact assessment, economic instruments, administrative reform and public education. Particularly, untimely and unnecessary conversion of agricultural land int urban uses that can be definitely detrimental to sustainable development must be avoided by all means. Ensuring urban sustainability ca not be left to market forces alone because the market pretends to govern within a short-term perspective whereas sustainability is long-term concern.

Policies to protect land assets from the encroachment of the harmful effects of urban sprawl can best be implemented by a dedicated political will which is not shaped by global forces. The main problem lies in the lack of a policy for national physical planning, lack of a national urbanization policy and the lack of a national policy integrating agricultural and industrial development.

Selected Bibliography

Goodall, Brian, *The Economics of Urban Areas,* Pergamon Press, Oxford, 1972.

Keleş, Ruşen, "Sustainable Urban Development under Unsustainable Conditions", in Derya Oktay (ed.), *Inquiry into Urban Environment: Issues Concerning Urban, Housing and the Built Environment,* Eastern Mediterranean University, Gazimağusa, 2006, pp.27-38.

Keleş, Ruşen, "Impact of Urbanization on Fertile Agricultural Land in Turkey", Driss Ben Ali, Antonio Di Giulio, Mustapha Lasram, Marc Lavergne (eds.), *Urbanisation et Agriculture en Méditerranée: Conflits et Complémentarités,* L'Harmattan, Ciheam, Paris, 1996, pp.145-154.

Keleş, Ruşen, "Sustainable Urbanization and its Policy Implications: The Case of Turkey", D.Camarda and L.Grassini (ed.), *Interdependency between Agriculture and Urbanization: Conflicts on Sustainable use of Soil and Water,* Ciheam-IAMB, Politecnico di Bari, Tunis, 2000, pp.113-128.

Keleş, Ruşen, "The Sustainability of Sustainable Urbanization" 30th International Symposium on Sustainable Spatial Development of the European Continent: Interdisciplinary Approaches, Willy Claus and Paul Trappe (eds.), *Nachhaltipe Raumliche Entwiclung auf dem Europaischen Kontinent Interdisziplinare,* Ansatza, Social Strategies, Vol.32, Peter Lang, Bern, 2000, pp.213-228.

Lean, William, *Economics of Land Use Planning: Urban and Regional,* The Estates Gazette Ltd., London, 1969.

Does Urban Sprawl Jeopardize Sustainable Development in Turkey?*

Introduction

In order to able to answer such a question, it is first necessary to clarify several concepts such as urban sprawl and sustainable development. Thorndike Dictionary defines the Word of sprawl as "spreading out in an irregular and awkward manner". In other words sprawl is understood as a kind of movement that does not take into account the considerations of planned intervention. In the context of either rural to urban migration or centrifugal expansion of the population from city centers, the cost of haphazard, irregular and unplanned population movements increased considerably. Urban sprawl is not only a costly process, but it also creates socio-cultural and environmental consequence. Some believe that urban sprawl has a number of positive economic effects such as increasing local economic growth, local property values and demand for automobiles.[1]

On the other hand, sustainable development is defined as the kind of development that meets the needs of the present

* Erwin Hepperle, Robert- Dixon Gough, Vida Maliene, Reinfried Mansberger, Jenny Paulsson, Andrea Pödür (eds.), *Land Management: Potential, Problems and Stumbling Blocks*, Vdf, ETH, Zurich, 2013, pp. 211-217.

1 George A. Gonzales, *Urban Sprawl, Global Warming and the Empire of Capital*, SUNY, New York, p. 50 and 197.

generation without compromising the ability of future generations to meet their own needs. Therefore, the problems caused by urban sprawl have to be assessed both from intragenerational as well as intergenerational equity viewpoints.

Rural to urban migration and urban sprawl have been the most important phenomena for sustainable use of the natural resources. Particularly the fertile agricultural land and almost all elements of the ecosystem are damaged as a result of the haphazard movements of the population and businesses. During the process of urbanization several interrelated changes take place in the use of landed property. Dwellings vacated by one occupant may be adopted for use by new occupant families, in accordance with a filtering- down process, or they may be demolished and replaced by different uses and structures. At the same time, businesses expand or decline according to the general macro-economic conditions.

Of course, it is the function of the land market to bring about the adjustment necessitated by urban growth or decline of urban activities and populations. If the urban growth brings an increase in demand for residential accommodation (house, dwelling), housing prices rise in the short run. If the price rise is sufficiently high, construction firm will be able to earn huge amount of profits. This certainly would encourage an increase in the supply of houses as vacant land is converted to residential use and certain sites are redeveloped for residential purposes.

Everywhere in the world, urban growth takes place either in a planned manner or spontaneously. The choice of urban areas as local or regional centers by political decisions, as in the case of Ankara, Brazil, Canberra or Islamabad, that can promote the further growth of the selected urban centers. But there are also numerous examples of unplanned growth of capitals or other metropolitan centers. Elimination of all kinds of inequalities require planned intervention in the development process. Because, growth does not affect all urban areas equally. While some areas will be increasing faster than others, some may be declining. Urban growth and structure are also affected by change in the economic base of an urban area, such as basic industries, exports, etc.

Normally, urban growth proceeds centrifugally (horizontally) along[2] major trans for growth[3] port routes. This leaves the core of the city as the oldest part of the urban area. Growth of an urban area is not a continuous and homogenous process. There are ups and downs in this process. It is generally consisted of a succession of jumps which may be related to the indivisibility of certain basic investments in infrastructure that is essential for growth 2. Economic rationality or the cost factor determines both the extent of vertical or horizontale expansion under normal conditions.

Patterns of Unplanned Growth

Sometimes, particularly in societies and times where planning instrument is not regarded as the guiding principle, physical growth takes the form of urban sprawl. Infilling takes place where the areas previously by-passed in the urban expansion of an urban area normally depends on the following factors: a) the size of the urban area, b) the rate of the

2   Brian Goodall, *The Economics of Urban Areas,* Pergamon, Oxford, 1972, pp. 185-187.

3   William Lean, *Economics of Land: Urban and Regional,* The Estate Gazette, London, 1969, pp. 147-165.

urban growth, c) the proportion of demand channeled into suburban preferences, and finally, d) the density of new development 3. In the absence of planning, the patterns of urban expansion are the direct outcome of haphazard growth. Expansion is the initial improvement of vacant land. This is usually confined to residential and industrial uses.

A major feature of outward expansion under the price mechanism is that there is a tendency towards discontinuity. This is the sprawl of haphazard development, which means unplanned growth of urban diffusion. This phenomenon is also called as leapfrog sprawl which means that areas of underdeveloped land separate new developments from each other and from the continuously built-up area. Dormitory settlements are examples of sprawl, the economic and non-material cost will certainly be on the shoulders of the inhabitants of the settlement ultimately. Ribbon development occurs when land on other side of a main road is converted from mainly agricultural uses to urban uses. This is also called conversion which would constitute a potential threat, if not appropriately controlled, to sustainable agriculture. This is one of the major drawbacks of urban sprawl for sustainable development in Turkey. It happens at the same time together with low-density continuous development.

Potential urban development has been a real threat to the existence of agriculture in the rural-urban fringe during the last decades in Turkey. Because, much underdeveloped land in the periphery is taken out of farming and allow to lie idle until such time as it is developed for speculative purposes. Such land derives its value from expectations of development. As a result, as we have witnessed in many regions in

Turkey, successful farming becomes increasingly difficult. Sprawl is largely determined by the scattering of manufacturing plants and residential blocks away from areas already too crowded into districts with good transport facilities. This is also called spatial diffusion process.

Criticisms of Urban Sprawl

Several criticisms have been levelled to urban sprawl that is relevant for the clarification of our subject matter. First of all, it is believed that sprawled or discontinued urban development is more costly and less efficient than a mere compact form of urban expansion. Ribbon development can lead to congestion of radial routes and consequently to higher transport costs. Perhaps this is one of the reasons behind the suggested guiding principles of the European institutions favoring *compact development.*

Secondly, where new development at the periphery occurs, it means that it bypasses large areas of usable lands in outward expansion. As a result, urban area may grow unnecessarily large. Then, transport, utilities and public services may all become less efficient and less economic.[4]

Thirdly, the prime farmland, market gardens and dairy farms may also be lost. This is at the same time the loss of the possibility of urban agriculture. In other words, a greater agricultural output is sacrificed in case that better lands are used for urban development instead of garming. This is what happens in major cities of Turkey, which puts the goal of sustainable development in peril.

---

4   Brian Goodall, *op. cit.,* pp. 188-199.

Fourthly, the sprawl is further criticised because it paves the way for land speculation. Sprawl which is often accompanied with land speculation is regarded as unproductive, absorbing of capital, manpower and entrepreneurial skills.

A final point to be made in this connection is that urban sprawl is regarded as unattractive, an aimless overspill into the countryside which is not compatible with ecological considerations. Not only prime farmland, but also the quality of air, water, landscape forests and touristic potentials are considerably affected by the sprawl.

Concrete Examples of the Impact of Haphazard Development on Sustainability in Turkey

Urban sprawl, as a phenomenon accelerated by an unplanned urban development is one of the major causes of unsustainable patterns of urbanization. Urban development that does not care for the principle of sustainability and the protection of natural resources, like the farmland, paves the way for the destruction of fertile agricultural lands, green and open spaces. Particularly in rapidly industrializing regions of the country, agricultural land is often expropriated for the purposes of industrial and urban development with no regard at all to the concerns for productivity and sustainability. An agriculturally viable belt of land surrounding agglomerations along the Mersin-Adana-Osmaniye axis in the Mediterranean Region has been totally appropriated recently for urban development purposes and for industrial plants, even though it would have been possible alternatively to locate these installations on less fertile agricultural lands somewhere else and still operate them efficiently.[5]

It has also been estimated that approximately 150 thousands hectares of the best quality of agricultural land has been converted into non-agricultural uses in these areas during the two decades between 1975 and 1995.[6] Relatedly, Turkey's experience show that squatting was an activity of genuine self-help and mutual aid during 1945 and 1965 while a partial commodification and commercialization began to establish itself in the squatter formation process thereafter.

Certain policies for the encouragement of tourism and pastures all over the country's territory, disregarding the vital role of the forestry, the fertile agricultural land, and other ecological assets have been put into practice during the last several decades.

There is no doubt that such policies and practices cannot be reconciled with the strategic imperatives of sustainable development which includes reviving growth, changing its quality, meeting essential needs of human beings, ensuring a sustainable level of population, conserving and enhancing the resource base and merging environmental and economic considerations in decision-making.

Therefore, care should be taken to ensure that the necessary change in the content of growth is made in such a

5   Ruşen Keleş, "Sustainable Urban Development under Unsustainable Conditions", in Inquiry into Urban Environment, (ed.) Derya Oktay, Eastern Mediterranean University, Gazimağusa, 2006. p. 32.

6   Ruşen Keleş, "Sustainable Urbanization and its Policy Implications: The Case of Turkey, in D. Camarda and L. Grassini (eds.), Intermedency between Agriculture and Urbanization Conflicts on Sustainable Use of Soil and Water, European Commission, INCO-DC (DG XII), Tunis, 2000, pp. 113-128.

way as to make it less material and energy intensive and more equitable in its impact, taking into consideration the fact that sustainable development involves more than simple economic growth.[7]

Land degradation has become a worldwide problem. Nearly two billion hectares of cropland, pastures and forests have become degraded over the past half century. This causes economic instability, nutrition problems and political unrest in the areas affected all over the world. The impacts fall disproportionately on poor segments of the societies in the developing world. Efforts are badly needed to be linked to measures fostering broad economic and social change to overcome the conditions that have resulted in degradation. It has been estimated that the amount of land suitable for agricultural production and the pastures decreased considerably during the last several decades.

The Role of the Planner

Since the sprawl represents a net disadvantage for the urban area and the nation as a whole, the planner must seek to redress the balance in favour of the public interest. The basic role of the planner in this process is to locate growing urban population and economic activities appropriately. The planner has a crucial tole to plan in certain in certain important issues: First, he has to decide, proactively, which lands will be developed. Secondly, the purpose for which the land will be developed has to be determined by the planner. Finally, the timing of development has to be determined by

---

7   Ruşen Keleş, "Sustainable Development and its Policy Implications", op. cit., p. 30.

him, taking into consideration the needs of the present and future generations. In this sense, one can justifiably argue without making the instrument of planning operational at all levels of the governance, the ideal of ensuring the sustainability of the ecosystem would just stay on the paper.

Concluding Remarks

Haphazard development taking place in the outskirts of metropolitan settlements like Istanbul, Ankara, Izmir, Bursa, Adana and other major centers is a kind of costly as well as unsustainable form of development. It does not comply with the principle of sustainable development as defined in the international legal documents. Both intra and inter-generational equity considerations are extremely important in this respect. These principles require that the needs of present and future generations be taken into consideration, limits be placed upon the use and exploitation of natural resources, and an integration of all aspects of environment and development must be ensured.

Sustainable urban development requires an integrated and multidisciplinary approach combining aspects of land use planning, effective development control, pollution control, transport planning, environmental impact assessment, economic instruments, administrative reform and public education. Particularly, untimely and unnecessary conversion of agricultural land into urban uses may be definitely detrimental to sustainable development, as we witness in metropolitan Turkey. Therefore, such practices must be avoided by all means. Ensuring urban sustainability cannot be left to the market forces alone, because the market pretends to govern within a short-term perspective whereas sustainability represents a long-term concern.

I believe that the policies to protect land assets and all other natural resources from the encroachment of the harmful effects of urban sprawl can best be implemented by a dedicated political will which is not conditioned essentially by global forces. The main problem lies in the lack of a policy for national physical planning, the lack of a national urbanization policy directed to the maximization of the public interest and the lack of well formulated national policy of sustainable development integrating agricultural and industrial development with ecological considerations.

Short Bibliography

Goodall, Brian, *The Economics of Urban Areas,* Pergamon Press, Oxford, 1972.

Keleş, Ruşen, "Sustainable Urban Development under Unsustainable Conditions", in Derya Oktay (ed.) Inquiry into Urban Environment, Eastern Mediterranean University, Gazimağusa, TRNC, 2006. pp. 27-38.

Keleş, Ruşen, "Impact of urbanization on Fertike Agricultural Land in Turkey", (eds.) Dris Ben Ali, Antonio di Giulio, Mustapha Lasram, Marc Lavergne, Urbanisation et Agriculture en Méditerranée: Conflits et Complémentarités, L' Harmattan, Chiheam, Paris, 1996, pp. 145-154.

Keleş, Ruşen, "Sustainable Urbanisation and its Policy Implications: The Case of Turkey", Domenico Camarda and Laura Grassini, Interdependency between Agriculture and Urbanization: Conflicts on Sustainable Use of Soil and Water, Ciheam-IAMB, Politecnico di Bari, Tunis, 2000, pp. 113-128.

Keleş, Ruşen, "The Sustainability of Sustainable Urbanization", (eds.), Willy Claus and Paul Trappe, 30 th International Symposium on

Sustainable Spatial Development of the European Continent: Interdisciplinary Approaches (Nachhaltipe Raumliche Entwicklung auf dem Europaischen Kontinent Interdisiplinare), Ansatza, Social Strategies, Vol. 32, Peter Lang, Bern, 2000, pp. 213-228.

Keleş, Ruşen, Hamamcı, Can and Çoban, Aykut, Çevre Politikası (Environmental Policy), (6 th ed.), İmge Pub., Ankara, 2009 .

Lean, William, Economics of Land Use Planning: Urban and Regional, The Estate Gazette Ltd., London, 1969.

Impact of Urbanisation on
Fertile Agricultural Land in Turkey[*]

Summary

Turkey is a rapidly urbanising country with a yearly increase of its urban population of 5 percent. This has a tremendous effect on the social and economic life, as well as on the land use. Increasing need for urban infrastructure and public services not only inflates the land price within municipal boundaries but it paves the way for an unprecedented expansion of the urban space into agricultural territories. It has been estimated that roughly 25.000 ha. of fertile agricultural land is converted into urban uses annually with no real control and protection by central or local authorities. In this paper, an attempt will be made to analyse this important issue and to evaluate the state policies formulated so far.

Resume

La Turquie est un pays à forte croissance urbaine avec un taux annuel d'environ 5 %. Cela a des répercussions énormes sur la vie sociale et économique du pays, ainsi que sur l'utilisation des terres. Le besoin croissant d'infrastructures urbaines et de services publics n'influe pas seulement sur les prix des sols au niveau des municipalités, mais prépare le chemin d'une expansion sans précédent de l'escape urbain

* This article was published in Deis Ben Ali Deis Ben Ali, Antonio di Guilio, Mustapha Lasram and Marc Lavergne (eds.), *Urbanisation et Agriculture en Méditerrannée: Conflits et Complémentarités*, L'Harmattan, Paris, 1996, pp. 135-154.

jusqu'aux terres cultivées. On a estimé qu'environ 25.000 ha de terres cultivables fertiles étaient transformes chaque année pour des besoins urbains sans rel contrôle ni protection de la part des autorités centrales ou locales Dans cette étude, un effort a été entrepris pour analyser cette importante question et pour évaluer les politiques de l'Etat énoncées jusqu'à présent.

Effects of Sprawl

Sprawl is most noticeable when urban areas are expanding rapidly and around the fastest- growing urban centers. Expansion involving the initial improvement of vacant land is usually confined to residential and industrial land uses. It is called **leap-frog sprawl** to indicate that areas of undeveloped land separate new developments from each other and from the continuous built-up area. Ribbon development occurs when land on either side of a main road is converted into urban use.

Potential urban development is a threat to the existence of agriculture in the rural-urban fringe. In this way, much undeveloped peripheral land may be taken out of farming and allowed to lie idle until it is developed. Such land derives its value from expectations of development. Urbanisation normally bids up the value of land far beyond agricultural value, but this need not render land immediately derelict for farming. Successful farming becomes gradually and increasing difficult. In some cases, only part of a farm may have been sold for development, leaving aa remnant too small to be a viable economic entity with the result that it too become derelict.[1]

---

1   Brian Goodall, The Economics of Urban Areas, Pegaman, London, 1972, pp. 186-187.

Several criticisms may be directed to this spontaneous transformation of land structure.

A. Sprawled or discontinuous suburban development is more costly and less efficient than a more compact form of urban expansion. Small fragmented developments may hinder progress towards optimum units in the provision of local public and utility services.

B. New development at the periphery is of lower density than other settled areas, which is an extravagant us of land. This, coupled with by-passing of large areas of usable land in the outward expansion, means that the urban area may grow unnecessarily large, and then transport, utility and local public services may all become less efficient and less economic.

C. The loss of prime agricultural land is perhaps the most important loss to society. Allowing that it is the best, most intensively farmed land, such as market gardens and dairy farms, which is most often taken, the protest of the public opinion is as much emotional as rational.

Where urban expansion on poor agricultural land would yield the same net benefit as on prime agricultural land, then from the community's point of view, the expansion should take place on the poor land.

A greater agricultural output would be scarified if the better land is misused, and this would need to replaced by extending the intensive margin of cultivation by bringing more land into farming or by increased inputs.

D. Sprawl is also criticised because the land speculation which accompanies it is regarded as unproductive, absorbing capital, manpower, and entrepreneurial skill.

E. Finally, urban sprawl is regarded as unaesthetic and unattractive, an aimless overspill into the countryside, from the perspective of urban form and environmental values.[2]

The peripheral spread creates far reaching effects upon the environment, upon agriculture, upon transportation, upon agricultural occupations and life styles. They are essentially irreversible, excepting only that agricultural land, once abandoned, can be put back into cultivation, even if it rarely is.

Agricultural areas near cities tend to comprise some of the nation's best quality lands not only because flat, well-drained lands are equally attractive for urban or for agricultural pursuits, but also because such lands have been made highly productive by generations of farmers supplying the city with agricultural foodstuffs. When such lands come under pressure for conversion to urban uses, then agriculture makes a number of different responses which seem quite universal.

One response is the further intensification of agriculture, usually by increased capitalisation. **A second response** is the development of new agricultural areas in the urban fringe. **Another response** is the maintenance of existing agricultural land use at roughly the same intensity but with a change of the household economy. Small farms near cities can often be maintained by substituting capital for labour

2   Ibid., 196-199.

on the farm and by obtaining urban employment, either full time or part-time, in order to balance the domestic budget. **A last response** is **deintensification** a somewhat ugly term that refers to the lowering of levels of labour or capital input while maintaining some form of agriculture. This is particularly the response in areas beyond the reach of daily commuting, but within reach of the weekender.[3]

Economic and political factors often conspire to lead to the abandonment of farming which in turn may lead to land lying unused. The differentials between farms profits and the urban wages may rise so high that farming is no longer an attractive proposition.

The Case of Turkey

Turkey is one of the most rapidly urbanising countries in the world. Its rate of urbanisation has been around 6 percent during the last three and a half decades, while the rate of annual population growth was only 2.5%. Its urban population increased from 7 million in 1960 to 35 million in 1994. The population of the cities with 100.000 and more population increased, within the same period from 3.5 to 25 million. The number of the cities with more than 100.000 inhabitants is around 50, and that with a population exceeding 1 million is 8. If one considers the remarkable increase in the number of cities (100.000 and over) during the last 35 years, from 150 to 500, one could easily imagine the extent of the damage given to most fertile agricultural land surrounding metropolitan areas. Because, as a result of haphazard and rapid expansion these areas are being converted

3   R. D. Hill, "Land Use Change on the Urban Fringe", Nature and Resources, Double Issue, Vol. XXII, No 1-2, (January- June 1986), pp. 26-28.

into buildings and installations necessitated by urban public services and utilizes, such as roads, industry, tourism, hospitals, schools, residences, infrastructure, and other public and private investments. Skyrocketing land prices inflated by land speculation without any serious control led to major public and private investments to take place in the outskirts of major metropolitan areas. The growth of cities occurs mainly in the mushrooming squatter settlements surrounding the city boundaries, instead of the centre, thus constituting a real threat for farms and agricultural productivity, as in other parts of the world.[4]

Land of high agricultural quality is being increasingly occupied by industry which is causing problems in the rational use of limited natural resources. The vast amount of industrial investment made especially in the Çukurova Region on both sides of the Içel-Iskenderun, Adana-Karatas and Adana-Tarsus-Mersin roads has had tremendous detrimental effects on the best agricultural land assets of Turkey. In terms of soil fertility and ecological characteristics, this region is one of the most important agricultural areas of Turkey. This area is the centre of production for cotton, a major export item of Turkey, and its contribution to the national economy is rapidly increasing especially after the completion of irrigation networks in the area. However, parallel to this agricultural development, the development in industry has not been based on rational planning, and as a result, industry has occupied valuable agricultural areas.

4   W. A. Befort, A. E. Luloff and M. Morrone, "Rural Land Use and Demographic Change in Rapidly Urbanizing Environment" Landscape and Urban Planning, 16, (1988), 345-356; and G. P. Wibberley, Agriculture and Urban Growth, Michael Joseph, London, 1959.

The lack of quantitative data in this field has also made it difficult to make the public awareness an effective pressure element in decision-making. What has happened in the Çukurova Region is taking place also in good quality agricultural land in the Western Regions and provinces, such as Bursa, Balikesir, Izmir and Manisa.

It is estimated that each year almost 400.000. ha fertile agricultural land is lost as a result of the misuse of land.[5]

The distribution of Turkey's land assets on the basis of suitability for cultivation is shown in the table I.

Table I: Turkey's Land Assets

Categories of quality	Ha	%
1. Suitable for cultivation	5,012,537	6.5
2. Suitable for cultivation	6,578,702	8.7
3. Suitable for cultivation	7,574,330	9.8
4. Part suitable	7,201,016	9.3
5. Unsuitable (non-arable)	166,547	0.2
6. Unsuitable (non-arable)	10,283,533	13.2
7. Unsuitable (non-arable)	36,288,553	46.7
8. Totaly unsuitable for cultivation	4,557,900	5.9
TOTAL	**776,663,127**	

Source: T.C. Başbakanlik Çevre Müstesarligi, Tarim Topraklarinin Amaç Disi Kullanilmasinin Onlenmesi Semineri, 1984, Ankara, s. 18.

---

5   Cemil Cangir, "Amaç Disi Arazi Kullanimi" (Misuse of Land), TMMOB, Ziraat Mühendisleri Odasi, Toprak, Insan, Cevre Sempozyumu, (Symposium on Land, Man and Environment), 3-4 June 1991, Ankara, 87.

Table II: Use Distribution of the
Most Valuable Agricultural Land (ha.)

	Category (I)	Category (II)	Category (III)
Cultivated Land	4.778.399 (95.3%)	5.986.866 (88.6%)	6.299.433 (82.7%)
Pastures	177.510	547.012	826.044
Forests	17.253	172.065	476.572
Settlements	39.375 (0.79%)	52.759 (0.78%)	42.281 (0.56%)

Source: T.C. Başbakanlik Çevre Müstesarligi, Tarim Topraklarinin Amaç Disi
Kullanilmasinin Onlenmesi Semineri, 1984, Ankara, s. 18.

Table III: Quality of Land in settled Areas

Quality Categories	Quantity (ha.)
I	40,000
II	53,000
III	42,000
IV	37,000
V	.
VI	49,000
VII	57,000
VIII	292,000
Total	**578,000 ha (0.7 % of the total)**

Source: T.C. Başbakanlik Çevre Müstesarligi, Tarim Topraklarinin Amaç Disi
Kullanilmasinin Onlenmesi Semineri, 1984, Ankara, s. 18.

In other words, the share of the settled areas in cultivable lands constitutes 30 percent of the total cultivable land. And only 0.7 percent of all arable land is occupied by human settlements.

Going back to the amount of the average annual loss of valuable agricultural land, one can safely assume that on the basis of 3,000 kg of wheat per hectare, the total annual loss to the economy would be 388,390 x 3,000= nearly 12 millions quintals.

The amount of the land loss is comparable to the total land assets of some of the major provinces of Turkey.

Table IV: Total Assets of Some Provinces

Istanbul	5,591	Sakarya	4,821
Hatay	5,57	Batman	4,694
Nevsehir	5,54	Trabzon	4,498
Amasya	5,452	Kirikkale	4,365
Usak	5,389	Bilecik	4,321
Total Missued Land	**3.884**		
Rize	3,920		
Bayburt	3,652		
Kocaeli	3,578		

Source: T.C. Başbakanlik Çevre Müstesarligi, Tarim Topraklarinin Amaç Disi Kullanilmasinin Onlenmesi Semineri, 1984, Ankara, s. 18.

Lost agricultural land is larger than the province of Van and 55 other provinces.

Policies

One can ask at this point what has been so far the response of the governments to this degradation.

Two clauses of the Turkish Constitution of 1983 possess stipulations concerning directly the agricultural land. The first is article 44, according to which, "the State shall take the necessary measure **to maintain and develop efficient land cultivation, to prevent its loss through erosion**, and to provide land to farmers with insufficient land of their own, or no land. For this purpose, the law may define the size of appropriate land units, according to different agricultural regions and types of farming. Providing of land to farmers with no or sufficient land shall not lead to a fall in production, or to the depletion of forests and other land and underground resources".

The second is the Article 45 of the Constitution. It stipulates that "the State shall assist farmers and livestock breeders in acquiring machinery, equipment and other inputs in order to prevent improper use and destruction of agricultural land, meadows and pastures and to increase crop and livestock production in accordance with the principles of agricultural planning".

The Constitution also refers to the right of citizens to a **safe and healthy environment**, which is indirectly related to proper use of agricultural land. The environmental Protection Law of 1982 and the law on land arrangements in the Irrigation Areas within land Reform Regions of 1984 contain stipulations for the protection of the agricultural land.

However, the most important guarantee for the protection of fertile agricultural land is the by-law concerning Improper Use of land (March 1989, February 1990, July 1994). This by-law classifies the land into 8 major categories and qualifies the first 4 groups as "valuable agricultural lands". According to the by-law, the permission of the General Directorate of Rural Services which comes under the Prime Ministry, is necessary (art. 4), in order to allocate agricultural land to the purposes of urban development. The first priority should be given to the land which is totally unsuitable for agriculture (category 8). An important principle of the by-law is that, the land which has been made irrigated land as a result of public investments, will definitely not be devoted to non-agricultural purposes. And finally, the land requirements for urban development, such as housing, education, health, industrial estates, shopping centres and state highways have to be met exclusively out of the land which is not suitable for cultivation.

It is regrettable that such protective and rational measures are not properly implemented all the time, and their implementation is interrupted by intervening political (partisan) or other factors.

Although another by-law issued by the government for the purpose of working out Environmental Impact Analysis before a major pollution investment, requires the detailed examination of the likely harmful effects of development projects, it can hardly be said that it is implemented properly. In most of the decision taken in such cases, short-sighted political considerations largely prevail and the official positions change from one administration to another.

The most recent example of such attitudes is a statement by the President of Republic, Mr. S. Demirel, who declared during the opening ceremony of a huge car factory, that will manufacture Japanese Toyotas right in the centre of one of the greenest and most fertile agricultural regions in the province of Sakarya that "Turkey can only develop by substituting potato cropping by manufacturing Toyota cars". What I mean by this is that policies to protect land assets from the encroachment of the harmful effects of urban development can best be implemented by a dedicated political will.

It seems that the main problem lies in the a) Lack of a policy for national physical planning, b) Lack of a national urbanization policy, and c) The lack of a national policy integrating agricultural and industrial planning.

As stated by Mustafa Kemal Atatürk during the 1930's, "Although the nations are the real owners of the territory they occupy, they have an absolute responsibility, as the representatives of the humanity, for present and future generations. Therefore, while utilizing the land, they should not forget that it is their duty to make humankind benefit this natural resource".

Short Bibliography

Brian Goodall, The Economics of Urban Areas, Pegaman, London, 1972, pp. 186-187.

Cemil Cangir, "Amac Disi Arazi Kullanimi" (Misuse of Land), TMMOB, Ziraat Mühendisleri Odasi, Toprak, Insan, Cevre Sempozyumu, (Symposium on Land, Man and Environment), 3-4 June 1991, Ankara, 87.

R. D. Hill, "Land Use Change on the Urban Fringe", Nature and Resources, Double Issue, Vol. XXII, No 1-2, (January- June 1986), pp. 26-28.

T.C. Başbakanlik Çevre Müstesarligi, Tarim Topraklarinin Amac Disi Kullanilmasinin Onlenmesi Semineri, 1984, Ankara, s. 18.

W. A. Befort, A. E. Luloff and M. Morrone, "Rural Land Use and Demographic Change in Rapidly Urbanizing Environment" Landscape and Urban Planning, 16, (1988), pp. 345-356; and G. P. Wibberley, Agriculture and Urban Growth, Michael Joseph, London, 1959.

The Growth of Ecological
Concerns in World Capitals[*]

Urban Growth and its Problems

The World population encountered an urbanization of unprecedented pace during the second half of the 20th century, which brought with it numerous problems of housing, infrastructure, transportation, land speculation, squatting and environment. Major public services are not being supplied in adequate standards for billions of people in major world capitals.

The number of metropolises with over a million inhabitants has tripled during the last thirty five years. In 1950, only 78 cities exceeded that size. The number has became 258 in 1985, and it is estimated that there will be 511 cities of this size in the year 2010 and 639 in the year 2025.

Their number will be increasing from 110 to 153 in advanced countries, and from 146 to 465 in the less developed countries between 1985 and 2025. By the turn of the century, the developing world might have 37 cities with a population of over 5 million.

Over 130 million of the developing world's poorest poor live in urban areas, and its great majority in capital cities.

---

[*] Paper submitted to the Third Conference of the World Capitals, Tokyo Metropolitan Government, Tokyo, Japan, October 26-28, 1993.

They cluster in slums and squatter settlements around the capitals or at the urban periphery. These areas are prone to hazardous natural and man- made environmental conditions, such as flood plains, slopes or land adjacent to harmful industries. Most of the residents live and work in hazardous exposure situations. They have to contend with bad sanitation, contaminated water, floods, or chemical pollution. According to WHO, an estimated 600 million urban dwellers in the developing world would live in what might be termed life and health threatening circumstances.[1] They are affected by water pollution, inadequate sanitation facilities, insufficient collection and disposal of solid and toxic wastes, in-door and out-door air pollution.

The problem of hazardous wastes in developing countries has been exacerbated by the transfer of products and technologies from developed countries. In many cases it is cheaper to relocate such industries to the developing countries than to meet the increasingly stringent environmental standards and regulations at home.[2]

One of the most striking description of environmental problems in the major cities of developing countries can be found in the Report called Our Common Future: "Out of India's 3.119 towns and cities, only 209 had partial and only 8 had full sewage and sewage treatment facilities. On the River Ganges, 114 cities each with 50.000 or more inhabitants dump untreated sewage into the river every day. DDT factories, tanneries, paper and pulp mills, petrochemical, fertilizer complexes, rubber factories, and a

---

1   Udo Simonis and Deonan Oodit, "Poverty, Environment and Development"; and Agni Vlavianos-Arvanitis and Ruşen Keleş (eds.), **The Bio-Environment,** Vol.4, Athens, 1993, pp. 11-12.

2   Simonis and Oodit, **Ibid,** s.12.

host of others use the river to get rid of their wastes. The Hoogly estuary (near Calcutta) is choked its untreated industrial wastes from more than 150 major factories around Calcutta. Sixty percent of Calcutta's population suffer from pneumonia, bronchities, and other respiratory diseases related to air pollution.

Chinese industries, most of which use coal in out-dated furnaces and boilers, are concentrated around 20 cities and ensure a high level of air pollution. Lung cancer mortality in the nation as a whole, and the difference is largely attributable to heavy air pollution.

In Malaysia, the highly urbanized Klang Valley (which includes the capital, Kuala Lumpur) has two to three times the pollution levels of major cities in the U.S. and the Klang River system is heavily contaminated with agricultural and industrial effluents and sewage".[3]

Methodological Considerations and Major Concepts

In a paper dealing with the Creation and Protection of a Pleasant Environment in Capital Cities, certain terms have to be clarified at the outset in order to avoid misunderstandings and methodological plausibilities. These concepts are the environment, the national capital city and the quality of urban environment. Before elaborating on each of these terms, I would like to make several assumptions with regard to the evaluations that will be based on the concepts just mentioned. These may avoid any methodological errors and misunderstandings.

3   World Commission on Environment and Development, **Our Common Future**, p.240.

1. Almost all big cities in the world are prone to adverse consequences of the environmental degradation. But the capital cities are more so, because of their size and the extra functions they assume. Therefore what will be said about the great cities of the world may be valid to a great extent for the capital cities as well.

2. Great majority of the capital cities are also the primate cities of the respective countries with minor exceptions.

3. Capital cities in the Third world countries have certain peculiarities which make them more vulnerable to ecological threats than the cities of the developed countries:

    aa) Their population increases more rapidly than that of the capitals of developed countries.

    bb) They are much less fortunate than the others in terms of financial means.

4. Most of the hardships faced by the inhabitants of the capital cities are imposed to them from above directly or indirectly by the central government or from outside by international firms or other organizations. Depending upon the degrees of centralization and upon the balance of the political forces, this may create extra problems for the capital cities and therefore the central governments should assume at least in part the responsibility to cure them.

Environment

Environment is defined by Charles Abrams as "the sum of all external conditions influencing the growth and development of an organism". Also all that is apart from and surrounds an observer or something being observed. A distinction is commonly made between the natural environment (air, water, trees) and that made by a man (a room, a street, a city). Urbanists who used to be primarily concerned with the improvement of the man-made environment have become increasingly concerned with the dislocations caused in the natural one.[4]

Ecology, on the other hand, is the study of the relationship between man and his environment. When it focuses on the urban environment, it is the study of spatial distribution in a community of people, groups and inhabitants; the relationships among them; and the changes that come about in the distribution through adaptation, competition, and accommodation. Just as patterns of development in the natural world occur in a series of phases, so human communities are held to develop and evolve over time and in space. First a certain balance among inhabitants is achieved, then this equilibrium is upset by some changes or intrusion, an a new balance is subsequently achieved.

Etymologically, the word environment points out that which environs (surrounds) and in this context, more precisely, that which surrounds human beings. This anthtropocentrist vision is in line with the spirit of our civilization of which the sole reference is human beings and of which all actions tend to master the totality of earth.

---

4   Charles Abrams, **The Language of Cities,** Avon Books, New York, 1972, p. 192.

This conception is one of the essential breaking points with ecological philosophy which perceives humankind as one organism among million others and considers that all forms of life have a right to an autonomous existence. [5]

Anthropocentrist (humanist) view of environment means what surrounds human beings; the periphery, but not the centre. In other words, environment is not considered as a subject of law, as an entity having an absolute value by itself. This is a view contradicting the observation of Gilberto Mastrinho, Governor of Amazonas State, who complained last year in the Rio Conference that "Ecologists care more about plants and animals than about people".[6]

On the other hand, utilitarian view is somewhat different. According to this approach, it is necessary not only to search for the interest of people, but to decrease the total hardships in the world more than to increase the quantity of welfare.[7] This view is well compatible with ecocentric approaches.

The approach of this paper is to perceive the concept of environment in its broadest sense. This is also the understanding of the Rio Declaration, according to which habitat and environment are inextricably linked. It also recognized that peace, development and environmental protection are interdependent and indivisible.[8]

One of the main environmental problems at present is the habitat of large numbers of the urban poor who lack

5   K.M.Meyer-Abish, **Wege zum Frieden mit der Nature,** Munich, 1984, pp. 90, 100, 187.
6   Internatiınal Society for Environmental Ethics, **Newsletter,** Summer 1992, p.8.
7   Luc Ferry, **Le nouvel ordre écologique,** Bernard Grasset, Paris, 1992, p. 33.
8   Principle 25.

accessible and secure land, water, sewerage facilities, healthy and basic services and access to financial and material resources to meet their basic needs. This implies the recognition of the right to a place to live in peace and dignity, and to healthy and affordable habitat. Therefore, as underlined in the Rio Declaration [9], the essential task is to eradicate poverty as an indispensable requirement for sustainable development.

Inspired by concrete facts and realities, İndira Gandhi, the last Prime Minister of India had declared in the Environment Conference of Stockholm in 1972: "Aren't poverty and unmet human needs the most important kinds of pollution? How can I explain the necessity of keeping the air, seas, and rivers clean to the masses living in their own villages, in slums, while their lives are badly contaminated? Environment cannot be improved in the conditions of poverty."

National Capital Cities

Capital cities are the principal headquarters of legislative, executive and judicial branches of governments. They are focal points of political and administrative activities essential to the daily lives of their residents. A second approach to perceive capital cities is to evaluate them by their multi-dimensional responsibilities. From this standpoint, capital cities perform economic and cultural functions, in addition to their political responsibilities.

The state capitals are not always the primate cities of the respective countries. But most of the time, both coincides. Exceptions like Washington D.C., İslamabad, Riyadh

9   Principle, 5.

and Ankara are few. With few exceptions, most of the capital cities are great cities or mega cities in the words of Mattei Dogan and John Kasarda.

A preferred site for state capital in federal states would avoid over association with any component units. Existing major urban centers are usually avoided there. In contrast to centralized states, the national capital in federal countries is not the primate city or even, as in some federal states (like Germany and Switzerland) among the first several centers of the urban hierarchy.[10]

Not only the size of the problems of capital cities increases, but also their numbers do as the demands of peoples in various parts of the world for statehood become reality. Relative importance of the populations of urban and total population is also a factor aggravating the dimensions of the problems especially in the middle-income countries.

Population in the Capital City as a Percentage of

	Urban Population	Total Population
1) Low-income countries	11 percent	3 percent
2) Middle-income countries	25	14
3) High-income countries	12	9
4) OECD countries	11	7

Source: The World Bank, *World Development Report, 1993* Washington D.C., pp.298-299.

---

10 Vienna is an exception. See Ronan Paddison, **The Fragmented State: The Political Geography of Power,** Oxford University Press, London, 1983, p. 122.

The Quality of Urban Environment

The quality of urban environment is a highly complex concept. When talking about the performance of an urban system, it is not possible disassociate great many factors from a much larger environment, which encompasses all activities and resources of man, as well as his surroundings. The concept of a pleasent environment is closely related with the quality of urban life of which quantitative and qualitative dimensions often cause considerable difficulties of measurement.

It is only through using a combination of physical, functional and administrative factors that one can clearly see whether the quality of the environment deteriorates or improves over time. All the relevant indicators should provide information on the average situation in the capital cities in our context, as well as on deviations from the average.[11]

Emphasis on numerical, quantitative indicators could be misleading. Value-reflecting, quality-oriented indicators measuring the divergence between desired states, or goals and current states are indispensable supplement to strictly quantitative indices of nature and magnitude of changes in the capital cities. Yet great caution should be exercised when trying to aggregate many social phenomena into a single measure.

It seem to me that the Resolution No: 234 of the Standing Conference of Local and Regional Authorities of Europe[12],

---

11   U.N., **Indicators of the Quality of Urban Development,** New York, 1977, pp.4-6; and Harvey S. Perloff (ed.), **The Quality of Urban Environment: Essays on New Resources in an urban Age,** Resources for the Future the normative Inc., Baltimore, 1969.

12   It was renamed as the Congress of Local and Regional Authorities at the middle of the 1990's.

Council of Europe (March 30, 1992), is highly helpful in better understanding and evaluating the normative characteristics of urban life in the capital cities.

The principles adopted by this resolution are grouped under the title of The European Urban Charter. The European Declaration of Urban Rights adopted similarly by CL-RAE (Conference of Local and Regional Authorities of Europe) on March 18, 1992, enumerates the individual urban rights of Europeans.[13] Each right seems to be one of the foundation stones of a healthy and pleasant urban life and environment in world capitals. Indicators of such an environment as expressed in the Urban Charter are the followings: Security, an unpolluted and healthy environment, employment, housing, mobility, health, sport, leisure, culture, multicultural integration, good quality architecture and physical surroundings, participation, economic development, sustained development, services and goods, natural wealth and resources, personal fulfilment, equality and the like.

As it is clearly seen from the above list, environment is considered in the largest sense of the term encompassing not only the right to an environment free from various kinds of pollution and protective of nature and natural resources, but also much broader elements are regarded as integral parts of a contemporary concept of a viable and pleasant environment.

13 The Council of Europe renewed the European Urban Charter in 2008, nearly 20 years after its first adoption, under the title of the European Urban Charter II: Manifesto of a New Urbanity. In the new text of the European Urban Charter, the concepts such as the role of citizens in local democracy, cities as center of sustainable development, the significance of adaptation to urban life and accumulation of scientific data attract the attention.

The European Urban Charter concentrates on qualitative aspects of urban environment and the quality of life considerations. It identifies a number of universal guiding principles, readily applicable from country to country in the whole world where the problems of capital cities are very much the same in nature, if not in scale. It must be added that the Charter insists that such urban rights are applicable to all urban dwellers without discrimination, in respect of sex, age, origin, race, belief, socio-economic or political position, physical or psychological handicap.

The Case for Capital Cities

Since the major theme of this Conference is the capital cities, but not the other metropolitan areas, the critical question is to know what actually makes the state capitals distinct from other metropolitan centers. The answer is given by the background paper (August 23, 1993), emphasizing that "The capitals retain many branches of government and establish themselves as the central focus of important political and administrative activities of national and international concerns." In other words, these critical political and administrative duties are reserved only for the capital cities.

Coupled with economic functions generated by their position in the national economy or as a part of the world economic system, their population size tends to increase abnormally. In great majority of world capitals, the optimum size of the city is considerably surpassed. This, in turn, does not fall to bring about adverse consequences as expressed by such terms as "external diseconomies" or "urban pathologies".[14]

---

14   Henry Teune, "Growth and Pathologies of Giant Cities", **The Metropolitan Era, Vol.I, A World of Giant Cities,** (eds.), M.Dogan and J.D.Kasarda, Sage, Beverly Hills, 1088, pp.351-376.

Increased population density is another source of complaint. Sir Raymond Unwin had drawn the attention to the socio-economic costs of density and disorderly urban growth at the beginning of the 20th Century in his well-known work entitled as *Nothing Gained by Overcrowding*. In fact, costs of density are considerable, and pollution alone from concentration exceeds physical capacities to absorb it. Density also increases the likelihood of contagious diseases. It also generates the need to substitute government for the social controls of family and kin. As a result, a number of improvisations and technologies are required in sewerage, sanitation, and disease control. High density makes it easier also to rope, steal, because of weakened societal controls and greater opportunity.

There are of course many examples of capital cities which function quite well and which provide their inhabitants with a satisfactory quality of environment. In these capital cities a balance is struck between economic development and retention of a high quality of environment. Most of the state capitals in the industrialized countries are in this category.

However, few would argue that the capitals of most of the Third World countries are good for all but a small number of their residents. Most of these capitals are not so well off and reflect a wide range of societal difficulties and painful adjustments, inner city decay, deterioration of historic centers, excessive traffic densities, noise, air and soil pollution, shortage of good quality and affordable housing, high unemployment, unfamiliar and alien surroundings and neighborhoods. Some of them no longer meet even the most elementary requirements of livability.

Undoubtedly urban pathology is a relative and complex concept loaded with value connotations. Its manifestations are usually attached to particular values. Capital cities can be bad for human health, but good for national economic development; destructive of family life, but an effective means to assure human services; harmful to environmental conditions, but good for individual opportunities.

A similar relativity of the concept of the costs of urban pathologies may be attributable to the nature of the locality. The benefits of Los Angeles may accrue to the residents of Southern California, not the citizens of the city; the costs to the citizens of Paris may redound to France; Amsterdam may drain western Europe; and Tokyo, whatever the losses to its residents for its huge size, may be vital to the world economy.[15] Therefore, suitability, livability and pleasantness of capital cities have to be seen from many different angles.

Ecological Concerns and Sustainable Development

The world has passed through four main stages in the progress of ecological thoughts during the last two centuries.[16] The first was associated with the rise of romanticism in the early 18 th Century. Poets and writers like Emerson, Muir, Chekov and Tolstoy judged human activity to be ethically linked to natural processes and purposes.

The second phase which occurred at the turn of the 19th Century following the economic depression of the 1920's. This was the era of the environmental manager who sought to manipulate the new understanding of natural processes

---

15   H.Teune, **op.cit.,**p. 363.
16   Timothy O'Riordan, "Future Directions for Environmental Policy", Wissenschatzentrum Berlin, IIUG Discussion Paper, 84-14., Berlin 1984.

in the interests of humankind. Nature was a usufruct, a substance capable of being transformed into economic and aesthetic wealth. They altered landscapes and intervened in natural processes to improve the well-being of man. In so doing, they regulated environmental damage and resource depletion in the interests of capitalistic enterprise.

In the mid 1960's, a period of rapid economic growth and ubiquitous communications began. This was a period of institution-building, regulation and the rise of politically articulate and legally active pressure groups. During 1968-1974, every major democratic nation saw the emergence of the new environmental scientists, a host of regulatory bodies and advisory committees. The ethos of romanticists was lost and skills of the environmental scientists were swallowed in interest groups lobbying and political indecision.

Finally came the modern era. This is the period of modern environmentalism. A very different picture is emerging in which a coalescence of the 19th Century romantic ideals, early 20 th Century technical expertise and scientific understanding of the late 20 th Century political lobbying and institution-building is taking place.

Concern of the public opinion for ecology in general has grown tremendously during the last two and a half decades all over the world. Alerted by global problems of environmental degradation, the world public opinion expressed great concern for the globalization of environmental problems following the publication of the *Limits to Growth*, a report prepared by the Club of Rome.

Two important international conferences, the first in Stockholm in 1972, and the second in Rio de Janeiro in 1992, called the nations of the world, at 20 year interval, to cooperate for the protection of the integrity of the global environmental and developmental systems.

In between, the Report of the World Commission on Environment and Development made it clear that there is the possibility for a new era of economic growth, one that must be based on policies that sustain and expand the environmental resource base. In other words, it was emphasized that sustainable is both necessary and possible. It is a process in which the exploitation of resources, the direction of investments, the orientation of technological development and institutional change are all in harmony and enhance both current and future potential to meet human needs and aspirations.[17]

Global environmental problems caused by socio-economic activities in developed countries are the depletion of ozone layer, global warming induced by the increase of carbon dioxide, and acid rains. On the other hand, global environmental problems of developing countries are tropical deforestation, desertification, erosion and various kinds of pollution, let alone the poverty. Finally, extinction of wildlife species and marine pollution are some of the global problems caused by the activities of both developed and underdeveloped countries.[18]

Rio Declaration proclaimed that "Human beings are at the center of concern for sustainable development. They are entitled to a healthy and productive life in harmony with

17   World Commission on Environment and Development, **Our Common Future,** Oxford University Press, London, 1987, p. 46.

18   **Japan Activities to Cope with Global Environmental Problems,** The Ad Hoc Group on Global Environmental Problems, June 1988, Tokyo, pp.4-32; and Sylvie Faucheux and Jean-François Noel, **Les menaces globales sur l'environnment,** Reperes, Paris 1990, pp. 10-38.).

nature".[19] It is emphasized that the right to development must be fulfilled so as to equitably meet developmental and environmental needs of present and future generations.[20] Therefore in order to achieve sustainable development, environmental protection should constitute an integral part of the development process and cannot be considered in isolation from it.

The Conference drew the attention to the role of participation by emphasizing that "Environmental issues are best handled with the participation of all concerned citizens, at the relevant level".[21] Therefore, each individual should have appropriate access to information concerning the environment that is held by public authorities, including information on hazardous materials and activities in their communities, and the opportunity to participate decision-making processes.

The role of international cooperation is extremely important in this respect. With the goal of establishing a new and equitable global partnership, the use of the sovereign right to exploit their own resources should not cause damage to the environment of other states or of areas beyond the limits of national jurisdiction.

The same spirit of global partnership requires the conservation, protection and restoration of the health and integrity of the Earth's ecosystem.[22] Consensus has to be relied upon for taking the environmental measures addressing transboundary or global environmental problems. But the

19   Principle 6.
20   Principle 3.
21   Principle 10.
22   Principle 7.

most important principle (No:14) is that states should effectively cooperate to discourage and prevent the relocation and transfer to other states of any activities and substances that cause severe environmental degradation or are to be harmful to human health.

Third world nations made it clear in the Conference that there was too much environment in the discussions and not enough development. Concern for nature directly was to be taken for an elitist luxury, an inhuman overlooking of the human poverty of the Third World. In fact, as mentioned above, Gilberto Mastrinho complained that "Ecologists care more about plants and animals than about people". This approach was at the source of many divisions and polarities observed in the Conference. It was expressing the just observation made by the Brundtland Report: "The Earth is one, but the World is not".

Aspects of Urban Ecological Issues in World Capitals

What is maintained in the European Urban Charter concerning ecological concerns is greatly valid for the capitals of the World. All the assertions laid down in that document may be said to be more correct and explicit in the capitals than in other localities.

In fact, the car dominates the capitals' transport policies and it degrades the whole public transport systems. Cars are killing the ecology of the capitals slowly, but surely. If nothing is done to change the status quo, road traffic will destroy not only the ecology of the capital cities, but contribute considerably to the destruction of global environment via the "greenhouse effect". Besides, cars threaten the capital cities through noise, discomfort, psychological and physical insecurity, loss of amenity and social space, atmospheric pollution. As a result, the domination of car in urban transport brings about cultural and social loss; and it contributes to the decline of town spirit as a place for living, for contact, and activities and culture.

Many capital cities are becoming more and more agglomerations of stone concrete, steel, glass and asphalt, with generally monotonous stretches of grass and wasteland of little use. The atmosphere and the ground have been polluted with noxious elements and emissions from industry, energy plants, traffic and private households. It must be kept in mind that nature and urban life are not mutually exclusive concepts.

The way in which the townscape is conserved and developed and the way in which inter-related issues of safety, comfort, convenience and appearance are dealt with are important considerations in the pursuit of an improved urban environment in capital cities.

On the other hand, the urban heritage constitutes an important and irrepleplaceable part of the urban fabric, crucial for the identity of the capital city and its inhabitants. It hands down to future generations a system of reference, composed of monuments, groups of buildings and sites. It is often threatened by disuse and deterioration.

Housing is an integral part of a decent environment. Access and the right to shelter is enshrined also in the Article 25 of the Universal Declaration of Human Rights. If its is deficient or inadequate, as in the case of most of the Third World capitals, it is the key element in insecurity, violence, segregation, intolerance and racism.

One of the fundamental rights of any citizen is the free access to all the social activities and facilities of the capital city without distinction of sex, age, nationality and physical and mental ability. Categories of citizens experiencing momentary or permanent problems of adjustment are often ignored. It is also important to ensure that everyone has the right to participate in sportive activities, thus improving their lives.

The promotion of cultural activities and the achievement of cultural democracy are integral parts of a sound ecological development. Architectural creation, language, the arts, music, and literature are all expressions of the rich storehouse of history, and the collective memory of the urban center, components of the cultural heritage and experience in the capital cities.

Full and active membership of the local community is becoming more and more important in a cosmopolitan world. However, this principle is not respected everywhere in our time. İmmigrant communities coming to capitals from other countries, minorities with different traditions, languages and religions are not always accepted or integrated into the community. Their experiences of urban life is usually synonymous with exclusion, solitude, fear and poor standards of living.

Leaders of large and capital cities have little power to make decisions on immigration policies laid down by national governments. This has a close bearing on the availability of employment opportunities in the capitals. Yet, it should be the right of every one of working age to participate through his own endeavors in the fruits of what the capital city has to offer. The Third World capitals are far from providing a certain standard of living, let alone promoting the quality of environment.

Policies
Solutions at Micro Level

Local leaders should find ways of providing cost-effective infrastructure and services, to prevent a further decline in the sanitary conditions, and to contain existing environmental hazards. Given that national and international mass migration will continue at varying degrees in the near future, the only way to relieve the pressure on environment is to ensure income growth and to alleviate poverty in the long run.

Since haphazard urbanization in developing countries turns economies of scale into diseconomies of scale, what is most needed now is a new paradigm for urban development, an ecological urban restructuring, appropriate institutions and a legal framework conducive to environmental city planning.

Highest priority should be given to urban poor which are directly affected by the negative side-effects for urban dynamics. They benefit little if at all from the industrial and commercial activities that degrade the environment, but bear the full costs of their adverse effects. They are the primary victims of municipal sewage discharged in water, of solid and toxic wastes dumps.[23]

Alternative Technologies

A full scale attacks on urban problems using conventional capital-intensive technology, would require large increases

---

23   Udo Simonis and D. Oodit, **Op.cit.,** p.12.

in investments. At such costs the crying need of urban sanitation cannot be met. Alternative Technologies which are
much cheaper have to replace the conventional ones.

Several possibilities exists for in-door air pollution control. For example, charcoal or biomass when fermented to
produce wood alcohol provide more energy per unit of fuel
than raw biomass, and reduce air pollution at the same time.

Solid waste minimization can ve achieved through modification of industrial processes and through change in the
design and use of products. Durable packaging instead of
single-used packaging can be made mandatory. Various
mechanisms for the implementation of user charges may
be experimented. In changing behavior, instruments such
as "pay per bag", "charge per can", "deposit refund system"
can be successful in reducing solid waste. Usually environmental costs are fully integrated in the price of a product.
As a result, market signals do not provide sufficient incentives for waste minimization. Therefore, efforts need to be
made for the full internalization of environmental costs also
in order to promote new technologies.

Transportation

As indicated above, it is essential that the volume of travel,
particularly by private car, be reduced. Highest priority should
be given to public and collective transport, bicycles, pedes-
trians instead of individual transport of people and goods.
The street must be recovered as a social milieu with gradual elimination of extraneous noise. Local authorities have
a clear responsibility to support and develop consciousness-
raising campaigns, in order both to shift behavioral patterns
and to inculcate in town dwellers the belief that the street

belongs to them, it is a communal property and it must be used harmoniously, and respected.

In fact, urban population problems are multiplying rapidly in the capitals of the Third World where automobile ownership symbolizes success and prestige. Chinese cities, with their traditional reliance on bicycles and buses for individual mobility, are perhaps the most efficient in their consumption of transport energy. Unfortunately, as Chinese living standards rise, autos are replacing bicycles, thus reducing energy efficiency and raising pollution levels.[24]

It is much appreciated that in Japan which is one of the biggest car producers in the world, the use of private car in daily life of the capital does not have the highest priority. Rail transportation dominates the scene. Japanese rationality necessitated to a certain extent by the dearth of urban land, has to be taken as an example by other developed and developing countries.

Some of the European capitals like Stockholm and Vienna have already banned traffic from various parts of the central city. Virtually all European capitals have some restrictions on auto use in force. In Hong-Kong and Singapore as well as in Korean cities, taxes and financial disincentives discourage auto use and encourage walking and biking.

Environment and Nature

The principle of sustainable development requires that local and regional authorities accept fully their responsibility for dealing within their boundaries with pollution,

24   Lester R.Brown and Jodi L.Jacobson, **The Future of Urbanization: Facing the Ecological and Economic Constraints,** Worldwatch Paper, No:77, May 1987, p.41.

domestic and toxic waste produced by them, rather than shifting them to other areas or leaving them as a legacy for future generations.

Capital cities should adopt policies to prevent pollution. Temporary, short-term measures, discharging solid and water wastes into rivers and lakes, burning or recycling waste, should be replaced by reduction of emission at source, application of clean technology, use of alternative fuels.

Establishing green belts within and around urban areas safeguards and increases local water supplies. A green belt strategy aimed at permanent protection of open land within and between cities can also mitigate pollution problems and increase urban self-sufficiency.

Priority areas for nature protection should be established. Greening roofs, walls, courtyards, city farms, and study gardens for children can play a valuable role in the establishment of direct contact with nature. This is essential if a responsible relationship with nature and natural resources is to be created.

Physical Forms of the Capitals

City centers must be safeguarded as important symbols of the cultural and historical heritage. The creation and management of open space should be neighborhood based, through partnership between the city governments, community groups and the population as a whole. Architectural characteristics of the city should be preserved as a sign of the quality of the urban townscape. Residential areas have to be protected against air, water, soil and sub-soil pollution. Environmental protection and buffer zones, parks, gardens should be established. Heavy traffic causing disturbance has to be avoided as much as possible.

The Protection of Architectural Heritage

A legal framework is needed to regulate respective rights, responsibilities and conflicts between the public authorities and the private owners in order to ensure protection of the heritage. In addition to the establishment of a comprehensive inventory of the urban architectural heritage, an increased awareness among the general public and the individual owners of heritage of its value is needed. Urban heritage must be interpreted into contemporary life via its incorporation as an essential element in overall planning.

Housing

Every person and family should be entitled to secure and salubrious housing. Capital cities should ensure diversity, choice and mobility in housing. Since the rights of persons and families in the most disadvantaged categories cannot be safeguarded by market forces alone, capital cities must cooperate with the central governments to intervene in the housing market.

Disadvantaged and Disabled Persons in Capital Cities

All commercial, administrative and public buildings must be accessible to all people, whatever their disability or handicap. Policies for this category of people should aim to integrate and not to over-protect. It is also important that houses and workplaces are suitably adapted to the requirements of the disadvantaged and disabled.

Sports and Leisure

Policy for sport and leisure in the capitals should be directed:

To remove all constraints which prevent many dwellers of the capital city from taking part in sport; to provide a network of basic sport facilities covering the whole of the city and to ensure that such facilities include small-scale units within easy reach of homes; and to plan in the city open spaces, wooded areas, playgrounds, stretches of water and cycle paths in order to foster and stimulate recreational activities.

Culture

The universality of cultural democracy is embodied in the Article 27 of the Universal Declaration of Human Rights. Therefore, culture should not be treated as a domain of a privileged for few or an elite, but rather a vehicle for stimulating the creativity and imagination of all special groups in the capital. Cultural exchange, as a powerful bond between peoples of different nationalities, regions and nations has to be encouraged. This should also include extensive collaboration between the capitals, other local authorities, community groups, the NGO's and the private sector.

Full and active membership of the local community is becoming more and more important in a cosmopolitan world. However, this principle is not respected everywhere in our time. Immigrant communities coming to capitals from other countries and minorities with different traditions, languages and religions are not always accepted or integrated into community. Their experiences in urban life is usually synonymous with exclusion, solitude, fear, insecurity and poor standard of living. Yet the New Leading City concept requires that capitals must be open in all senses, within the limits of domestic and international law, reflecting global solidarity among peoples of the world.

Multicultural Integration

Capital cities should adopt or reinforce legislation against discrimination, in order to ensure equal access to all citizens-irrespective of race or ethnic origins to public places. This right should be guaranteed by joint bodies composed of representatives of the capital city, those of neighborhood associations, and the representatives of different communities. Central government policies should be revised accordingly.

At the beginning of the 21 st Century, capital cities should be encouraged to put into operation at least of the principles of the European Convention on the Participation of Foreigners in Public Life at Local Level, which recognizes the right to vote and be elected in local elections for foreigners having legally resided in the capital city for a specific period of years.

Finally, multicultural integration implies full integration of important communities into the social and physical urban environment.

Health

The urban environment in the capital city must be conducive to good health for all citizens. This can be done by developing a comprehensive urban environment policy; managing waste, monitoring air, water, soil, and sub-soil pollution; by totally eliminating dangerous waste, by keeping the most sensitive urban areas and populations under constant review, by generally promoting community development and social renewal. A reliable and durable supply of goods, including a healthy and safe supply of drinking water is a major factor in ensuring good health. Monitoring the supply and distribution of non-durable consumer goods, issuing precise regulations regarding the manufacture of foodstuffs and the cleanliness of places where food is consumed, and by issuing precise policy statements regarding the priority of supply and distribution of major public utility infrastructure.

Broader Policies

Towards the last decade of the 20th Century, nations realized that economic development is important, but it is not everything. Economic and social development are inextricably linked, and the concept of sustainable development itself emanates from such a need. Sustainable development is striking a balance between economic development, environmental protection and social improvement. Urban economic growth in world capitals with regard to inadequate ecological consequences can not contribute to the prosperity of mankind.

From the standpoint of human welfare ecology, sustainable development means not merely sustaining the natural resource base systems for human production, but also sustaining biological support systems for human reproduction. This is the reason why the stream of human welfare ecology has been so much critical of economic growth per se and the idea that science and technology alone can deliver the humankind from the ecological crisis.[25]

25 Robyn Eckerseley, **Environmentalism and Political Theory: Toward an Ecocentric Approach,** State University of New York Press, Albany, 1992, p.37.

Numerous NGO's, including the Biopolitics International Organization, have been alerting the public opinion all over the world about the impact of technology and economic growth on the bio-environment, and emphasizing that in the present meta-industrial era, society is undergoing a crisis of values, realized by everyone since it affects our daily lives.[26]

In fact, the present destruction rate of the bio-environment threatens not only the aesthetic values, but also the very essence of bio-diversity in our planet. In the late 1960's, ecology was developed as a reaction to the destruction of the ecos (the house, habitat), that was endangered. However, what is in danger nowadays is bios, the life itself. Humanity has no right to destroy within one or two generations the gift of bios, the most precious possession on the planet.[27] Inhabitants of the capital cities are more than anybody else the victims of such degradations.

Then, it is only through the sustainable development that people living in capital cities can survive. Only under the conditions of sustainable development that eco-citizens, members of the eco-society, visualized by Joel de Rosnay, can benefit from the symbiosis of economy and ecology.

In other words, the sequence is from the primitive society, through industrial society to eco-society, or post-industrial society. This new society will be constructed from bottom-up, not from up to bottom. This society recognizes the private ownership of the means of production and the

26 Agni Vlavşanos-Arvanitis, "Bios in the Next Millenium: Reversing the Crisis of Values", in A.V.Arvanitis and Ruşen Keleş (eds.), **Biopolitics: The Bio- Environment,** Vol. IV. Athens, 1993, pp.1-10.

27 Martine Rémond-Guilloud, **Du droit de détruire,** Presses Universitaire de France, Paris, 1989, pp.11-56.

state ownership at the same time. It accepts adaptation capacity of free enterprise, but it puts it under strict control of the community of consumers and users. Eco-society, in the words of Joel de Rosnay is a participatory and decentralized society. Its cities are profoundly reorganized. The most ancient quarters are given to people, rescued of the cars, the atmosphere became breathable again and silence is respected everywhere. On the streets, in the parks, people take their time. Very little medicine is consumed; very infrequently people recourse to doctors. They go to hospitals in exceptional cases.[28]

In the 19th Century, mere size was regarded as a desirable attribute of the cities, and "the bigger, the better" was a maxim which embodied public opinion on the subject. There was little or no attempt to limit or control urban growth. Today, the overblown, dropsical city of elephantine proportions can no longer be regarded as desirable or even tolerable in present conditions. As pointed out by Robson and Regan more than twenty years ago, "The period of unqualified acceptance and unfettered growth of metropolitan city is passing".[29]

An increasing gap exists between the fiscal and ecological costs of supporting urban development in its present context and the resources required to sustain it. All countries now need a new norm of urban development- one that embraces the concept of the city as an ecosystem in which population size and urban form are matched to available resources. The question policy-makers face now is how capital

28   Joel de Rosnay, **Le macroscope,** Points, Ed. Seuil Paris, 1975, pp.313-321.
29   William A.Robson and D.E.Regan (eds.), **Great Cities of the World,** Vol.I, George Allen and Unwin, London, 1972, p.125.

cities should be in a world that depends primarily on renewable resources.

It seems that the optimum city size will be reduced as the age of oil slowly fades and the age of renewable energy begs to unfold. Oil is a concentrated resource easily transported in huge quantities that large cities require. In contrast, renewable energy sources, whether firewood, solar collectors, or small-scale hydro, are more geographically diffuse. Both the ecology and economics of these energy sources suggest that the future will favor smaller cities rather than the giant urban centers.[30]

The problem we face, on the eve of the 21 st Century, largely emanates from rapid population growth, industrialization and urbanization. Solutions must be searched for within the context of these and similar variables. David Hume has anticipated in the 18 th Century that the ideal city of future would not exceed 700.000 population. Jules Vernes, in his turn, saw the possibility of emerging big cities of nearly ten million inhabitants. It was only the contemporary Japanese architect Kenzo Tange, who, more realistically, talked about super metropolises of ten million each, comparable to Mexico City and Shanghai of the year 2.000, which are expected to reach 30 million and 25 million by then, respectively.

Certainly, we are now faced not only with a simple issue of numerical magnitude. What confronts us has widespread qualitative consequences as well. Despite all new developments with respect to ideological differences between East and West, what seems to be almost certain is that only those countries with strict control over the ownership and

30   L.Brown and J.Jacobson, **op.cit.** . p.45.

use of resources, including the urban land, have a better chance to effectively grasp the ecological problems of present-day capital cities and human habitat.

Normally, the actual costs of unprecedented urban growth has something to do with surpassing the human scale in human habitats. That is why present-day city life in most of the capitals tends to alienate man from his environment. Planners of future societies have to design capitals not for machines alone, but for the needs of human beings. As rightly put by Laborit, the French thinker, "Because the road we have followed has brought us to the conclusion that all serious problems confronting contemporary man could find their solutions only in the transformation of man's own behaviour.[31]

On the other hand, one can find the ways of striking a balance between the goals of economic growth and environment by trying to modify life styles without being forced to accept the exaggerated view that these two variables are essentially contradictory objectives. As pointed out by Johan Galtung, this depends to a large extent upon self-sacrifice of industrialized countries, and on their formation of new life styles.[32]

It is essential to modify the attitudes of developed nations towards satisfying themselves with lower standards of living as far as their habits of nutrition, clothing, housing, education, health, transportation and communications are

31   Henri Laborit, L'homme et la ville, Flammarion, Paris, 1981, p.201.
32   "Perspectives on Environmental Policies in Overdeveloped and Underdeveloped Countries", , pp.9-21: and Ignacy S.Sachs, "Developing with Harmony with Nature: Consumption Patterns, Time and Space Uses, Resources Profiles and Technical Choices",pp.205-227, in Bernard Gleaser(ed.), Ecodevelopment, Pergamon, New York, 1984.

concerned. In other words, developed countries must visualize that they have certain responsibilities towards poor nations.

Not only the developing countries but also the developed World suffers from the overgrowth of their capital cities. Many search for alternative settlement patterns to be created only in accordance with well-prepared long-term plans.[33]

For example, Japan looked for alternative locations to remove its capital out of Tokyo in recent past. In a gold-prize winning essay, submitted to a contest organized by the Daily Japanese newspaper Asahi some years ago, the authors seriously had recommended putting the functions of the capital city in several "giant ships", one ship carrying the legislative and executive departments of the state apparatus, to spend two years in each of Japan's major harbours around the islands, in accordance with 21st Century concept of "rotating capital".[34]

They recommended that increasing need for the internalization of Tokyo must be met by the establishment of an economic ward (keizai-ku) and a world ward (sekai-ku), forming the basic spatial structure of the metropolis, in addition to the existing 23 wards (ku).

Let alone such science-fiction like products of creative human imagination, it is a well-known fact that plans are in preparation for at least part of the rapidly increasing population and economic functions of the capital city to

33 Tokyo Metropolitan Government, **Protecting Tokyo's Environment,** Tokyo, 1985: TMG., **2nd Long-Term Plan of the capital city Metropolis,** TMG. Library, No: 25, Tokyo, 1991.

34 **Asahi Evening News,** Editorial, "Ease Congestion in Tokyo", January 7, 1988.

be settled on and under Tokyo Bay at the beginning of the 21st Century.[35]

Some years ago, the urban land crisis in Tokyo reached incredible dimensions so as to involve even the works of several diplomatic missions, and some of them expressed even publicly their intention to close off their offices in the capital, in order to avoid the financial difficulties caused by increasing rents and speculated land prices.

Finally, a few nations have experimented in the past to transfer their state capitals elsewhere. Some of them are trying to decongest administrative offices, research institutions and the like, that should no longer be located necessarily in the capital. However, the core of the problem is essentially an economic one, and it obviously needs economic remedies. It is the large companies that are responsible for the tremendous land price increases in the capitals. Most of those companies anticipate enormous profits from land speculation game, to be realized as a result of new office building booms. Therefore, it seems that unless the governments are determined to intervene actively in the urban land market, proposals of decentralization and decongestion will remain ineffective. In this connection, it must be admitted that inherent conflict between the public and the private interests cannot be kept under control without a determined intervention of the state as an arbiter to correct imperfections of the market mechanism.

Environmental Ethics and the Capital Cities

The growth of ecological concerns in world capitals is closely related, in the final analysis, to ethical responsibility

35   Y.Yasoi, "Tokyo on and under the Bay", **Japan Quarterly**, Vol.35, No:12, April-June 1988, pp.118-126.

of individuals living in the capital, towards the ownership and use of urban land and environmental assets. Humanity needs to find a social criterion to be used in his search for the rightest way between maximizing the public and the private interests. The trend from Aristoteles to Léon Duguit signifies a progress from individualism and selfishness toward a system more or less socialized, where the public interest is in balance with private concerns, if not totally superior to it.

Contemporary formulations of the concept of intergenerational solidarity charge individuals with a social responsibility for future generations in their use of present day values.[36] It is commonly recognized that the owner or user of an environmental value could not have an unlimited right over it, if the use of that right injures the social interests represented by the state. A civilized society, explicitly embedded in the concept of the New Leading City mentioned above, demands more than any other, that people be guided by a sense of responsibility which extends beyond the duties exacted by law.

As Ciceron said several centuries ago, "You will not prevent the river from flowing, because it is a common good for all, and it belongs to no one (res nullius). It is so for the air, because it can not be seized." The first task of the justice should be to guarantee the use of these common goods by all the peoples of today" and by future generations.

---

36 Philip Hansen, **Environmental Ethics: Philosophical and Policy Perspectives,** Simon Fraser University, Institute of Humanities for the Burnaby, B.C., 1986; Frédérick Lenoir, **Le temps de la responsabilité: entretiens sur l'éthique,** Fayard, Paris, 1991; Richard E.Hart (ed.), **Ethics and the Environment** , University Press of America, New York, 1982.

What is morally right or wrong, good or bad, is ultimately determined by looking to see what happens to human beings, other living things and the ecology. Therefore, an environmentally ethical action has to be understood as the one that seeks the greatest number of people and ecological values belonging to humanity.

Where the ethical guide to shape the conduct of human beings, as the prime destroyer of environment, can be found? From Montaigne to Fénélon, from Bentham to Léon Say, from Condorcet to Jules Perry, liberal thinkers always recognized a primordial role to human education. John Stuart Mill accorded an undeniable importance to the development of moral and intellectual capacities of citizens through education, in order to ensure the operation of all political institutions.

All these observations are well substantiated by the fact that the countries which are the most successful ones in the protection of their environment are those which are able to educate their citizens adequately, using the all means, to cope properly with the disposition and preservation of the national assets. Growth of concerns for the ecology in world capitals can only be evaluated safely in such a broader context.

Bibliography

Abrams, Charles, *The Language of Cities,* Avon Books, New York, 1972.

The Ad Hoc Group of Global Environmental Problems, *Japan Activities to Cope with Global Environmental Problems,* Tokyo, June, 1988.

Brown, Lester R. And Jodi L. Jacobson, *The Future of Urbanization: Facing the Ecological and Economic Constraints,* Worldwatch Paper, No: 77, May 1987.

De Rosnay, Joel, *Le Macroscope,* Points, Ed.Seuil, Paris, 1975.

Eckersley, Robyn, *Environmentalism and Political Theory: Toward and Ecocentric Approach,* State University of New York Press, Albany, 1992.

Faucheux, Sylvie et Jean-François Noel, *Les menaces globales sur l'environnement,* Reperes, La Découverte, Paris, 1990.

Ferry, Luc, *Le nouvel ordre écologiqye,* Barnard Grasset, Paris, 1992.

Galtung, Johan, "Perspectives on Environmental Policies in Overdeveloped and Underdeveloped Countries", in Bernard Gleaser (ed.), *Ecodevelopment,* Pergamon, New York, 1984.

Hansen, Philip, *Environmental Ethics: Philosophical and Policy Perspectives,* Simon Fraser University, Institute of Humanities for the Burnaby, B.C., 1986.

Hart, Richard E. (Ed.), *Ethics and the Environment,* University Press of America, New York, 1987.

International Society for Environmental Ethics, *Newsletter,* Summer 1992.

Laborit, Henri, *L'homme et la ville,* Flammarion, Paris, 1991.

Lenoir, Fréderick, *Le temps de la responsabiliité: entretients sur l'éthique,* Fayard, Paris, 1991.

Meyer-Abisch, K.M., *Wege zum Frieden mit der natur,* Munich, 1984.

O'Riordan, Timothy, "Future Directions for Environmental Policy", Wissenschaftszentrum Berlin, Internationales Institute für Umwelt und Gesellschaft, Discussion Paper, 84-14, Berlin, 1984.

Paddison, Ronan, *The Fragmented State: The Political Geography of Power,* St. Martin's Press, New York, 1983.

Harvey, Perloff S. (ed.), *The Quality of Urban Environment: Essays on New Resources in an Urban Age,* Resources for the Future Inc., Baltimore, 1969.

Lepage, Corinne, *Vivre Autrement,* Grasset, Paris, 2009 (translated into Turkish under the title of *Başka Türlü Yaşamak,* by Ruşen Keleş and Can Umut Çiner and published by İmge Publishers in 2020, Ankara).

Robson, William A. and D.E.Regan (eds.), *Great Cities of the World,* Vol.I, George Allen and Unwin, London, 1972.

Rémond-Gouilloud, Martine, *Du droit de détruire,* Presses Universitaires de France, Paris, 1989.

Sachs, Ignacy S., "Developing in Harmony with Nature: Consumption Patterns, Time and Space Uses, Resources Profiles and Technical Choices ", in Bernard Glaeser (ed.), *Ecodevelopment,* Pergamon, New York, 1984.

Simonis, Udo and Deonan Oodit, "Poverty, Environment and Development", in Agni-Vlavianos Arvanitis and Ruşen Keleş (eds.), *Biopolitics: The Bio-Environment,* Vol. 4, Athens, 1993.

Teune, Henri, "Growth and Pathologies of Giant Cities", in Mattei Dogan and John Kasarda (eds.), *The Metropolitan Eraf*: Vol. I: *A World of Giant Cities,* Sage, Beverly Hills, 1988.

Tokyo Metropolitan Government, *Protecting Tokyo's Environment,* Tokyo, 1985.

Tokyo Metropolitan Government, *2nd Long-Term Plan for the Tokyo Metropolis,* TMG Library, No:22, Tokyo, 1987.

Tokyo Metropolitan Government, *3rd Long-Term Plan for the Tokyo Metropolis,* TMG Library, Mo:25, Tokyo, 1991.

U.N., *Indicators of Urban Development,* New York, 1977.

Vlavianos-Arvanitis, Agni, "Bios in the Next Millenium: Reversing the Crisis of Values", in A. Vlavianos-Arvanitis and Ruşen Keleş (eds.), *Biopolitics: The Bio-Environment,* Vol.4, Athens, 1993.

The World Bank, *World Development Report 1993,* Washington D.C., 1993.

World Commission on Environment and Development, *Our Common Future,* Oxford University Press, London, 1987.

Yasoi, L., "Tokyo on and under the Bay", *Japan Quarterly,* Vol.35, No:12, April-June, 1988.

Quality of Urban Life in Turkey as Affected by The Policies of Urbanization and Environment[*]

Introductory Remarks on the Concepts

The quality of life is a broad concept which is concerned with the overall well-being in society. However, there is no agreed- upon definition of the term in academic and policy discourses. Rather the tendency is towards divergence. According to one of the definitions, "well-being reflects not only living, but also the ways in which people respond and feel about their lives in those domains.[1] The concept of the quality of life has three main characteristics: First, it reflects the individuals' life situations and their perceptions rather than a country's quality of life; secondly, it is a multidimensional concept, covering multiple life domains such as housing conditions, education, employment, work-life balance, Access to institutions and public services and their interplay; and finally, it brings together objective information on

---

[*]   Naples, Italy, 2012.

[1]   T.Fahey, C.Whelan,and B.Maitre, *Quality of Life in Europe: First European Quality mof Life Survey, 2003,* Eurıopean Foundation for the Improvement of Living and Working Conditions, Office of Official Publications of the European Communiities, Luxemburg, 2005. P.14.

living conditions with subjective views and attitudes to provide a picture of overall well-being in society.[2]

It should be noted that the micro concept of quality of
life has perhaps been most widely used in relation to health
conditions where it is essentially used to extend the assessment of clinical outcomes beyond simple physical survival. It is also argued that the concept of the quality of life
needs to be used in a context beyond an economic perspective privileging income and wealth in measuring well-being.[3] Dieter Frick draws our attention to different qualities
of urban life: Objective and subjective. Objectively, it can
be measured by the level of physical and mental health enjoyed by the inhabitants of an area. On the other hand, sub-
jectively, the presence or absence of the quality of urban life
is measured by the sum of the perceptions and experiences
of those who live in, work in and visit a city or a neighborhood and the judgments resulting from these perceptions
and experiences.[4]

As rightly observed in one of the publications of the
Turkish Academy of Sciences on the indicators of Quality
of Life, the concept may be approached from more than one
angles, in addition to philosophical, ethical and psychological ones, such as human rights, health considerations and
environmental concerns.[5] Environmental quality has always

---

2   M.Shucksmith, S.Cameron, T.Merridew ,and F.Pichler, Urban-Rural Dif-
     ferences in Quality of Life Accross the European Union,*Regional Studies,*
     43, 2009.,*p.1276.*

3   Ibid, p.1276.

4   Dieter Frick (ed.), *The Quality of Urban Life: Social, Psychological and Phys-
     ical Conditons,* Gruyter, Berlin, 1986, p.2.

5   Türkiye Bilimler Akademisi (Turkish Academy of Sciences), *Yaşam kalitesi
     Göstergeleri: Türkiye İçin Bir Veri Sistemi Önerisi (Indicators of the Quality
     of Life: A Proposal for a Data Base System for Turkey),*Ankara, 2004.

been one of the most important components of the quality of life. Although this reality is not faced with any reaction, the measurement of qualitative and effective evaluation of environmental quality has been a bit of a headache for social scientists.[6]

It is because of the increasing role of the health conditions in defining the concept of the quality of life that Parliamentary Assembly of the Council of Europe has recently voted for an Additional Protocol to the European Convention on Human Rights concerning the right to a healthy environment.[7] From another point of view, one has to remember that economists use the term negative *externality* to express misallocative or disagreeable effects of the free interplay of the market forces. In the source of most of the environmental disturbances, hazards, degradations and dilapidation are found the impacts of such externalities that can be overcome only by paying *a* certain price to the transacting party.

In order to analyze the relationships between the quality of life and environmental conditions adequately, it would be appropriate to have a brief look at urban environmental stresses affecting the rapidly urbanizing world at the beginning. Rapid population growth and urbanization, industrialization and technological change, increased expectations caused by rising affluence, gaps between the level of expectations and actual consumption patterns, lack of adequate public awareness concerning the deterioration of environment and dilapidation of resources and finally persisting human egoism make both the protection of the environment

---

6   T. O'Riordan, *Environmentalism*, Pion Ltd., London, 1976, p.178.

7   11 September 2009, Doc. 12003.

as well as the quality of urban life difficult goals to reach. Environmental stresses are linked to one another, they are dependent upon the nature of the economy, and the dichotomy of environment-economy causes, at the same time, occasionally social tensions and political unrest. The international aspects of the issue are no less important. Because the fact that pollution recognize no national boundaries and no country seems willing to give up any of its freedoms makes the problems of transboundary linkages extremely important. At the Millennium Summit in 2000, the members of the United Nations had reaffirmed their commitment to working towards a world in which eliminating poverty and sustaining development would have the highest priority. Millennium Development Goals focused the efforts of the world community on achieving significant and measurable improvements in the quality of life.

Integration of the principle of sustainable development, which is defined as the kind of development which meets the needs of the present, without compromising the ability of the future generations to meet their own needs, into policies and programmes and reserving the loss of environmental resources is not an easy task. Environment which is an essential component of the quality of urban life is too often overlooked by policy makers and planners, as a key resource for sustainable growth and poverty alleviation. It must urgently be integrated into the decision-making. Unless this is done successfully, many aspects of the quality of urban life will be affected diversely, as observed in many parts of urban environments in Turkey. Since environmental values are affected considerably by our culture and cultural characteristics of the inhabitants which are also shaped by the environment, there is a pressing need to strengthen the interdependence between bio-culture and the environment.[8]

General Setting of Urban Governance in Turkey

Turkey is a rapidly urbanizing country in the Middle East, with 76.6 percent of its total population (76 million) living in urban centers. Its level of urbanization was only 20 percent in 1950 and 43.9 percent in 1980. The number of cities having 10.000 or more inhabitants is 528, and those with 100.000 population and over is 138. There are seven cities with a population of one million and over. The distribution of cities among various city-size categories seems to be rather unbalanced, in the sense that more than three fours of the urban population is concentrated in the size category of 100.000 and over. A similar inequality exists between the level of urbanization in different geographical regions. For instance, while the degree of urbanization is as high as 91 percent in the Marmara Region, with İstanbul at its center, and 83 percent in Central Anatolia, it is not higher than 55 percent in such regions as Eastern Anatolia and the Black Sea. There is no doubt that such inequalities reflect at the same time relative socio-economic underdevelopment of the regions concerned.[9]

On the other hand, the Constitution of Turkey requires the establishment of a territorial organization based on the principles of centralization and decentralization (Art.123). Decentralized institutions are a) municipalities, b) departments

---

8   Agni Vilavianos-Arvanitis and Ruşen Keleş, "Biopolis: An Urban Development Model: Networking, Education and Culture", Paper presented to International Ekistics Conference on Human >settlements, Mumbai, 2010.

9   Ruşen Keleş, *Kentleşme Politikası (Policy of Urbanization)*, İmge, Ankara, 2012, (12 nd ed.).

and c) village administrations (Art.127). Municipalities which are established in settlements in settlements with 5.000 or more inhabitants are in charge of meeting the common service needs of local communities. At present there are 2950 municipalities, 81 departments and nearly 36.000 village administrations in Turkey.

According to the Quality of Life Survey carried out by the European Foundation for the improvement of Living and Working Conditions in 2007, the majority of Turks reported overall satisfaction with their life. They are least satisfied with domains for which the State is directly responsible, such as health services, education and Standard of living. In view of the fact that Turkey is a developing economy with more than 10.000 US Dollars per capita GNP, local authorities have to possess necessary resources to finance the construction of urban infrastructure, major urban facilities and services, without increasing their dependency upon the central government funds. However, a certain amount of funds from the national budget is allocated to local authorities every year, in accordance with the constitutional principle requiring that they have to be provided with necessary financial means in proportion to their competencies (Art.127).

Policies of urban development and environment have a close bearing upon the level of subjective and objective satisfaction with the quality of urban life. Therefore it is useful to have a brief look at each of these policies.

Policies of Urban Development

Policies of urban development in Turkey have to be assessed from the point of view of the principle of subsidiarity. This principle defined in the Article 5 of the Amsterdam Treaty

(Article 3/b of the Maastricht Treaty) and its major aim is to bring the decision-making as near as possible to the level where citizens can influence it. The same principle is also defined in the European Charter of Local Self-Government. Yet, in Turkey policies of urban development are essentially formulated by the central government. The central government is assisted by the State Planning Organization (Ministry of Development) in this endeavor. The main executive organ in charge of formulating urbanization, regional development and environmental policies is the Ministry of Environment and Urban Development.

In principle master plans of the cities are prepared and approved by the municipal councils with no approval at all by the central government. However, legal arrangements put into effect during the last several decades demonstrate that the preparation of the existing centralized system is completely incompatible with the principle of subsidiarity.

The Law on Urban Development (No: 3194) requires that cities with 10.000 or more inhabitants should work out master plans in order to ensure a balanced and healthy urbanization. A satisfactory level of quality in urban life can only be reached by effective implementation of city master plans aiming at the maximization of the public interest. Although the city councils have the final say in the plan preparation stages, exceptionally, the Ministry of Environment and Urban Development and several other central government departments have been given broad planning powers under different circumstances. The major problem of urban development and management is to deal with upgrading of expanding squatter settlements. Especially from the end of the Second World War, in parallel with accelerated urbanization, the need for supply of urban land to meet growing demand for urban social housing increased enormously. It is remarkable to note that the number of squatter houses (gecekondus) increased from 50.000 in 1955, to 2.5 million in 2010. It can be safely estimated that as much as 29 percent of the urban population, a total of 12.5 million people is actually living in 2.5 million gecekondus, considerably deprived of most of the urban public services and facilities. This can be regarded as one of the most striking indicators of the unsatisfactory level of the quality of urban life in Turkey.

The Mass Housing Administration, in cooperation with municipalities, play an important role in meeting the housing needs. The main target groups of the housing policy are socially underprivileged segments in the society which need financial and other kinds of assistance to resolve housing problems. The role of the housing cooperatives, as non-profit housing organizations, is rather negligible at present. Despite the fact that the Constitution provides (Art.35) that the right to property shall not be used in contravention of the public interest, there is no real restriction upon the rent-seeking efforts of landowners which make the solution of the problems of homelessness almost impossible. Under these conditions, another provision of the Constitution regarding the right to decent housing (Art.57) is deemed to remain just on the paper.

In the implementation stage of their master plans, cities benefited for the last several decades from the financial and technical assistance of a central finance agency, namely the Bank of Local Authorities. This Bank carried out certain major local public services such as the installation of sewerage and heating systems, mapping and drinking water on behalf of the municipalities. However, large- scale privatization of the public services both at central and local levels, and the reorganization of the Bank for the same purpose may no longer allow central authorities to help cities to improve the quality of urban life. Particularly in metropolitan centers, housing conditions, transportation and sewerage systems, drinking water needs of the cities will suffer from the lack of intelligent design as well as sufficient financial resources. No matter whether services are provided by central or local authorities, inhabitants of almost all major settlements seem highly unsatisfied with the quality of urban living. Main reasons can be attributed more to the pace of rapid urbanization, ways in which local public services are provided, unplanned and haphazard urban development, lack of resources than the urban living itself.

One cannot talk about the existence of a long-term regional development and urbanization policy which aims at balanced distribution of urban settlements over the national territory and a division of labor between the central and local governments to ensure at least a minimum level of quality in urban settlements.

Policies of Environmental Protection

Everyone has the right to live in a healthy and balanced environment according to the Article 56 of the Turkish Constitution. The Constitution emphasizes at the same time that it is the duty of the State and the citizens to improve the natural environment and to prevent environmental pollution. In addition to this, several other articles in the Constitution provide legal guarantees to the for the protection of natural

and man- made environmental values. One of these prohibits the exercise of the right to property in contravention
of the public interest (Art.35). Another puts the coastal areas under the sovereignty and at the disposal of the State
with the consequence that in the utilization of the sea cost,
lake shores and river banks, and of the coastal strip along
the sea and lakes, public interest is to be taken into consideration with priority (Art.4).

To prevent the loss of cultivable agricultural land is also
the duty of the State (Art.44). Similarly, providing land to
farmers with insufficient land could not lead to a fall in
production or to the depletion of forests and other land
and underground resources. The responsibility of the State
to ensure the conservation of historical, cultural and natural assets and wealth is also underlined in the Constitution
(Art.169). More specifically, the State is charged with the
duty to enact the necessary legislation and to take appropriate measures for the protection of forests and the enlargement of their areas. No amnesties or pardons to be granted
for offences against forests shall be legislated. The restraining of forest boundaries is also prohibited by the Constitution (Art.169), except in respect of areas of which preservation as forests is considered technically and scientifically
useless, but their conversion into agricultural land is found
definitely advantageous.

Within the framework designed by the Constitution,
the Environment Law (No:2873, amended in 2006 by the
Law No: 5491) reflects the main principles of environmental protection. It defines the concept of environmental protection as the activities for the preservation of ecological

balance, prevention of degradation and pollution in the air, water and land, and for their improvement. According to the general principles of the Environment Law, it is the duty of the citizens to protect the environment and to comply with the measures taken for that purpose. Health of all human beings is to be taken into account to protect and improve the environment.

Sustainable environment and sustainable development are the fundamental concepts of the Environment Law guiding the formulation and implementation of environmental policies. In addition to the principle of sustainable development, Environmental Law adopted several other guiding principles such as participation, prevention and polluter pays. All economic enterprises and other institutions are required, in their decisions of land and resource use, and project evaluation, to strike a balance between the goals of environmental protection and development. They must choose the most appropriate methods and technology in order to achieve that end. An environmental impact analysis has to be made by all the entrepreneurs for their planned establishments, in order to avoid their adverse impact upon environmental values.[10]

Those who damage the environment are held responsible for their acts or neglect, even the negative impact is caused without their fault (the principle of objective responsibility). Citizens have the right to recourse to administrative authorities and to ask to stop any activities which degrade the environment whenever they are informed or

10   Ruşen Keleş, Can Hamamcı and Aykut Çoban, *Çevre Politikası (Environmental Policy)*, İmge, Ankara, 2012, (7th ed.), pp.548-564.

affected by hem. A specific Law on the Right to Information (No: 4982) passed in 2003, allows them to be informed about anything that affects the environment. In principle, tools available to public authorities for the protection of the environment are mainly market-based instruments, such as taxes, charges, participation fees, financial incentives, carbon trade, and the like. A final policy instrument is education for environmental protection and increasing public awareness. For this purpose, public radio and TV channels are required to broadcast at least two hours a month programmes on environmental protection.

In addition to the Environmental Law and the Law on Public Health, numerous special legislation possess rules to be applied for the protection and the preservation of environmental assets. The Law on the Protection of Cultural Values (No: 2863), The Law on the Protection of the Bosphorus (No:2960), the Law on the Protection of Coastal Areas (No: 3830), Urban development Law (No: 3194), the Law on the Encouragement of Tourism (No: 2634), the Forests Law (No: 6831), the Law on Water Products (No:1380), the Law on the Protection of Animals (No: 5199), and the Law on the Protection of Land Resources (No: 5403) are a few of these legislation.

There are nearly 300 associations actively working in the fields of the protection of flora and fauna, biological diversity, and all natural assets and historical and architectural heritage. Although and actual, personal and legitimate interest in the issue at stake is a precondition for seeking the annulment of an administrative act or decision in the court, the Procedural Law on Administrative Suits make an important exception for those methods of public interest like city master plans, historical buildings and the protection of the environment.

Concluding Remarks

It is beyond any doubt that proper protection of the environment can only be ensured through the effective involvement of the citizens in decision-making processes regarding urban development and environmental issues. Channels of participation for associations, foundations, labor unions, cooperatives and Professional organizations have to be widely open for the success of urbanization and environmental policies. Effective contribution depends upon the level of consciousness of the public as a whole towards the environmental values, complementarity of economic development and environment, in other words, concern for sustainable development. So far, the public opinion played an important role in influencing the legislative and executive bodies. Judiciary has been playing, in its turn, an important function to ensure sustainable urbanization.

In addition to increasing public awareness, consciousness of decision-makers is of utmost importance. Unless they are well informed about the exact nature of such concepts as sustainable development, quality of urban life, intergenerational equity, precautionary principle, common but differentiated responsibility, the principle of participation and prevention, and the like, it would be practically impossible to carry out the suggestions laid down in the international declarations or conventions. Turkey is still witnessing a kind of indifference at least on the parts of such decision-makers to such issues of nuclear and hydroelectric power plants, protection of historical and natural assets in general.[11] One has to keep in mind that one can talk about the quality of urban life so long as there exists some ecological, biological and urban values that one can consider to raise their quality.

Turkey is signatory of party to nearly 50 of the international conventions or treaties concerning the quality of urban life and environment in general. Being a candidate for the full membership of the European Union, she needs to adjust her legislation and practices to the norms prevailing in the European Community in a relatively short time.[12] She has the obligation to put into effect the legal norms of all ratified legal instruments, which charge Turkey, like full member states, to protect the environment not only for present, but also for future generations and the mankind as a whole.

Inadequate interest all over the world in planning at all levels (national, regional and local) is gradually attracting more reaction of those who have deep concern for sustainable development. The anti-planning attitude observed in many countries up to now is being encouraged and supported by some international finance institutions. The prejudged and excessive emphasis upon the uselessness of the public sector and planning and the increasing anti-planning

11   Ruşen Keleş, "Sustainable Urban Development under Unsustainable Conditions", Derya Oktay (ed.), *Inquiry into Urban Environment: Issues Concerning Urban, Housing and the Built Environment,* Eastern Mediterranean University, Famagusta, 2006, pp.27-38.

12   Nesrin Algan and Ayşegül Mengi, "Turkey's Sustainable Development Policies in the EU Accession Process", *European Environment Law Review,* Vol.14, No:4, April 2005, pp. 89-116.

attitude may end up with leaving the shaping of urban environments completely to the free play of the market forces,
which may be neither economically more efficient, nor acceptable from a social justice point of view. This seems to be
absolutely contradictory with the principle of prevention as
a rational component of the concept of sustainable development. Quality of urban life is no more than a result of these
and similar socio-economic and political considerations.

The Quality of Life and
The Environment*

On the Concept of the Quality of Life

Quality of life is a broad concept which is concerned with the overall well-being in society. However, there is no an agreed-upon definition of the term in academic and policy discourses. Rather, the tendency is towards divergence. According to one of the definitions, "well-being reflects not only living, but also the ways in which people respond and feel about their lives in those domains. (Fahey,T., Whelan, C., and Maitre, B.,2005, p.14).The concept of quality of life has three main characteristics: First, it reflects the individuals' life situations and their perceptions rather than a country's quality of life; secondly, it is a multidimensional concept, covering multiple life domains such as housing conditions, education, employment, work-life balance, access to institutions and public services, and their interplay; and finally, it brings together objective information on living conditions with subjective views and attitudes to provide a picture of overall well-being in society. (Shucksmith, M., Cameron, S., Merridew,T.,Pichler, F.,2009, p.1276).

---

* Keynote Speech, ASIA Pacific International Conference on Environment-Behavior Studies Salamis Bay Conti Resort Hotel, Famagusta, North Cyprus 7-9 December 2011.

It should be noted that the micro concept of quality of life has perhaps been most widely used in relation to health conditions where it is essentially used to extend the assessment of clinical outcomes beyond simple physical survival. It is also argued that the concept of quality of life needs to be used in a context beyond an economic perspective privileging income and wealth in measuring well-being. (Shucksmith et al., p.1276). An American environmental activist and writer, Hazel Henderson argued, without ignoring the decisive role and function of the economy in improving the quality of living, that per capita income was a very weak indicator of human well-being, and therefore she suggested that it should be replaced by less tangible measures such as political participation, literacy, education and health.

Maslow's theory of the classification of human needs developed in the 1960's is taken as a starting point in most of the investigations extensively. As rightly observed in one of the publications of the Turkish Academy of Sciences on the Indicators of Quality of Life, the concept may be approached from more than one angles, in addition to philosophical, ethical and psychological ones, such as human rights, health considerations and environmental concerns. (Türkiye Bilimler Akademisi, (Turkish Academy of Sciences, 2003, pp.9-19).

Environment quality has always been one of the most important components of the quality of life. Although this reality is not faced with any reaction, the measurement of qualitative and effective evaluation of environmental quality has been a bit of a headache for social scientists (O'Riordan,T., 1976, p.178). Evaluation of such values as beauty, fresh air, noise, fumes, and congestion cannot be precisely determined because people themselves are not very specific about their likes and dislikes. As rightly emphasized by O'Riordan, no device, no matter how carefully thought out, can overcome the inherently contradictory psychological and social processes which cause any assessment of environmental quality to be problematic (O'Riordan, T., p.178).

In a worldwide survey carried out recently by French researchers, it was found out that the basic preconditions of good living in cities included security, health, mobility, sanitation, cost of living. And these conditions were far more important in the eyes of the respondents as compared with such factors as beauty and attractiveness of the community (Damon, J., 2011, p182). Robert Marans and his Turkish colleagues carried out important studies on the quality of life on the basis of scientific criteria they developed, both in İstanbul and Famagusta, North Cyprus. Their aim was to provide useful information for developing planning and design strategies that will foster sustainable urbanization. At the same time, they made an effort to explore the impact of environmental, economic, social, physical and health related indicators on quality of life satisfaction among İstanbul and Famagusta residents. (Oktay, D., Rüstemli A., Marans, R. W., 2009, pp.6-20; and Türkoğlu-Dülger, H., Bölen, F., Baran,P,.K.,Marans, R.,W., 2008, pp.103-113).

It is because of the increasing role of the health conditions in the concept of the quality of life that Parliamentary Assembly of the Council of Europe has recently voted for an Additional Protocol to the European Convention on Human Rights concerning the right to a healthy environment (11 September 2009, Doc.12003).

From another point of view, one has to remember that economists use the term *negative externality* to express misallocative or disagreeable effects of the free interplay of the market forces. In the source of most of the environmental disturbances, hazards, degradations and dilapidation are found the impacts of such externalities that can be overcome only by paying a certain price to the transacting party.

Numerous factors contribute to the improvement or worsening of the quality of life from an environmental point of view. (Görer, N. and Uğurlar, A., 2007, pp.225-234). First and the most critical threshold is undoubtedly the access to environmental infrastructure and services. These include water and sanitation systems, solid waste management, drainage, and transportation. When people do not have adequate access to these amenities or when their quality is poor, a set of important health consequences occurs immediately. Secondly, pollution from urban wastes and emissions caused by city-based activities affect daily life considerably. The examples are the air, water pollution and land degradation. It has been estimated that 300 to 700 million premature deaths could be avoided each year, if the WHO's minimum clean air standards are taken into consideration in practice. According to the statistics of the WHO, environmental conditions are responsible for one quarter of the deaths from respiratory and other infectious diseases (Keleş, R., 2010, Bodrum, p.10).

Resource degradation is the third factor affecting the quality of life. For instance, urban development can damage surrounding ecosystems through construction on sensitive and fertile lands, as well as through improper disposal of urban and industrial wastes. Cultural and historical heritage is another resource which may be lost as a result of neglect and ignorance. Fourth is the environmental hazards coming from both natural sources, like earthquakes, floods, etc., and human sources, such as accidents caused by industries, traffic, municipal facilities, and fires. Finally, environmental problems of a global nature, like greenhouse gases, sea level rise, climate change and pollution of international waters create important risks for the living environments (Leitman, J., 1999, pp.60-73). Among the factors mentioned above, urban land use decisions are critically important determinants of the environmental security, and consequently urban and rural life. Distortions in land markets, combined with ineffective land management policies and practices result in degradation of environmentally fragile lands. (Leitman, J, op.cit., p.83).

A certain level of quality which guarantees the inhabitants a sustainable welfare may have, from another point of view, socio-cultural, economic and spatial characteristics. The fact that the people have numerous wishes constitutes the socio-cultural dimension of the issue. On the other hand, if they desire to be able to consume certain material and immaterial goods at the desired level, this points to the essentially economic nature of the problem. Finally, by realizing their wishes, they use space to live in, to work in and to recreate in. The fact that they create the physical conditions, in other words, the built environment for living, working and recreation, it means that spatial factors too will have a special role to play in raising the level of the quality of life. There are strong signals that we are destroying the equilibrium between the processes in biotic and non-biotic spheres. Therefore there is a need to work together in such a way that the results of one part do not cross the results of the others. (van der Heuvel, H.,M.,M., 1992, p.215).

An Introduction to the Concept of Environment

In order to analyze the relationships between the quality of life and environmental conditions adequately, it would be appropriate to have a brief look at urban and environmental stresses affecting the rapidly urbanizing world at the beginning. Rapid population growth and urbanization, industrialization and technological change, increased expectations caused by rising affluence, gaps between the level of expectations and actual consumption patterns, lack of adequate public awareness concerning the deterioration of environment and dilapidation of resources and finally persisting human egoism make both the protection of the environment as well as the quality of life difficult goals to reach.

Environmental stresses are linked one to another, they are dependent upon the nature of the economy, and the dichotomy of environment-economy causes, at the same time, occasionally social tensions and political unrest. The international aspects of the issue are no less important. Because, the fact that pollutants recognize no national boundaries and no country seems willing to give up any of its freedoms and sovereignty make the problems of transboundary linkages extremely important. This is the main source of the need for close cooperation among nations. As noted by René Dubot in the early 1970's, "The Earth is one, but the World is not". Different parts of the World, in other words, the North and the South, the States, sailing in the same Spaceship Earth possess moral responsibilities towards each other. "The

Principle of Common but Differentiated Responsibility" of the Rio Declaration is just an expression of this need.

At the Millennium Summit in 2000, the members of the United Nations had reaffirmed their commitment to working towards a world in which eliminating poverty and sustaining development would have the highest priority. The Millennium Development Goals, which had grown out of the agreements and resolutions of successive world conferences organized by the United Nations in the past decades, had been commonly accepted as a framework for measuring development progress. The goals focus the efforts of the world community on achieving significant and measurable improvements in the quality of life. They establish yardsticks for measuring results, not just for developing countries but also for the rich countries that help to fund development programs and for the multilateral institutions that help countries implement them.

It is an undeniable fact that the eradication of poverty all over the world must be the starting point for any kind of improvement in the quality of life. Therefore, an emphasis on some global ecological challenges which might create important consequences for the quality of life in cities and for keeping the man-environment balance in general seems highly important in this respect. Let us look briefly at the Millennium Development Goals with this objective in mind. The first seven goals directed at reducing poverty, in all its forms, are mutually reinforcing. The eight goal, which is called as the global partnership for development is about the means to achieve the first seven. Many of the poorest countries will certainly need additional assistance and must look to rich countries to provide it. Countries that are poor and heavily indebted will need further help in decreasing their debt burden. And all countries will benefit if their trade barriers are lowered, allowing freer exchange of goods and services.

The environment is an essential component of the Millennium Development Goals. The Millennium Development Summit's Declaration dedicated a section to environmental protection, making explicit reference to climate change, desertification, biodiversity, forestry and water management. The Millennium Development Goals framework captures the environmental concerns in Goal seven, namely Ensuring Environmental Sustainability. The targets associated with that goal refer to mainstreaming the environment in policies and programs, reversing the loss of environmental resources, and improving access to environmental services. It makes sense to try to achieve the goals together, because of the many synergies among them. Addressing environmental issues would help to ensure environmental sustainability. The centrality of the environment to the Millennium Development Goals is reinforced by its strong linkages to the rest of the goals. Promoting non-farm sources of income and technological improvements in agriculture is essential to reducing income poverty in rural areas. But it is difficult to imagine the achieving this reduction where land is degraded and water absent. Reductions in child mortality will be more likely if households have access to adequate water supply, sanitation facilities, and modern fuels. Ready access to fuels and water lessens the time demands on women and girls, facilitating their engagement in productive activities and school attendance. Climate change will favor the spreading of vector borne diseases and increases the likelihood of natural disasters. Those disasters, in turn, reduce income and destroy the infrastructure for education and health.

In order to ensure environmental sustainability, a) we have to integrate the principle of sustainable development into national policies and programs and reverse the loss of environmental resources, b) reduce by 2015, the proportion of people without sustainable access to safe drinking water, and c) have achieved by 2020, a significant improvement in the daily lives of at least 100 million slum dwellers all over the world.

The attainment of this goal may help to ensure that future generations enjoy the benefits from development and the achievement of the other Millennium Development Goals. The goals comprise three targets referring to mainstreaming the environment in policy and programs, reversing the loss of environmental resources, and improving access to environmental services, with special reference to slum dwellers.

Integration of the principle of sustainable development, which is defined as the kind of development which, meets the needs of the present, without compromising the ability of the future generations to meet their own needs, into policies and programs and reversing the loss of environmental resources is not an easy task. Environment which is an essential component of the quality of life is too often overlooked by policy makers and planners as a key resource for sustainable growth and poverty alleviation. It must urgently be integrated into decision-making. The loss of environmental resources has far reaching implications for the welfare of the current generation and for the ability of future generations to maintain and improve the welfare and living conditions of human beings. This has a close bearing on ensuring sustainable development. The focus should perhaps be on a few natural resources now being rapidly degraded or polluted, or are at risk of further deterioration: These are land, water, forests, biodiversity, clean air, and climate change and ozone depletion.

Land degradation has become a global problem. Nearly 2 billion hectares of cropland, pastures and forests worldwide have been degraded over the past fifty years. Desertification causes economic instability and even political unrest in the areas affected. More than one million people are at risk from desertification in the world. The impacts fall undoubtedly disproportionately on the shoulders of the poor. Efforts to tackle land degradation must be linked to measures fostering broad economic and social change, to overcome the conditions that have resulted in degradation.

The challenges for sustainable development of water management are formidable. While the world population tripled in the past century, the aggregate use of water increased sixfold. Some rivers no longer reach the sea. Half of the world's wetlands disappeared in the past century. It is estimated that water use will increase fifty percent in the next thirty years. And half of the world population will be living under severe need for substantial improvements in managing water sources.

Biodiversity is another important issue. This is often understood as a wide variety of plants, animals and micro-organisms. But it also includes genetic differences within each species. It provides many goods and services that sustain our lives. The quality of living has much to do with sustaining its existence in the future. Local communities benefit from biodiversity in many ways. However, it is often not protected or managed sustainably. It is faced with increasing risk of extinction or genetic erosion. Carefully designed institutions, including forms of man-made environment, are a prerequisite for capturing the full value of biological resources, avoiding their overexploitation.

While most developed countries have recently made good progress in addressing urban air pollution, clean air can no longer be taken for granted in the developing world. Pollution from transport is a major concern. There are adverse health effects of exposure to air pollution in urban areas as a result of increasing number of motor vehicles. And there are the effects on global climate change. Every year an estimated one million people throughout the developing world die prematurely from respiratory and other illnesses associated with urban air pollution.

Many ecological purposes are global public goods and their degradation affects people across the world. Addressing them effectively requires coordinated international action, as in the cases of climate change and ozone layer depletion. Many less developed regions are especially vulnerable to climate change and within these countries the poorest of the poor are likely to suffer most. Dealing successfully with climate change requires major reductions in emissions of greenhouse gases. In the Millennium Declaration, the International Community committed itself to making every effort to implement the Kyoto Protocol, which sets precise targets for reductions in greenhouse gases.

Ozone layer depletion is a similar and related topic. The depletion allows more radiation to reach Earth, with severe consequences for human health, plants and marine ecosystems. The Montreal Protocol on Substances that Deplete the Ozone Layer, signed in 1987, has proven successful in reducing the emissions of human-made ozone depleting substances by ceasing their production and consumption. It is estimated that with the implementation of the Protocol, more than 20 million cases of skin cancer and nearly 130 million cases of cataracts will be avoided.

In order to avoid altogether or to reduce adverse consequences of all these global environmental challenges, a number of principles developed by International Environmental Law, in addition to the principle of Sustainable Development. These include the Precautionary Principle, and the principles of International Cooperation, Prevention, Integration, Common but Differentiated Responsibility. Concern for the Rights of Future Generations (intergenerational equity) is also crucially important in this respect. Of course, reciprocal responsibilities of the States (intragenerational equity) in ensuring sustainable development and use of natural resources are of utmost importance too.

There is no doubt that effective implementation of the principles of International Environmental law depends upon a number of factors. Their incorporation into the domestic legislation may not be enough. There is also a need to get them properly enforced. Enforcement may be defined as a set of actions that governments and other authorities take to achieve compliance within the regulated community and to correct and halt situations that endanger the environment or human health. In addition to legal action, to compel compliance and to impose some effective sanctions for violating law, non-governmental groups should become involved in the enforcement process. Finally, we have to remember that moral and social values for environmental quality in general, lack of public support for environmental problems, societal respect for the rule of law and a clear government will to enforce rules and regulations are of prime importance. Much will depend upon the normalization of economic and ethical relationships between the North and South in order to ensure the proper implementation of the principle of common but differentiated responsibility adopted in the Rio Summit.

Culture is an essential element of a sustainable city. The environmental conditions are affected by our culture, which is, in turn, shaped by the environment. Bio-culture represents a conscious effort to reach this interdependence. Aesthetic values, music, science, the arts, politics, economics, and determination to changing the existing consumption patterns shaped by contemporary capitalist development and globalization, can all come together on the struggle for a better quality of life (Vlavianos-Arvanities, A. and Keleş, R (2010).

Action Taken at the International Level
The United Nations

A number of international organizations are making considerable and constant efforts to internalize all environmental costs and negative externalities, and not to transfer problems and tensions into shoulders of the future generations. Since the United Nations Organization is keenly concerned with physical, social, economic well-being of human beings since its establishment, the first step taken in that direction was to insert a specific provision in the text of the Universal Declaration of Human Rights adopted by the General Assembly in 1948. According to the Article 25 of the said Declaration, "Everyone has the right to a standard of living adequate for the health and well-being of himself and his family, including food, clothing, housing and medical care and necessary social services, and the right to security in the event of unemployment, sickness, disability, widowhood, old age and other lack of livelihood in circumstances beyond his control". Of course, concrete realization of all these fundamental rights depends upon each nation's ratification of the concerned international covenants concerning these rights. I must underline that the efforts of the United Nations and its specialized agencies in this field are of utmost significance for any concrete improvement in the quality of life.

A few examples are the world conferences convened by the U.N. in Vancouver (1976), İstanbul (1996), Stockholm (1972) and Rio de Janeiro (1992) and the declarations and action plans adopted in these conferences. The Vancouver Declaration on Human Settlements drew the attention of the world public opinion, among its general principles, "to the continuous improvement in the quality of life of all people, beginning with the satisfaction of the basic needs of food, shelter, clean water, employment, health, education, training, social security without any discrimination as to race, color, sex, language, religion, ideology, etc." Similarly, Action Plan, namely the Habitat Agenda, adopted during the United Nations Conference on Human Settlements (Habitat II) in İstanbul, in 1996, emphasized once again (par.36) that "Human health and quality of life are at the center of the efforts to develop sustainable human settlements". World leaders participating in the Conference expressed "their commitment to promote and attain the goals of universal and equal access to quality education, the highest attainable standards of physical, mental and environmental health, and the equal access of primary health care, making particular efforts to rectify inequalities relating to social and economic conditions." (UNCHS, 1997, p.20).

International conferences on the protection of the environment organized by the United Nations in 1972 (Stockholm) and in 1992 (Rio) drew attention of the public opinion to the relationship between the quality of life and the environment. The first principle of the Stockholm Declaration stresses that "Man had the fundamental right to freedom, equality and adequate conditions of life, in an environment of a quality that permitted a life of dignity and well- being, and he bore a solemn responsibility to protect and improve the environment for present and future generations". Similarly, in the Principle 1 of the Rio Declaration on Environment and Development, it is stated that "Human beings are the center of concern for sustainable development. They are entitled to a healthy and productive life in harmony with nature".

The United Nations continued its efforts to improve the quality of life on Earth through a series of world urban forums towards the direction of what it called "harmonious urbanization." The first of these forums was held in Nairobi in 2002, followed by the Second World Urban Forum in 2004, which was convened in Barcelona, and the third one in Vancouver in 2006. The location of the Fourth World Urban Forum was Nanjing, the Peoples' Republic of China, which was taken place in 2008. Fifth meeting took place in Brasilia in 2010.

The concept of harmonious urbanization, dealt with in these forums, which is closely related with increasing the level of quality of life, can be regarded as a kind of urbanization that possesses entirely opposite features of unbalanced and disorderly urbanization which largely neglects ecological considerations and the concern for the quality of life. *Socially harmonious cities* (equity, inclusiveness, income, poverty reduction, cheap land and social housing), *Economically harmonious cities* (infrastructure development, financing urban development, foreign direct investment, urban informal economy), *Environmentally harmonious cities* (climate change, energy and resources savings, bio-diversity, water, sanitation and transport, green buildings and cities), *Spatially harmonious cities* (urban planning, urban and rural linkages, integrated regional development, mixed land use), *Historically harmonious cities* (heritage, culture, architecture and urban renewal), *Harmonious cities for all age groups* (youth, aging population, internet and ICT, education and health care, sports and music) are the basic characteristics of cities where human beings enjoy a quality of life consistent with their dignity.

On the basis of these characteristics, harmonious of urbanization may be defined as a policy option which aims at ensuring the sustainability of the nature, to provide opportunities for living, shelter, employment, entertainment, health and education, to eradicate poverty without alienating people from their natural environment. (Keleş, R., 2008, p.3).

Contributions of the European Institutions

Raising the level of quality of life by improving environmental conditions has been always at the center of concern of the European institutions. For example, the principle of sustainable development has been included as a requirement in the Article 37 of the Charter of Fundamental Rights of the European Union which determines that "A high level of environmental protection and he improvement of the quality of environment must be integrated into the policies of the Union and ensured in accordance with the principle of sustainable development". Brought into force by the Treaty of Lisbon on 1st December 2009, the Charter itself has acquired the strength of a Treaty with the purpose of imposing penalties in instances of its infringement. According to the Article 191 of the consolidated version of the Treaty on the Functioning of the EU, "the policy of the European Union in the sector of the environment will seek to achieve the following goals: a) The conservation, protection and improvement of the quality of the environment, b) The safeguarding of the health of the individual, c) The sensible and rational use of natural resources, and, d) The promotion at international level of measures to deal with regional or global environmental problems and in particular to combat climate change".

Earlier than the Lisbon Treaty, in 1999, in another EU document, in the European Spatial Development Perspective (ESPD, Towards Balanced and Sustainable Development of the Territory of the European Union), attention was drawn to the fact that, despite all efforts to combat environmental problems such as noise, air and water pollution, traffic congestion, waste production and excessive water consumption, the quality of the environment was still in need of further improvement in many respects. It was pointed out that urban development measures had often diminished the historic fabric of many cities and eroded their identity. This not only had a negative effect on *the quality of life* and the health of their inhabitants, but also had an economic impact due to the loss of attractiveness and reduced investment, employment and municipal financial resources. (European Commission, 1999, p.66).

The European Urban Charter adopted by the Council of Europe in 1992 and revised in 2008 under the title of *Manifesto for a New Urbanity* underlines the fundamental rights of urban residents and describes almost all material and non-material components of what is called the quality of life in urban centers. This Charter is not a kind of international convention open to ratification of the States, but a document addressing to local authorities, bringing together necessary guiding principles for a reasonable level of quality of life in cities. (Conseil de l'Europe, 1993).

Concluding Remarks

The problem of the quality of life is a multidimensional phenomenon. It has numerous linkages with economic, social, cultural, psychological and environmental factors. None of these dimensions can be taken and assessed in isolation from each other. Therefore there is a pressing need for a holistic approach in reaching a just and enduring solution as far as the quality of life is concerned. From an environmental point of view, the solution has something to do with reversing the present selfish attitudes of some States and to ensure close cooperation among nations as stipulated by the United Nations Charter. Steps must be taken by the world community in order to ensure that the Rio principle of common but differentiated responsibility be respected by all States, particularly the developed ones. The determining role of economic conditions in raising the level of quality of life in all spheres should not be overlooked. Eradication of poverty must be the fundamental goal of everyone to deal with the improvement of the quality of life. This certainly requires something more than the implementation of legal rules. Ethical considerations are also involved to a greater extent. An ethically inspired conscience, independent of external pressures from legislation and the courts must shape the behavior of the individuals. Therefore, the cultivation of an environmental conscience, which must begin as early as from the primary school, is a prerequisite for the strategy to be successful.

Despite all the efforts reflecting the goodwill of the United Nations and other international organizations and individual States, there is still a wide discrepancy between what the governments said and what they did. "The speeches are beautiful, but the reality awful." It was rightly noted in the World Urban Forum 3 in Vancouver some years ago that all urban players must do their part in this respect rather than simply transfer responsibility to others. Planners, architects, designers, decision-makers, teachers and scientists must cooperate closely to deal with such worldwide phenomena such as rapid urbanization, eradication of poverty, rational settlement patterns, problems of sanitation, nutrition, shelter needs of the poor, environment friendly urban growth and development. All components of the quality of life require a planned intervention into the process of the free play of the market forces, not only in developing but also in developed countries.

References

Conseil de l'Europe, Conférence Permenante des Pouvoirs Locaux et Régionaux (1993), *La Charte Urbaine Européenne*, Strasbourg.

Damos, J., (2011), *Les Villes a Vivre: Modes de Vie Urbaines et Défis Environnementaux*, Odil Jacob, Paris.

European Commission, (1999), *European Spatial Development Perspective (ESDP)*, Council of Minister responsible for Spatial Planning, May 1999, Potsdam.

Fahey,T., Whelan,C.,and Maitre,B.,(2005) , *Quality of Life in Europe: First European Quality of Life Survey 2003*, European Foundation for the Improvement of Living and Working Conditions, Office of Official Publications of the European Commun,,t,es, Luxembourg.

Frick, Dieter (Ed.), (1986), *The Quality of Urban Life*, de Gruyter, Berlin.

Görer, N. and Uğurlar,A., (2007), Yaşam Kalitesi ve Kentsel Yaşam Göstergeleri Üzerine Bir Yazın Denemesi (An Essay on the Quality of Life and Indicators of the Quality of Urban Life), *Yerellik ve Politika: Ruşen Keleş'e Armağan IV, (Localism and Politics: In Honour of Ruşen Keleş IV)*, Ayşegül Mengi (ed.) İmge Publishers ,Ankara, pp.225-234.

Keleş, R.(2010), Küreselleşme ve Ekolojik Değişiklikler (Globalization and Ecological Changes), paper presented to the 20th Congress of Spiritual Health and Diseases, Bodrum.

Keleş, R. (2008), Harmonious Urban Settlements in the Light of the Principles of Ekistics, Keynote Speech made during the Fourth Session of the World Urban Forum, Southeast University, Nanjing, Peoples' Republic of China, 5-6 November 2008.

Leitman, J. (1999), *Sustaining Cities: Environment Planning and Management in Urban Design*, McGraw-Hill, New York,

Oktay, D., Rüstemli, A., Marans, R.W., (2009), Neighborhood Satisfaction, Sense of Community, and Attachment: Initial Findings from Famagusta Quality of Urban Life Study, *AIZ, İTÜ Journal of the Faculty of Architecture: Quality of Urban Life*,6,1, pp.6-20.

O'Riordan,T.,(1976), *Environmentalism,* Pion Ltd., London,

Shucksmith,M., Cameron,S., Merridew,T., and Pichler, F.,(2009), Urban-Rural Differences in Quality of Life Across the European Union, *Regional Studies,* 43, 10.

Türkiye Bilimler Akademisi (Turkish Academy of Sciences), (2004), *Yaşam Kalitesi Göstergeleri: Türkiye İçin Bir Veri Sistemi Önerisi (Indicators of Quality of Life: A Proposal for a Data Base System for Turkey),* Ankara.

Türkoğlu-Dülger, H.,Bölen.,F.,Baran,P.,K.,and Marans,W.,R. (2008), İstanbul'da Yaşam Kalitesinin Ölçülmesi (Measuring Quality of Life in İstanbul), *İTÜ Dergisi/a,Mimarlık, Planlama, Tasarım (Architecture, Planning and Design),*7, 2,pp.103-113.

UNCHS, (1996), *İstanbul Declaration and the Habitat Agenda,* UN Conference on Human Settlements (Habitat II), İstanbul, 3-14 June 1996.

Van der Heuvel,H.M., (1992), The Quality of the Daily Environment: Ways of Cooperation, *Urban Ecology,* UN Commission for Europe, Seventh Conference on Urban and Regional Research, Ankara.

Vlavianos-Arvanitis, A. and Keleş,R., (2010), Biopolis: An Urban Development Model.Networking, Education and Culture. Paper presented to International Ekistics Conference on Human Settlements, Mumbai.

The Relevance of Ekistics Principles for The Present Problems of Spatial Development[*]

Ekistics means the Science of Human Settlements. Ekisticians are those who study, teach or practice the principles of the Science of Human Settlements. The general conceptual framework of Ekistics is designed by the principles falling under five major categories, such as 1. Anthropos (peoples as individuals), 2. Natura, 3. Society, 4. Shells (buildings) and 5. Networks (roads, utilities, transportation, communication and administrative boundaries.

The main aims of this emerging discipline is 1. To initiate basic research in these fields, 2. To bring together specialists from all relevant disciplines to work together with an interdisciplinary approach on projects in this field, 3. To work out new methods of training those who can assume leadership and responsibility in the sphere of action; and finally, 4. To attract some of the best young and promising minds into this new area of research, development and practice.

Delos Symposia played an important role in developing the Ekistics principles. Twelve symposia have been

[*] Paper to be presented to WSE 2014 Meetings on Bringing Ekistics to New Generations, WSE Bogota, Colombia, 3-5 April 2014. The World Urban Forum 7, Medellin, Colombia,6-11 April 2014.

held during 1963-1975, ten on board ship, and the last two in Athens and the Apollonion Porto Rafti. More than 200 hundred eminent planners, architects, philosophers, geographers, scientists have attended and made considerable contributions to the successes of the progress of Ekistics.

I have the privilege to attend one of the last meetings taken place in Athens, in 1972, (42 years ago), and had the honour to meet Constantinos Doxiadis personally.

Worldwide problems of urbanization in both developing and developed countries, growth of cities and planning, regional development, urban identity, social housing, resource conservation, transport and communications, local self-government and a variety of similar issues concerning human settlements have been dealt with intensive concern for making human beings happier in their living environments.

The ideas developed by the Ekisiticians led not only to the establishment of the United Nations Center for Human Settlements (UNCHS) in order to integrate fragmented aspects of policy and to combine them in a genuine strategy in the field of human settlements, but also deeply affected the main themes of the various UN HABITAT Conferences in the following years, such as the vancouver (1976) and İstanbul (1996) Conferences on Human Settlements, Stockholm (1972) and Rio (1992) Summits on the Protection of the Environment and even the Johannesburg (Rio+10) Declaration on Sustainable Development, as well as the Urban Charter of the Council of Europe (1992 and 2008), and the Guiding Principles of Spatial Development prepared by CEMAT (Conference of the Ministers responsible for Spatial Development).

1. *Holism.* Emphasis on developing a holistic approach
    to the study of human settlements was one of the
    fundamental contributions of Ekistics. Actually, the
    Ekistics Grid is the best expression of such an ho-
    listic approach. It was assumed that the application
    of basic sciences in the universities to human wel-
    fare is extremely fragmented and this is no longer
    acceptable. Parts of human life as health, nutrition,
    education could not be dealt with in isolation, but
    the whole man, man in the society had to be stud-
    ied. This holistic approach requires that not the but-
    terfly, but its habitat as a whole has to be studied.

This understanding is reflected in the 1996 İstanbul
Declaration adopted at the end of the HABITAT II Conference in the following way: "Human settlements problems
are of a multi-dimensional nature. It is recognized that adequate shelter for all sustainable human settlements development are not isolated from the broader social and economic development of countries and that they cannot be set
apart from the need for favorable national and international
frameworks for economic and social development, and environmental protection, which are indispensable and mutually reinforcing components of sustainable development."

2. *Right to Adequate Shelter.* Before the First UN Con-
    ference on Human Settlements (Vancouver), Delos
    Eleven declared that a Charter for Human Settlements
    has to be formulated and three basic human rights
    have to be included in it. These were a) the right to
    shelter, b) the right to equality, and c) the right to
    dignity. It was clarified that the ultimate goal of the
    right to shelter must be one person/one room, an

done family/one dwelling. During the HABITAT II Conference, the heads of state or government have reaffirmed their commitment to "the full and progressive realization of the right to adequate housing as provided for in international instrument, namely Universal Declaration of Human Rights.

Attention was drawn to the deteriorating role of "the unregulated urban land markets and inflated land values". It is because of these phenomena that massive high-rise buildings are designed as offices in such a way as to paralyses city life. Apartments break up local intimate relationships, imprison mothers and young families and impoverish the imaginative life of a whole generation of children. The misuse and abuse of the right of ownership in land created adverse socio-economic, cultural an even psychological consequences.

The trend from Aristoteles to Léon Duguit signifies a constant shift from pure individualism towards a system more or less socialized where public interest is reconciled and harmonized with the private concern. Principles of Ekistics provided vast opportunities for the incorporation of such ideas into the very definition of harmonious urbanization and adequate housing as a fundamental human right.

3. *Regional Imbalances.* As early as 1965, the participants of the Delos Three Symposion had drawn the attention of the world public opinion to the need to tackle with the problem of regional underdevelopment. It was stated that the problems urban sprawl and mass migration to urban centers could not be dealt with on a local scale. They need to be handled within larger systems of planning and administration

at regional levels. To redress economic imbalances and to reduce regional disparities and to get all regions contribute to the overall growth of the national economy were mentioned among the fundamental goals of territorial development. Such considerations were included in the concerned international declarations and in legal instruments adopted in Vancouver and İstanbul much later.

Balanced territorial development as the sub-heading of the main theme of the World Urban Forum 4 (Nanjing 2008) was one of the most important policy issues. It has become a very important policy concern later on in the European organizations such as the European Union and the Council of Europe. European Spatial Development Perspectives (1999), the Territorial Agenda of the European Union (2007), Leipzig Charter (2007), the Guiding Principles for Sustainable Development of the European Continent are some of the European instruments influenced by the Ekistics principles regarding balanced territorial development. In all these documents, due regard is given to the role to play by regional planning in meeting the needs of human settlements.

4. *Planning and Public Participation.* Perhaps for the first time in planning history, a reference was made, in the Delos Symposia, to the quality of the planning targets, in the sense that they should be flexible enough to be changed in the course of implementation by a continuous process of trial and error. Of course, a natural corollary was the need for a maximum involvement in the planning process, which has come to be known in the coming decades as

public participation in planning. According to Delos Five Declaration, public participation requires giving citizens the chance of access to the widest possible range of free choice, that is called the freedom to be consulted about their choices. Here we find a fair and balanced reconciliation of planning with democratic values.

Delos Seven suggested that representation based on geographical units and social classes was unsatisfactory and therefore we needed a representation of group interest, such as the poor, the miserable, the disadvantaged, handicapped and greater possibilities for individual choice, for quality of human contacts and multiple group relationships had to be created. Thirthy years after the Delos Seven, the HABITAT Agenda devoted a whole section to the needs and the role of vulnerable groups and the people with special needs among its strategies (pp.93-98).

Similarly, at the beginning of the 1990's, the vital role and the participation of such groups as women, youth, indigenous people and underprivileged has been underlined in the underprivileged has been underlined in the Rio Declaration on Environment and Development (1992, Principles 20-22). The respective chapters of the European Urban Charter (1992, 2008) deals also with public participation and the need for Access of vulnerable groups and the underprivileged in the planning process.

The suggestion of the Declaration Delos Ten to bring local government closer to the people and to ensure active participation in decision-making had an indirect impact upon the formulation of the principle of subsidiarity in the Maastricht (1993), Amsterdam (1997), and Lisbon (2009)

Treaties, and the European Charter of Local Self –Government of the Council of Europe of the Council of Europe of
the Council of Europe (1985). This principle requires that
public responsibilities must be carried out, preferably, by
the authorities as close as possible to the citizens. One can
find similar commitments made by the well-known NGO's,
such as the European Cities and Towns towards social equity for urban sustainability, sustainable land use patterns,
sustainable urban mobility patterns, etc.

5. *Environmental Concerns.* Numerous principles adopted in various Delos Symposia and embedded in
the traditional components of the Ekistics Grid reflect basic guidelines for sustainable urban and spatial development. a) Respect for human scale and
dignity in urban settlements, b) concern for the
protection of historic and cultural assets of the settlements as a part of the heritage of humanity were
constantly emphasized in those documents. c) The
Ekisticians deplored the destruction of irreplaceable
cultural values through careless stewardships, thus
predicting the significance of the concept of sustainable development long before the appearance of the
concept in the agenda of the environmentalists. d)
As early as Delos Three Symposion, certain consequences of the population growth and technological
progress were blamed as factors causing visual monotony, lack of satisfaction in urban design and the
pollution of air and water. Similarly, Delos Four underlines the stress on natural resources, wilderness
for recreation, untouched habitats for biological research, water tables and circuits and unpolluted air.

Ideas underlying interconnectedness of peace, development and environment were incorporated into the text of the Rio Declaration on Environment and Development, only one and a half decade after the Delos Six which had emphasized the search for a world order to eliminate war, the need to check the population explosion, to provide food to prevent starvation, to halt the contamination of the environment, and to deal with the discrepancy between resources and expectations that existed in so many countries of the world.

Even an instrument as specific as recycling was in the agenda of Ekisticians during the Delos Eight. They have recognized that components of many products made by man for his use must be recycled. Because the prevailing trend was towards use and re-use, rather than ownership, and sequential multiple use rather than merely individual use in order to overcome the scarcity of non-renewable natural resources. This was an early announcement of sustainable development that was going to be used in international legal instruments as late as sixteen years after Delos Eight.

This was of course related to a more substantial issue in environmental protection which concerned the rights of future generation over the resources of the planet. Such concepts as "children yet unborn", have been used in Delos Declarations as early as in the 1960's; and the need was expressed for immediate change in environmental conditions and the nature of our society without waiting for infants still unborn.

As you know, the principle of intergenerational equity of the International Environmental Law suggests that the instrument of sustainable development be adopted and respected, as a kind of development, which while meeting the needs of present generation, without comprising the ability of future generations to meet their own needs.

6. *Social Justice.* Another principle which was extensively relied upon by Ekisticians is the social justice. Social justice is emphasized as a tool to assist the establishment of the public order both horizontally (domestically, and at the international level) and vertically. It was suggested that inside the cities, wealthier citizens pass on some of their surplus to poorer neighborhoods through taxation, investment and social assistance. Inside the country, poorer regions should be assisted in the same way, inspired by solidarity considerations. However, one could assume that under the impact of globalization and further liberalization of the world economy today, intervention in economic and social life will no longer be encouraged; rather requirements of social justice will be left, more and more, to the market forces. This shows us that the need emphasized in Delos Declarations more than three decades ago is more pressing today than before.

Suggestions made during the Delos Symposia have had their impact on the formulation of certain legal principles concerning the moral responsibilities of rich nations towards the poor with respect to environmental protection and sustainable development. For example, the principle 7 of the proposed legal principles of the Brundtland Report declares that "States shall ensure that conservation is treated as an integral part of the planning and implementation of development activities and provide assistance to other States, especially to developing countries, in support of environmental protection and sustainable development.

Conclusion

The most important problems waiting for solution in the world are unsatisfactory living conditions, deteriorating environmental quality and the impact of irrational and contradictory human settlement policies.

A number of selected and distinguished scholars, philosophers, authors, and practitioners of planning architecture and environmental sciences, under the leadership of Constantinos Doxiadis have greatly contributed to both theory and practice of the Science of Human Settlements (Ekistics) during the Delos Symposia convened during 1963-1975. I believe that the intellectual quality of the ideas developed during those debates, reflected in the Delos Declarations, is extremely high and their content is relevant to the understanding and solution of the most pressing territorial problems facing the world today. Thank to their contributions, decision-makers, planners, teachers and students all over the world, of the 21st century will have no difficulty to find the most appropriate solutions to such contemporary problems as rapid urbanization, national settlement pattern, regional underdevelopment, sustainable architecture and urban development, eradication of poverty within cities, deteriorating environmental conditions, housing for the poor and middle-income families, bringing local authorities as close as possible to the citizens, and the like.

Harmonious Human Settlements in The Light of The Principles of Ekistics[*]

A Conceptual Introduction

According to the concerned resolution of the United Nations General Assembly (56/2006) the Urban Forum 4 will constitute "a non-legislative technical forum in which experts can exchange views in the years when the Governing Council of the United Nations Human Settlements Programme does not meet". Our major goal is certainly to discuss at length the problems of urbanization facing the world, to assess the degree of efficiency to deal with them and to make necessary recommendations to guide the policies of both developing and developed nations in the direction of harmonious urbanization. The first of these forums was held in Nairobi in 2002, followed by the Second World Urban Forum in 2004, that was convened in Barcelona, and the third one in Vancouver in 2006. They have been attended by 1.200, 4.100 and 11.418 participants from more than 150 countries, respectively.

A brief explanation may be required at the beginning in order to find out what is meant by harmonious human

[*] Keynote Speech, Fourth Session of the World Urban Forum Draft Paper presented to the 2008 Meeting of the World Society for EKISTICS Southeast University, Nanjing, The Peoples' Republic of China, 5-6 November 2008.

settlements. Until present, we have talked about unbalanced, unhealthy, disorderly and unplanned urbanization. The idea of balance in all of these terms had something to do with the imbalances, disparities and inequalities between geographical regions, city size categories and between more or less prosperous communities within metropolitan areas. Of course, such an understanding does not exclude the possibility that urbanization movements in Third World countries are coupled with high rates of unemployment and disguised unemployment and with an expanded informal sector in major urban centers. Discrepancy between the public consciousness for a clean, well preserved and livable environment and the concern for rapid economic development was also an integral part of the concept of unhealthy urbanization.

What we have began to hear now under the title of harmonious urbanization can be regarded as a kind of urbanization that possesses entirely opposite features of unbalanced and disorderly urbanization. One can argue that the fundamental components of harmonious urbanization have to be regarded as the followings as announced in the general information sheet of the World Urban Forum 4 : *Socially harmonious cities* (equity, inclusiveness, income, poverty reduction, land and social housing), *Economically harmonious cities* (infrastructure development, financing urban development, foreign direct investment, urban informal economy), *Environmentally harmonious cities* (climate change, energy and resources savings, bio-diversity, water, sanitation and transport, green buildings and cities), *Spatially harmonious cities* (urban planning, urban and rural linkage, integrated regional development, mixed land use), *Historically harmonious cities* (heritage,culture,architecture and urban renewal), *Harmonious cities for all age groups*

(Youth ,aging population, internet and ICT, education and health care, sports and music).

From an ideological point of view, private interests of certain social classes such as the bourgeoisie can be blamed for the obstacles before the realization of harmonious urbanization. Because, according to such an exaggerated view, the philosophy of capitalism itself would not allow ensuring a harmonious, balanced and healthy urbanization. Its priorities are on maximizing the private interests of the bourgeoisie, sustaining the existence of the capitalist system itself, but not on the preservation of natural, environmental and cultural values.

Apart from such debates, harmonious urbanization may be defined as a policy option which aims at ensuring the sustainability of the nature on which we live, to provide opportunities for living, shelter, employment, entertainment, health and education, to eradicate poverty without alienating people from their natural environment. This environment friendly definition of harmonious urbanization ensures needed harmony between ecology and economy, the interests of the individuals and the society on one hand and the concerns for the present and future generations on the other. This definition is in line with the understanding of the newly adopted of the European Urban Chapter (2008) of the Council of Europe which takes as the starting point a new concept of urbanity which is based on sustainable, cohesive and knowledge-based towns and cities.

The Principles of Ekistics Revisited

Since the establishment in the early 1960's The World Society for Ekistics and the Athens Center of Ekistics have focused their efforts on various aspects of the issues which had direct and indirect impact upon the kind of urbanization that is called "harmonius" within the context of the World Urban Forum 4. It is certainly not possible to cover all of the principles of Ekistics within the context of this meeting. Rather a selection is made and an effort will be made here to show how relevant are these principles for the main theme of the World Urban Forum 4, namely Harmonious Urbanization: Balanced Territorial Development. The main source of information is numerous publications of the Athens Center of Ekistics, the Journal of Ekistics, and the Declarations of Delos Symposia that have taken place between 1963 and 1975.

Institutional and Methodological Issues
An Emerging Discipline

The first is of course the attempt to develop a new discipline of human settlements that is called Ekistics. It was going to include such sub-systems as anthropos (peoples as individuals), nature, society, shells (buildings) and network (roads, utilities, transportation, communications and administrative boundaries) (C.A.Doxiadis, "Action for a Better Scientiific Approach to the Subject of Human Settlements: An Anthropocosmos Model", Ekistics, Vo9l.38, No:229, December 1974, pp.405-412; Institute of Architectural and Urban Studies, Tsinghua University School of Architecture, Tsinghua University, Wu Liangyong and Sciences of Human Settlements in China, 2008) . To initiate basic research in these fields, to bring together specialists from other relevant discipline to work together with an interdisciplinary approach on projects in this field, to work out new methods of training those who can assume leadership and responsibility in the sphere of action and finally to attract some of the best young minds into this new area of research, development and practice.

Revision in the Institutional Set-Up of the United Nations

A second impact of Ekistics works was to help development of the institutional set-up of he UN system to enable it to respond better to the problems of human settlements. It was suggested that a) human settlements be recognized within the UN system as a separate sector or activity, and that b) appropriate organizational measures be taken within the framework of the United Nations to meet the needs of this new individual sector and that c) the proper share of the UN funds be allocated to the sector of human settlements and further finance be sought on a scale more adequate to the extent of urban crisis.

The need to establish a United Nations Agency or a major programme was constantly stressed by the participants of Delos symposia. As a result of the accumulation of pressures towards that direction resulted in the creation of the United Nations Center for Human Settlements (UNCHS) following the Vancouver Conference in 1976. It was hoped that the new agency would integrate fragmented aspects of policy and would combine them in a genuine strategy in the field of human settlements. The UNCHS urged many international agencies "*to adopt the Ekistic approach*" in their own work and to collaborate closely with each other to produce integrated policies.

A Holistic Approach to the Study of Human Settlements

Actually, the Ekistics grid is the best expression of an holistic approach to the study of human settlements. The view that the application of the basic sciences to human welfare is extremely fragmented is no longer acceptable. Therefore, parts of human beings as health, nutrition, education could not be dealt with in isolation, but the whole man, man in the community had to be studied. What is needed is not to examine the butterfly itself, but to study its habitat as a whole, as a requirement of the holistic approach. This methodology which is perfectly embedded in the Ekistics grid assumes that it is only by looking at all aspects of these Networks as parts of a whole system of human settlements that we can hope to rationalize and develop these Networks so as to provide a framework for the future well-being of man". This approach fits quite well to spatial (territorial) and temporal (intergenerational) equity issues and it is based on the ethical responsibility of the citizens. The concepts of comprehensive development and planning have been considerably influenced by this approach during the last several decades.

Substantial Issues Related to Harmonious Urbanization
Making Cities the Real Engines of Growth

As pointed out in the İstanbul Declaration adopted at the end of the Habitat II Conference (1996), rapid urbanization, the sprawl of cities and the rapid growth of mega-cities are among the most significant transformations of human settlements. The urban population has increased from less than 30 percent of the total in 1950 to more than 47 percent at the beginning of the 20th century. It is estimated that by the year 2006, more than half of humankind will begin to

live in urban areas. During the course of history, urbanization has been associated, in principle, with economic and
social progress, the promotion of literacy and education,
the improvement of general health conditions, greater access to social services, and cultural and political participation. As rightly stressed in the same document, cities and
towns have been the engines of growth and incubators of
civilization and have facilitated the evolution of knowledge,
culture and tradition, as well as industry and commerce.

However, particularly the developing countries with
least financial resources suffer considerably from the adverse consequences of excessive urbanization, manifested
through enormous backlogs in shelter, infrastructure and
services, increasingly crowded transportation systems, unsustainable consumption patterns, deteriorating sanitation
and environmental pollution. All these are often associated
with general conditions of urban poverty, insecure land tenure, unsatisfactory housing conditions, urban crime and
homelessness. Only if handled in an appropriate manner
and with a planned approach, as advocated by Ekisticians
for years, the range of opportunities can be broadened and
equal rights can be favored.

Housing and Urban Land

Long before the Vancouver Conference on Human Settlements, in Delos Eleven Declaration, Ekisticians declared
that a Charter of Human Settlements has to be formulated
and three basic human rights have to be defined there.
These were *The Right to Shelter, The Right to Equality,* and
The Right to Dignity. The ultimate goal of a human right to

shelter has to be understood as one person/one room, and in the first stage, one family/one dwelling.

Although the Article 25 of the Universal Declaration of Human Rights adopted by the UN General Assembly in 1948 has defined the right to housing, among others, as the following: "Everyone has the right to a level of life sufficient to guarantee his feeding, well-being, of himself and his family, particularly for nutrition, dressing, *housing,* health care, and necessary social services…".Even after twenty years following the Vancouver Conference on Human Settlements, humanity has observed that it was far from having reached the targets set during the Conference. However, one has to keep in mind that the provisions of the Universal Declaration of Human Rights and similar documents are of "soft law" nature and their becoming binding for particular States depends upon their ratification by national parliaments. Therefore, it is necessary to ratify the International Covenant on Social, Economic and Cultural Rights of 1966 in order to enable the citizens to claim that right. Besides, as reaffirmed in the Habitat II Conference, the provisions of the Covenant require that the States commit themselves "to the *full and progressive realization of the right to adequate housing* as provided for in international instruments.

An inseparable element of harmonious urbanization is undoubtedly the fact that urban land must be used in the public interest. This principle has been defended by WSE since the beginning. The role of the landownership in urban development is so crucial that the name of the main themes of the Congress of the International Union of Architects that was convened in 2005 was "Who owns the land? Who owns the city ?". This sentence may be correct in the sense that who owns the land has also the power to control what happens in the city. However, the impression that both land and the city may be owned by individuals in the absolute sense is false. This is more than a semantic phenomenon. Both the land and the city are not owned by present generations. They are and should be regarded to be in their possession, not in their ownership. Because as collections of material and non-material assets, they are inherited from past generations, and they will be transmitted to future generations in no worse conditions than when they are obtained.

Land is both "a physical commodity" and "an abstract concept". Land may be owned by one person, may be in possession of another, and may still be occupied by a third. Ownership means the right to enjoy the use of something, the ability to dispose of it, and to benefit from the rights associated with it. On the other hand, possession involves the ability to enjoy the use of the land and in some circumstances to exploit the products on or below its surface. Possession implies the physical power to control an object. Possession may be legitimate or illegal. It may be based on formal agreements such as leases or rental arrangements.

The right to ownership in land is one of the economic and social rights recognized to human beings. John Locke, 17th century philosopher, had indicated that the land, in its natural state, was un-owned. Some of the well-known philosophers like Karl Marx and J. Proudhon had called private ownership over the production factors as a theft (La Propriété, c'est le vol). On the other hand, others believed that it is the right of ownership that makes the societies to succeed in achieving rapid development. It was regarded as a flight to increased welfare and prosperity (La Propriété, C'est l'Envol pour la Prosperité).

The land has become subject to ownership when labor is added to land. It took quite a long time to abandon the idea that the land belonged to God. However, as different from its conception in the 19th century, it is now widely accepted that the right to ownership in land, like other properties subject to private ownership, can be restricted by the considerations of public interest, public safety and public order. Ethical considerations require that ownership rights to land should be used with due regard to the public interest. In other words, no one could use his private ownership right in land in contravention of the general interests of the society and humanity. Despite the fact that since the last quarter of the 20th century widespread privatization efforts in the world undermined considerably the importance of the above mentioned socially motivated restrictions, more efficient safeguards are still needed in order to ensure sustainability in urban development, in the management of land stocks, housing design, architecture and environmental protection. The trend from Aristoteles to Léon Duguit signifies a constant shift from pure individualism towards a system more or less socialized where public interest is reconciled and harmonized with the private concerns. Principles defended by Ekisticians provide vast opportunities to incorporate such ideas into the very definition of harmonious urbanization.

Balanced Territorial Development

As early as in 1965, participants of the Delos Three Symposium had drawn the attention of the world public opinion to the need to tackle with the problem of regional underdevelopment. It was stated that the problems of urban sprawl and mass migration to urban centers could not be dealt with locally. They need to be handled within larger systems of planning and administration at the regional levels. To redress economic imbalances and to reduce regional disparities and to get all regions contribute to the overall growth of the national economy were mentioned among the fundamental goals of territorial development. Such considerations as balanced territorial development were included in the concerned international declarations like Vancouver and İstanbul much later. In the Ekistics publications, one can find references to some successful regional development projects carried out in various parts of the world like Mezzogiorno in Italy, Guayana Project in Venezuela, and the Lakish Project in Israel. Balanced Territorial Development as the sub-heading of the main theme of the World Urban Forum 4 is one of the most important policy issues occupying the European institutions such as the European Union and the Council of Europe. European Spatial Development Perspectives (1999), the Territorial Agenda of the European Union (2007), Leipig Charter (2007), Guiding Principles for Sustainable Development of the European Continent (2000) are some of these Europen institutions which contain relevant principles for balanced territorial development.

Sustainable Development and Environmental Considerations

Numerous principles adopted in various Delos symposia and embedded in the traditional components of the Ekistics grid reflect basic guidelines for sustainable urban and spatial development. Respect for human scale and dignity in urban settlements, concern for the protection of historic and natural assets of the settlements as a part of the heritage of humanity were constantly emphasized in those documents. The Ekisticians had deplored "the destruction of irreplaceable cultural values through careless stewardship" thus predicting the significance of the concept of sustainable development long before the concept appeared in the agenda of the environmentalists.

More specifically, as early as Delos Three Symposion, certain consequences of the population growth and technological progress were blamed as factors causing visual monotony, lack of satisfaction in urban design and the pollution of air and water. Similarly, Delos Four underlined the increasing stress on natural resources, wilderness for recreation, untouched habitats for biological research, water tables and circuits and unpolluted air. All these were, in varying degrees, in need of protection against the encroachment by human beings. It continued to emphasize that "the present (as early as the 1960's) chaotic combination of over density and sprawl added to the production of *unacceptable urban landscape.*" Repeatedly, the attention was drawn into the fact that if we treat the living ecology of the planet as a seamless web, within which breaks are disastrous, we can plan for the ways in which man's construction of an artificial environment can complement and improve the natural environment of this planet.

A final but not least important consideration that might shed light into the formulation of harmonious urbanization policies as well as balanced territorial and sustainable development is certainly concerned with the rights of future generations over the resources of the planet. The need was insistently expressed for an immediate change in environmental conditions and the nature of our society without waiting for infants still unborn (Ruşen Keleş,"The Relevance of the Delos Declarations for the Problems of Urbanization and Environment Facing the World Today", Paper presented to the International Conference on Constantinos A. Doxiadis and His Work organized by the Association of Collaborators and Friends of Constantinos A.Doxiadis, Athens, 19-21 January 2007, New Benaki Museum).

Ekisticians have always paid due attention to the considerations for the needs of future generations. Volumes 67 (1999) 68 (2000) of the Ekistics Journal were devoted to the discussion on the future in general and on human settlements. In his introductory notes to these volumes, Mr. Psomopoulos had attempted to conceptualize the ways in which the future can be shaped. He had distinguished four major forces actually shaping the city of the future.

The first of these was *the constant* one, represented by things like mountains, which we cannot change, or the fundamental properties of matter and energy. The second future was represented by those elements which were inherited from the past but which were declining and will be gradually eliminated such as the present generation of people, or houses which are in a dilapidated state, or the cultural traits and technological inventions which have been superseded: that is *the declining past*. The third future was represented by *the continuing past*, such things as the children of the present generation who are influenced by parents now alive, houses being built according to the patterns of existing ones or roads which exist today and will go on being used. The fourth and final future is *the creative future*. This is the future which will come into being because of things that do not exist at all today: new ideas, new technology, new developments. It is this creative future which in fact makes all the real difference between the past and the future, and which marks the difference between Anthropos and animals, since they cannot influence their future in this way, whereas Anthropos can." (Panayis Psomopoulos, "The Editor's Page", *Ekistics*, Futures 1 (Triple Issue). The Four Future of Human Settlements).

The principle of *intergenerational equity* of the International Environmental Law suggests that the instrument of sustainable development be adopted and respected, as a kind of development, which, while meeting the needs of present generation, should not compromise the ability of the future generations to meet their own needs.

Public Participation, Local Involvement and Subsidiarity

Making urban growth subject to planned intervention, ensuring the flexibility of both the planning process and of the instruments available to decision-makers and the maximum degree of public participation have been major concerns of the World Society for Ekistics for a long time. Delos Five Declaration emphasized the achievement of the goals of public participation and the need to have the freedom to be consulted about the choices. Similarly, Delos Nine Declaration underlined the fundamental ideology behind public participation as the following: "The settlements' pattern should not come to the citizen in a shape so fixed and predetermined by external authority that there can be no free play or creativity for development and change" Again, according to Delos Ten Declaration, "involvement of the citizens in the solution of ekistical problems is indispensable". All these requirements had an undeniable impact upon the inclusion of the basic principles of public participation in the planning process. In fact, The Habitat Agenda (1996) devoted a whole section to the needs and the role of the vulnerable groups and the people with special needs among its strategies. Similar provisions have been incorporated into such international instruments as the Rio Declaration on Environment and Development (1992) and the European Urban Charter (1992, 2004 and 2008).

Bringing local governments closer to the people and ensuring active participation were among the recommendations of Delos Ten Declaration. This suggestion was reflecting the same ideology of the principle of subsidiarity which has been guiding the policies of the European Union since the adoption of the Maastricht Treaty in 1993. The Amsterdam Treaty (1997), the European Charter of Local Self-Government and several other international legal instruments possess the same principle which requires that public affairs have to be carried out at the levels of authority that are closest to the citizens. A recent report prepared by the Governing Council of the United Nations Human Settlements Programme (4-8 April 2005, "Dialogue on Effective Decentralization and the Strengthening of Local Authorities") has resulted in a Resolution (20/18) with a view "to develop the concept of a global observatory that would assess, monitor and evaluate the state of decentralization and accountability to people at the local level and local governance in the world, as important conditions for achieving the goals of the Habitat Agenda". One can find similar commitments made by the well-known NGO's such as the European Cities and Towns towards social equity for urban sustainability, sustainable land use patterns, sustainable urban mobility patterns, etc. The Aalborg Charter (1994) and the Aalborg+10- Inspiring Futures (2004) of the same Association, and the European Urban Charter (1992, 2004,2008) of the European Council are full of commitments for strengthening local democracy to contribute to harmonious urbanization and balanced territorial development.

Lessons to be Learnt from European Experiences

Occasionally references have been made to the provisions of several international legal instruments throughout the intervention. It was assumed that a considerable accumulation of valuable information could be found in the sources of several European institutions like the European Union and the Council of Europe. Therefore, a reciprocal and constant exchange of ideas, experiences and assessments with regard to harmonious urbanization and balanced territorial development between the UN and the individual member states on one hand and those institutions on the other would be highly rewarding.

The directives of the European Commission on the European Urban Environment Strategy, the Environment Action Programmes of the Union possess valuable guidelines for a sound urbanization policy. The document called the European Spatial Development Perspectives (ESDP) (1999) may provide a suitable policy framework for balanced and sustainable spatial development. Such principles of this document as a) the development of a *polycentric and balanced urban system* and a partnership between and urban areas, b) the promotion of integrated transport and communications concepts and c) the development and conservation of the natural and cultural heritage seem to be highly relevant in terms of the objectives of the World Urban Forum 4.

On the other hand, Leipzig Charter on Sustainable European Cities (2007) and the Territorial Agenda of the European Union (2007) provide essential guidelines for integrated urban development, strategies for upgrading the physical environment, strengthening local economy in deprived urban areas, efficient and sustainable use of resources.

Similarly, Guding Principles for Sustainable Spatial Development of the European Continent adopted by the Ministers Responsible for Spatial Development of the Member States of the Council of Europe (Hannover, 2000) contains main traits of the theme of the World Urban Forum 4, as embedded in the sentences of socially, economically, environmentally, spatially, historically harmonious cities and cities for all age groups. Territorial cohesion, harmonized urban-rural relationships, equal accessibility to public services, reducing environmental risks and damages, protecting natural resources and cultural heritage are some of the major objectives of this document.

Principles of the Aalborg Charter (1994) and the Aalborg+10: An Inspiring Future (2004), the European Charter of Local Self-Government (1985), and the Valencia Declaration of Good Local and Regional Governance all stress the need to strengthen territorial authorities for better implementation of the idea of harmonious urbanization. Finally, the European Urban Charter (1992, 2004, 2008) of the Council of Europe must be added to this list.

Concluding Remarks

Considering that at least two thirds of humanity will be living in towns and cities in the next fifty years, the keen interest of the United Nations to examine the impact of rapid urbanization on human settlements, economies and policies becomes more meaningful. The humanity will be necessarily more concerned with burgeoning poverty in cities, improving the access of the urban poor to basic facilities such as shelter, clean water and sanitation, nutrition, controlling skyrocketing prices of urban land, achieving environment-friendly and sustainable urban growth and development. All these require a planned intervention into the free play of the market forces not only in developing but also in already developed countries.

On various occasions and particularly in the Habitat meetings (Habitat II, İstanbul, 1996), the world leaders have committed themselves to sustainable patterns of production, consumption, transportation and settlements development, pollution prevention, respect for carrying capacity of ecosystems, and the preservation of opportunities for future generations. In this connection, the pressing need for cooperation among nations in a spirit of global partnership to conserve, protect and restore the health and integrity of the Earth's ecosystem was repeatedly emphasized. And in view of different contributions to global environmental degradation, the principle of common but differentiated responsibility and the precautionary principle have been inserted into the agenda of the humanity.

Despite all the efforts reflecting the goodwill of the United Nations and other international organizations, there is still a wide discrepancy between what he governments said and what they did. "The speeches were beautiful, but the reality awful". Yet, it was rightly noted in the World Urban Forum 3 in Vancouver two years ago that all urban players must do their part in this respect rather than simply transfer responsibility to others. Planners, architects, designers, decision-makers, teachers and scientists coming together under the umbrella of the World Society for Ekistics (namely the problems and science of human settlements) have made on their part undeniable contributions during the last half century to the development of a conceptual model suitable for the analysis and solution of such worldwide issues as rapid urbanization, rational settlements patterns, regional underdevelopment, eradication of poverty in cities, problems of exclusion, deterioration of environmental conditions, addressing the shelter needs of the poor, and strengthening local authorities.

Holism, comprehensiveness, future orientation, rational planning, respect for cultural heritage, rational use of land, and participation were some of the features of the Ekistics approach. Doubts have been expressed recently (Amos Rapoport, "The Need for an Ekistics Research Program: A Proposal",31.1.2003-4.2.2003, Berlin) about the analytical and operational utility of the Ekistics grid. It was noted that the main elements in the grid were "extremely general, broad and vague" and "there was a need to dismantle them" in order to make them operational, I believe that the level of generality as well as the relevance of the components of the grid have still the chance to serve as a suitable framework.

Squatting, Slum Upgrading and Prevention in Turkey[*]

Introduction: Concepts and Definitions

Throughout the second half of the 20th century a rapid urbanization characterized the development process all over the world, including the developing countries. Turkey is one of the countries facing the problems brought about by rapid urbanization mainly due to her structural characteristics. However, urbanization in Turkey has also its own peculiarities. In addition to its features such as its extent, pace and imbalances in the geographical distribution of population and economic activities, Turkey's urbanization manifests itself as an essentially demographic phenomenon, a constant flow of population from rural to urban centers, which caused not by an essentially rapid industrialization that might create extensive employment opportunities in urban centers to justify its pace. Instead, a substantial portion of the population migrating to cities had a chance to begin working in a variety of employments which is called the "informal sector".

---

[*] JAICA (Japan International Cooperation Agency), The Consulting Service of the Third Country (Turkey) , by Holding Lecture Sessions and Workshops on Urban Planning and Urban Development of Turkey and Afgan Government Officials, Ankara, 2020.

The main reasons for rural-urban migrations are identified as high population growth, mechanization of the agricultural sector and uneven economic development which have caused disparities among geographical regions and between rural and urban areas. In this respect, while the share of urban population in the total was 25.1 percent in 1960, this ratio rose to 55.4 percent in 1990. With the rapid increase in rural-urban migration, the share of urban population in the total has become 61.7 percent in 2000 and 93.0 percent in 2014. As the migrants concentrated in urban centers realized that their individual benefits they receive in their new environment in addition to their incomes far exceed the amount of their revenues in the rural sector, rural-urban migration thus becomes more or less justified and legitimized.

Rapid urbanization created numerous bottlenecks in meeting the increased service needs of new migrants as well as those of the existing inhabitants of cities. These included housing, transportation, urban infrastructure, public health and education, environmental security, and the like. It was assume for a long time that most of such unmet needs could be attributed to the imperfections of the market mechanism. However, it was finally realized that uneven income distribution was the main variable causing the crisis and therefore measures of long-term had to be taken for its improvement. This is also the most important suggestion made in the Quito (Ecuador) HABITAT III Conference in 2016.

Socio-economic marginality seems to be the major reason for the emergence of squatter settlements in metropolitan centers of Turkey. In our surveys on Ankara and Gaziantep squatters revealed that those interviewed were overwhelmingly expecting that their living conditions will be either worsened or remained unchanged in the future. The percentages of the pessimistic heads of households were 66.7 percent for Ankara, the State Capital, and 62.5 percent in different districts of the city of Gaziantep. Similarly, the findings of our surveys conducted in 11 sites of Turkish cities during 1985-1986 indicated that the inhabitants of the poorest squatter settlements possess a "loss accepting attitude" and incline towards "a culture of poverty".

Despite the fact that squatting was generally regarded a rational action of the homeless poor, attempts have been made to indicate that the expenditures made for building squatter houses were, to a great extent, a waste on the part of the national economy.

Squatter houses of Turkey are called as "gecekondu", simply meaning that they are built overnight. As such, the term gecekondu does not refer to the characteristics of the shack houses constructed but rather to the procedure and the timing of its building. From another perspective, gecekondu denotes to the dwelling unit or the end product of the gecekondu formation process rather than the settlements where gecekondu buildings constitute the overwhelming majority of the built-up territory.

The Dictionary of Town Planning defines the gecekondu as a dwelling unit which is constructed without a building licence, in contravention of the building and construction regulations, on the lands owned by public authorities or private individuals, against the will of the landowner, to be used by the poor and lower-income families which the State or local authorities are unable to meet their housing needs. According to another definition, gecekondu is the name of an unhealthy and primitive shack house which is built in violation of building regulations in an uncontrolled manner. Official sources define gecekondu as a dwelling unit constructed swiftly on the lands unowned by the gecekondu builder in contravention of the building regulations and the rules concerning engineering and public health.

Finally, the Gecekondu Law of 1966 (Number: 775) defines the gecekondu as a building constructed on land belonging to others than the gecekondu builder in violation of the legislation concerning development and construction. The official definition does not possess such elements as being unhealthy and having being constructed swiftly. It is likely that these components of the definition were assumed to be normally included in other elements of the definition which are direct result of being built in violation of the building and development legislation.

Both slums and squatter houses (gecekondus) are non-conventional types of housing which do not comply with legally established standards and procedures. They are usually constructed outside the conventional institutions of building industry and they are frequently built-in contravention of the existing building legislation. As such they are almost always unacceptable in terms of the established and prevailing values in capitalist societies.

Slums and squatter houses are the formations which possess most of the physical and socio-economic qualities attributed to marginal populations. They reflect those characteristics in more pronounced and aggravated measures of magnitude. Although they are often used in the literature interchangeably, the terms of slums and settlements are entirely different concepts.

The term of slum is mainly used in western industrialized countries to denote substandard and rundown dwellings
and the structures the dwelling unit and the neighborhood.
They are situated in the central parts of the cities. They are
built by common methods of house production in accordance with the building standards and regulations in effect
in time of erection. Therefore, their status as being a slum,
a sort of undesirable residence or neighborhood is *ex post*
qualification acquired later than the state of construction.

People living in slums are usually considered as lower
strata of the society. Tenancy rather than home-ownership
characterizes the type of occupancy of slums. Their inhabitants are generally transients. Dwellings are designed and
constructed by others than the occupants of the slum dwellings. Most of them are the multi-family units. On the other
hand, squatter dwellings are located primarily in the outskirts of the cities where building site is not as scarce and expensive as in the center. However, squatting in central areas
is also extensive in almost all Middle Eastern metropolises,
as in Turkey. At the same time, outlying areas are more advantageous to squatters, for they can easily escape the control of municipal and national authorities. Squatter dwellings are illegal structures starting from the beginning, *ex
ante*, because they are constructed consciously in violation
of the building codes, zoning and subdivision regulations.

Squatters are essentially homeowners and also low-income groups. They live in these houses nor temporarily, but
permanently. The structures which are often one, rarely two
stories, which some small gardens around them, suitable for
poultry growing and urban agriculture, are designed partly
or wholly by their own residents. Either these latter characteristics or the fact that these structures are built socially,

through self-help and mutual aid have to be understood as in the original qualifications of the squatter settlements which may hold true for the squatter houses all over the Third World at present.

Therefore, the term of slum has to be understood as meaning the dwellings of which the characteristics expressing exactly the *gecekondus* of Turkey.

One of the policy measures regarding the squatter settlements is called upgrading. The concept of upgrading has something to do primarily with improving the physical conditions of the individual squatter houses or neighborhoods or communities of which the whole or the great majority of the dwellings have the characteristics of gecekondu. One should keep in mind that such a perception of the concept of upgrading, while expressing the need of making up of the deficiencies in the physical features of the shack houses or the gecekondu settlements such as infrastructure, land-ownership, running water, electricity, cultural opportunities, environment and the like, it tends to neglect the economic aspects of the problem. As rightly pointed out many years ago by Manuel Castells, although slum clearance and urban redevelopment experiments of industrialized western nations accomplish a certain improvement in the conditions of the slums as a whole, what actually they achieve is just "to transfer the poverty from one location in the city to another". What is more important is to meet the need to eliminate poverty conditions which create the slums. Therefore, upgrading should be understood in its broadest sense to include both improvements in physical conditions as well as the social and economic rehabilitation of the squatter settlements.

All socio-economic indicators reveal that squatter settlements in major Turkish cities house the great majority of
the unemployed, disguised unemployed individuals, which
are reflected in the size and structure of the informal sectors in those centers.

One of the important variables that are directly related
to the growth of the illegally built housing stock is the uneven income distribution in Turkey in general and in the
city of Ankara. According to the figures provided by the
State Planning Organization, the share of the poorest 20
percent of the households decreased from 5.24 percent in
1987 to 4.86 in 1994, while the share of the richest 20 percent of households increased from 49.9 percent to 54.9 percent during the same period.

Inflated land prices make access by the poorest families
to the formal land market practically impossible. Land is
supplied by such institutions as the Mass Housing Administration (TOKİ) and the municipalities in accordance with
the procedures set by their own legislation. Formally, land
development takes place in four different ways: a) Through
city development plans in accordance with the City Planning Law. b) Outside municipal boundaries, through partial urban development plans worked out by different public and private agencies. C) Through partial development
plans prepared for areas outside the boundaries of the city
development plans. And finally, d) through legalization of
the title deeds by improvement plans worked out for squatter settlements in the course of the so-called planned transformation.

The last category is composed mainly of the illegally
constructed housing that provides considerable profit to
the holder of the title deed, who had occupied the land

illegally. In settlements that have been formed entirely informally through outright invasion, by squatters, legalization of titles is not permitted in principle, until the enactment of a legislation pardoning the squatters. There is no doubt that there is always a large gap between the needs and the formal supply. But for the city of Ankara, it would not be misleading to assume that the gap filled out by illegal housing does not increase percentage-wise, although it does not decrease either.

Proliferation of gecekondu settlements in Turkey goes back to the years following the World War II. In 1948, there were only 25-30.000 gecekondus in major centers. This figure increased to 80.000 in 1953, where a Gecekondu Law was put into force. It has become 240.000 in 1960 and 1.5 million in 1983. Despite the fact that squatting was forbidden by the legislation in force, their number kept constantly increasing. It was estimated that the number of these dwellings has been 2.200.000 in the early 2000.

A remarkable feature of the gecekondu formation process in Turkey which has shaped its proliferation throughout the last half century is its changing nature. This feature not only affected the expansion of squatter settlements in major metropolitan centers, but also influenced the formulation of official policies regarding these settlements. In order to make this observation more concrete and easier to understand, it is appropriate to underline the changes taken place in different stages.

1. First of all, until the early 1960's, the self-help and mutual aid aspect of the squatting process was clearly evident. Building a squatter dwelling was a joint venture of family members, friends and relatives, with no assistance from public authorities. The structures

used to be built primarily for self-use. Renting out with the purpose of the enjoyment of the exchange value of the property was an exceptionally rare phenomenon. Use value was the main driving force behind the attempts to build squatter houses.

2. However, during the late 1960's and 1970's, although the self-help and mutual aid component of the total building cost remained high, the squatting process became gradually commercialized in the sense that attempts of letting out of the units with the purpose to profit from their exchange value, became gradually common. The squatter has become an entrepreneur, and squatting became a sort of new culture. No longer as a poverty of culture, but a culture of profit-making.

3. In the final stage, namely, from the late 1970's onward, the process of this petty commodity production became entirely commercialized, and private firms have taken over the tasks such as securing the plot, designing the project, and actually constructing the dwelling units. In other words, the self-help nature of squatting has been totally replaced by the concern for more profit out of the exchange value of the house.

Analysis of Past and Current Gecekondu Upgrading and Prevention Approaches

It is appropriate to draw a dividing line between the major approaches of upgrading and prevention adopted and implemented in the past and those that are being carried out at present. However, one must be aware that the origins of the current strategies go back to the political and intellectual developments that have started in the early 1980's. Therefore, approaches that are actually followed have to be understood as those being implemented not only at present but also carried out in recent past, namely since the beginning of the 1980's.

The Pre-1980 Period

The beginning of the slum upgrading and prevention approaches adopted during the pre-1980 period may be taken to the post-war years where the phenomenon of squatter formation had emerged. Of course, the first attempts have focused on prevention rather than upgrading because it was assumed that squatting could be prevented by strict measures to be implemented by police power of the State and the municipal authorities. Two different periods at this stage may be distinguished from each other, namely the period up to 1960 and the planned period that started in the beginning of the 1960's.

The Pre-Planned Period (up to 1960)

In this period, the State has made an attempt to resolve the squatting problems by enacting certain laws which reflect its basic philosophy in this matter. The first law was dated 1948 (No: 5218). Its aim was to ameliorate the conditions of Ankara's squatter houses and to prevent the construction of the new ones. The primary tool to be used for the prevention was to provide cheap land for the likely squatter builders. In the allocation of land the priority was given to those families with more children, those that are homeless, having a regular occupation in Ankara, being residents of the city for the most extended period, and the lowest level income groups which need financial assistance from the State. The price of the land allocated was going to be paid back within ten years on the basis of equal installments. A complementary Law (No: 5228) passed in the same year in order to provide loans to the applicant families in need as much as 75 percent of the cost of the building with an interest rate of 5 percent. This second law expanded the scope of the implementation of this preventive measure to encompass all cities. The families had to finish the construction of the dwellings within a period not exceeding two years.

Another law of 1949 (No: 5431) authorized local authorities to tear down the illegally built dwellings could not be implemented successfully. However, a law of 1953 (No: 6188) which has been in force nearly fifteen years aimed to encourage construction of social housing by allocating public lands (state or municipal) to homeless families. It aimed to "legalizing" the squatter houses constructed until the promulgation date (1953) of the law, and prohibited building new ones.

In order to facilitate the provision of lands to the homeless, a law of 1959 (No: 7367) made it possible the free transfer of the state lands suitable for housing to the municipalities. The aim of the law was to prevent squatter building and the formation of squatter settlements.

Three characteristics of the approaches adopted during the pre-planned period can be summarized as a) the prevention of gecekondu building by providing urban land to be acquired by cities to the homeless, b) the prohibition of the construction of new illegal houses, and c) to legalize the already built ones.

The Planned Development Period (1960-1980)

This is the period where the major approaches to "slum" upgrading and prevention have been shaped by Five-Year Development Plans prepared by the State Planning Organization. Starting with the First Five-Year Development Plan (1063-1967), almost all plans had recommendations to provide these settlements of unauthorized housing with missing social and technical infrastructure in addition to banning the construction of new ones. This approach is also reflected into the Law on Gecekondu of 1966 (No: 775) which is still in force. Therefore, looking at the basic principles of this law would make it easier to understand the official approach adopted in the Planned Development Period.

Four topics are worth to look at briefly in this context.

1. First is designating the squatter settlements in the city where upgrading, prevention or demolition works will take place. The Law on Gecekondu empowered municipalities to determine such settlements in the city within six months through all means available to them including aerial photographs, etc. Municipalities were also authorized to demand technical assistance from the central government, namely from the Ministry of Public Works and Settlement (presently Environment and Urban Development) for that purpose. It was decided that once determined by the standing committees of the municipalities, decisions and schemes concerning these areas should be made public in appropriate places in the city for a period of 30 days.

2. The second issue is to increase the land stocks of the cities in order to make them powerful enough to help the families in need of decent housing conditions. The Law on Gecekondu made possible the free transfer of all suitable public lands (land belonging to the Treasury, to Provincial Local Authorities, etc.) within the municipal boundaries to municipalities to be used with the aim of slum prevention. Even the urban lands possessed by the pious foundations were going to be allocated to municipalities at a reasonable price unless they were designated to be used for a certain public service in the city's master plan or they had buildings on them which constituted a part of historical and cultural heritage.

Such lands transferred to municipalities could exclusively be used for the purpose of building social dwellings regularly licensed by the city authorities. Selling out or renting out of these lands could only be permitted on the conditions that they are not suitable for house building, they are designated for a public service in the master plan, or they were situated in the central business districts of the cities.

Since the fundamental goal of the gecekondu policy is to assist the poor to meet their accommodation needs, it is vital to select the members of the group in greatest need. This task is rendered enormously difficult to carry out as the number of applicants exceeds considerably the amount of available urban land that can be developed and allocated. Therefore, the legislator set certain priorities in the allocation of parcels to citizens, including the followings: a) those squatters who are or will be left without accommodation because of the demolition of their gecekondu. b) other families without shelter. c) Homeowners in gecekondu upgrading or prevention districts, who prefer to replace their gecekondu with social dwellings.

In principle, individual families are the final beneficiaries of the titles of the lands to be allocated to them by cities. Therefore, the system functions in a direction that causes the municipalities lose the lands they possess. Since the amount of lands owned by municipalities are not unlimited, it is not unrealistic to expect that in view of the rapid increase of the applicants for suitable and cheaper lands, the achievement of the goals of the Gecekondu Law will become unlikely to a considerable extent. Only the families with law income and those who are homeless have been considered eligible for land allocations, a by-law has been issued to guide implementation. The Ministry of Public Works and Settlement through making periodical amendments in the respective by-law seeks to adjust the criteria used in describing poor families taking into account the inflation rate. The principe is to set a fixed account as the net annual income of a family of two persons with the addition of a certain amount for each child. In addition to the income criterion, it is required that the head of the household who requests the allocation of land, his or her partner and their children should neither own a house nor an apartment/flat somewhere in the country, nor possess a parcel of land suitable for building shelter.

3. A third feature of the Law on Gecekondu was the creation of two funds, one in the control of municipalities and the second at the central government level, to be used for upgrading of squatter settlements and for providing housing credit to build social housing. Municipalities were also authorized to use the funds for expropriation in addition

to their duties to improve the quality of urban public services in unauthorized settlements. In its turn, the Ministry of Public Works and Settlement was authorized to provide loans out of its own funds to municipalities trying to upgrade the slums and squatter settlements. Individual households could receive housing credits from the Ministry under this scheme for a period not exceeding 20 years and with an interest rate not lower than 5 percent.

The implementation of the provisions of the Gecekondu Law with respect to the utilization of these funds during the last four decades revealed that success in upgrading and prevention was rather negligible.

4. Fourth instrument in the Law on Gecekondus was concerned with the obligation of the residents of squatter settlements to participate in financial expenditures incurred to municipalities in connection to such public services as sewerage systems, road construction, water installations, electricity and the like. Not only the residents but at the same time the absentee owners of the squatter houses were obliged to pay the necessary fees and charges in accordance with the rules prescribed by the local finance legislation. These contribution shares had to be paid in ten years with equal installments.

In order to ease the financial burden of low-income families living in those settlements, the law provided exemptions for the services realized with expenses made out of the national budget. Moreover, municipal councils were authorized to decide to assume the responsibility to pay a certain part of the expenditures to be made for basic infrastructure, facilities and amenities. At the same time they could extend the ten year period prescribed for payment by installment to twenty years. Getting the residents of squatter settlements to contribute to the expenditures for infrastructure and other public services was in line with cost recovery principle. It had also contributed to strengthening of their self-reliance.

5. Demolition of illegally built houses is the last instrument introduced by the Law on Gecekondu. The power to demolish such buildings lies with municipalities in principle. However, local authorities have the opportunity to ask the representatives of the State, namely the governors and sub-governors to provide them with the assistance they need to demolish gecekondus.

If the squatter houses are built or are being built on publicly owned lands they are demolished by respective authorities without any decision of any organ or a court. If they are built on the lands of private individuals, their owners are invited to present their titles or equivalent certificates. If they cannot, they are demolished as in the same way as the dwellings built on publicly owned land.

Three stages seem to be important in the evolution of squatter formation in Turkey: a) Prior to 1960, unauthorized building was regarded almost as a right of the poor families, realized mainly by self-help activities and by the support of their relatives and friends. Owner-occupation at this stage was the most common use. Renting out of the gecekondus was exceptional. The priority was given to the use value of the shelter. b) The self-help feature of the building process prevailed during the period of 1960-1980, but the degree of renting out for profit-making purposes increased considerably. One family build one and then another gecekondu in order to increase the family income. Gecekondus began to be built not only by the labor of the family members and relatives, but also by hired workers. c. After the 1970's and especially 1980's, partial commercialization and commodification of the gecekondu building process was replaced by complete commercialization. In this period, gecekondus were no longer an output of self-help or mutual-help initiatives. Labor by the individual and his family members is almost completely removed from the production process. The design and the production of dwellings, the provision of the building plot and the realization and safety of the illegal process of production were taken over by commercial firms to a large extent. In this stage, it has become obvious that gecekondu building process is preferred in order to increase the exchange value of the dwelling. Perhaps inevitably, considerations of public interest lost their significance considerably in this evolution.

Starting from the late 1960's, the State played an indirect role in urban housing and land market through the Land Office. This has been established to function as a regulatory institution in the land market with Powers to undertake land transactions and provide land for such public investments and services as housing, industry, public health and tourism. One of the majör reasons why the Land Office has not become a successful agency is that is capital was insufficient to operate efficiently in the land market. A related reason is the unwillingness to the functioning of the State in land market on ideological grounds. That is the reason why the Land Office has been abolished at the beginnings of the 2000's.

The Post 1980 Period

In general, the fundamental principles adopted by the Law on Gecekondu of 1966 did not change substantially in the post 1980 period. However, new concepts and practices such as the sites and services, and public-private partnership have been added to them. The tradition of providing occasional amnesty to already built dwellings, in other words, pardoning them by law mainly for political considerations has continued during the period. Almost all of the legislation enacted during the last five decades possessed a provision that authorized the government pardoning illegally built houses by legitimizing them and by trying to upgrade their conditions. Although a strict prohibition to build was introduced by all these laws, none of them was appropriately implemented as clearly expressed in the increase of their numbers.

Pardoning of illegally built houses has been all the time in the agendas of newly formed governments in Turkey. There is no doubt that some sort of legalization is needed in order to integrate these settlements and their residents with the larger society and economy. However, enactment of pardoning laws which usually coincides with the years of local or national elections gives the impression that this issue is largely exploited by partisan considerations. Experiences of Turkey clearly indicate that each attempt of pardoning illegal action of squatters tends to encourage new attempts for illegal building.

Although increasing emphasis was put on urban transformation projects in Ankara and elsewhere during the period starting from the 1990's these are subject to the analysis of other presentations within the context of this Project.

Lessons Learnt: What has worked and what not?
How sustainable have the various interventions been?

1. Slum upgrading and prevention issue has been taken up by public authorities, namely the central government and local authorities, and it has not been left to the interplay of the market forces since the beginning. This positive approach lasted until the 1980's where, although the government preserved its initiative and control apparently, its will has been actually substituted by the free play of the market forces.

2. The coordination of the efforts towards improving the conditions of the squatter houses and squatter settlements has been successfully provided thanks to the General Directorate of Housing and its division in charge of squatter settlements.

3. Particular attention has been given to the incorporation of the squatter settlements into the development plans of major metropolitan cities.

4. Planning controls and building prohibitions required by the legislation on the protection of natural assets and historical heritage, protection of coastal areas, protection of the Bosphorus, disaster management, and national forests in addition to the controls laid down in the Law on Urban Development helped to some extent prevention of the expansion of squatter settlements.

5. Although the Ministry of Public Works and Settlement played a leading role in formulating the housing policies and the policies concerning squatter settlements, the ultimate responsibility for planning these communities remained essentially with municipalities. This practice was in line with the universal principle of local autonomy requiring

that public affairs of local nature must be carried out by the authorities closest to the citizens.

6. However, there are a number of issues that have not worked well. One such bottleneck had something to do with planning regulations, planning standards and procedures. As in many developing countries, a considerable proportion of these regulations, standards and procedures were mostly imported from Western countries and they are followed properly in real life. The fact that most of them did not correspond to the realities of a developing country restricted to a considerable extent the chances for success of upgrading efforts. In a more general context, one can assume that the ways in which these regulations, standards and procedures are set forced the poor to break the law or regulations. In other words, the regulatory framework played a significant role in influencing Access into legal housing negatively.

7. One important lesson to be taken from the Turkish experience is that it has proved that the distribution of land titles to squatters can not be regarded as a sustainable technique of intervention in the housing market. For, land is a scarce natural resource and its amount cannot be increased at all. Therefore, it must be used with maximum care and every possible measure must be taken to avoid its wasteful use. Even a policy is adopted in order to allocate urban land to squatters, its implementation in the medium and long-term would face serious bottlenecks simply because matching the supply and demand would never be possible in view of the enormous magnitude of the need. Such a practice was in complete contradiction with the principle of sustainable development which denotes a kind of development that meets the needs of the president generation

without compromising the ability of future generations to meet their own needs.

8. Another lesson that can be taken has something to do with the real nature of the legislation on gecekondus. As touched upon above, each gecekondu law aimed at pardoning the squatters and the act of squatting taken place until the promulgation of these legislations. About a dozen laws and law amending ordinances enacted during the last half century to regulate the gecekondu building process and to ensure their upgrading, while providing them with land titles, urban public services, infrastructure and other amenities, aimed at forbidding the construction of the new ones. Legalizing the squatter houses built up tona certain date produced a consequence which can be considered as meaning de facto encouragement of the acts of squatting. This is the fundamental reason behind the constant increase of the number of squatter houses in Turkey during the last six decades.

9. Long-term solutions of the social and economic problems lie with the eradication of poverty rather than the enforcement of legal rules. Since slum formation and squatting are the consequences of poverty, simple implementation of the provisions of the gecekondu laws were not enough to ending the problem in the absence of majör measures of macro-economic nature. Slowing down the rapid growth of metropolitan centers caused by rural to urban migration and distribution of population and economic activities more evenly over the territory of the State have not accompanied the implementation of the physical tools needed for upgrading and prevention.

10. The slum prevention question has aways been taken as a political issue which might provide benefits to the

political parties in power and those controlling municipalities. Partisan considerations hampered the proper implementation of the objective rules set by the laws. Therefore, national or local election periods were full of examples of the reflections of patron-client relationships on the practice. Impartial assessment of the facts and a non-partisan implementation of the rules would ease reaching a fair solution.

11. Finally, The Turkish experience suggest that if the public authorities give up their leading role with respect to the implementation of slum upgrading and prevention policies in favor of the private firms, the objective of public interest is rapidly turned out to be replaced by the profit maximization concerns which spoil greatly the social goals to be attained.

Short Bibliography

Bayraktar, Erdoğan, *Gecekondu ve Kentsel Yenileme (Gecekondu and Urban Renewal)*, Ankara, 2006.

Geray, Cevat, "Toplumsal Konut Yöneltisi ve TOKİ'nin Tutum ve Yöneltilerindeki Son Değişiklikler (Social Housing Policy and the Recent Changes in the Position and Policies of the Mass Housing Administration), *Ruşen Keleş'e Armağan, (In Honour of Prof. Dr. Ruşen Keleş, Vol.II)*, Ankara, 2007.

Görk, Reyhan Varlı, "Gecekondu Bölgeleri ve Yerinde Islah Projelerine Sosyolojik Bir Bakış (A Sociological Approach to Gecekondu Settlements and Projects of in-site Upgrading), TMMOB Şehir Plancıları Odası (Chamber of City Planners), *Yoksulluk, Kent Yoksulluğu ve Planlama (Poverty, Urban Poverty and Planning)*, TMMOB, Chamber of Planners, Ankara, 2002, pp. 231-250.

Keleş, Ruşen, *Kentleşme Politikası (Urbanization Policy)*, İmge Pub., Ankara, 2021 (3rd. ed.).

Keleş, Ruşen, *Urban Poverty in the Third World: Theoretical Approaches and Policy Options,* AJİKEN (Institute of Developing Economies), VRF Series, No:152, Tokyo, Japan, December, 1988.

Keleş, Ruşen, "Dar Gelirli Kentliler İçin Bir Konut Edindirme Yöntemi: Evini Yapana Yardım" (A Housing Method for Low-Income Urban Families: Self-Help Housing), *SBF Dergisi (Journal of the Faculty of Political Sciences),* Vol.43, No:1-2, January-June 1988, pp.81-112.

Keleş, Ruşen, "The Culture of Squatting, Land Rights and the Realities of Globalisation", in Ruşen Keleş and Hagen Henry (eds.), *On the Systematics of Old and New Land Tenure Rights in their Cultural Context: Ecological, Economic and Societal Aspects,* Peter Lang, Bern, 2004.

Keleş, Ruşen and Kano, Hiromasa, *Economic Development and Social Consciousness: Turkey under Developmentalism,* AJİKEN (Institute of Developing Economies), M.E. Series No:17, Tokyo, 1986.

Keleş, Ruşen and Mengi, Ayşegül, *Kent Hukuku (Urban Law),* İmge Pub., Ankara, 2021 (2nd ed.).

Keleş, Ruşen and Mengi, Ayşegül, *İmar Hukuku (Urban Planning Law),* İmge Pub., Ankara, 2019 (3rd.ed.).

Keleş, Ruşen, Görer, Nilgün, Yankın, Birsen, "Regulatory Gidelines for Affordable Shelter: A Case Study of Ankara, Turkey", Geoffrey K. Payne and Associates, March, 2004.

Mühürdaroğlu, Akın, *De-Regulatory Urban Redevelopment Policies in Gecekondu Areas in Turkey: The Case of Dikmen Valley,* Ankara, 2005.

Payne, Geoffrey K., "Lowering the Ladder", *Land, Rights and Innovation: Improving Tenure Security for Urban Poor,* ITDG, London, 2002.

PART **II**

SUSTAINABLE URBANIZATION

The Contribution of Ernst Reuter to the Culture of Turkish Urbanization[*]

Observations Concerning His Personality

Ernst Reuter had come to Turkey in June 4 of 1935, where the author of these lines was two and a half years old. After having worked for some time in the Ministries of Economy and Transportation, he began to teach at the School of Political Sciences, upon the request of Mr. Emin Erişirgil, the Director of the School. His mission continued for eight years from 15 November 1938 to 19 September 1946. When he left Turkey, I was a junior high school student at 13 years of age. This is the reason why the main sources of my knowledge concerning Reuter consist of his numerous books and articles, Professor Fehmi Yavuz, who was his assistant and my teacher, with whom I have worked with for more than 35 years, several bureaucrats, statemen, politicians who had been his students, and the writings about him.

[*]   Former Director of Ernst Reuter Center for Urban Studies, Faculty of Political Sciences, Ankara University
      Draft Paper to be presented to the Symposium, On Ernst Reuter als Kommunalpolitiker, 1922-1953.
      Technische Universitaet Berlin, Center for Metropoitan Studies und Landesarchiv Berlin, Berlin, Deutschlan, 23-24 Marz 2007.

His colored portrait designed by the well-known painter Georg Löwel, and donated to the university by the German Embassy in Ankara, which decorates the wall of my office at the Ernst Reuter Center for Urban Studies, of which foundations were laid down by him, is one of the moral ties between me and Ernst Reuter. Although I did not know him personally, I had the honor of meeting his distinguished wife during her visit to Ankara at the beginnings of the 1970's and of course his son, Mr. Edzard Reuter in 1986. As pointed out by my distinguished colleague and friend Prof. Dr. Klaus-Detlev Grothusen in his book on Scurla Bericht, I am his "second-generation successor".[1] It is rightly called "second-generation" because between him and me, there is Professor Fehmi Yavuz.

Ernst Reuter is both a politician and a scholar who is the founder of the Chair and the Institute of Urban Studies at the University of Ankara. Since 1986, the name of the Institute was changed to be the Ernst Reuter Center for Urban Studies. Until 1982 Professor F. Yavuz, during 1982-1999 myself, from 1999 to 2006 Professor Can Hamamcı have served as the Director of the Center. Its present Director is Professor Ayşegül Mengi. By all of us in the university, the Institute of Urban Studies was regarded as a gift given by Ernst Reuter.

Reuter has learned Turkish in a very short time and to the extent that enabled him to conduct his classes in Turkish. He used to talk about Turkey as "my country" in his books and other publications. Yet, paradoxically, he used to

---

1   Klaus-Detlev Grothusen, *Der Scurla Bericht: Die Taetikeit deutscher Hochschullerer in der Türkei: 1933-1939,* Zentrum für Türkeistudiendien, Dağyeli Verlag, 1987, Frankfurt am Main, pp.55-56.

refer to Western European countries, including Germany, as "foreign countries". This distinguished personality, scholar and action man who had escaped from Nazi Germany by accepting the invitation of Mustafa Kemal Atatürk, not because he was a jew, but with the hope to see the return of the days where human dignity and the freedom of thought would be respected again in his country.

Reuter was not a regular immigrant or a scientist in Turkey. His true mission was the one of a real diplomat representing his nation in Turkey with great success. I would wish that I could have the chance, happiness and honor to know Ernst Reuter personally, as I had the opportunity to meet some other immigrant scholars such as Fritz Neumark, Ernst Hirsch and Edward Schwartz. My personal closeness to him has reflected entirely in our classes, in the contents of our books, in our understanding of the role of discipline in education and training. We are still continuing to be loyal to the tradition of "oral examinations" in the school which was initiated and implemented for years by Ernst Reuter.

The basic guiding values in his personal and academic life were rationality, scientific method, honesty, modesty, tolerance and humanism. It is mainly because he had a modern, autonomous and impartial mind that he had discontinued his friendship with Vladimir Lenin, who had criticised him "as being a very intelligent and very talented young man, but a person who is too much jealous of his freedom".[2]

Reuter is one of the German immigrants in Turkey who has contributed greatly to the development of a contemporary, secular and humanist academic tradition. He developed, in a

---

2   Hans E.Hirschfeld und Hang J. Reichhardt , *Ernst Reuter Aus Reden und Schriften*, Colloqium Verlag, Berlin, 1963, p.35.

relatively short time, an image of a scholar with an independent and modern mind, in a school which was attached to the Ministry of National Education, and in a period where academic autonomy did not exist and it was absolutely unknown. His modest manners and attitudes made him a respected personality not only in the university, but also in the eyes of his neighbours and the public at large.

The topics he tought at the School (Faculty) of Political Sciences[3] are Town and Country Planning, Municipal Management, and Municipal Finance. He had also accepted to provide advisory services in professional matters when requested by the government. Great many people who have become his students at the School of Political Sciences during the 1940's, have began to occupy very influential positions in politics and public administration or in the public life in general particularly during the 1950-1990 period as Sub-Governors, Governors, General Directors, Undersecretaries of the Ministries, Members of the Parliament, or Ministers. Turkey had learned much from him, both as a stateman and politician and as an academician. But his contribution not less important than these, was undoubtedly his reflecting to the attitudes and behaviour of his students certain highly respected ethical values.

Mr. Ziya Müezzinoğlu, who was one of Reuter's student during 1938-1940, and later become the Undersecretary of the State Planning Organization, Ambassador of Turkey in Bonn, and the Minister of Finance, once said that "when he had mentioned that he was the student of Ernst Reuter, his official relationships with Chancellor Willy Brandt had

3   The School was attached to the University of Ankara in 1952 as a new and
     autonomous Faculty.

turned out to be one of close friendship". And he also added that "If Mr. Reuter was happened to be the Chancellor in Germany in the years where mass immigration of Turkish workers to Germany started, the economic, social, and cultural problems faced by millions of Turkish migrant workers would be much less than those encountered at present".[4] I would have one more point to add to this prediction: If Reuter was not passed away untimely and if he could have been elected as the Chancellor of Germany in the late 1950's, I think that the doors of the European Union would absolutely be more open to Turks and Turkey than they are today."

Although Prof. Dr. Horst Widmann tells us that the biggest legacy of Ernst Reuter, namely the Chair of Town Planning in Ankara University was realized after his return to Germany in 1946, as I have mentioned earlier, this observation reflects the reality but it needs to be complemented. Because Reuter did not leave Turkey without having completed all preparations for the establishment of the Institute of Town and Country Planning, or in its new name, the Ernst Reuter Center for Urban Studies.

His Contributions to the Turkish Urbanization and Town Planning

What I am going to say in this section relies largely on my previous talks elsewhere and publications came out in different times.[5] The fact that the contribution of Ernst Reu-

---

4   Ruşen Keleş (Herausgeben), *Zum Gedenken An Ernst Reuter*, SBF İskan ve Şehircilik Enstitüsü ve Alman Kültür Merkezi, Ankara, 1986, pp.178-183.

5   Ruşen Keleş, "Ernst Reuter ve Türk Kentbilimi"(Ernst Reuter and Turkish Town Planning), *Amme İdaresi Dergisi(Public Administration Journal)*, Vol.19, No:3, September 1986, pp.81-98; Ruşen Keleş(Herausgeben), *Zum Gedenken An Ernst Reuter*, İskan ve Şehircilik Enstitüsü ve Alman Kültür

ter to the development of a Town Planning discipline with essentially an economic and sociological background is undoubtedly not less important than his contribution to the formation of a generation of outstanding images in Turkish politics and bureaucracy. It is Ernst Reuter himself who ensured teaching the scientific disciplines concerning the growth, planning and administration of cities within the framework of social sciences for the first time in Turkey. It has become necessary to wait for at least another 20 years, until the beginnings of the 1960's, to see the opening of Town Planning Departments and similar courses in other higher educational institutions.

His publications on urbanization and urban land policies, planned development of cities, urban public transportation, ecologically oriented urban development, autonomous local authorities and local public finance are of such a high caliber as to create enthusiasm even among contemporary town planners. Using the urban land with a view to giving priority to the public, but not private interest, prevention of high-rise building construction and providing housing as a public service, and through non profit-making housing organizations, making local authorities less dependent upon central government are the main themes of modern Town Planning which were emphasized constantly by Ernst Reuter. It is useful to look at briefly his views on each of these issues.

Merkezi, Ankara, 1986; Ruşen Keleş, "100. Yaş Gününde Ernst Reuter" (Ernst Reuter in his 100 th Anniversary), *Cumhuriyet (Daily Cumhuriyet)*, 29 July 1989.

The Pace and Patterns of Urbanization

In his works that he carried out, by using the results of the population censuses taken during the period between 1927 and 1945, he found out that there was no significant urbanization in Turkey.[6] However, he had warned the decision-makers about the likeliness of the problems of urbanization that might be faced in the years to come. The criterion that he used in defining an urban community, which was the threshold of 10.000 inhabitants, has also been used by the State Planning Organization (SPO) and the State Institute of Statistics (SIS) for many years in their official studies and publications. Even today, great many researchers use his 10.000 population criterion in distinguishing the city from the village.

Even at the beginning of the 1940's, an objective assessment of the concept of optimal city size, which is at present used by town planners can be found in his writings. He emphasized that the existence and growth of cities was inescapable, and cities and towns had their own advantages and disadvantages. He generally used a socialist discourse meaning that the developments and movements which aim to change psychological and moral conditions of the nations are initiated not in the villages but in cities.[7] The following words taken from his book complement his views concerning the optimal city size[8] : "It has been told us that the optimal city size was somewhere between 20.000 nd 25.000

6   Ernst Reuter, "Şehirlerimizin Nüfus Gelişmesi" (Population Growth in Cities), *Siyasal Bilgiler Okulu Dergisi*, Vol.1, No:4, 1946, pp.775-776.

7   Ernst Reuter, "Türkiye'de Şehirleşme Temayülleri", (Urbanization Tendencies in Turkey), *Siyasi İlimler Mecmuası*, 1941, pp.244-245.

8   Ernst Reuter, *Yakın Münakale (Intra-urban Transportation)* (unpublished book), Ankara. Siyasal Bilgiler Okulu, 1941, pp.8-9.

(Gustav Feder, *Die Neue Stadt)*. The effect of optimal city size has a significant impact upon all thoughts concerning social development. It is not desirable for a great number of people to be concentrated in agglomerations of several million inhabitants for many reasons. But we have to emphasize that all criticisms and shortcomings originated from the mistakes regarding urban development had been committed during the 19th century. What is more important is not to repeat these mistakes. No modern state could afford to abandon its great cities. Large cities must continue to exist for many cultural, economic and social reasons. Contemporary life cannot sustain itself without cities. But one must refrain from accelerating the pace of urban growth artificially. Otherwise, urban life would face undesirable consequences for the society as a whole"[9]. He maintained, in accordance with these views that "Nowadays there is no local official who explains his success by unlimited growth of his town".[10]

Without undermining the role of industrial development which is the primary pushing factor behind urbanization, he pointed out that it would accelerate rural to urban migration, and more important than this, without industrialization it would not be possible for a nation to continue to be independent forever nationally and culturally. One can find similar views in the introductory chapters of all Town Planning textbooks even today.

In his writings, Reuter always emphasized that city and village were two complementary forms of living, and the major aim of Town Planning was to reduce the distance existing between them. What he wanted to draw the attention

9   Ernst Reuter, "Türkiye'de Şehirleşme Temayülleri", op.cit, p.4.
10   Ernst Reuter, *Ibid, p.245.*

to by this view was not to "ruralize cities", as happens in the cities of less developed countries of today, but "marrying cities and villages" as suggested by Ebenezer Howard at the beginnings of the 20th century. In the Garden Cities to be created thus, it was going to be possible for each of the rural and urban centers to complement the shortcomings and inconveniences of the other. In accordance with this view, Reuter's definition of Town Planning has always included the element of orderly growth and development of the villages too. This indicates that Reuter was not only informed about contemporary Town Planning movements, but he knew also the social structure of Turkey quite well.

Housing and Urban Land Policy

The part of his publications devoted to the study of the problems of housing and urban land is of significant magnitude. In this context, as experienced in many European countries in the postwar period, he recommended the control of rents and to authorize Turkish municipalities in this field where the general conditions of the economy had been largely effected by the World War II. This recommendation played a decisive role in the enactment of laws concerning the control of the rents of residences and workshops in Turkey following the war years. He had often drawn attention to the need for the authorization and enabling of local authorities in meeting housing needs of local communities. His thesis was based on both technical and economic grounds.[11] In view of the fact that housing policy could not be formulated and implemented without the initiative and support of public au-

---

11   Ernst Reuter, *Mesken Meselesinin Hal Çareleri (Solutions of the Problem of Housing)*, Türk Ekonomi Derneği, Ankara, 1946.

thorities, one could understand more easily to what extent were right his assessments. He also emphasized the need for the government to be engaged as much in planned development of cities as in house building, in order to compensate the costs caused by the World War II and to carry out the reconstruction of the cities in western Europe. He recommended that the supply of housing for the large masses of population be realized with an understanding of public service and with the initiative of government.

The three preconditions for a successful housing policy, that he had recommended, namely a) the provision of cheap urban land, b) the provision of housing credit with easy terms and c) the technical assistance by the state and local authorities, have been used as the starting points of housing and squatter policies for a long time in Turkey. Reuter maintained that although land speculation seems to cause a certain increase in national wealth at first glance, it was also resulting in rendering residential settlements poorer, more deprived of satisfactory health conditions and modern social services. He insisted that environmental consequences of land speculation will be consisted in "settlements deprived of sunshine and fresh air under the shadow of polluting chimneys and at the same time a generation unable to understand the meaning of human life".[12] The readers of these lines will be able to quickly see the close connections between the thoughts of environmental protection reflected into the world public opinion only after the 1970's, the Declarations of the UN Conferences of Stockholm (1972), Van-

---

12   Ernst Reuter, "Şehirlerimizin Gelişme Problemleri" (Development Problems of Our Cities), *A.Ü.Dil ve Tarih-Coğrafya Fakültesi Dergisi*, No:5, July-August 1943, p.154.

couver (1976), Rio de Janeiro (1992) and İstanbul (1996) on one hand, and the views of Ernst Reuter.

Reuter has regarded selling off publicly owned lands as a wrong policy from the point of view of the success of social housing policy, recommended that leasing out should be preferred to selling off, if necessary. He believed that uncontrolled price increases exceeding rational and natural dimensions were indirect consequences of land speculation. He insisted that the true success in Town Planning would lie, to a great extent, in increasing the land stocks of public authorities, including municipalities. For example, during 1924-1931, the city of Berlin had bought all farms within its boundaries at relatively reasonable prices. He had pointed out that these lands would facilitate grately the reconstruction of Berlin in the postwar period. As touched upon above, Reuter always recommended leasing out of public lands must be preferred to selling off and underlying the fact that German cities owned, on the average, nearly half of the land within their boundaries. His examples include Magdeburg in Germany and Vienna in Austria where the urban land is rented for extended periods of time, 40 years, 66 years, respectively.[13]

Reuter's proposal regarding financial assistance for making housing policy a successful one is to encourage the establishment of "savings associations" which had a tradition of 150 years in western Europe. These are the institutions that, as the owners of the mortgage rights of first order, they allocate a certain percentage and often half of their savings to house building purposes to be used as loans on a

---

13   Ernst Reuter, *Mesken Meselesinin Hal Çareleri*, Türk Ekonomi Derneği, Ankara, 1946, p.13.

long-term basis. The legislation called "Mortgage Law "which was passed recently (March 2007) in Turkey is based on the same principles of housing finance. Through this method which was first recommended by Reuter, Turkish Real Estate Bank was able to finance the construction of thousands of social housing during 1945-1985 period.

Reuter emphasized that financial assistance for housing must be based on correct principles from social and economic points of view. Therefore, he drew the attention to the fact that financial assistance should never be a free donation (a fonds perdu). He recommended that assistance must me provided only for certain types of building, within certain limits, and their rents must be as small as the amount of financial assistance. These views are similar to those which require that financial assistance should not be a burden on the national budget.

Reuter, emphasizing the role of non-profit housing associations and housing cooperatives in the implementation of housing policy, suggested that dwelling standards appropriate for the needs and opportunities of the country, optimal dwelling sizes, prefabrication, the use of local building materials and low-rise building must also be taken into consideration. The kind of housing cooperatives that he recommended to support are the ones which continue to be in close cooperation with the city authorities after the construction of the dwellings is terminated. He underlined that this characteristic of the cooperatives is particularly important from the point of view of the planning of housing environments. This was a vision expressed in the 1940's, which Turkey was not able to realize during the 1980's through its mass housing arrangements. One can conclude that both his

views on the role of non-profit organizations and his recommendations regarding the role of social security agencies
in housing have affected, to a great extent, various models
such as OYAK (Pension Fund for Army Officers), MEYAK
(Social Security for Public Servants), BAĞ-KUR (Social Security Organization for the Self-Employed), and the Mass
Housing Administration and Fund.

Planned Approach to Urban Development

He tried to teach his students the need for the development
of cities according to a plan based on a detailed and substantial study of local conditions.[14] He particularly emphasized
the protection of identity and historical tissue of settlements
in the process of preparation of the city development plans.
He recommended the extension of the coastal road along
the Bosphorus and the Golden Horn. Turkey was able to
begin to realize this recommendation and making this road
usable by everyone only 45 years later. He also asked for the
protection of the ribbon development in İzmir, alongside
the Bay of İzmir, indicating that it was meeting the need of
addressing more than one of the urban functions. He drew
the attention to the need for planning Edirne as the Selim-
iye Mosque being taken as its center. In Ankara, the biggest problem was the protection of the form of the Citadel
and to ensure that its image should not be lost. Allocating
at least one third of its lands for roads and parks, the increase of the land stocks[15] were among the recommenda-

14   Ernst Reuter, *Komün Bilgisi* (*Municipal Management*), Siyasal Bilgiler Okulu, Ankara, 1940, p.141-142.
15   Ernst Reuter, "Şehir Planlamasında İktisadi Kaideler" (Economic Pinciples
in Town Planning), *Belediyeler Dergisi*, No:64, 1942, pp.21-22.

tions of Reuter, which he believed that this would increase the chance of success of the master plans. He is one of the first scholars emphasizing for the first time the economic rules that should shape urban planning. He believed that it was wrong "to leave the task of planning the towns to artists alone". Economists must be employed in this process. He suggested that population density in urban Turkey should not exceed 150-200 persons per hectare, and consequently he recommended that low and extended systems of urban development should be preferred to the construction of high-rise apartments. Yet, during the years that followed, due to the density permits exceeding at least two times the density standards approved by Reuter, construction of apartment flats has become almost the destiny of Turkish cities. As a result, cities turned out to be piles of stones and in many cities children became deprived of finding even a tiny open space to be used as their playgrounds.[16]

His advices to the future of public administrators in the field of Town Planning included the following: "Since *our* country is full of historical buildings and monuments, these have to be taken into consideration in the process of plan-making. It is among the duties of the communes to enlighten the public about their values...Therefore, while preparing development plans for the communes in the future, it is necessary to take these considerations into account and to integrate them into the plans." One may conclude that Reuter's book entitled *Komün Bilgisi* is not simply a classical textbook aiming at dealing with scientific topics by a descriptive approach and systematically, but a very valuable guidebook of which each page contains the rules and principles

16   Ernst Reuter, *Komün Bilgisi, s.198.*

that are very useful for the future public administrators in creating modern and well developed cities and towns.

Urban Public Services and Ecological Issues

The first systematic classification of urban public services was made by Reuter in Turkey in his book *Komün Bilgisi*. In this source book, urban public services were classified into four main groups:

a) Those services meeting the general and necessary needs of the inhabitants (Versorungsbetriebe). These are such classical public services as water, gas, electricity and transportation.

b) Services addressing the public health needs. Cleaning the streets, garbage collection, slaughterhouses, market places, sewerage systems and stables for animals.

c) Enterprises with different characteristics operated by local authorities in different ways.

d) Specific economic enterprises of local authorities such as hotels and touristic enterprises. Reuter has objectively studied the advantages and disadvantages of each of these category of services in the 1930's and 1940's Turkey. He concluded that in the prevailing conditions of that period, it was inescapable for the municipalities to assume increasing responsibility. He is the one who for the first time recommended that a distinction should be made between the large communes in developed regions and those in less developed areas, and special programmes have to be prepared to meet the specific needs of the communes in each category.

When ecological problems were not as much alarming as today, some 60 years ago, Reuter had made important warnings for Turkey. One of these assessments seem extremely realistic even in the present age of globalization. "Peoples have a false impression at this age of revolutionary growth of cities that machines and factories mean impressive progress. Chimneys surround cities one after one; they rise above the high-rise, unhealthy and narrow apartment buildings (Mietkasernen). In accordance with the theoretical thinking that neither the State nor local authorities should prevent development, the most valuable lands of the cities are being used wastefully....In the Meiers Hof, Ackerstrasse, Berlin, more than thousand people live in seven buildings on one subdivision , separated from each other by courtyards is the most striking example of this insane development...There exists neither a tree nor a branch in these courtyards and backyards... Children do not recognize anything else as playground other than the backyards and garbage baskets... Houses are deprived of the sunshine".[17] And he adds the following highly justified assessment to the foregoing observations : "If the early development of capitalism, not taking into consideration any standards and forms, with no regard to social conditions did not cause such disastrous appearances in the slums of the city of New York and Chicago, Mietkasernen of German cities and British slums , the one-sided world view of Karl Marx would never be justified".[18] In these sentences, Reuter has touched upon the need to assess the problems caused by capitalism with

17   Ernst Reuter, "Şehirlerimizin Gelişme Problemleri" (Development Problems of our Cities), A.Ü. Dil ve Tarih-Coğrafya Fakültesi, No:5, July-August 1943, p.154.
18   Ibid.

a socialist approach and to draw the attention to the duties of the social welfare state as early as within the first half of the 20th century.

To ensure that thinking of social justice guide political decisions in a rapidly urbanizing world was a fundamental principle in his life. He paid no less attention to such vital principles as the fundamental rights and freedoms, rule of law, human rights and respect for the requirements of science than the others. In fact, Reuter has been always against the extravagencies of politics and religion threatening free thinking.[19] According to him, human beings are the creatures that must be free and regain their freedoms all the times.[20]

Intra-Urban Transportation

In his unpublished book entitled *Yakın Münakale* (Intra-urban Transportation) written in 1941, of which only one copy is available in the library of the Faculty of Political Sciences (No: B-415), Reuter deals with transportation from the perspective of administration, management and transportation techniques and he does not enter into technical engineering discussions.[21] He has indicated that the number of experiences from which lessons could be taken were two. The first is the integration of all organizations in Berlin, which were in charge of transportation; the second is the establishment of a greater transportation trust in London.

19   F. Yavuz, 24 April 1969, the text of the speech given in German Library in Ankara, 1969, pp.12-13.

20   The Congress of Cultural Freedom, *Science and Freedom*, Martin Secker and Warburg ltd., London, 1953, p.283.

21   Ernst Reuter, *Yakın Münakale*, Siyasal Bilgiler Okulu, Ankara, 1941, p.21.

The major topics of *Yakın Münakale* which concern to-day most town planners and transport planners are the followings: Transportation techniques, transportation planning, choice of vehicles, organization and management techniques for transportation enterprises. Reuter explained very clearly, 65 years ago, the understanding that intra-urban transportation should not be regarded as a management and engineering issue that could be solved in the junctions in the transportation systems, but as a subject which shapes the use of urban land, and which concerns also the complex economic and social structure of the city. He pointed out that the most appropriate transportation system was the municipal bus system for Turkish cities and the most rational choice for the future was to turn it into a railed network. These views reflect the same philosophy of contemporary Town Planning and also the rationale behind the proposals in the European Urban Charter of the Council of Europe (1992).

He had also underlined the fact that the major factor which makes the solution of urban transportation problems more difficult is the fact that the settlement pattern is rendered unsuitable for transportation as a result of excessive fragmentation of the structure of urban land ownership. His views concerning the fact that intra-urban transportation systems like all other economic enterprises have to be able to meet their expenditures with their own revenues and they are not "charity organizations" are in line with the views of the present day planners and economists as well as with the principles of international donor institutions. However, he did not forget to add that in the preparation of general service tariffs, for social reasons, cheaper transportation systems must also be available in order to enable everyone, all classes in the society, to benefit from the service.[22]

Economic Enterprises of the Communes

It seems that Reuter had been influenced by the movement that is called *municipal socialism*, which was very popular at the beginnings of the 20th century, and was put forward by two British scholars, namely Sydney and Beatrice Webb. This movement was aiming to increase the role of local authorities in economic life. Reuter, drawing attention to the fact that even the politicians who were against all kinds of socialist thinking, seemed to approve the performance by the communes of certain public services of economic nature. One example given by Ernst Reuter in this regard is the acceptance by the majority of the Conservative Government which had come into power in the 1930's, of the law project that was initially prepared by the Labor Government in the 1920's with respect to the municipalization and unification of the intra-urban transportation system in London.[23]

According to Reuter, economic enterprises of the communes worked generally for a narrower market and they do not, in principle, aim at the socialization of the production factors, as required by the theory of "socialism". Their aims are limited to certain auxiliary sectors of the national economy. Reuter pointed out that cooperative movement had a positive impact upon municipal economy, and this, in turn,

22   *Ibid.*,p.90.
23   Ernst Reuter, "Mahalli İşletmelerin Ehemmiyeti ve Problemleri", Siyasal Bilgiler Okulu, Ankara, *Kaymakamlık Kursu Ders Notları*, 18 June 1942, p.13.

encouraged the tendencies towards development of public economy. According to Reuter, all these developments "weakened the opinions that the State is unable to cope with economic affairs".[24] He thought that Local Public Economy has merely the objective to prepare the required preconditions for the development of the national economy. Though, it is not a branch of the economy which affects and even manage general development directly. Municipalities try to carry out services to replace or to complement the private enterprises by realizing at smaller scales what the State carries out at a larger scale. Among these what Reuter tends to recommend most is to increase the limited role of the municipalities in the field of the production of housing. In addition, his recommendations with regard to the economic activities of the communes included the purchase and the increase of urban land, participation indirectly in lending housing credit, in the encouragement of the citizens to increase their savings in order to be able to play a certain role through savings associations.

When the issue of increasing economic activities of the communes in the early 1970's, under the slogan of "municipalities as producers" in Turkey, rules and regulations in the Turkish legislation enabling the communes to undertake economic enterprises were already existent. Reuter, influenced by the concept of "municipal socialism" had transmitted to his students as future administrators, in the early 1940's, similar thoughts, together with their potentials and limitations. He thought that economic activities of the communes must be subject to certain conditions, although he was in favor of their encouragement:

24   *Ibid*, p.28.

a) The aim of the initiative must be the performance of the service in the public interest.

b) This service should not be carried out better by other authorities.

c) The initiative must be in conformity with financial capacity and needs of the municipality.

d) Economic enterprise must provide a certain revenue, and this should suffice financing its expenditures.

e) The municipality should also undertake such works that are beyond the everyday needs of the inhabitants. I believe that what he wrote some 60 years ago are quite meaningful, relevant and significant at present where "widespread privatization of local public services" are so much in fashion.

In the light of the experiences during the World War II, while recommending on one hand the intervention of the municipalities in economic life through negative means, such as fines and various controls, he suggested, on the other hand, that they should be engaged in productive activities in a positive manner through monopolies and partnerships.[25]

Another view of Reuter which is quite relevant for the clarification of the activities of mass housing has something to do with his interest in building enterprises. He believed that all municipalities with a population over a certain size threshold must have a building enterprise of a certain scale. This should not be regarded as an obstacle to bidding for construction works by private entrepreneurs. Reuter has maintained that municipalities will be in a better position to control the performance of the building enterprises in terms of prices and quality by benefiting the experiences of

---

25 Ernst Reuter, "Belediyelerin İktisadi İcraatı" (Economic Activites of the Communes), *Türkiye Ekonomisi,* No:7, 1944, pp.225-226.

building enterprises.[26] He was in favor of the intervention of
the local authorities directly in the field of house construction. He also warned that building high-rise apartments with
more than three stories should not be permitted.[27]

Municipal Finance and *Finanzausgleich*

It can be safely assumed that the concept *finanzausgleich*
which denotes the establishment of a fair and just financial
relationship between the State and the communes has been
introduced into the Turkish social science literature for the
first time by Ernst Reuter. He had insisted that this balancing
must be based, in principle, on the division of the competencies between the State and local authorities. This principle
requires that the State should provide additional revenues
and revenue sources proportional with their competencies,
and their amount must be increased whenever their duties
are increased by the State. As an example, Reuter reminds
us the fact that at the beginnings of the 1940's, as a result
of the decision of the Celal Bayar Government reducing the
meat prices, the city of İstanbul had also to reduce the prices
of meat in the slaughterhouses and consequently the city's
budget was adversely affected by this development. As result, following the decision of the government, the Ministry of Health has assisted the municipality by transferring
two municipal hospitals to the Ministry, thus relieving the
commune of the burden of costly services of the hospitals.
This was a sort of compensation paid by the State to the
municipality of İstanbul. In Germany, according to a law

---

26   Ernst Reuter, "Belediyelerin Yapı İşletmeleri", *Arkitekt*, Vol.13, No:1-2,
     1943, p.28.
27   *Ibid*,p.29.

of 1925 of the Reich, the State could not assign new duties and competencies to the communes without providing corresponding financial means.

One can also assume that Ernst Reuter had been influenced by some German scholars and practitioners like Rudolph Gneist, Lorenz von Stein, Otto von Guericke, and Freiherr vom Stein [28], with respect to the relationships between the State and the communes. These people had regarded the communes as instruments able to increase the interaction between the State and local authorities, accelerating economic and social development, preventing social tensions, and strengthening local communities.

Reuter accepts, in fact, that the view requiring that the communes must be completely autonomous financially is "old-fashioned".[29] However, he emphasized the following two principles of the integrated fiscal relationships:

a) Communes must have financial resources that they can determine and dispose of, as a result of their financial autonomy, and under the control and supervision of the State and on their own responsibility.

b) Secondly, central government must leave a certain a part of its resources to the communes, contribute to certain activities of the communes, recognize their rights to collect some of the State taxes themselves. In collecting this second

28 Ayşegül Mengi, "Freiherr vom Stein'ın Modern Kent Yönetim Anlayışının Gelişmesine Katkısı ve 1808 Prusya Kentsel Şartı" (The Contribution of Freiherr vom Stein to the Development of Modern Urban Management and 1808 Urban Charter of Prussia), *Siyasal Bilgiler Fakültesi Dergisi*, Vol.58, April-June 2003, pp.117-132.

29 Ernst Reuter, "Belediye Maliyesinin Umumi Meseleleri" (General Problems of Municipal Finance), *Siyasal Bilgiler Okulu Dergisi*, Vol.1, No:1, 1943, p.116.

category of revenues which the communes cannot decide by themselves, they are free to fix additional percentages to be put over the national taxes.

His view concerning "the outmoded quality" of the financial autonomy of the communes is based on his vision that it is a fact that even today no local authority could continue to exist merely on its own financial resources. This truth has been understood better in the following years both in developing and developed countries. Isn't this understanding that it is found in the roots of the financial assistance of the State to local authorities?.[30]

We must accept that those who were influenced by his lectures and publications played a significant role in inserting the Article 116 in the 1961 Constitution, concerning the *finanzausgleich* he defended so much. The sentence "Local authorities shall be provided with financial resources commensurate with their competencies" was written by his assistants and former students, who happened to be the members of the Consultative Assembly during 1960-1961. The same sentence was also put in the Article 127 of the 1982 Constitution. One can argue that this recommendation made by Ernst Reuter played an important role in Turkey after 1980 to support local authorities financially.

It is generally accepted in modern municipal finance that compliance with rational principles in spending public funds is as important as making sufficient amount of resources available to municipalities. Besides, Reuter made significant proposals in order to safeguard municipalities

---

30   Ernst Reuter, "İstanbul Belediyesi'nin Mali Durumu:1937-1942" (Financial State of the Municipality of İstanbul), *Siyasal Bilgiler Okulu Dergisi,* Vol.1, No:3, pp.26-27.

against the uniformity of the local finance system. For example, he talked about the shortcomings of making all municipalities subject to the same budget formula. He pointed out the need to classify municipalities on the basis of their size, geographical regions in which they are situated, and their levels of economic development.[31] It is a pity that no change in that direction in the legislation of municipal finance has been realized so far. No rules are provided in the law project concerning local finance, which has been brought recently to the Parliament by the Government.

Reuter had tried to carry out serious scientific researches on municipalities by himself. His works on the financial state of the İstanbul municipality is the product of a serious research. In this study he makes a classification of the topics that have to be taken up, the methodology to be used in a study of local finance. Among the proposals he made with a view to provide municipalities with a strong financial structure are the register of buildings, an objective reassessment of land values, and a better use of the municipal property. He believed that more than half of the increase of municipal revenues can be provided from this source. He concludes in his study on the Financial State of the İstanbul Municipality with the following sentence: "İstanbul is the most beautiful city in the world. But without a strong financial base even the greatest administrative personality may not be able to make this city to live in conditions commensurate with its natural beauty. Therefore, this should be the guiding principle of our country".[32]

31   Ernst Reuter, *Ibid*, p.537.
32   Ernst Reuter, +İstanbul Belediyesi"nin Mali Durumu : 1937-1942", *op.cit*, p.537.

Municipal Banking and the Bank of the Provinces
(*İller Bankası*)

When talking about municipal finance in Turkey, the first institution that comes into mind is undoubtedly the Bank of the Provinces (The Bank of Local Credit). Reuter expressed his opinions on the Bank of the Provinces in some of his publications and reports. In one of his writings he referred to the Bank of Municipalities (its original name) as "an obligatory savings association of Turkish municipalities". And he underlined that the aim of the legislation establishing this bank was "to safeguard municipalities against being obliged to recourse to the private banks for their credit needs". The Bank of the Provinces is a bank of which the capital is composed of the contributions of local authorities, and which lends credits to the communes at low interest rates and with easy terms whenever they need. The role of the Bank in supporting small communes is particularly important. However, Reuter noted that municipalities did not benefit properly from the services of the Bank, the expenditures of the Bank seemed as an additional cost on the shoulders of the municipalities as a criticism of the practice.[33] Reuter's writings must be read and utilized at present very carefully because the Bank of the Provinces is going to be radically reorganized in such a manner to lose its original identity.

The Bank was established in 1933 as the Bank of the Municipalities and it was reorganized in 1945 under the title of the Bank of the Provinces. The Government asked Ernst Reuter to study and prepare a report on the ways in which

---

33   Ernst Reuter, "Belediyeler Bankası" (Bank of the Municipalities), *İstanbul Üniversitesi İktisat Fakültesi Mecmuası, Vol.4, No:1, 1943, s.16.*

the Bank could carry out its functions better and more efficiently. The request of the Government was made in the days where he was preparing to leave the country. Reuter had submitted this report during the summer of 1946 by postponing several weeks his return to Germany. In this report, Reuter recommended that the Bank of the Provinces should function in accordance with the regular principles and procedures of banking. However, he also noted that the municipalities will be in need of the technical services supplied by the Bank *for a long time to come.* In my opinion, this "long time." has not ended even today. Since the Bank is about to be reorganized at present, it is in order to suggest that the preservation of the social functions of the Bank should not be forgotten.

Reuter recommended that in order to make the Bank as a real bank of the communes, it should have a mission to lend short-term loans to a certain extent. Besides, he suggested that it should assist municipalities in meeting their needs such as large-scale purchases and the realization of their imports. This proposal is still valid, because it should be remembered that all functions of he bank are being abandoned to be guided by international lendind institutions. By drawing the attention that the communes possess a powerful purchasing capacity, he argued that the savings to be obtained thus could create new and more extensive service opportunities for municipalities. One can assume that Reuter's views had significant impact upon the earlier reorganization of the Bank in 1945 and on the inclusion of the Provincial Local Administrations among its partners. Finally, Ernst Reuter said that large-scale investments concerning municipalities must be taken care of by a specialized and powerful institution; and this would not increase the financial tutelage over local authorities.[34] According to Reuter adequacy of financial control over municipalities depends more on the nature and the form of the control itself than through which institution it is exercised.[35]

Conclusions

Ernst Reuter has contributed to Turkish urbanization in three major ways: The first is his contribution to teaching and training of the administrators who will be in charge of the practices of urban development and Town and Country Planning. Many of the one time Sub-Governors and Governors, General Directors, Undersecretaries, Members of the Parliament, even the Ministers, have successfully transmitted the light they have received from him to the cities and towns, provinces and the villages.

Secondly, Reuter made it possible, for the first time in Turkey, teaching the disciplines concerned with development, planning and administration of cities within the framework of the Social Sciences. He competently dealt with certain topics closely connected with technical disciplines such as Urbanization, Municipal Finance, Local Government from economic and social perspectives.[36]

The establishment of the Institute of Town and Country Planning, which he had completed all its preparations while in Turkey was realized after his return to Germany.

---

34   Ernst Reuter, "Belediyeler Bankası" (The Bank of Municipalities), *op.cit*,p.23.

35   *Ibid*,p.27.

36   Fehmi Yavuz, "Professor Ernst Reuter", *İnsan Hakları Armağanı, Turkish Association of the United Nations*, Ankara, 1983, pp.1-2.

Even the statute of the Institute was prepared by him. This Institute, since the 1950's has realized important contributions in such fields as Town Planning, Municipal Administration, Local Public Finance, Urbanization, Housing and Urban Land Policies. The concepts and terms he used, the principles he defended, which have also been used by his assistant Professor Fehmi Yavuz, and his assistants, namely Reuter's second-generation successors, still preserve their validity.[37]

Thirdly, his dozen books and numerous articles which address scholars, administrators, economists, municipal officers are very important sources for those who are to study the recent past of the urbanization process in Turkey, and for the administrators, town planners and planners in general. These books and articles might suffice to entitle these people, who never had a chance to know him, as his students. It would undoubtedly be an excellent contribution to translate all his publications ton German and to English, and make them available for a larger audience.

It is obvious that Ernst Reuter's views on urban development and municipal management have been shaped over a period encompassing the pre-war years, the war years and the post-war era. The formation of these views coincides with a period where there was a pressing need for an understanding of the Social Welfare State. As a result, in view of the anti-governmental tendencies of the globalization

---

37 Fehmi Yavuz, Ruşen Keleş and Cevat Geray, *Şehircilik: Sorunlar, Politika, Uygulama (Town and Country Planning: Problems, Policies and Implementation)*, Siyasal Bilgiler Fakültesi, Ankara, 1978, (2nd ed.); Ruşen Keleş, *Kentleşme Politikası (Urbanization Policy)*, Imge Publisher, Ankara, 2006 (9th ed.); Michael N. Danielson and Ruşen Keleş, *The Politics of Rapid Urbanization*, Holmes and Meier, New York, 1985.

era which affect the world since the early 1980's, one may question whether these views of Reuter could or should be re-evaluated and questioned. I believe that, despite all these developments many of the views maintained by Reuter are still valid for Turkey and for the peoples of a large number of states in the world.

Bibliography

The Congress for Cultural Freedoms, *Science and Freedom,* Martin Secker und Warburg Ltd., London, 1955.

Danielson, Michael N., and Keleş, Ruşen, *The Politics of Urbanization: Government and Growth in Modern Turkey,* Holmes and Meier, New York, 1985.

Glase, Bentley, *Ethical Basis of Science,* Technion, IIT, The Joseph Funch Lecture, 1969.

Grothusen, Klaus-Detlev (herasgegeben und eingeleitet von), *Der Scurla Bericht,* Zentrum für Türkeistudien, Dağyeli Verleg, Frankfurt am Main, 1987.

Hirschfeld, Hans E. und Reichardt, Hans, J., *Ernst Reuter, Aus Reden und Schriften,* Colloqium, Verlag GmbH, 1963.

Keleş, Ruşen, *Kentleşme Politikası (Urbanization Policy),* Ankara, 2006 (9th ed.).

Keleş, Ruşen, *Yerinden Yönetim ve Siyaset (Decentralization and Politics),* Cem Yayınevi, İstanbul, 2006 (5th ed.).

Reuter Edzard, *Ernst Reuter: Ein Leben für Freiheit und Sozialismus,* Verlag Arani, Berlin, Grünewald.

Reuter, Ernst, *Komün Bilgisi,* Siyasal Bilgiler Fakültesi, Ankara, 1940.

Reuter, Ernst, "Mahalli İdarelerle Devlet Arasındaki Münasebetler", *Siyasi İlimler Mecmuası,* 1940, No:116, pp.387-392 and No:117, pp.446-452.

Reuter, Ernst, "Belediye İktisadiyatının Ehemmiyeti ve Meseleleri",*İ.Ü. İktisat Fakültesi Mecmuası,* 1941, No: 3-4, pp.382-411.

Reuter, Ernst, "Türkeye"de Şehirleşme Temayülleri", *Siyasi İlimler Mecmuası*, 1941, No:126, s.243-249.

Reuter, Ernst, *Yakın Münakale*, Siyasal Bilgiler Fakültesi, Ankara, 1941.

Reuter, Ernst, "Şehir Planında İktisadi Kaideler", *Belediyeler Dergisi*, 1942, No:64, pp.19-27.

Reuter, Ernst, "Mahalli İşletmelerin Ehemmiyeti ve Problemleri", *Kaymakamlık Kursu Ders Notları*, 1942, 18 June 1942.

Reuter, Ernst, "Türk Eknomisinde Belediyelerin Önemi", *Türk Ekonomisi*, 1942, No:2.

Reuter, Ernst, "Belediyelerin Mali Durumlarının Denkleştirilmesi ve İslahı İmkanları", *İdare Dergisi*, 1943, No:173, pp.48-71.

Reuter, Ernst, "Şehirlerimizin Gelişme Problemleri", *A.Ü.Dil ve Tarih-Coğrafya Fakültesi Dergisi*, 1943, July-August, No:5, pp.149-163.

Reuter, Ernst, "Belediyelerin Yapı İşletmeleri", *Arkitekt*, 1043, Vol.13, No: 1, pp.27-32.

Reuter, Ernst, "Belediye Maliyesinin Umumi Meseleleri",*Sosyal Hizmetler Okulu Dergisi*, 1943, Vol.1, No: 1, pp.108-142.

Reuter, Ernst, "Belediyeler Bankası", *İ.Ü. İktisatFakültesi Mecmuası*, 1943, Vol.4, No:1, pp.1-27.

Reuter, Ernst, "Kasabalarımız", *Arkitekt*, 1943, No:9-10.

Reuter, Ernst, "Belediye Masrafları", *Siyasal Bilgiler Okulu Dergisi*, 1944, Vol.1, No:2, pp.319-341.

Reuter, Ernst, "Belediyelerin İktisadi İcraatı", *Türk Ekonomisi*, 1944, No:7, pp.225-228.

Reuter, Ernst, "Küçük Belediyeler Meselesi", *Arkitekt*, 1944, No:5-6.

Reuter, Ernst, "İstanbul Belediyesinin Mali Durumu: 1937-1942", *Siyasal Bilgiler Okulu Dergisi*, 1945, Vol.1, No:3, pp.489-503.

Reuter, Ernst, *İller Bankası Raporu*, Ankara, 1946.

Reuter, Ernst, *Mesken Meselesinin Hal Çareleri*, Türk Ekonomi Derneği, Ankara, 1946.

Reuter, Ernst, "Şehirlerimizin Nüfus Gelişmesi", *Siyasal Bilgiler Okulu Dergisi*,1946, Vol.1, No:4, pp.775-790.

Reuter, Ernst ve Ergin, Necmettin, *Belediye Maliyesi*, İstanbul, 1945.

Schwenger, Hannes, *Ernst Reuter,* Piper, München, 1987.

Yavuz, Fehmi, "Prof.Ernst Reuter", *Siyasal Bilgiler Fakültesi Dergisi,* 1968, Vol.23, No:3, pp.135-192.

Yavuz, Fehmi, text of the speech given in German Library in Ankara, April 24, 1969.

Yavuz, Fehmi, "Professor Ernst Reuter", *İnsan Hakları Armağanı,* Birleşmiş Milletler Türk Derneği, Ankara, 1983, pp.71-83.

Yavuz, Fehmi, Keleş, Ruşen and Geray, Cevat, *Şehircilik: Sorunlar, Politika ve Uygulama,* Siyasal Bilgiler Fakültesi, Ankara, 1978 (2nd. Ed.).

General Legal Framework for Sustainable Land-Use and Management as Designed by International Environmental Law*

Introduction

Sustainable development was defined by the Brundtland Commission (World Commission on Environment and Development) as a kind of development that meets the needs of present without compromising the ability of the future generations to meet their own needs. Serious efforts have been made since the adoption of the report by the UN General Assembly in the early 1980's at both international and national levels, in order to make the principle of sustainable development both applicable and respected. The concept has been widely used in such international legal instruments as the Rio (1992) and İstanbul (1996) Declarations, Agenda 21(1992) and The Habitat Agenda (1996), and in a series of conventions adopted during the Rio Summit on Environment and Development.

On the other hand, land as a scarce and non-reproduceable natural resource is essential for the provision of food, water and energy for many living systems. Therefore, it is

---

*   36th International Symposium of the European Faculty of Land-Use and Development, (EALD), Core Problems of Sustainable Land Management, Zurich, 25-27 September, 2008.

critical to human activity. In rapidly growing urban areas, access to land is rendered increasingly difficult by the potential demands of housing, industry, commerce, infrastructure, transport, agriculture and the need for open spaces and green areas and the protection of fragile ecosystems.[1] The rising cost of urban land and other factors prevent persons living in poverty from gaining access to suitable land. Bringing the development of urban areas into harmony with the natural environment and the overall system of settlements is one of the basic tasks in achieving a sustainable urbanized world. In other words, there is always a tension between two variables: "demand management depends essentially on the argument that environmental capacity... is limited. The planning system, required on the one hand to make provision to meet demands and on the other to be an instrument of environmental protection, is unavoidably implicated in this tension".[2] The tools for achieving a physically more balanced development include not only specific urban and regional policies and legal, economic, financial, cultural and other measures, but also innovative methods of urban planning and design and of urban development, revitalization and management. Integration of national, subnational and local policies is no less important goals to attain.

In this regard, a number of principles developed by international environmental law, in addition to sustainable development are worth to mention. These include the precautionary principle, and the principles of international cooperation, prevention, integration, common but differentiated responsibility. Concern for the rights of future generations

1   The Habitat Agenda, Nairobi, 1996, p.42.
2   Susan Owens, "Interpreting Sustainable Development: The Case of Land Use Planning", in Michael Jacobs (ed.), **Greening the Millennium: The New Politics of the Environment,** Blackwell, London.

is crucially important in this respect. Of course, reciprocal responsibilities of the States in ensuring sustainable development and use of the natural resources are of utmost importance too and it will be taken up below under UN activities. Let me briefly refer to one relevant observation made in the Agenda 21 which is extremely relevant to our topic: "Expending human requirements and economic activities are increasing pressures on land resources, creating competition and conflicts and resulting in suboptimal use of both land and land resources. And it is essential to resolve these conflicts and move towards more effective and efficient use of land and its natural resources to meet the human requirements in the future. So, integrated physical land use planning and management is an important practical way to achieve this."

Many cities are using peripheral and agricultural land for urban-related purposes in a wasteful manner while existing serviced land and infrastructure may not be adequately developed and used. As recommended by the Habitat Agenda in 1996, it is necessary to promote land-use patterns that minimize transport demands, save energy and protect open spaces. Appropriate urban density and mixed land use guidelines are of prime importance for urban development. Green and open spaces and vegetation cover in urban and peri-urban areas are essential also for biological and hydrological balance and economic development. The fact that the nature is so constructed that it is impossible to create more land. Since land is a finite resource[3], it must be used more carefully than any other natural resource

---

3   Christopher P. Mooney, "Property Rights and the Environment", in Richard E.Hart (ed.), **Ethics and the Environment,** University Press of America, New York, 1982, pp.33-34.

that is renewable. It is because of this reason that the World Summit on Sustainable Development (Johannesburg) emphasized in 2002 that fundamental changes were needed in the ways societies produce and consume limited natural resources. Plan of Implementation adopted in Johannesburg has put an emphasis on such issues as combatting desertification, managing the natural resources in an integrated manner, promoting sustainable tourism development, ensuring sustainable forest management, protecting mining, minerals and metals.

A study carried out in 1992-1993 by the UNEP found that an area of 1,2 billion hectares, nearly 11 percent of the earth vegetated surface suffers from soil degradation. This has been defined as a process that describes human-induced phenomena which lower the current and future capacity of the soil to support human life. It occurs in the forms of light, moderate, severe, and extreme degradation. In the severe degradation agricultural use is no longer possible and restoration is possible only at a high cost. However, in extreme degradation, the area becomes completely unsuitable for agriculture and beyond restoration. All forms of degradation are caused by agricultural activities, deforestation, over-exploitation, industrial and bio-industrial activities and overgrazing.[4]

Key significance of the landed property as a finite natural resource led some scholars to suggest that it should be placed into a kind of "public trust" for the benefit of present and future generation. Jeremy Rifkin's point of view is remarkable in that respect: "...whole areas of the planet's

---

4   Philippe Sands, **Principles of International Environmental Law,** 2nd. ed., Cambridge University Press, Cambridge, p.555.

landmass need to be placed into public trust, to preserve what remains of the earth's genetic diversity. He recommended, at the same time, to increase land reserves of the public: "Developed nations like the United States need to match international initiatives with ambitious domestic programs to buy up large tracts of land from the private sector and place them in public trusts. The commercial leasing of all public lands to the private sector should be conditional on meeting rigorous sustainable production processes established by the government. Local communities and regional planning authorities ought to be able to place zoning restrictions on any private commercial use of publicly leased land".[5] He goes on further to provide reasons for this policy stand as the followings: "Only by placing ecosystems in public trusts will it be possible to reverse the process of rampant short-term exploitation of the environment, which endemic to private commercial ownerships. Of course, there is no automatic guarantee that public ownership will ensure preservation and sustainable development. That will depend upon the public's willingness and commitment in every country to protect the ecosystems under their charge".[6]

The legal norms of international law can be found in international treaties and conventions, resolutions of the international institutions, the texts of the declarations adopted by the conferences of such institutions. Some of these legal rules are binding and some are non-binding. A growing number of treaties do not include immediate obligations for the contracting states, instead they develop programmes for action. The multilateral conventions were multiplied during

5   Jeremy Rifkin, **Biosphere Politics,** Harper, San Francisco, 1991, p.312-313.
6   **Ibid.**

the 1970's and 1980's [7]and their number kept increasing rapidly also during the 19906. On the other hand, the enormous importance of "soft law" instruments lies in the fact that while they play a more technical role through the "resolutions", "recommendations", "guidelines", etc., they may be evaluated by the States and may be included either in a formal international treaty or introduced in national legislation.

Principal Guidelines for Sustainable Land-Use and Management
The United Nations

Legally binding or non-binding norms available for the sustainable land-use and management cover a vast area ranging from the ownership right to land, to landscape, erosion, soil degradation, forests, national parks, the protection of fertile agricultural lands, urban development, etc. As a general rule, in such legal instruments as the Stockholm (1972) (Art.21) and Rio (1992) (Art.2) Declarations, duties of the States are emphasized in such a way that "States have sovereignty over their national resources and the responsibility not to cause transboundary environmental damage beyond national jurisdiction". Of course, such a principle does not exclude their responsibility towards their own citizens and future generations. Sustainable use of natural resources is an important component of the Rio Declaration. National legal responses to address soil degradation have been relatively limited. Apart from the commitments which establish general obligations, a 1998 Protocol on Soil Protection to the Alpine Convention and a solitary EC Directive, no

---

7   Alexandre Kiss, "The Implications of Global Change for the International Legal System", Edith Brown Weiss (ed.), **Environmental Change and International Law,** The United Nations University, Tokyo, 1992, pp.317-318.

legally binding instruments have been adopted which have, as their primary aim, specific measures to conserve, improve and rehabilitate soil, and prevent erosion and other forms of degradation.[8]

World Soil Charter

But some non-binding instruments establish general guidelines in this respect. The FAO's Council adopted the World Soil Charter. Its includes the principles and guidelines to improve productivity, conservation and rational use of soils and to promote "optimum land use", recognizing the responsibility of the governments to ensure long-term maintenance and improvement of soil productivity.[9] Governments are invited a) to develop policies for wise land use according to land suitability, b) to incorporate principles of national land use, management and conservation of soil resources into appropriate resource legislation, c) to monitor and supervise soil management, d) to implement education, training and extension programmes, e) to establish links between local governments, administrations and land users, f) to create socio-economic and institutional structures favorable to rational land uses, and finally g) to conduct research programmes.[10]

World Charter for Nature

The World Charter for Nature which was adopted by the UN General Assembly in 1982 contains several important principles concerning sustainable land use and management.

8   Philippe Sands, **Op.Cit** ,p.555.

9   **Ibid.**

10   FAO, World Soil Charter, Land and Water Development Division of FAO, Rome, 1982.

After drawing the attention to the fact that "Mankind is a part of nature", it lays down the general principles of protection of natural resources, including the land as the followings: "Nature shall be respected and its essential processes shall not be impaired. All areas of the earth, both land and sea, shall be subject to these principles of conservation. The productivity of soils shall be maintained and enhanced though measures which safeguard their long-term fertility and the process of organic decomposition and prevent erosion and all other formes of degradation. Natural resources shall not be wasted."

Convention to Combat Desertification

In 1992, the UN General Assembly established an intergovernmental negotiation committee to elaborate an international convention to combat desertification in those countries experiencing draught and desertification, particularly in Africa. The UN Convention to Combat Desertification in Countries Experiencing Serious Draught and Desertification was adopted in 1994, entered into force in 1996. Affected country parties are required to develop national action programmes to combat desertification in accordance with regional criteria set out in four annexes to the Convention. These programmes should be integrated with other national policies for sustainable development, in accordance with the principle of the integration of International Environmental Law.[11]

Agenda 21 and the Habitat Agenda

Problems of draught and desertification are other problems dealt with in the Agenda 21, according to which "Land

---

11   Philippe Sands, **Op. Cit.**, p.557.

degradation in arid, semi-arid and dry sub-humid areas resulting from various factors, including climatic variations and human activities." Therefore, the Chapter 12 of the Agenda 21 establishes 6 programme areas to combat desertification.[12]

The HABITAT Agenda adopted during the Habitat II Conference in İstanbul in 1996 made important recommendations as to the sustainable urban land-use patterns and planning, which include the followings:

1. Legal frameworks have to be established to facilitate the development and implementation of public plans and policies for sustainable urban development and rehabilitation, land utilization, housing and the improved management of urban growth.

2. Efficient and accessible land markets have to be promoted that are responsive to demand and meet community deeds.

3. Fiscal incentives and land-use control measures, including planning solutions for more rational and sustainable use of limited land resources have to be developed.

4. Greater attention has to be paid on meeting capital investment requirement through resource mobilization strategies that facilitate investment in urban development in locations that contribute to sustainable land-use patterns.

5. Partnerships among the public, private and voluntary sectors in managing land resources for sustainable urban development has to be encouraged.

12   Philippe Sands, **Ibid**, p.556.

6. Urban planning, housing and industrial siting initiatives that discourage the siting of hazardous industrial facilities in residential areas have to be promoted.

7. Urban planning, housing and industrial siting initiatives that discourage the disproportionate siting of polluting industrial facilities in areas inhabited by people living in poverty or those belonging to vulnerable and disadvantaged groups have to be promoted.

8. The implementation of improved land-management practices that deal comprehensively with competing urban land requirements for housing, industry, commerce, infrastructure, transport, green spaces and forested areas, taking into account the need for spaces for everyday activities-for playgrounds, parks, sports and recreation areas suitable for gardening and urban agriculture must be developed and supported.

9. The integration of land-use, communications and transport planning to encourage development patterns that reduce the demand for transport has to be promoted.

10. Integrated coastal zone management to ensure the proper development and conservation of coastal resources has to be developed and implemented.

11. Tools for transparent urban monitoring and reporting activities based on appropriate indicators for the environmental, social and economic performance of cities have to be promoted.

12. Participatory approaches to sustainable human settlements have to be institutionalized.

13. Capacities in integrated environmental management have to be strengthened.

In order to be able to develop and support improved and integrated land management systems, governments have been invited, during the Habitat II Conference in İstanbul, to develop integrated land information and mapping systems, to establish structures for the enforcement of land management laws and regulations, to develop the land market through the establishment of an effective legal framework that incorporate environmental concerns and encompasses the diversity of tenure systems, and finally, to develop comprehensive and environmentally sound land-use strategies at the local level.[13]

In 1992, the Committee of Ministers of the Council of Europe adopted a Recommendation on Soil Protection which set four fundamental principles:

a) Soil protection should be declared of general public interest and integrated into development planning,

b) Soil should be recognized by the States as a common heritage and a natural, non-renewable resource,

c) Soil should be taken into consideration in all other policies, including agricultural, forestry, industrial, transport and town planning, and finally,

d) The public should have access to information on soil and be permitted to participate in relevant procedures.[14]

---

13 The Habitat Agenda, İstanbul, 1996, p. 44.
14 Philippe Sands, **Op.Cit.,** p.556.

The European Union

The land policy of the European Union is embodied in the Environment Policy of the Union together with 16 other policy areas, including air and water. The European Commission has a role to play in ensuring the Member States take environmental concerns into account when putting together their land use development plans. The Commission has five major tools in this area, namely, a) The Directive on Environmental Impact Assessment, b) The Directive on Strategic Environmental Assessment, c) Infrastructure for Spatial Information in Europe and Global Monitoring for Environment and Security, d) European Urban Environment Strategy and d) Integrated Coastal Zone Management. All these make sure significant environmental impacts are identified, assessed and taken into account throughout he decision-making processes.

The Sixth Environment Programme of the EC for the period 2001-2010 contains commitment by the European Commission to develop a thematic strategy for soil with the ultimate goal of raising the political importance of soil issues at the EU level. No announcement was made as to whether such a strategy has already been formulated.

In the field of land-use planning and management, following principles have been adopted by the Sixth Environment Action Programme:

- Publishing a communication on the importance of integrating the environment into land-use planning and management
- Improve the implementation of the Environment Impact Assessment Directive

- Spreading best practice and fostering the of exchanges and experiences on sustainable development, including urban development.

- Boosting agri-environmental measures within the Common Agricultural Policy.

- Developing a partnership fort the sustainable management of tourism.

In connection to the Sixth Environment Action Programme, the European Commission, in a communication to the Council and the European Parliament as well as to the Economic and Social Committee and the Committee of the Regions underlined the fact that "Land use planning and management decisions in the Member States can have major influence on the environment leading to fragmentation of the countryside and pressures in urban areas and the coast." Similarly, one of the main objectives of sustainable use of natural resources and management of wastes is mentioned in the same document as "to ensure the consumption of renewable and non-renewable resources does not exceed the carrying capacity of the environment."

In the new Environment Action Programme, a clean and healthy environment is regarded as part and parcel of the prosperity and quality of life. It was also underlined that this was a desire "for ourselves and for our children in the future." The Sixth Environment Action Programme emphasized that "In the complex interplay of different forces and pressures...the role of land-use planning and management is crucial. This covers a wide range of decisions, usually made at local and regional level, determining the character and intensity of land uses and activities which may often have a major impact on environmental conditions. Such impacts may be direct, for example by way of destruction of habitats and landscape, or indirect such as influencing the generation of additional traffic and hence contributing to congestion, air pollution and greenhouse gases. These impacts are of particular concern in urban and coastal areas where the greater pressure and conflict for land use and development is taking place."

It has been pointed out that the Community Directive on Environmental Impact Assessment and the Proposal on Strategic Environmental Assessment, which aim to ensure that he environmental implications of planned infrastructure projects and planning are properly addressed will also help ensure that the environmental considerations are better integrated into planning decisions. The implications of these rules for the candidate countries are important because they may be regarded as preconditions for full membership. According to the respective principle of the Action Programme, the use of urban planning in candidate countries should be encouraged so must help to ensure that urban expansion can be better controlled and not at the expense of the environment.

European Spatial Development Perspectives (ESDP)

In view of the fact that over 80 percent of the EU's nearly 400 million citizens live in cities and towns, urban land use planning and management become a crucially important policy issue for the EU. In fact, land use is one of the strongest determinants of an urban area's character and its environmental performance. For example, land use policies which encourage urban sprawl can lead to dependence on private car use, greater land use per capita and correspondingly higher levels of resource use.[15] That is the reason why, the Community's Sixth Environmental Action Programme called the Commission to develop a new "Thematic Strategy on the Urban Environment" to help promote a more integrated approach and support action at local level. Long before, as early as in 1999, the Ministers responsible for Spatial Planning in the Member States of the European Union and the members of the European Commission responsible for regional policy emphasized in Potsdam that the conclusion of the political debate on the European Spatial Development Perspective (ESDP) was an important step in the progress towards European integration. The basic aim of spatial development policies is to work towards a balanced and sustainable development of the territory of the European Union. a) Economic and social cohesion, b) conservation and management of natural resources and the cultural heritage, and c) more balanced competitiveness of the European territory are three fundamental goals of the ESDP.

The Ministers adopting these perspectives made it clear that these principles will neither be legally binding for the European Union nor its Member States and their local and regional authorities. The document simply provides a suitable policy framework and a reference for the Member States and it is expected that it would contribute to the balanced and sustainable development through social and economic cohesion. For, as pointed out in the Brundtland Report, sustainable development requires not only a healthy economy

---

15   Commission of the European Communities, Commission Staff Working Document, Annex to the Communication from the Commission to the Council and the European Parliament on Thematic Strategy on the Urban Environment. Commission of the European Communities., Brussels, 2006, p.47.

from the environmental point of view, but also from a balanced spatial development.

As a legally non-binding document, the ESDP provides a policy framework for better cooperation between Community sectoral policies with significant spatial impacts and between Member States, their regions and cities. The principles of the document are consistent with the political principles adopted by the concerned Ministers as early as in 1994. These principles are as the followings:

-Spatial development can contribute in a decisive way to the achievement of the goal of economic and social cohesion

-The ESDP may contribute to the implementation of Community policies which have a territorial impact, but without constraining the responsible institutions in exercising their responsibilities.

-The central aim will be to achieve sustainable and balanced development.

-It will be prepared respecting existing institutions and will be non-binding on Member States.

-It will respect the principle of *subsidiarity*.

-Each country will take it forward according to the extent it wishes to take account of European spatial development aspects in its national policies.

The most important treaty headings providing the European Commission with the basis for action with implications for spatial development in the EU include a) Community Competition Policy, b) Trans-European Networks, c) Structural Funds, d) Common Agricultural Policy, e) Environment Policy, e) Research, Technology and Development, f) Loan Activities of the European Investment Bank.

Policy aims for the territory of the EU are centered around three fundamental issues. The first is the development of a polycentric and balanced urban system and strengthening of the partnership between urban and rural areas. This involves overcoming the outdated dualism between city and the countryside.[16] The second is the promotion of integrated transport and communication concepts, which support the polycentric development of the EU territory and an important pre-condition for enabling European cities and regions to pursue their integration into EMU. Finally, development and conservation of the natural and cultural heritage through wise management is expected to contribute both to the preservation and deepening of regional identities and the maintenance of the natural and cultural diversity of the regions and cities of the EU in the age of globalization.

The Leipzig Charter (2007)

A number of legal documents adopted by various EU bodies, other than the ESDP, contain provisions with respect to land-use planning and management. One of them is the Leipzig Charter on Sustainable European Cities which was adopted by the Ministers responsible for Urban Development. Integrated urban development as a prerequisite for successful urban sustainability, strategies for upgrading the physical environment, strengthening the local economy and local labor market policy in deprived urban areas, proactive education and training policies on children and young people

---

16   European Commission, **ESDP European Spatial Development Perspective: Towards Balanced and Sustainable Development of the Territory of the European Union,** Potsdam, May, 1999.

in the same urban areas and sustainable urban transport. A compact settlement structure is regarded by the Charter as one of the prerequisites for efficient and sustainable use of resources. The Charter suggested that urban development policy be laid down at the national level and the European structural funds be utilized by the Member States.

The Territorial Agenda of the European Union (2007)

Ministers responsible for Regional Development, met in Leipzig during 24-25 May 2007, adopted a document entitled as the Territorial Agenda of the European Union: Towards a More Competitive and Sustainable Europe of Diverse Regions. In the light of the general goal of ensuring the territorial coherence, the Territorial Agenda, as an action-oriented political framework for future cooperation emphasizes on strengthening of regional identities and better utilization of spatial differentiation. This Agenda accepts the fundamental principles of the ESDP, namely a) development of a balanced and poly-centric territorial system and rural-urban partnership, b) ensuring equity in the access to infrastructure and information, and c) sustainable development, careful use and management of the nature and historical heritage. Basic principles of the European Territorial Agenda can be summarized as the followings:

1. To strengthen polycentric development and innovation through networking of city- regions and cities,
2. New forms of partnership and territorial governance between rural and urban areas,
3. To promote regional clusters of competition and innovation in Europe,

4. Strengthening and extension of trans-European Networks,

5. To promote trans-European risk management including the impacts of climate change,

6. Strengthening of ecological structures and cultural resources as the added value for development.

In order to be able to realize these ends, a more active involvement of the European institutions, a closer cooperation between the European Commission and the States and finally strengthening territorial cohesion within the boundaries of Member States is necessary.

The Council of Europe
Guiding Principles for Sustainable Spatial Development of the European Continent

The Treaty of Rome set the major goals of the European integration as a) the development of the backward regions, b) ensuring economic and social development, c) improvement of living and working conditions and d) the elimination of welfare differences. These goals have been retained in all the amendments that have taken place later on. Reducing spatial inequalities preserved its place all the time in the agenda of the Council of Europe. Reflecting the major goals of social cohesion, these principles have been incorporated into the document called as the Guiding Principles for Sustainable Spatial Development of the European Continent by the Ministers in their meting taken place in Hannover during 7-8 September 2000.[17]

17 European Conference of Ministers responsible for Regional Planning (CE-MAT), **Guiding Principles for Sustainable Development of the European Continent,** adopted at the 12th Session of the European Conference of

The goal of these principles is to determine spatial development measures that would ensure an acceptable level of living in all Member States of the Council of Europe, briefly to define the human rights and democracy. In the legal instrument of the Council of Europe concerning these principles, it was stated that these principles were inspired by the philosophy behind such documents as the Torremolinos Charter (1983), the European Regional Strategy adopted in Lausanne in 1988 by CEMAT, The European Charter of Local Self-Government (1985) as well as the Draft Charter of Regional Democracy(1997).The document also takes account of the European Union's European Spatial Development Perspective (ESDP)(1999), the Baltic Agenda 21 (1998), the Vision and Strategies around the Baltic Sea(1994) and existing regional development strategies for individual areas of Europe, the Structural Scheme for Benelux(1998) and the Strategy for Integrated Spatial Development in Central, Adriatic and Danubian Europe.

Europe represents a multiplicity of cultures with a regional, national and international impact, of which the 60 languages spoken are simply an indication. This diversity represents also an inestimable potential for sustainable spatial development. In the context of economic integration and globalization, economic growth impetus is being generated as well as negative impacts, for instance on environmental conditions and social cohesion.[18] It is pointed out

the Ministers responsifor Integrated Spatialble for Regional Planning on September 2000 in Hannover.

18   CEMAT, **Guiding Principles for Sustainable Spatial Development of the European Continent, adopted at the 12th Session of the European Conference of Ministers responsible for Regional Planning on 7-8 September 2000 in Hannover, CEMAT, (2000)7, p.2-3.**

that Europe has the potential for realizing a polycentric development pattern, with a number of significant growth areas, including ones on the periphery, organized as urban networks, which will create an impetus and the necessary external economies of scale to attract further investment. Polycentric development is expected to contribute also to the lowering environmental pressure and of social tension.[19] Another remarkable point in the introductory part of the document on guiding principles of spatial development is the role of the private development. It was referred as a driving force that might contribute to increasing the attractiveness of municipalities and regions for private investment at regional and local levels. Therefore, it is recommended that support be given to public-private partnerships that are developing in areas formerly confined to the public sector.

Let us look briefly at the content of the principles themselves.

1. Promoting territorial cohesion through balanced social and economic development of regions and improved competitiveness.

2. In this context, it is suggested that the attractiveness of Europe's metropolises and gateway cities should be further developed and that the attractiveness of structurally weak regions for economic investment should be strengthened. Prerequisites are the existence of democratically legitimated territorial authorities, a high standard of administrative practice and applied policy, as well as a stronger involvement of the citizens and societal groups in spatial development planning.

19   **Ibid.**, p.5.

3. Encouraging development generated by urban functions and improving the urban-rural relationship. Urban systems and functions should be developed so as to facilitate country dwellers' access to them. The establishment and strengthening of urban networks increases the complementarity of these towns and creates synergy and economies of scale, encourages specialization and creates benefits through economic competition while avoiding the associated pitfalls. Urban-rural partnerships have an increasingly part to play in the fields of balanced settlement structure, development of public transport networks, revitalization and diversification of the economy of rural areas, the increase in the productivity of infrastructures, the development of recreation areas, the protection and enhancement of the natural and cultural heritage.

4. Promoting more equal accessibility. This principle requires that the Pan European Transport Network has to be completed as a prerequisite for ensuring good accessibility anywhere in Europe. It is suggested that to achieve a regionally more balanced development, links between small and medium-sized towns as well as rural areas and the main transport routes and centers be improved.

5. Developing access to information and knowledge. The emergence of the information society is the most significant phenomenon reshaping society and its territorial structure. It is recommended that particular attention be paid to all regions to make sure that access to information is not restricted by physical and

other constraints. Improvements should be made to telecommunications networks and encouragement should be given to national and regional interfaces between information suppliers and potential users.

6. Reducing environmental damages. Environmental problems that may result from inadequate co-ordination of sectoral policies of local decisions have to be prevented. Spatial planning policy must give support to less damaging agricultural or forestry practices, to encouraging more environmentally friendly forms of transport, to such as wetlandsand to regenerating areas damaged by industrial pollution.

7. Enhancing and protecting natural resources and the natural heritage. Natural resources contribute not only to properly balanced ecosystems but also to the attractiveness of regions, their recreational value and general quality of life. Therefore, they must be protected. The Convention on the Conservation of European Wildlife and Natural Habitats (1979) and the Pan-European Biological and Landscape Diversity Strategy must also be taken into account in a sustainable spatial planning policy. Spatial planning is also concerned with reconstituting ecological networks. Appropriate measures are also needed for he protection of environmentally sensitive areas.

8. Enhancing the cultural heritage as a factor for development. Increasing local and regional appeal for investors, tourists and the population makes an important contribution to economic development and to strengthening regional identity. Not only the conservation of the past is at stake, but also harmony

and creativity in the spatial relationship between modern architecture and urban design and the historical heritage. Spatial development policy has to preserve and respect the memory of every nationality and religious group when a specific aspect of cultural heritage is enhanced.

9. Developing energy resources while maintaining safety. Spatial development policy as coherent, environmentally friendly systems and completion of the Pan-European Energy Networks. Priority must be given to more efficient use of energy and equipment already available. The safety of older nuclear power plants should be increased. There are nuclear power plants the life of which will come to an end in the coming decades. The sites where they are located have to be rehabilitated. New tasks for spatial planning will result from this.

10. Encouraging high-quality, sustainable tourism. The aim of the spatial development policy is to use the development opportunities originating in tourism, in particular in the case of disadvantaged regions. Priority should be given to developing forms of high-quality and sustainable tourism. The most needed is eco-tourism. Forms of soft tourism that are carefully adapted to local and regional circumstances can provide many regions with a major opportunity for development which should be exploited.

11. Limiting the impacts of natural disasters. Natural disasters such as earthquakes, hurricanes, flooding, avalanches and mudslides, cause considerable damage in Europe every year with serious consequences, for

people's lives and health, for the economy, for the settlement structure and for the landscapes. Preventive measures should be taken in the context of spatial development policies aiming at limiting the extent of damage and at making the settlement structure less vulnerable.

In addition to the principles related to a sustainable spatial development policy, more detailed spatial development measures concerning the following issues are proposed: cultural landscape, urban areas, rural areas, mountain regions, coastal and island regions, Eurocorridors, river basins and alluvial valleys, reconversion areas; and a closer cooperation between the Member States of the Council of Europe and participation of regions, municipalities and citizens is proposed.

Within the framework of the implementation of the guiding principles, not only the cooperation between the nation states and local authorities but at the same time collaboration between the Council of Europe and the European Union is recommended. With this purpose in mind, the European Commission established such programmes as INTERREG, PHARE, TACIS, MEDA, SAPARD, etc. In addition, the World Bank, European Development Bank, European Bank for Reconstruction and Development, and the European Investment Bank provide financial opportunities for the achievement of the goals of sustainable spatial development policy.

Within the framework of interstate cooperation and the cooperation between the States and international institutions, vertical and horizontal cooperation become important. The aim of the *horizontal cooperation* is to integrate sectoral policies having territorial impacts with spatial development projects. These include policies concerning infrastructure, social security, economy and public finance. A special kind of horizontal cooperation concern cross-border cooperative initiatives between the States, regions and local authorities. On the other hand, *vertical cooperation* can be defined as the cooperation between various administrative levels. It is organized in a way that enables local and regional authorities to adapt their planning decisions to measures decided on at a higher level. National authorities in turn try to adapt their decisions to locally and regionally derived plans and projects. This is called the principle of reciprocity.

The subsidiarity and reciprocity principles in spatial development can only function if appropriate statutory powers have been given to the regional level. Regional and local authorities have, according to the European Charter of Local Self-Government and to the Draft European Charter of Regional Democracy, a particular responsibility in spatial development.[20] The involvement of younger generations and the role of societal consensus in the planning process are also emphasized in this document.

Several other legal documents that are adopted in different international meetings possess relevant principles in terms of sustainable land use, although they are indirectly, but not directly concerned with the subject matter.

Aalborg Charter and the Aalborg+10: Inspiring Futures
The representatives of the European cities and towns met in Aalborg, Denmark in May 27, 1994 and have adopted

20   CEMAT, Council of Europe, **Guiding Principles. op.cit., p. 17.**

important decisions concerning sustainable spatial development. Ten years after the first meeting, they have revised those principles in 2004 in the same place and have added new provisions to the previously adopted ones. They have referred to "man-made and natural threats to our communities and resources", and set their own responsibilities as "harmonising environmental, social, cultural and economic objectives". They have expressed their commitment "to accelerate efforts towards local sustainable development, drawing inspiration from the sustainability principles set out in the Aalborg Charter". Particularly, they have emphasized that their aim was "to translate our common vision for sustainable urban futures into tangible sustainability targets and action at the local level".

The major previous legal instruments on which the Aalborg Charter relied extensively were the Lisbon Strategy, the European Sustainable Development Strategy, the Sixth Environment Action Programme, the forthcoming EU Thematic Strategy on the Urban Environment, and European initiatives on climate change, on health, on governance, and in implementing the UN Millennium Development Goals and the Johannesburg Plan of Implementation. The major themes of the Aalborg Charter included increased participatory democracy (governance), local management towards sustainability, natural common goods, responsible consumption and lifestyle choices, planning and design, better mobility, less traffic, local action for health, vibrant and sustainable local economy, social equity and justice, and connections between the local and global. It was also stressed that they were committed "to improve soil quality, *preserve ecologically productive land,* and promote sustainable agriculture and forestry. In addition, they have emphasized on re-using and regenerating derelict or disadvantaged areas, on avoiding urban sprawl by achieving appropriate urban densities and prioritising brownfield site over green field site development. Finally, they have stressed the need to ensure appropriate conservation, renovation and use/re-use of our urban culture heritage.

The definition of the notion of sustainability that is made in 1994 is particularly important and worth to remember. According to understanding of the Charter, economic sustainability requires environmental sustainability as well, and the environmental sustainability is defined as "maintaining the natural capital". Such an understanding demands from us that "the rate at which we consume renewable material, water and energy resources does not exceed the rate at which the natural systems can replenish them, and that the rate at which we consume non-renewable resources are replaced".

From the point of view of sustainability of land-use patterns, the Aalborg Charter emphasizes that "we recognize the importance of effective land-use and development planning policies by our local authorities which embrace the strategic environmental assessment of all plans. We should take advantage of the scope of for providing efficient public transport and energy which higher densities offer, while maintaining the human scale of development. In both undertaking urban renewal programmes in inner urban areas and in planning new suburbs we seek a mix of functions so as to reduce the need for mobility. Notions of equitable regional interdependency should enable us to balance the flows between city and countryside and prevent cities from merely exploiting the resources of surrounding areas".

The European Charter of Local Self-Government

The European Charter of Local Self-Government adopted in 1985 aims at strengthening autonomous local authorities all over Europe as the most efficient actors of genuine democracy. The Charter contains provisions with regard to the nature and scope of the concept of local autonomy, types and limits of the central supervision and control over local authorities, their financial resources, cooperation among the units of local governments and the legal protection of the rights and freedoms of local authorities. It can be assumed that really autonomous local authorities may be in a better position to manage their landed property more rationally and in favor of the public interest within a policy framework to be formulated by national authorities.

Valencia Declaration: Good Local and Regional Governance (The European Challenge)

Another document recently adopted by the European Ministers responsible for Local and Regional Government in Valencia during 14-16 October 2007 is called Good Local and Regional Governance which sets the principles of democratic participation and public ethics at local and regional level.[21] The very definition of the concept of autonomous local government as formulated by the European Charter of Local Self Government (Art.3, par.1) is regarded as a precondition for the implementation of the fundamental principles of good democratic governance which are the followings: 1) fair conduct of elections, representation and

---

21   Council of Europe, **Conference of European Ministers Responsible for Local and Regional Government,** 15the Session, 15-16 October 2007, MCL-15(2007)5 Final, 16 October 2007.

participation, 2) responsiveness, 3) efficiency and effectiveness, 4) openness and transparency, 5) rule of law, 6) ethical conduct, 7) competence an capacity, 8) innovation and
openness to change,9) sustainability and long-term orientation, 10) sound financial management, 11) human rights,
cultural diversity and social cohesion, 12) accountability. All
these principles are analyzed in detail and the respective
duties at the European and national levels for their proper
implementation are clarified in the text of the Declaration.

Several principles which seem quite relevant in terms
of sustainable use and management of urban land have to
be underlined in this respect: The public good is placed before individual interests", "the needs of future generations are
taken into account in current policies", "Decisions strive to
internalize all costs and not to transfer problems and tensions, be they environmental, structural, financial, economic
or social, to future generations", "charges do not exceed the
cost of services provided and do not reduce demand excessively, particularly in the case of important public services.

The European Urban Charter

The European Urban Charter was adopted by the Council of Europe's Congress of Local and Regional Authorities in 1992 and it has been revised in 2004. Its main goals
were to provide practical urban management advice for local authorities and citizens alike, to identify the principal
elements for a future Council of Europe Recommendation
on towns in Europe, and finally to announce the Council
of Europe's views on matters relating to the built environment. The Charter was prefaced with by a European Declaration of Urban Rights, which underscored the commitment

of the Congress to participatory democracy. The principles of the original Charter have been revised in the light of new global developments and the new concepts have been incorporated into the text. Sustainability, the urban village, distinctiveness, reconciliation of different needs, balancing the past with the future, solidarity, responsibilities, mutual dependence of the town and its surroundings, political will and professional skills and cooperation between towns are the main topics and considerations which inspired the formulation of the new text.

Particularly, the theme of sustainability concerns closely the subject matter of this paper. The European Urban Charter suggests in this respect that a firm commitment to sustainable policies must be introduced and maintained. In addition, the approach to planning cities must be focused on sustainable policies which support clear, interlinked environmental, social and economic objectives. A related recommendation of the European Urban Charter with regard to sustainability is that public authorities have a responsibility to husband and manage natural and energy resources in a coherent and rational manner. Because the principle of sustainable development requires that local and regional authorities accept fully their responsibilities in limiting their use of non-renewable resources and increase the use of secondary products from recycled waste and from renewable resources. Of course, the role of urban land as a non-renewable and non-reproducible resource has to be kept in mind in this respect.

The Charter also stresses that in the past, zoning and separation of the main urban functions of housing, industries and transport was often seen as the ideal solution.

However, such separation of activities into single land use zones leads to larger volumes of transport and greater use land. More transport implies more pollution; and more extensive built-up areas of land reduces land available for agriculture, water catchments, forestry and adversely, damage natural habitats. Local authorities should formulate land use plans for compact and denser urban development and a mix of functions. Large disused areas, often former industrial land, may provide the possibility of regeneration, once removal of ground and water contamination has taken place. This brownfield development makes use of previously developed rather than open green field.

European Soil Charter

In parallel with the World Soil Charter, the European Soil Charter of the Council of Europe contains provisions which are considerably relevant to the topic of sustainable land-use and management. First of all, it stresses that the soil is one the humanity's most precious assets and as such it allows plants, animals and man to live on the earth's surface. Secondly, it is emphasized that the soil is a "limited resource" (non-renewable) which is easily destroyed. Therefore, a regional planning policy must be conceived in terms of the properties of the soil and the needs of today's and tomorrow's society. The need is stressed in the Charter for the farmers and foresters to apply methods that preserve the quality of the soil. And the soil must be protected against erosion and pollution. Perhaps a more important principle of the European Soil Charter is the one concerning urban development. It requires that urban development must be planned in such a way that it causes as little damage as possible to adjoining areas. Therefore, it is suggested that urban development must be concentrated and so planned that it avoids as far as possible taking over good soil and harming or polluting soil in farmland and forest, in nature reserves and recreational areas. Other recommendations of the Soil Charter aim at assessing the effects of the civil engineering projects on adjacent land, making an inventory of soil resources, fostering research and educational levels and planning and administering soil resources by public authorities.

These principles reflected the same ideas enshrined in the text of the Recommendation on Soil Protection which was adopted by the Committee of the Ministers of the Council of Europe as early as in 1992. Four fundamental principles laid down in that Recommendation are particularly worth to remember: 1) Soil protection should be declared of *general public interest* and integrated into development planning, 2) Soil should be recognized by the States *as a common heritage and a natural, non-renewable resource,* 3) Soil should be taken into consideration in all other policies, including agricultural, forestry, industrial, transport and town planning and finally, 4) the public should have Access to information on soil and be permitted to participate in relevant procedures.[22]

European Convention on Transfrontier Cooperation

The European Outline Convention on Transfrontier Cooperation between Territorial Communities and Authorities which has been adopted by the Council of Europe in 1980 contains some provisions that can be used indirectly as an helpful device for sustainable land use through cooperation

22   Cited in Philippe Sands, **op.cit.,** p.556.

between local communities and authorities. According to this Convention that has been signed so far by nearly half of the full membership of the Council of Europe (23 out of 47) and ratified 15 out the 47 Member States of the Council of Europe, the smooth functioning of transfrontier cooperation between municipalities and regions may enable them to carry out their tasks more effectively and enable frontier areas to be improved and developed more harmoniously. The model interstate agreement there are provisions showing the main areas of cooperation such as urban and regional development, nature conservation, and housing.

Concluding Remarks

Effective implementation of the principles of International Environmental Law depends upon a number of factors. The most important is the legal nature of rules concerned. Legal instruments adopted by international organizations may be simply the kind of *soft law* that are not, in principle, legally binding for the signatory states. They may serve merely as guidelines for the formulation of official policies. In order to make them applicable, they have to be ratified by the parliaments in an appropriate manner. As a result they may acquire the status of *hard law* that are legally binding. Secondly, the incorporation of international principles into the domestic legislation may not be enough. There is also a need to get them properly enforced. Enforcement may be defined as a set of actions that governments and others take to achieve compliance within the regulated community and to correct and halt situations that endanger the environment or the public health. Enforcement by the government usually includes inspections, negotiations, and legal action.[23] Thirdly, international conventions may possess provisions regarding the monitoring of implementation of the principles of conventions. In addition to legal action to compel compliance and to impose some consequence for violating the law, non-governmental groups may become involved in enforcement by detecting non-compliance taking legal action also against a violation for non-compliance or against the government for not enforcing the requirements. Fourthly, the principle of integration of the environmental law is particularly important for sustainable management of land use, because it requires the integration of the sector with all other related sectors of the economy, like transportation, urban and regional development, siting. Finally, we have to remember that moral and social values for environmental quality in general o lack of public support for environmental concerns, societal respect for the law in general and a clear government will to enforce land use and environmental laws are of prime importance.

Short Bibliography

Council of Europe, CEMAT, Guiding Principles for Sustainable Spatial Development of the European Continent, adopted at the 12th Session of the European Conference of Ministers responsible for Regional Planning on 7-8 September 2000 in Hannover, CEMAT, (2000) 7.

Council of Europe, Conference of the European Ministers Responsible for Local and Regional Government, 15th Session, 15-16 October 2007, MCL-15, (2007) 5 Final, Valencia,16 October 2007.

---

23 US Environment Protection Agency, **Principles of Environmental Enforcement,** Washington DC, 1999, p.xiii.

European Commission, ESDP, European Spatial Development Perspective: Towards Balanced and Sustainable Development of the territory of the European Union, Potsdam, May, 1999.

European Commission, Annex to the Communicate from the Commission to the Council and the European Parliament on Thematic Strategy on the Urban Environment, Commission Staff Working Document, Brussels, 2006.

Kiss, Alexandre, "The Implications of Global Change for International Legal System", in Edith Brown Weiss (ed.), *Environmental Change and International Law*, The United Nations University, Tokyo, 1992.

Mooney, Christopher P., "Property Rights and the Environment", in Richard E. Hart (ed.), Ethics *and the Environment*, University Press of America, New York, 1982.

Owens, Susan, "Interpreting Sustainable Development: The Case for Land Use Planning", in Michael Jacobs (ed.), *Greening Millennium: The New Politics of Environment*, Blackwell, London.

Rifkin, Jeremy, *Biosphere Politics*, Harper, San Francisco, 1991.

Sands, Philippe, *Principles of International Environmental Law*, 2nd ed.,Cambridge University Press, Cambridge, 2001.

U.N., *The Habitat Agenda*, İstanbul, 1996.

U.S Environment Protection Agency, *Principles of Environmental Enforcement*, Washington D.C., 1999.

Sustainability of Sustainable Urban Development Under Unsustainable Conditions[*]

Introduction

The Concept of Sustainable Development

I would like to begin with expressing my gratitude and congratulations to the organizers of this important symposium that will provide a new opportunity to discuss once again the problems concerning closely the future of mankind. During the last four decades, sustainable development and long-term orientation have become the guiding principles of a rational spatial development strategy and democratic governance at all levels of authority. The need for future generations are more increasingly taken into consideration in formulating current policies of urban development, in addition to its implications for national social and economic policies, thanks to the contributions of certain international institutions such as the United Nations, the European Union and the Council of Europe. Particularly, the European institutions are making considerable and constant efforts to

[*] Ruşen KELEŞ, Ph.D. Professor of Local Government, Urbanization and Environmental Policies, Ankara University, Faculty of Political Sciences (Em.) 4th International Buildings Symposium 18-20 July 2019, Crown Plaza Hotel, Dallas, Texas, USA.

internalize all costs, and not to transfer problems and tensions into the shoulders of future generations.

The very definition of sustainable development made by the Brundtland Commission on Environment and Development towards the end of the 1980's had put an emphasis on meeting the needs of the present generations without compromising the ability of the future generations to meet their own needs. Almost the same thesis was defended by Mustafa Kemal Atatürk, the founder of the Turkish Republic, in 1919, nearly 70 years earlier than the publication of Brundtland Report, in the following words: "Nations live on the territories that they occupy not solely as the holders of the ownership right but also as the representatives of the whole humanity. Therefore, in using this right, they should never forget that the future generations will also have the right to use these territories in the future."

These ideas will have far reaching consequences for the protection of natural resources and cultural assets of the countries all over the world. Sustainability adds new dimensions to spatial development. Conversely, urbanization, depending upon its pace and patterns, creates numerous problems or opportunities that will need special treatment. In this context, the concept of sustainable development needs to be clarified further. As early as in 1972, there was a reference to the same concept in the principle 13 of the Declaration of the Rio UN Conference on Environment and Development, without mentioning the term of sustainable development, simply saying that; "States should adopt an integrated and coordinated approach to their development planning so as to ensure that development is compatible with the need to protect and improve environment for the benefit of their population". Brundtland Report published in 1987 drew the attention rather to the rights of future generations stating that sustainable development is to meet the needs of the present generation without compromising the ability of future generations to meet their own needs.

The United Nations has brought forward a new set of global targets to replace its Millennium Development Goals which were expected to reach their deadline by 2015. Collectively known as the Sustainable Development Goals, this new set of targets comprises 17 universal goals that will require all countries to consider when formulating their national policies as they contain indicators that every government will be obliged to work towards. These goals cover the broad themes such as ending poverty and hunger, and improving health, education and gender equality. They also include specific proposals to reduce inequality, make cities safe, address climate change and promote peaceful societies.[1] Most of these targets coincide with the principles laid down in Action Plan, called the New Urban Agenda adopted during the HABITAT III Conference held in Quito, Ecuador in 2016.

In fact, sustainable urbanization may be defined as the maximization of economic efficiency in the use of scarce resources including water, air, and soil, maintaining natural resource stocks at or above their present level, ensuring social equity in the distribution of development costs and benefits, and avoiding unnecessary foreclosure of future development options.

---

1   Agni Vlavianos-Arvanitis, *Biopolicy: The Bioethics of Climate Change Mitigation,* **B.I.O,** Athens, 2015.

Climate Change and the Limits to Growth

Common environmental problems facing almost all countries include the loss of biological diversity, deforestation, ozone layer depletion, climate change, air and water pollution, using the most fertile agricultural lands for building purposes, the need to integrate ecological considerations with the processes of building and planning, reducing energy consumption, particularly the use of fossil fuels, and dealing properly with the unhealthy and unplanned urbanization and disorderly building activities in urban, semi-urban and rural areas.

In addition to domestic legislations, International Environmental law provides us several guiding principles of high relevance for the analysis as well as for the formulation of appropriate strategies concerning all these issues. Most of them are reflected in the international legal instruments such as the Stockholm Declaration (1972), legal principles proposed by the Brundtland Commission (1987), the Rio Declaration (1992), Framework Convention for Climate Change and later the Kyoto Protocol. Therefore, it is appropriate now to remember the following legal concepts: Common heritage of mankind, environmental security, common but differentiated responsibility of the states, the rights of future generations, and international cooperation.

A civil society organization called the Club of Rome had been set up in 1968 by several academicians and businessmen for the encouragement of the studies on the protection of the environment. The well-known report published under the title of the Limits to Growth and written by Donella Meadows, Jorgen Randers and Dennis Meadows has drawn the attention of the world public opinion to the fact that not later than 100 years, (namely by 2072) humanity will definitely reach the limits of the physical growth and it will be necessary both to slow down the population growth as well as the pace of economic growth if we are going to ensure the livability of mankind and the ecosystem. That is the reason why that the main suggestion made in the book called The Limits to Growth was "zero growth".

Nearly 30 years later than the publication of the Limits to Growth, in 2004, the authors of the book called the Limits to Growth, succeeded to publish a new version of their book, under the title of "Beyond the Limits: Confronting Global Collapse Envisioning Sustainable Future". They maintain that in case the neo-liberal economic system continues to exist as it is, a global economic collapse will be inevitable. We clearly observe that both for the utilization of natural resources and for the pollution of nature, limits of sustainability have already been left behind.

Global warming and the climate change threaten the future of the humanity. While the average temperature in the world remained as 14 centigrade degrees during the last 10.000 years, it began to change during the last 20-25 years. The increase in temperature has been 0.74 degree during the last century, namely between 1906 and 2006, while it doubled during the last half century. And it reached unbelievable limits during the last fifteen years. Europe, lived the hottest summer in 2003. The basic reason is not the impact of the natural factors, but it derives from human activities, including greenhouse gas emissions. It is estimated that the total cost created as such is greater than the cost of the 1929 world economic crisis to the humanity. It seems that global warming will continue in the coming several decades, because of the existence of the existing gases in the atmosphere.

It has become almost impossible to draw boarder lines between various seasons. As different from several decades ago, no one could tell us today when the winter ends and the spring begins. Qualifications of different seasons have been mixed up altogether. There is no doubt that famous Vivaldi, if he was to live in our century, could not be able to compose again his great masterpiece called "Four Seasons".

The basic requirements of the concept of sustainable cities and urban development have been conceptualized by French academician Olivier Godard in the following categories: a) Reduction of consumption of energy, spaces and natural resources of the cities, b) definition of new spatial units of planning, regional development and urban management, c) searching for a new urban landscape which puts an end to the rupture between a city which is no more than a city and a countryside that is no more than "the nature", and finally, d) taking into consideration of the long term needs of urban populations.[2] It is worthwhile to search for several relevant examples concerning this matter.

When applied to the field of urban development, it is assumed that sustainable urbanization can be secured only when master planning is directed to minimize travel needs, to promote public transportation, to conserve fertile agricultural lands, to avoid wasting other sensitive and non-renewable ecological resources and to enhance savings in building designs and layouts, in other words, to take measures to render effective all strategies required by the slow city

2   Olivier Godard, "Projets et recomposition par les échelles territoriales", *Pouvoirs Locaux,* Paris, No:34, 1997, pp.36-37.

(Cittaslow) movement. This would certainly require carrying out sustainability programmes and projects and also incorporating analysis and measures of regional sustainability in city planning practices through regional resource inventories, vertical and horizontal coordination among all public authorities and private entities involved in regional resource management and the development of renewable resource strategies within a holistic vision.

Appropriate land-use planning can provide substantial environmental benefits ranging from better living environments to lower greenhouse gas emissions. In case land-use planning fails to achieve its objectives, it often pushes low-income households to the periphery and to lands still poorly controlled by owners or regulators. This may result in untimely and unnecessary conversion of fertile agricultural land into urban uses that can be detrimental for sustainable development.

Economic Commission for Europe of the United Nations has published in 1996 an important document called *Guidelines on Sustainable Human Settlements* which suggests highly relevant rules for sustainable urban development. Some of these principles are the followings: a) Conservation, protection and enhancement of natural areas and life forms. b) Promotion of compact community development policies. c) Encouragement of the utilization of already built-up areas so as to limit urban sprawl. d) Optimization of density potential of existing urban areas. e) Limitation of the use of private car through the maximization of the use public transport alternatives, including commuter rail, buses, bicycles and walking. f) Promotion of a sense of community and creation of opportunities for social interaction.

g) Ensuring that environmental considerations and precautionary principle become an integral part of the plans, programs and projects. h) Integration of the "net environmental gain" in assessing development. i) Preservation of the coherence of the landscape. j) Encouragement of the development of medium- size cities as a network of complementary urban settlements to big cities, in order to develop a more balanced hierarchy of human settlements.[3]

Similar guiding principles have been proposed by the European Urban Charter of the Council of Europe in 1992, revised later in 2008 under the title of *The European Urban Charter II: Manifesto for a New Urbanity*. In each of its chapters, the principles proposed coincide to a large extent with the above mentioned rules which reflect the fundamental urban rights and the main philosophy of sustainable urban development. The rights connected with the transport and mobility, environment and nature in towns, the physical forms of cities, urban architectural heritage, housing, urban security and crime prevention, disadvantaged and disabled persons, sports and leisure in towns, citizen participation, urban management and urban planning, economic development of cities are all regulated there with due regard to the principle of sustainability, reflecting the contemporary trends. Particularly the role of local authorities, as fundamental agents of sustainable urban development is highly emphasized in the text.[4]

---

3   Derya Oktay (ed.), *Inquiry into Urban Environment,* p.35.

4   Ruşen Keleş, "Sustainable Urban Development under Unsustainable Conditions", in Derya Oktay (ed.), *Inquiry into Urban Environment: Issues concerning Urban, Housing and the Built Environment,* Eastern Mediterranean University, EMU Press, Gazimağusa, 2006, pp. 35-36.

What we observe in many parts of the world is not in line with the required strategies already mentioned. For example, most of the countries in the Mediterranean Basin were not able to realize the principles formulated in the agenda 21, particularly with respect to sustainable urban development. Turkey is not an exception to such an observation. Urban development there is considerably influenced qualitatively and quantitatively by rapid urbanization. Rural to urban migration is not only rapid, but also one-directional, unbalanced and disorderly. It operates to increase the rate of unemployment and underemployment in major cities and to inflate the informal sector. Rapid urban development is also characterized during the last several decades by a rapid increase of informal dwellings (squatters) that surrounded major cities.[5]

National economic policies particularly followed in developing countries could not cope adequately with the task of providing employment opportunities, technical and social infrastructure such as housing, transportation, communications, sewerage, public health, educational and cultural services to meet the needs of rapidly urbanizing populations. Policies of urbanization, migration, housing, urban land and informal settlements have not succeeded in realizing the kind of urban development that might be regarded as the outcome of a sustainable urban management. Related to this issue is the inadequacy of the planning techniques used. The traditional comprehensive master planning techniques that have been in use during the last decades failed

5   Michael N. Danielson and Ruşen Keleş, *The Politics of Rapid Urbanization: Government and Growth in Modern Turkey:* Holmes and Meier, New York, 1985.

in achieving the aims of the resource conservation and rational management. The concern for maximizing the private rather than the public interest in using the urban land dominated the practice of urban planning. National and local politicians do not hesitate to cooperate with major actors who have significant private interests in land speculation. Under such conditions, the constitutional provisions concerning the protection of natural resources such as land, water, forestry, historical, cultural and architectural assets could not be implemented properly.

Legal and Ethical Considerations

The right to land ownership, like all other rights and freedoms requires that the owners of the rights must have certain responsibilities towards the society and future generations. Urban land ownership is particularly important in this respect. The success of land use planning and all kinds of regulatory measures for the protection of natural resources depend upon the acceptance of putting rational limits on the use of land ownership. In the theory of Political Science, the following sentence is often used to prevent the emergence of dictatorial tendencies: "Power corrupts, absolute power corrupts absolutely". There is no doubt that land ownership too has a corrupting effect. But, its most dangerous impact may be expressed in the following sentence: "Land ownership corrupts; absolute land ownership corrupts absolutely". Especially in the implementation of land use plans, only a sensitive balance between the private interests and the public interest can ensure the sustainability of a sustainable urban development.

The main objective of the Reference Framework of Climate Change adopted in Rio de Janeiro in 1992 was to set up definite limits to the greenhouse gas emissions. It was put into effect in 1994 by the ratification of more than 194 states. The related Kyoto Protocol was put into effect in 2005. Major states have taken different positions vis a vis the Kyoto Protocol. a) The first category of the European states including Germany, Italy, France, The Netherlands, Denmark, Finland, Sweden and Japan was depended to a certain extent to the imported energy sources while at the same time they could not say no to the diminishing the use of fossil fuels in order to preserve the quality of their living standards. b) In the second category were such states as the U.S.A., the Russian Federation, Peoples' Republic of China, Mexico, and Brazil which possess cheap energy sources, but their "culture" of energy use was not developed sufficiently. c) In the third category are Norway and Australia in addition to oil producing Arab countries. In all these categories, those states which seem definitely against to carry out their international commitments were The U.S.A., The Russian Federation, Brazil and the Peoples' Republic of China. Of course, the national interests in the narrow sense of the term influenced these official positions. The position of the European Union is quite clear. According to the principle of "Common, but differentiated responsibility", the states must assume the responsibility in this field in proportion to their part in the atmospheric pollution.

Industrialized states which ratified the Kyoto Protocol have accepted to reduce their greenhouse gas emissions between 2008 and 2012 by at least 5 percent of the 1990 levels. The U.S.A. was against such position. However, the problem has been solved to a large extent during the Paris Summit on Climate Change in December 2015 upon the acceptance by more than 196 states the responsibility to reduce their levels of greenhouse gas emissions. The Agreement has been put into effect definitely in April 2016. If its principles are going to be implemented properly, more than 80 percent of the countries which use fossil fuels at present, will begin to use renewable energy sources by giving up using coal and natural gas. We must keep in mind that buildings that not only conserve energy but meet their own requirements through renewable energy sources, could transform urban centers in such a way so that they can get the most out of the land, water and energy they actually use.

Over-Consumption and Bioethics

Over-consumption fostered by the meta-capitalist period and globalization has resulted in excessive exploitation of the Earth's resources. Former French Minister of Environment, Madame Corinne Lepage, in her book entitled *To Live in a Different Way (Vivre Autrement)* [6] drew the attention of the world to the fact that the survival of the ecosystem can only be ensured by radically changing the consumption patterns of human beings which have been shaped mainly by meta capitalist development and the goal of private interest maximization. She suggests that consumption patterns in each sector, such as energy, housing and building, education and public health, transportation and communications and the like have to be changed in order to guarantee the livability of the ecosystem as a whole. Actually, we do

6   This book has been translated into Turkish (y Ruşen Keleş and Can Umut Çiner) and published by İmge Publishers, Ankara in 2019.

not propose the abolition of the capital, but as suggested by Madame Arvanities, we advise using it wisely. This requires to put into effect a global mission to convert material power games into games of ethics and values.[7] French writer and journalist Hervé Kempf went even further, in his book entitled as *To Safeguard the Planet, Escape Capitalism (Pour Sauver la Planete, Sortez du Capitalisme),* to propose the abandonment of the capitalist system itself. This attitude was of course completely opposite to the suggestion made by the World Bank in 1996 requiring that all kinds of plans must be replaced by the market forces.[8]

The position of the European Union was quite clear since the beginning. Its clear position was reflected into its Fundamental Charters. The importance of sustainable development has been underlined in the Section called Solidarity in the Charter of Fundamental Rights appended to the Lisbon Treaty (2009). The Article 37 of the Treaty stipulates that" A high level of environmental protection and the improvement of the quality of environment must be integrated into policies of the Union and ensured in accordance with the principle of sustainable development". According the Article 191 of the consolidated version of the Treaty of Lisbon on the functioning of the European Union, "The policy of the European Union in the sector of the environment will seek to achieve the following goals which reflect morally defensible values": a) "The conservation, protection and improvement of the quality of the environment, b) safeguarding of the health of individual, c) the sensible

7   Agni Vlavianos-Arvanitis, *Biopolicy: The Bioethics of Climate Change Mitigation,* B.I.O., Athens, 2015., p.23.

8   World Bank, **World Development Report, 1996, From** *Plan to Market,* Washington D.C., 1996.

and rational use of natural resources, and d) promotion, at
the international level, of measures to deal with regional or
global environmental problems, and in particular, to combat climate change."

The climate change crisis, which is global in nature, demands that world leaders move beyond their comfort zone
and assume greater responsibility and action. Nations must
begin to balance their short-term national self-interests with
a greater sense of our universal bioethical responsibilities as
human beings on this planet. We must keep in mind that
it is urgent to identify common bioethical concerns across
a broader spectrum of society and to develop conservation
strategies and climate change mitigation policies that stem
explicitly from bioethical values.[9] In other words, the conti-
nuity of bios should be regarded as a primary profit in our
daily life. Green buildings, clean urban transport and agriculture in the city are the preconditions of creating an environmentally sustainable biopolis in which human and natural populations live in harmonious balance.

Concluding Remarks

There are a number of factors that seem to be responsible
for the ineffectiveness of present policies of sustainable urban development.[10]

First of all, there can be no urban sustainability in the
absence of socio-economic sustainability. Socio-economic

---

9   Agni Vlavianos-Arvanitis, *Biopolicy,* p.9.
10 Ruşen Keleş, "Sustainable urban development under Unsustainable Con-
    diitions", in Derya Oktay (ed.), *Inquiry into Urban Environment: Issues
    concerning Urban, Housing and the Built Environment,* Eastern Mediter-
    ranean University, Urban Research and development Center, EMU Press,
    Gazimağusa, 2006, pp. 27-38.

sustainability may be understood as the development of a society that ensures and reconciles social justice, economic efficiency, democratic participation, cultural diversity and rational environmental governance. Sustainable development is a holistic concept, like total quality, and its success depends upon people's behaviour, value systems, transparency and accountability in both public and private decision-making.

A second factor affecting the chances for the sustainability of urban development has something to do with globalization. In other words, sustainable urban development depends on the normal functioning of the political economy in favor of the public interest. At present, we witness a regression phenomenon in this respect. The public sphere is shrinking and the space reserved for the private interest and the market forces is expanding. Competitiveness, technological innovation, liberalization, deregulation and privatization have become the new commandments of our times and the concern for sustainable urban development has no chance to get the support of European and other international financial institutions in case they attempt to resist them. As a result, their chances to reach the balance may be bound to be curtailed considerably.

A third point is that urban sustainability cannot be left to the market forces alone, because the market pretends to govern within a short- term perspective whereas sustainability is a matter of long-term concern. In this framework, only the largest cities have significant political power to play with and to pursue their own global metropolitan strategies, entering into alliance with global firms and competing with each other to be the most effective location for global firms. As a result, the free application of market principles and mechanisms make the cities other than the metropolitan ones quite important to govern the ongoing process in the direction towards sustainability.

Finally, basic obstacles before ensuring the sustainable development cannot be overcome simply by acting in accordance with the principles of national and international law. What is needed is to complement the compatibility of legal rules with strengthening human behaviour by ethical considerations. With this important point in mind, the principle of sustainable development must be integrated into national policies and programmes. The loss of environmental resources has far reaching implications for the welfare of the current generation as well as for the ability of future generations to maintain and improve the welfare and living conditions of human beings. Because most of the natural resources are now being rapidly degraded or polluted, or are at risk of further deterioration.

Selfish or individualistic interests do not transform themselves spontaneously into collective interests, and if followed unconsciously, rapidly end up with creating ecological crises. One cannot talk about the public interest without taking into consideration the future. It becomes meaningless, in case it does not go beyond the sum of the private interests of the present generation.

There is no doubt that the realization of all beautifully formulated goals and principles depends upon the awareness, will and willingness of the people. This is the reason why democracy was defined by Abraham Lincoln as the governance of the people, by the people and for the people. As we had emphasized together with my late and distinguished

Greek colleague Professor Agni Vlavianos-Arvanitis, The Founding President of the Biopolitics International Organization, in a meeting organized by the World Society of Ekistics (Human Settlements) in Mumbai some years ago, "Culture is an essential element of a sustainable city. The environmental conditions, as part of the survival of humanity, are affected by our culture, which is, in turn, shaped by the environmental conditions. Culture as defended by the Biopolitics International Organization represents a conscious effort to ensure necessary interdependence. Aesthetic values, music, science, the arts, politics, economics, and determination to change the existing consumption patterns, shaped by behavioral consequences of the contemporary capitalist development and globalization can all come together on the struggle for a better quality of life."

Bibliography

Algan, Nesrin, Pınar, Nur Münevver, Özel Demiralp, Duygu and Çörtoğlu, Feza Sencer (eds.), *İnsanların Doğayla Kenetlenmesi: Kentte ve Doğal Alanda, Kutuplardan Ekvatora* (Uluslararası Sempozyum: 8-9 June 2017), (*Connecting People to Nature in the City and on the Land, From the Poles to the Equator*), Ankara University, Ankara, 2019.

Ascher, François, *Les Nouveaux Principes de L'Urbanisme*, Ed. L'Aube, Poche Essai, Paris, 2004.

Birnbacher, Dieter, *La Responsabilité envers les générations futures*, Presses Universitaires de France, Paris, 1994.

Bourg, Dominique et Whiteside, Kerry, *Vers une démocratie écologique*, Ed. Seuil, Paris, 2010.

Brown-Weiss, Edith, *In Fairness to Future Generations*, United Nations University and Transnational Publishers, Tokyo and New York, 1988.

Cengiz, Vural, "Carbon Dioxide Emmissioms Embedded in Exports for 40 Major Economies in 2000 and 2009; Calculating a Suggested Export Carbon Tax Rate for Major Economies and Their Sectors", Ph.D. Disseration, Çukurova University, Adana, 2010.

Danielson, Michael and Keleş, Ruşen, *The Politics of Rapid Urbanization: Government and Growth in Modern Turkey,* Holmes and Meier, New York, 1985

Ecologie Politique: Les Villes Durables, Paris, No:13, Printemps, 1993.

Ergönül, Sema, Gündeş, Selin ve Erbaş, A.Erdem, *Green Age, 1st International Symposium,* 6-8 December, 2010, Mimar Sinan Fine Arts University, Faculty of Architecture, İstanbul, 2010.

Eryıldız, Semih, *Ekokent: Çevreyi Geliştirici Kentleşme,* Gece Yay., Ankara, 1995.

European Commission, *European Spatial Development Perspectives: Towards Balanced and Sustainable Development of the Territory of the European Union (ESDP),* Potsdam, May 1999.

Godard, Olivier, "Projets et recompositions par les échelles territoriales", *Pouvoirs Locaux,* Paris, No: 34, 1997, pp. 36-37.

Jepon, Edwards Jr., Edwards, Mary M., "How Possible is Sustainable Urban Development? An Analysis of Planners' Perspectives about New Urbanism. Smart Growth and Ecological City", *Planning Practice and Research,* Vol. 25, No:4, August 2010, pp. 417*437.

Jonas, Hans, *Une Ethique pour la Nature,* Desclée de Brouver, Paris, 1993.

Jonas, Hans, Le Principe responsabilité, Flammarion, Paris, 1995.

Keleş, Ruşen, "Urban Planning and Sustainable Land Management in Turkish Municipalities", *Local Land and Soil News,* Zurich, No:44-45, 1/13, 2013.

Keleş, Ruşen, "The Sustainability of Sustainable Urbanization", paper presented to the 30th International Symposium on Sustainable Spatial Development of the European Continent: Interdisciplinary Approaches, June 15-16, 2000, Strasbourg.

Keleş, Ruşen, "Impact of Urbanization on Fertile Agricultural Land in Turkey", Driss Ben Ali, Antonio Di Guilio, Mustapha Lasram et Marc lavergne (sous la direction de…), *Urbanisation et Agriculture: Conflits et Complémentarités*, L'Harmattan, CIHEAM, Paris, 1996, pp.145-154.

Keleş, Ruşen, "Urban Development and Sustainable Management for the Mediterranean Towns", Paper prepared for the meeting of Working Group *for Urban Management, Mediterranean Commission for Sutainable Development*, Split, Croatia, April 26-27, 1999.

Keleş, Ruşen, National Protection: The Case of Protected Areas in Turkey", *Naturopa*, Council of Europe, No:85, 1997, pp. 23-24.

Keleş, Ruşen, "Sustainable Urban Development under Unsustainable Conditions", Derya Oktay (ed.), *Inquiry into Urban Environment: Issues Concerning Urban, Housing and the Built Environment*, Eastern Mediterranean University, Urban Research and Development Center, EMU Press, Gazimağusa, 2006.

Keleş, Ruşen," Our Ethical Duties Towards Future Generations in a Globalising World", VIII. World Conference on Bio-Ethics, Universal Bioethics, Principal Dimensions, Gijon, Spain, 13-16 May 2013.

Lepage, Corinne, *Vivre Autrement*, Grasset, Paris, 2009.

Kempf, Hervé, *Pour sauver la Planete, sortez du capitalisme*, Ed.Seuil, Paris, 2009.

Kural, Nerkis, "A Proposal for the Analysis of a Design Process for Urban Sustainability", Ergönül, Sema, Gündeş Selin and Erbaş, A. Erdem, (eds.) *Green Age,*pp.10-21.

OECD, Environmental Performance Review, Turkey, 2019, Paris, 2019.

Oktay, Derya, *Planning Housing Environments for Sustainability: Evaluations in Cypriot Settlements*, Yapı Endüstri Merkezi, İstanbul, 2001.

Oktay, Derya (ed.), *Inquiry into Urban Environment: Issues Concerning Urban, Housing and the Built Environment*, Eastern Mediterranean University, EMU Press, Gazimağusa, 2006.

Owens, Susan, "*Interpreting Sustainable Development: The Case of Land use Planning*", The Political Quarterly, 1997, pp.87-97.

Paquot, Thierry et Younes, Chris (eds.), *Philosophie de l'Environnement et Milieux Urbains,* La Découverte, Paris 2010.

Petrella, Ricardo, "Is it Possible to Promote Intermediate Cities, Sustainability within the Present Context of Triumphant Global Market Competitive Capitalism?", *Intermeditae Cities in Search of Sustainability,* European Foundation for the Improvement of Living and Working Conditions, *The* Research and the Attica Workshop, Lavrion, 4-6 October 1995, Luxembourg, 1996.

Petrini, Carlo, "The Rights of Future Generations in Environmental Ethics", *International Journal of Ethics,* Vol.7, No:3-4, 2011.

Rémond-Gouilloud, Martine, *Droit du Détruire: Essai sur le Droit* de *LEnvironnement,* Presses Universitaires de France, Paris, 1989.

The United Nations, Economic Commission for Europe, *Guidelines on Sustainable Human Settlements: Planning and Management,* Geneva, 1996.

The World Bank, *From Plan to Market, World Development Plan 1996,* Washington D.C., 1996.

The World Bank, *The State in a Changing World, World Development Report 1997,* Washington D.C., 1997.

The World Bank, *Entering the 21st Century, World Development Report,* Washington, D.C., 2000.

Tuğaç, Çiğdem, *Türkiye'de Kentsel İklim Değişikliği İçin Eko-Kompakt Kentler,(Eco-Compact Cities for Urban Climate Change in Turkey),* Ankara University, Faculty of Political Sciences, Ernst Reuter Center for Urban Studies, No:23, Ankara, 2019

Vlavianos-Arvanitis, Agni, *Environmental Education for Sustainable Development in Turkey,* B.I.O in cooperation with Ankara Univrsity and Municipality of Çankaya, Ankara, 2010.

Vlavianos-Arvanitis, Agni, *Biopolicy: The Bioethics of Climate Change Mitigation,* B.I.O., Athens, 2015.

Vlavianos-Arvanitis, Agni and Keleş, Ruşen (eds.), *Biopolitics: The Bio-Environment,* Vol. IV., Fifth BIO International Conference, İstanbul, 1992.

World Commission on Environment and Development, Brundt-land Report, *Our Common Future*, Oxford University Press, London, 1986.

Yılmaz, Meltem, "The Concept of Sustainability in European Urban Charter-The City of Malmö as a Sample", Ergönül, Sema, Gündeş, Selin, Erbaş, A.Erdem (eds.), *Green Age*, pp.29-37.

Yılmaz, Meltem and Tüfekçioglu, Dilara, "An Approach Proposal in Sustainable Design: Design from Waste Materials in Context of Re-Use Method", Sustainable Innovation 2019, Road to 2030: Sustainablility, Business Models, Innovation and Design, Abstract under title, Re-use, Repair and Remanufacturing.

Draft Report of the Delegation in Charge of Monitoring Local and Regional Democracy in Russian Federation[*]

Mr. Christopher NEWBURY[**],
Mr. Knud ANDERSEN[***],
Prof. Dr. Ruşen KELEŞ[****]

Introduction

The Delegation of the Council of Europe in charge of monitoring the practice of local self-government in Russian Federation has paid two visits to Russian Federation during 16-17 December 2009 and 14-15 April 2010. During both monitoring visits, the team had contacts with the representatives of the Federal Government, local authorities, various professional organizations, the NGO's and the members of the Russian Delegation to the Congress of Local and Regional Authorities of the Council of Europe. In both visits, the members of the delegation have visited Moscow, Chelyabinsk and Miasskoye, a rural settlement near Chelyabinsk. We had contacts with the Union of Small Cities and Towns,

[*] Report submitted to the Council of Europe, The Congress of Local and Regional Authorities of Europe by Christopher Newbury (UK), Knud Andersenn (Denmark), Prof. Dr.Ruşen Keleş (Tırkey), Strasbourg, May, 2010.
[**] United Kingdom.
[***] Denmark.
[****] Turkey.

European Club of Municipal Experts, EU Delegation in Moscow, leading figures of the Press, Moscow Helsinki Group and some politicians representing the opposition.

The last monitoring of Russian Federation by the Congress was conducted in 2004 resulted in Recommendation 143 and Resolution 171 on local and regional democracy in Russia in the same year. The main focus of the Congress Recommendation were financial resources and municipal properties, delegation of State powers, central control and supervision over local authorities, their legal protection, the participation of foreigners in public life, federal supervision of regional governance, the concept of regional sovereignty, as well as the power sharing between various levels of government.

The Congress had close concern with the development of local democracy in Russia during the last decade. Since Russia ratified the European Charter of Local Self-Government in 1998, a report was adopted by the Congress Bureau with regard to the compliance with the principles of the Charter by the constituent legal entities of the Russian Federation. Similarly, a fact-finding mission has been accomplished by a Congress Delegation in 1999 to look on the procedure for dismissing local authority officials and the disputes between the mayors and the regional governors. The strengthening of the principle of vertical command (democratic centralism) and limiting of the prerogatives of local government were the main findings of such missions.

More recently, two complaints have been in the agenda of the Institutional Committee of the Congress (October 2009). (One) of these complaints was from the members of the Tula City Council alleging violation of the right of local authorities to be consulted on issues that concern local governance. This right of local authorities originated from the Article 4/6 of the European Charter of Local Self- Government. The subject of (the second) complaint were the amendments to the Federal law on the General Principles Governing the Organization of Local Self-Government in the Russian Federation (131-FZ), concerning the dismissal of mayors by municipal councils on the initiative of the regional governors.

General Legal Framework of Local Self-Government Constitutional Provisions

Most of the legal principles governing local and regional democracy in Russia can be found in the Constitution. As a general rule, Article 3 of the Constitution stipulates that the people exercise their power directly, and also through organs of State power and local authorities. According to the Article 12 of the Constitution. "Local self-government shall be recognized and guaranteed in Russian Federation Local self-government shall operate independently within the bounds of its authority. The bodies of local-self government shall not be part of the State power bodies". The Article 72 (m) of the Constitution, on the other hand, lays down the main rules concerning the establishment of common principles of organization of state authorities and local self-government bodies. There is a reference here to the principle of "shared competences" between the Federation and its subjects, in other words, the local and regional entities. According to his principle, the regions may adopt their own legislation on local self-government provided that this is compatible with federal legislation.

The Article 130-133 of the Constitution possess, pursuant to the provisions of the European Charter of Local Self-Government, detailed rules concerning certain rights and prerogatives of local authorities. Namely, a) local self-government in the Russian Federation shall ensure independent solution by the population of issues, the ownership, use and disposal of municipal property. Local self-government shall be exercised by the citizens through referendums, elections and forms of expression of their will through elected and other bodies of local self-government (Art. 130).

b) Local self-government shall be exercised in the cities, rural areas and other localities taking into account historical and other local traditions. The structure of bodies of local self-government shall be determined by the population independently. The borders of territorial entities under local self-government shall be changed only the consent of their population (Art. 131).

c) The bodies of local self-government shall independently manage municipal property, form, approve and execute the local budget, establish local taxes and levies, ensure law and order and solve any other local issues. The bodies of local self-government may be delegated under law with certain State powers with the transfer of material and financial resources required to exercise such powers. The exercise of the powers transferred shall be supervised by the State (Art. 132).

d) Local self-government in the Russian Federation shall be guaranteed by the right to judicial protection and compensation for any additional expenses arising from the decisions passed by the bodies of State power and the ban on the restrictions of the rights of local self-government established by the Constitution and federal laws (Art. 133).

Fundamental Laws on Local Self-Government

The main laws on local self-government include a) "the Federal Law on the General Principles of Local Self-Government in the Russian Federation" (Law No: 131-FZ, 6 October 2003), and b) "the Federal Law on the General Principles Applying to Legislative and Executive Bodies of the Constituent Entities of the Russian Federation" (Law No: 184-FZ, 6 October 1999). In addition to these framework laws, several other laws have been put into force between 2000 and 2009, which contain certain fundamental provisions regarding local self-government:

1. Federal Law on the Guarantees of the Access to the Information about the State Authority Bodies 'and Local Self-Government Bodies' Activities, (Law No: 8-FZ, 9 February 2009, entered into force in 1 January 2010).

2. Federal Law on Municipal Public Service in the Russian Federation (Law No: 25-FZ, 2 March 2007).

3. Federal Law on the Basic Guarantees of the Russian Federation Citizens "Electoral Rights and Right to Vote in Referendums" (Law No: 67-FZ, 12 June 2002).

4. Federal Law on the State Registration of the Municipalities' Statutes (Law No: 97-FZ, 21 July 1995).

5. Federal Constitutional Law on the Referendums in the Russian Federation, (Law No: 5-FKZ, 28 June 2004).

6. Federal Law on the State and Municipal Unitary Enterprises, (Law No: 161-FZ, 14 November 2002).

A large proportion of the powers of local self-government is governed by the following legislations: Civil Code of the Russian Federation (1994); The Land Code (2001), and the Town Planning Code (2004). The basic legislation regulating **financial matters** of local self-government includes the Budget Code (1998) and the Tax Code (1999). In order to complete the legal bases of local self-government in Russia, two more laws have to be added to the list. The first is the Law on the Organization of Local Self-Government in Moscow, the City with Federal Status (Law No: 56, November 2002), and the second is the Law on the Organization of Local Self-Government in St. Petersburg, the City with Federal Status (Law No: 420-79, 23 September 2009).

Territorial Divisions

The territory of the Russian Federation is composed of 21 republics, 6 territories (kraya), 49 regions (oblasti), 2 cities with federal status (Moscow and St. Petersburg), 1 autonomous region, and 10 autonomous districts (okrugi). According to the municipal reform carried out following the promulgation of the Federal Law on the General Organizational Principles of Local Self Government in the Russian Federation (Law No: 131-FZ, 6 October 2003), the number of municipalities in Russia doubled from 12.000 to 24. 244. The distribution of municipalities to different territorial entities on the basis of their legal status is as the followings: 516 urban districts (okrugs), 1.801 municipal districts, 1.732 urban settlements, 19. 849 rural settlements, and 236 intra-city municipal districts (territories) of cities with federal status (Moscow and St. Petersburg).

Selected Problems of Local Self-Government in Russian Federation

Relationships of Regions with Local Authorities

Russian Federation is not a unitary state and therefore regional entities enjoy broad legislative and executive powers emanating from the Federal Constitution. But the ways in which the regional entities use their powers may have far reaching implications for the autonomy of local authorities. It is observed that where subjects of the Federation (regions or republics) operate largely or entirely subservient to the regional authority. It has been noted that the more a regional authority inclined towards an absolute patrimonialism the more local authorities were likely to be under pressure. In some regions such as Vologda and Tambov where the regional administrations were supportive of local autonomy, but there were many others where local autonomy was kept to the absolute minimum (Adrian Campbell, Satoshi Mizobata, Kazuho Yokogawa, Elena Denezhkina, "Institutional Transition and Local Self-Government in Russia", Kier Discussion paper Series, Kyoto Institute of Economic Research, No: 640, October, 2007, pp. 11-12). There seems to be a struggle for supremacy between mayors and governors. Local-regional tension sometimes tends to manifest itself through individualized conflicts between governors and mayors which ultimately end up with de facto restriction of local autonomy. Such tensions endemic to the system prevent local authorities to be really autonomous entities. Support for a balance of power between various levels of government would have helped to ensure proper operation of constitutional democracy. "Recentralization" of resources and administrative recentralization taken place after the beginnings of 2000 seem to have led to the weakening of local self-government.

If this trend is not reversed through suitable means, the relationships between the regions and local self-government would continue to be problematic and incompatible with international commitments of Russian Federation. Namely, the Reference Framework for Regional Democracy of the Council of Europe provides certain obligations for the member states. According to the Resolution 299 (18 March 2010) of the Congress, this Reference Framework has to be used in monitoring activities of the Congress. This legal document requires that "The relationships between regional authorities and other sub-national territorial authorities be governed by the principles of regional self-government set out in this document, and local self-government set out in the European Charter of Local Self-Government and the principle of subsidiarity". Similarly, according to the Congress Recommendation 240 (2008) (Art. 8.3), "Regional authorities shall cooperate with local authorities in the pursuit of objectives of general interest and to meet citizens' needs". There is no doubt that increasing intervention in the affairs of local self-government by upper- level (regional) authorities is incompatible with the Article 4(3) of and the expressions in the Preamble of the European Charter of Local Self-Government, regarding the principle of subsidiarity.

Sharing Competencies between Different Levels of Government

Our common observation is that competences of local authorities are not always adequate, nor they are always clearly defined. There is often a large gap between competencies and resources that will be taken up further below. The Constitution of the Federation determines the main areas falling within the jurisdiction of the Federation and the subjects, and the right of the subjects to enjoy full State authority outside those areas. The local authorities are empowered to carry out all public services of local interest. These include socio-economic development of the municipality, pre-school, primary, general and vocational education, public health and the sanitary welfare of the population, maintenance of the public order, land use planning, social protection and employment, environmental protection, and the safeguarding against the fire. Federal legislation entitles municipal authorities to fulfill certain state functions delegated to them. The delegation of state competencies to local authorities is governed by federal law and the legislation of the Federation's subjects.

It was initially intended to define clearly the competencies of all types of municipalities and thus to avoid duplications in the public service. However, as a result of recent legislative amendments, the scope of shared competencies is broadened. It was reported that 42 amendments to the Law on Local Self-Government have taken place during several years following its promulgation in 2003. Type of public services falling in this category such as public transport, support for agricultural production, management of emergency situations, civil defense, etc., were not matched by the required financial and human resources. Consequently, local authorities have been forced to bear the responsibility of performing numerous additional services without having necessary resources to carry them out. As a result, there has been a problem of the forced transfer of competencies from both urban and rural settlements to the larger municipal districts with the accompanying financial resources.

Recent legislative proposals to amend further the Federal Law No: 131 on the General Principles of Local Self-Government as well as the Federal Law No: 184 on the General Principles of Organization of Legislative and Executive Organs of the State aim at setting up a regime of substitution by Subjects of Federation of Local Authorities and to ensure the joint responsibility of the State and local authorities in performing local public services of high quality. In the case where the federal law allows the regional parliaments to adopt a law on the power of substitution in the regional capitals, this would not only undermine the strength of the law itself, but also the guarantees recognized to local authorities. It would fully undermine the right of citizens to local self-government in capital cities. Compatibility of such developments with the **Article 3(1)**, requiring that local authorities regulate and manage a substantial share of public affairs, and with the **Article 4(4)**, stipulating that powers given to local authorities shall normally be full and exclusive and they may not be undermined or limited by another, central or **regional** authority.

Regulating and managing a substantial share of public affairs under their own responsibility clearly means that local authorities should not be limited to acting as agents of other levels of government, which to a larger extent seems to be the case.

Financial Resources of Local Authorities

Many settlements have an acute lack of financial resources to carry out their functions assigned to them by specific legislation. Financial problems of local authorities include not only the insufficiency of financial resources, but at the same time, the freedom to determine expenditure priorities, the exercise of political choices and the determination of local taxes and charges by them. We have real doubts about the effective working of local accountability, especially in smaller municipalities. In the light of the **Article 9 (2, 3 and 4)** of the Charter, such practices can hardly be defended. Arrangements for equalization seems to exist, but are primitive, so that it makes a great difficulty for a locality whether it has local industries to contribute to its tax base. There seems to be a pressing need to make the equalization system work more efficiently and equitably in order to comply with the **Article 9 (5)** of the Charter. Ineffectiveness in the implementation of the equalization mechanisms exists also at the regional level. Besides, there seems to be far too much use of sector-specific grants and grants earmarked for specific project. Such a situation undermines undoubtedly the freedom of local authorities to exercise discretion within their own sphere of competence which is guaranteed by the **Article 9 (7)** of the Charter. Finally, it appears to us that not all local authorities have access to the national capital market. This neglect cannot be reconciled with the **Article 9 (8)** of the Charter.

The share of the own resources in total budgets of the municipalities is between 30 to 50 percent, of which 10 to 20 percent comes from local taxes, mainly from the property tax. The remaining part is composed of the federal and regional transfers. As a general observation, revenues are not proportional to the competencies of the municipalities. The Congress had stressed, in its 2004 Recommendation (No:

171), that the economic and financial base of most local authorities were not adequate for the performance of local public services. The Russian authorities were called by the Congress to supplement the framework laws by amendments to the Tax Code and the Budget Code so that local authorities were provided with necessary financial resources.

In the meantime, certain steps have been taken by the Federal Government to reduce own resources of local authorities and to increase their dependence on the transfer from central and regional government resources which has resulted in further reducing their fiscal autonomy. This move was parallel to increasing the scope of local competencies during the period 2005-2008, resulting in increased expenditures of local authorities without a matching increase in local revenues. In a report submitted to the Parliamentary Assembly in March 2009, it has been pointed out that local government reform has, paradoxically, led to increased centralization of financial flows. For example, the share of the transfers in the consolidated budget of the Russian Federation increased from 44 percent in 1999 to 66 percent in 2007. Equally, according to the figures provided by the Ministry of Finance for the year 2006, only 2 percent of the municipalities were financially self-sufficient while 60 percent received more than half of their revenues from the transfers.

We have to be point out that rural settlements, which constitute the great majority in total local government entities, also have been stripped of a substantial part of their revenue base. Since nearly two thirds of their territory is owned by the state, rural settlements are deprived of receiving the land tax to increase their budget revenues. As a result, rural settlements are forced to, in many regions, to transfer their competences and financial resources to municipal districts.

Such a situation is certainly not compatible with the provision of the **Article 9 (1) and 9 (2)** of the Charter which stipulate that local authorities shall be entitled, within national economic policy, to adequate financial resources of their own, of which they may control freely within the framework of their powers. Moreover, local authorities' financial resources shall be commensurate with the responsibilities provided for by the Constitution and the law. The Recommendation 228 of the Congress (2007) on the Draft Additional Protocol to the European Charter of Local Self-Government underlines the need to provided foreseeable and sufficient resources to local authorities for the effective discharge of the competencies and responsibilities. According to the same Recommendation, where local authorities are discharged with additional responsibilities, they have to receive transfers of adequate resources or they will be authorized to raise new resources. In the event of a transfer, the resources shall be at least equivalent to those which the higher-level authority allocated to them.

Changes in Local Authority Boundaries

The European Charter of Local Self-Government requires **(Article 5)** that the changes in local authority boundaries shall not be made without consultation of the local communities concerned, possibly by means of a referendum where this is permitted by statute. This article is about "changes in local authority boundaries", which must include mergers, and the need for "prior consultation of the local communities concerned". This consultation has failed to happen in

Russia as intended by the **Article 5** mentioned above. Given the huge number of municipalities with very small populations, we recognize the desirability of real change in this respect. Besides, the **Article 4 (6)** stipulates that local authorities shall be consulted in so far as possible, in due time and in appropriate way, in the planning and decision-making processes for all matters which concern them closely. It should also be stressed that the obligation to consult with respective bodies of local authorities in not only a requirement laid down in the **Article 4 (6)**, but also in the **Articles 5** and **9 (6)** of the Charter.

Recommendation 228 of the Congress (Art. 11), requiring that any decision by a higher level authority concerning one or more local authorities must be adopted means of a procedure comprising, at least, **prior notification** of the proposed decision to the local authorities concerned, their right to access to the relevant administrative documents, their entitlement to state their own positions within a reasonable time and the obligation to give reasons for the decision, taking account of the positions expressed by the local authorities.

It is known that 12 local referendums and 146 voting were organized on changes to municipal boundaries in 79 Russian regions on 1 March 2009, according to the above mentioned rules. At first glances, this was reflecting a compliance with the provisions of the Charter. However, there have been many other cases where local authorities concerned have not been consulted on the boundary changes connected with merging decisions of higher level authorities. Mr. Timchenko referred to a recent e-mail message by Mr. Markwart drawing the attention to the fact that "referendum

on the merger of municipalities had been abolished and replaced by the consent of the municipal councils."

Mr. Emil Markwart warned that the new amendments
to law 131-FZ will allow local authorities to merge without consulting their populations. Such a stand cannot be
regarded as compatible with the democratic principles enshrined in Charter of Local Self-Government and the repeatedly expressed legal position of the Constitutional Court
of the Russian Federation.

As a part of the local government reform in Russian Federation there is a pronounced trend towards merging rural
and urban settlements into larger municipal districts. The
main reasons expressed in favor of such enlargement in the
absence of revenue resources and the need for increasing
efficiency in the performance of local public services. Some
of the recent amendments to Law 131-FZ serve to facilitate
the merging of settlements and to oblige local authorities
to proceed with a referendum on the issue even where they
have no interest in a merger. The delegation heard that many
small settlements are in favor of mergers since the lack of
resources sufficient to provide services.

In November 2007, the Congress was informed about
the boundary change in one of the largest and richest municipal districts (Odintsovsky) in the Moscow Region. This
was regarded as an attempt to change the boundaries of a
local authority without the consent of the local authorities
concerned. It required to dissolve 16 constituent municipalities and to merge them into a new legal entity. This move
was not supported by 4 out of the 16 communities concerned. The initiative was put to referendum and the result
was against the merger.

The case of Tula complaint is closely related with the boundary changes in municipalities without the consent of the community and to merge them into larger units. It was upon the adoption of a new legislation in 2008 by the Tula Regional Parliament that several members of the Tula Municipal Council lodged a complaint to the Congress in 2009. The said legislation was changing the electoral system of municipal elections for cities of more than 400.000 inhabitants from majority to proportional system. At the same time, Law No: 1024-ZTO of 9 June 2008, namely, the Law on the Types of Election Systems, the Manner and Conditions for their Application in Municipal Elections in the Tula Region, as contested in the court, on the grounds that the local authorities in Tula had not been consulted and as a result, the **Article 6 (4)** of the European Charter does not prohibit taking a decision without consultation with local authorities. According to the Court, consultations with local self-government in adopting the laws on local self-government are simply optional but not obligatory. In march 2009, the Prosecutor of the Tula Region rejected the case on the grounds that the Framework Law on Local Self-Government in Russia (No: 131-FZ) stipulates that systems for municipal elections are determined by the regional law (Art. 23) and the requirement in the Charter to consult local authorities "in so far as possible" does not mean that a decision taken without such consultation is null and void. Similarly, the Supreme Court of the Russian Federation, in its turn, upheld the decision by the Tula Regional Court. When the attmpt to bring the issue to the Constitutional Court of the Russian Federation is failed, the case was referred to the

European Court of Human Rights in Strasbourg. Its decision is still pending.

We have to remind that the Congress Recommendation 171 (2005) had stressed that "consultation of local authorities has to be a required part of policy-making and administrative processes, enabling the wishes of local authorities to be known in good time and properly taken into account in the decisions of central and regional authorities".

Dismissal of Mayors

The Federal Law on Local Self-Government (Law No: 131-FZ) stipulates the specific grounds for the state bodies to temporary takeover of some powers of local self-governments. The dismissal procedure is a part of this process. These pertain to the cases when local governments run a fiscal debt exceeding a certain proportion of their own revenues or when appropriations assigned to them by the State bodies for carrying out delegated State power have been disbursed for other purposes. In all these cases a proper court decision is needed. The dismissal procedure can be initiated by at least one third of the municipal councilors or by the regional governor. If the council finds the annual report unsatisfactory with a two thirds majority of its members, the dismissal is confirmed. If the attempt of the council for dismissal fails, it may be repeated two months later.

The list of grounds for dismissal are as the followings: a) decisions, actions by the head of the municipality which entailed the consequences ser out by Article 75, Part 1, Paragraphs 2 and 3 of the Federal Law 131-FZ; b) failure to carry out for a period of at least three months, the responsibilities in regard to federal legislation and by the municipal statute or in regard to powers assigned to local governments by federal or regional authorities; c) negative evaluation of the mayor's activities by the representative assembly for two consecutive years, following the presentation of this activity report.

The new law was passed by the Federal Assembly of the Russian Federation in April 2009 and entered into force in May 2009 (Law No: 90-FZ). This Law amended the Articles 35, 36, 37, 40 and 74 of the Federal Law No: 131- FZ which deals with the powers of the representative body and the chief executives, whether the mayor or the head of the municipality elected directly by popular vote or from among the councilors or the head of the head of local administration contracted by the representative body. The major aim of the new law was to enhance the authority of the elected local assembly by making the head of the local administration more responsible and accountable to the representative body. A requirement was introduced for the mayor to present an annual activity report to the municipal council which must deal both with local public affairs and specific stat functions devolve to local authorities by federal or regional laws.

In so far as the requirement for the submission of an annual activity report is concerned, there seems to be no compliance problem with the European Charter of Local Self-Government, since the Article 3 (2) authorizes "the councils or assemblies composed of members freely elected by secret ballot on the basis of direct, equal, universal suffrage and which may possess organs responsible to them". One may argue that the amendment aims to improve the quality of the governance at the local level. However, the amended law, at the same time, enlarges the scope of the powers of local assemblies to dismiss the mayor upon the initiative of members of the council and the governor of the region (Art. 74. 1).

Apart from the compliance with national legislation, compliance with international conventions and the interests of civil society, the fact that obedience to certain procedural requirements seems to be neglected needs to be emphasized. For example, it is reported that following the adoption of the amendments, local assemblies have removed from office the mayors of certain towns such as Chaikovsky (Permsky krai), Ozersky (Chelyabinskaya oblast), Kupino (Novosibirskaya oblast), Suzdai (Vladimirskaya oblast) upon the initiative of the respective governors. Not much care has been showed to observe the procedures prescribed by the law which required that the assemblies. Similarly, the dismissed mayors have been denied the possibility to express their own view before the assemblies. The electorate was not even informed about the decision.

According to the arguments in favor of the amendments, there is neither specific legal restraints nor interdictions concerning the procedures of dismissal of elected members of the municipal bodies. Therefore, these issues can be resolved by the local self-government concerned by itself in accordance with the national legislation in force. Secondly, it was argued that by these amendments an important innovation has been created to enhance the authority of the local assembly, and the head of municipality was made more responsible to the representative body. Presenting an annual activity report on public affairs and on specific state functions devolve to local authorities by federal or regional authorities would enhance the quality of local democracy. Thirdly, the introduction of an annual report was first initiated by the federal legislation. Such changes in the legislation had no other aim than improving local governance. Therefore, this does comply with the European Charter. Because the Charter requires that the rights of local government shall be exercised by democratically constituted councils or assemblies. Finally, one of the arguments in favor of the amendments is concerned with the absence of judicial procedures in calling off the powers of the head of municipality. The argument is that local self-government bodies have the right to appeal in court any time in accordance with the Article 47 of the Russian Constitution.

On the other hand, numerous criticisms may be lodged to the amendments made to the basic legislation on local self-government. First of all, it can be argued that these innovations allowing the dismissal of mayors by the local council upon the initiative of the regional governor contradict the fundamental principle of the interdependence of local self-government and introduce extrajudicial procedures for mayor's dismissal. Secondly, these amendments do not take into account the mechanism of the election of the mayors. If the mayor is elected directly by the population of the municipality, the right of the electorate to local self-government is undermined. Thirdly, the regional governor is granted the power to initiate the procedure of dismissal of the mayors only in cases where the head of municipality breaches his duties to exercise certain state powers devolve to him. Although the administrative supervision by the chief executives of the regions with respect to the execution of the state functions delegated to local authorities is legitimate, their intervention in their purely internal affairs is unacceptable. This would contradict the provision of the **Article 8 (3)** of the Charter. Otherwise, intervention in local affairs by controlling authorities could not be kept in proportion to the importance of the interests which it is intended to protect. Fourthly, no consultation with the electorate is prescribed by the new legislation. This is a position that cannot be reconciled with the **Article 4 (6)** of the Character. Fifthly, by the amendments, "a new institution of out-of-court dismissal" is created along with the existing mechanism of "removal from office only by court decision". This increases the dependence of mayors on the political party in power. As a result, the autonomy of local authorities guaranteed by the Constitution of the Russian Federation and the European Charter of Local Self-Government is considerably restricted (the **Article 8 (2)**). Finally, such frequent changes in legislation make the rules governing local government exceedingly complex. There are too many amendments and amendments of amendments. In these circumstances even the lawyers specialized in municipal affairs are having difficulty to keep up with the changes. There is a clear need to publish a consolidated text of law 131-FZ.

The dismissal of mayors seems to create a serious problem from the standpoint of the provisions of the **Article 7 (1)**, which provides that the conditions of office of local elected representatives shall provide for free exercise of their functions. This is an area in which recent amendments to the law have created some areas of real problems, especially with regard to the removal of heads of municipalities.

Since the amendment to the Article 74. 1. 2 of the Federal Law infringes the principle of the free exercise of local functions, it must be regarded as incompatible (the **Article 4 (4)**). As expressed openly in the Recommendation 228 (2007) on the Draft Additional Protocol to the European Charter of Local Self-Government (Art. 3), the responsibility of the elected or appointed chief executives of local authorities to the council or assembly representing the local authority shall be guaranteed by law in an effective manner. Although these guarantees shall, in particular, ensure that the council or assembly has the deciding say in matter of prime importance to local authority in question, this does not entitle certainly the respective authorities to dismiss the chief executives arbitrarily or under the influence of partisan pressures.

Consultation

The European Charter of Local Self-Government stresses the need to consult local authorities not only with respect to the changes in their boundaries and in connection to the ways in which redistributed resources are to allocated, but also for all matters which concern local authorities directly (the **Article 4 (1)**). Consulting local authorities, regarding all these matters during the decision making and planning stages in due time and in an appropriate way is one of the important preconditions of local autonomy. Numerous evidences exist to show that this obligation, which is inseparable of the principle of subsidiarity, is not fully done.

The right to be consulted has been furthest by the Additional Protocol to the European Charter of Local Self-Government on the Right to Participate in the Affairs of a Local Authority (Parliamentary Assembly, Doc. 11935, 4 June 2009), which stipulates that "In the planning and decision-making processes concerning measures to be undertaken to give effect to the right to participate in the affairs of local authority, local authorities shall be consulted insofar as possible, in due time and in an appropriate way" (Art. 2 (4)).

Problems connected with the Electoral System and its Operation

The members of the monitoring mission have had some real doubts based on their interviews during their meetings with numerous concerned people in Russia both in large and small settlements whether the right of self-government to regulate and manage a substantial share of public affairs **through democratically constituted authorities** is fully honored. These doubts are mainly based on their observations regarding the problems associated with the electoral arrangements. First of all, we are unhappy about the possibility of "closed party list" elections and also the de-registration of all but the very largest parties (those which can prove more than 50.000 members). In particular, local and regional parties cannot now exist at all or put forward candidates in elections at any level, and sometimes independent candidates are prevented from standing in local elections. For example, in rural settlement of Hamatina in October 2009 several people were prevented from standing in local elections because of the closed party list. Concerns were raised with us in the Chelyabinsk Region that some of the seven major parties impose candidates on municipalities from above who are not chosen locally.

On the other hand, it has been pointed out that recent local elections were widely perceived as being flawed. There are many allegations of vote-rigging and abuse of

administrative resources. There were expressions of popular disillusion with the election process. Lack of real choice
and strong opposition in elections were the major complaints. Particularly, local NGO's are no longer allowed to
send official observers to the elections. Similarly, no international observers were present at the last elections. It was
also reported that there were certain irregularities in recent
local elections. For instance in one voting station, a district
with 8000 voters, 2000 people apparently voted in the last 3
minutes. In another district, an extra 5000 votes were cast
in the final 5 minutes of voting. Vote counting seems to becoming les less transparent. Social and public monitoring
of voting should not be prevented. We have been told that
in some places there were different versions of the same
list circulating.

A draft law was presented to the State Duma in 2006 in
order to replace elections of the mayors in regional capitals
by a system of direct appointment. Municipalities which are
the regional administrative centers were going to be treated
differently from other municipalities. Although according
to the Article 3 (2) of the Charter the executive organs of
local authorities need not to be elected directly by the people, the major tendency in contemporary liberal democra-
cies is to elect the executive organs as well. The reaction of
the Congress was positive to then Deputy Prime Minister's
promise that the government was not going to support such
an initiative in favor of appointment.

In 2008, the mandates of two Congress members were
contested on the grounds that they do not have an elected
mandate, because they were not be elected directly by the
people and they were not be accountable to an elected

assembly. Both of these members were representatives of regional administrations in the Federation Council. As such, they were nominated by regional governors and their nomination was confirmed by regional legislators. The fact that they are not held accountable to regional assemblies makes their status questionable in terms of the principles of local democracy. Therefore, an effort has to be made to realize necessary changes in the composition and the status of the Federation Council through a reform procedure as promised by Russian authorities to take place in 2011 in order to make the status of the Federation Council unquestionable.

To sum up, one can argue that several amendments to the Electoral Law (No: 67-FZ) that have been put into force during the last several years caused increasing doubts about their real contribution to the strengthening of local self-government. These changes include a) the introduction of a system of proportional representation in municipal elections, b) a ban on local non-governmental organizations from presenting their own candidates in municipal elections, c) a prohibitively high threshold for the political parties to be represented in the municipal councils.

There is no doubt that the introduction of proportional system into local elections may lead to a degree of instability in local governance while raising threshold levels in the elections may counterbalance the effects of the proportional system. From the point of view of the compatibility of the amendments with the principles of the Charter, only argument may be that they may affect adversely the functioning of the local self-government to achieve the fundamental aims mentioned in the Preamble of the Charter by reducing the enthusiasm of electors and candidates for local democratic processes.

It can be argued that these changes altogether have led to decreasing levels of participation and activism on the part of both electors and candidates. Although a Round Table in Miasskoye where the members of the Monitoring team were present showed that there was a strong interest and enthusiasm at the local level for people to run their own affairs by even setting up street committees, young local democracy in Russia began as something from above. As such it has not taken root. Some of the resulting structures are perceived as even artificial. On the other hand, as mentioned above, there is increasing grassroots activity at the local level. Local activists seem to becoming increasingly articulate and resisting or criticizing what they perceive as government moves to claw back the powers that they were given in the original Law No: 131-FZ. Recent amendments to this Law pave the way for local authorities to decide whether or not to proceed with elections for a directly elected mayor or whether more powers can be invested in "an appointed city manager". Some sectors in the society perceive this as a decline in local democracy.

Observations of the members of the Monitoring Group do not make it possible to conclude that electoral processes at the local level operate in such a way to regard local councils or assemblies, as decision making bodies representing the local people, as democratically constituted institutions. Such practices certainly could not be regarded as compatible with the **Article 3 (2)** of the European Charter of Local Self-Government. Moreover, this issue is highly important from another point of view which is the requirements of the European Convention on Human Rights. Because the rights and freedoms constitute a whole and they cannot be separated from each other. Absence of one may affect the enjoyment of others considerably. For example, the harassment of journalists may have far reaching effects not only upon the freedom of expression but also on the quality of democratic elections. It has been reported that while media in Russian Federation are very active they are constantly and increasingly threatened. Russia figures 153 in the 2009 Worldwide Press Freedom Index (47th out of the 47 Council of Europe member states).

Although the Russian Federation has signed but not ratified the Protocol 12 of the said Convention, several obligations emanating from other provisions of the Convention make the practices connected with the local electoral processes highly questionable. **The Articles 10, 11 and 14** of the European Convention on Human Rights are particularly important in this respect. The first (Art. 10) deals with the freedom of expression which entitles everyone with the right to freedom of expression. This right includes "the freedom to hold opinions and to receive and impart information and ideas without interference by public authority". The second (Art. 11) is concerned with the freedom of assembly and association. Both of these freedoms which are under the guarantee of the above mentioned Convention are recognized to everyone. Everyone has the right to freedom of peaceful assembly and to freedom of association with other. Both are extremely important for the local councils or assemblies to be democratically formed. Finally, dealing with the prohibition of discrimination (Article 14) stipulates that "the enjoyment of these rights shall be secured without discrimination on any ground such as sex, race, color, language, religion, political or other opinion, national or social origin, association with a national minority, property, birth or other status". Practices encountered during the local election processes in Russian Federation can be hardly reconciled with all these provisions of the Convention. As a result, democratic nature of the process of constituting local decision-making bodies is considerably affected by these practices in an adverse manner.

Inter-municipal Cooperation

The general principles of inter-municipal cooperation are laid down in the Articles 66-69 of the Federal Law No: 131-FZ (October 6, 2003) on the General Organizational Principles of Local Self-Government in the Russian Federation. A council of the municipal formations of Russian Regions is expected to be formed in each Russian region. Powers of the Council are shown in the Article 66 of the said Law. The Council of Municipal Formations is neither entitled to interfere into the activities of municipal formations, nor to limit the activities thereof. Besides, The Article 67 empowers the Council of Municipal Formations to form a single All-Russia Association of Municipal Formations on the condition that it incorporates the councils of municipal formations of at least two thirds of the Russian regions. This umbrella association may also incorporate other associations of municipal formations. The All-Russia Association has the power to make proposals concerning the nomination of the members to the delegation of the Russian Federation that will attend the Congress of Local and Regional Authorities of Europe. Like the Council of Municipal Formations, the single All-Russia Association is neither entitled to interfere in the activities of municipal formations, councils of the municipal formations of Russian regions, other associations of municipal formations, nor to limit the activities thereof.

The Law No: 131-FZ empowers also the representative bodies of municipal formations to establish inter-municipal companies (either in the form of joint stock companies of limited liability companies) in order to jointly resolve issues of local significance. The lack of necessary financial resources makes their initiatives in the economic and commercial fields rather ineffective. Similarly, they may decide to form non-commercial organizations in the form of autonomous non-commercial organizations and funds (Article 68 and 69). There are no limitations in the Law to the right of local authorities to associate internally or externally. Although this formulation in the law is quite in conformity with the Article 6 (1) of the Charter, requiring that local authorities shall be able to determine their own internal administrative structures in order to adapt them to local needs and "ensure effective management", the obligation to set up associations of municipalities in all regions, in other words, to make the establishment of association mandatory may be regarded as questionable from the point of view of its compatibility with the **Article 10 (2)** of the Charter. The latter article concerning the right of local authorities to associate entitle them to belong to an association for the protection and promotion of their common interests and to belong to an international association of local authorities cannot be regarded as empowering the State to pressurize local authorities to unite according to their own needs and by their own will.

Before 1990 there were no national association of local authorities in Russia. By the initiative of the Federal Government various national associations have been sat up. At present there are several. Since this a top-down method of instituting national associations of municipal formations, one may ask to what extent they represent the real will and interest of their members. In almost all 83 Russian regions, regional associations of local authorities have been set up in recent years. But, in fact, they are under the guidance and authority of the regional governors. This situation prevents them to lobby for their own interests. It is reported that most of the mayors and councilors have no experience of national association of local authorities.

The Council of Federation, as an NGO, plays an active role in the legislative process. It interacts with federal authorities and informs them of developments in the regions. No prior authorization is needed to join external networks and to establish relations with counterparts in other countries. The Council of Federation is composed of two members from each region. There is also a second nationwide association which is called the National Congress of Municipalities. Of course, having such national associations established is one thing, but consulting them in appropriate times and manners is another. We have learned that the representative of the National Council was consulted by Duma Committees, but only after the concerned decisions had been taken.

Another non-governmental organization which is called the Civic Chamber represents the interest of the civil society. Its main task is to help enforce legislation, shape local communities, and assist local people to set up local self-government bodies. It is a sort of institution which functions as a link between the civil society and the decision-making bodies. Awareness raising activities of the Civic Chamber are expected to contribute to nurture the democratic culture in local communities. It has also a function of monitoring the implementation of the Law No: 131-FZ. It present legal opinions on new legislation. Out of its 129 members, the number of those appointed by the President, those chosen by the first group (from a list of candidates presented by Pan-Russian civil society organizations) and the ones chosen by the first two groups (representing regional organizations) are 43 each.

We have observed that there is clearly a right in the Russian Federation to associate as required by the Charter, but we have some concerns about the "top-down" development of the structures of association. A "top-down" approach may be seen as compatible at first glance with the expression in the Article 6 (1) regarding "without prejudice to more general statutory provisions", that would not suffice to adapt internal administrative structures "to local needs" and may not ensure "effective" management". Therefore, a "bottom-up" approach would benefit more elected representatives would make it possible to adapt the implementation of this principle to the spirit of the **Article 10 (2)**. Because through only a "bottom-up" association as mentioned above would ensure a real "protection and promotion of the common interests" of local authorities.

Rules Concerning the Creation of Agglomerations

In several regions in the Russian Federation there are preparations to create agglomerations. For example, seven municipalities around the city of Krasnoyarsk, regional capital, will be agglomerated in 2020. However, the possibility to create agglomerations is not clearly defined in the Federal Law No: 131-FZ. The rules concerning the legal status of agglomerations and of the bodies of local self-government do not exist. It is not known whether the general public will be consulted or not during the process of setting up agglomerations. Therefore, it would be advisable to set detailed provisions in order to shed light into these to avoid hesitations in practice.

Corruption

Corruption is perhaps the most challenging area that one may address. As the Mission heard from some of those it met, including the editor of a major regional newspaper, there are undoubted problems with corruption in local and regional self-government. There are, of course, existing laws in the Russian Federation which should control corruption especially on conflicts of interest. The existence of such legislation is welcome. But it seems from what we heard that such laws are easily evaded, especially if the wives of elected representatives treated as being beyond regulation.

It was reported that the ruling party is perceived as having strong links to business. There are many allegations of corruption at the local level. News regarding the involvement of the relatives of local politicians is abundant. There is the phenomenon of "billionaire wives", perceived as the result of Russian President obliging politicians to declare their income. We have been told that the cost of public works is 5 to 7 times greater than for similar projects in the west, which imposes a huge burden on local and regional authorities.

We had drawn the attention earlier to the fact that Russian figures up on the high in terms of the Transparency International Corruption Perception Index (46 out of 47 Council of Europe member states). Such practices can be regarded as a complete violation of the rule of the Charter concerning the very definition of the scope of local self-government requiring that public affairs must be regulated and managed "in the interest of local population" as mentioned in the **Article 3 (1)**, in other words, in the public interest. Reference Framework for Regional Democracy reiterates the same rule almost in the same manner, referring to "the interests of the regional population". In the European Code of Conduct of Local and Regional Elected Representatives, a Council of Europe document, it is stressed that individual favoring must be banned. The Article 8 goes on as the following: "Elected representatives shall not perform their functions or use the prerogatives of their office in the private interest of individuals or groups of individuals, with the aim of deriving a direct personal benefit therefrom". Similarly, in the Article 13 there is a ban on bribery, urging local representatives to refrain from any conduct qualifying as active or passive bribery".

New mechanisms for decision-making to reduce corruption may be recommended. New forms of compulsory competitive tendering that are in use in some developed countries would be worth exploring in this respect.

The Right to Determine Their Own Administrative Structures

The European Charter of Local-Self-Government entitles local authorities to determine their own administrative structures in the light of local needs and to regulate the conditions of service of their employees **(the Article 6)**. The recruitment of high quality staff on the basis of merit and competence, providing adequate training opportunities, remuneration and career prospects are inseparable preconditions of this right. We satisfactorily observed that in some regions, for example in Chelyabinsk, that training courses are organized matters are offered to newly elected heads of all settlements, including the rural ones, through an Academy for training local staff. This is an important step taken in view of the fact that many of the problems encountered by local authorities are connected to the lack of qualified managers and competent staff, in addition of the training needs and problems of local politicians. There is no doubt that exceptional attempts to emphasize training may not be sufficient. More can and should be done. Under the circumstances where necessary in-service training opportunities and knowhow are not provided to local officials and elected representatives, strong tendency for local authorities to transfer their competences to higher authorities may continue. The establishment of a federal training centers or a chain of regional training centers to be in charge of meeting this need would contribute to the achievement of the task defined in the **Article 6 (2)** of the Charter.

Legal Protection of Local Self-Government

While the Article 11 recognizes the right of local authorities to a judicial remedy in order to secure free exercise of their powers, real concerns were raised with us about the independence of the judiciary. For instance, representatives of the Transparency International asserted that it is now impossible to protect the rights of the individual citizens and autonomous institutions, because the judiciary is no longer independent, or impartial. The Article 6, 7 and 13 regarding the right to fair trial, no punishment without law and the right to effective remedy of the European Convention on Human Rights may be meaningful only where the independence and impartiality of the judiciary is ensured.

Landed Property

The transfer of public property to local and regional authorities continues to be a major concern for many local communities. A large proportion of land which is the main source of finance in rural settlements remains State owned, and is therefore not subject to local planning controls. There are complaints that local authorities do have necessary powers to manage their land properly. Little land is owned by local and regional authorities. In particular, the federal authorities are hanging on most of it. Two points may be worth to be underlined in this respect. The first is that land planning and implementation of city master plans are the tasks of local nature and therefore they have to be handled by local authorities without intervention of the State. Secondly, the Article 6 of the Draft Additional Protocol to the European Charter of Self-Government provides that "local authorities shall be entitled to acquire and utilize property, including the right to transfer of the management thereof to inter-municipal cooperation structures, public services or other bodies". On the other hand, the Article 1 of the Additional Protocol No 1 (20.03.1952) to the Convention for the Protection of Human Rights and Fundamental Freedoms is very clear on the protection of the property, it emphasizes that "every natural and legal person is entitled to the peaceful enjoyment of its possessions. No one shall be deprived of his possessions except in the public interest".

Conclusions and Recommendations

On our two visits to Russian Federation during December (16-17) 2009 and April (14-15) 2010 we have been informed that despite the achievements taken place through reforms on local self-government, numerous amendments have been made later on to the basic legislation in such a way that they highly overshadowed the positive steps taken to improve local democracy. The period of rapid legislative development that has brought the former Russian system from "democratic centralism" towards an autonomous system of local government in line with the principles of the European Charter of Local Self-Government up to the 2003. However, the number of amendments of the Law on Local Self-Government No: 131-FZ increased to 49 in relatively short period of time. It seems obvious that it is not easy to transform the traditionally centralistic characteristics of a political system to a system based on the principles of decentralization and subsidiarity immediately. Among the amendments to the legislation in force the most important ones are the broadening of the scope of the shared competences between local governments and higher-level authorities without providing additional financial resources to carry out these competences, increasing dependence of local authorities upon central funds, increasing trend of merging rural and urban settlements into larger units, dissolving smaller municipalities or changing the boundaries of local authorities without consulting local communities, enhancing the authority of elected local assemblies to dismiss mayors, increasing political and administrative problems as a result of changing electoral systems. Although Russian Federation has made important efforts to align itself with the fundamental principles of the European Charter of Local Self-Government, it should keep away from taking backward steps. Therefore, we would recommend that harmonization must be effectuated not only on paper, but also in practice, based on the findings described in this report, bearing in mind the rules and principles of the European Charter of Local Self-Government as well as those of the European Convention on Human Rights.

1. Suggestion made in 2004 by the Recommendation 143 and the Congress Resolution 171 on local and regional democracy in Russia have to be taken into consideration seriously.

2. The right of local authorities to be consulted on issues that concern them closely guaranteed by the Charter must be observed strictly. Incases where there are even justifiable grounds for changing the boundaries of local authorities for more efficient management of local affairs, local communities concerned or their representative bodies must be consulted by all means available.

3. Complaints regarding the recent amendments to the Federal Law on the Organization of Local Self-Government in Russia Federation, concerning the dismissal procedure of mayors by municipal councils upon the initiative of regional governors must seriously be taken into consideration and necessary revisions be made in both legislation and practice.

4. Particularly important is to meet the need to provide necessary financial resources to local authorities, commensurate with their competences, as required by the respective rules of the Charter. The lack of transparency with regard to the allocation of funds at the local level cannot be reconciled with the essence of local self-government. Apart from this general principle, local authorities have to be provided with matching funds or they should be authorized to raise new resources in cases where they are delegated certain State functions to be carried out on behalf of the higher- level authorities.

5. Measures have to be taken to realize necessary changes in the status and composition of the Federation Council through a reform procedure in order to make their representative characteristics unquestionable.

6. There is also a need to realize necessary revisions in the local electoral system in order to minimize the existing prohibitively high threshold levels for political parties to be represented in the municipal councils.

7. The provisions of the Federal Law on the General Principles Governing the Organization of the Local Self-Government make the establishment of municipal associations mandatory in order to jointly resolve the issues Article 10(2) of the Charter would not allow the State to pressurize upon the autonomous local units formally or informally to unite. To make such choices has to be left to the discretion of freely elected local assemblies.

8. De jure and de facto measures have to be taken to ensure that autonomous local authorities are not completely controlled by the regional authorities. Regional governors have to be prevented from constantly interfering into the affairs of local authorities. There are provisions in the Council of Europe Reference Framework for Regional Democracy preventing local authorities to become inferior legal entities vis a vis regional authorities even in the federal states. The said Reference Framework underlines the obligation that regional democracy must not be achieved at the expense of the autonomy of local authorities, but must be accompanied by measures designed to protect such authorities and fully respecting what has been achieved through the European Charter of Local Self Government.

9. Small settlements deprived of necessary financial resources and the landed property to carry out their responsibilities for public services are encouraged to transfer their competences to higher-level authorities. This should be avoided by appropriate measures in order to protect the institution of local self-government itself.

10. We think that new mechanisms for decision-making to reduce corruption may be recommended. For example, new forms of compulsory competitive tendering that are in use in some developed countries would be worth recommending in this respect.

11. Existing programs and organizations for training local officials and elected representatives have to be

expanded and strengthened in order to render public service provision at local level more efficient.

12. The Draft Law that aims to authorize the regional parliaments to pass laws to substitute the powers of local authorities concerning a number of municipal duties of local importance by the government of the Subjects of the Federation has to be examined once again in detail, in cooperation with the staff of the Council of Europe, since it may undermine the philosophy of the local government reform in Russia, which was based on the Article 130 of the Federal Constitution stipulating that local government shall manage public affairs of local importance under its own responsibility. This would also prevent a deviation from the fundamental principle laid down in the Article 4 (4) of the Charter which emphasized that powers given to local authorities shall normally be full and exclusive.

Urban Governance and Environmental Policies: The Case of Turkey*

Introduction

Turkey is a rapidly urbanizing country in the Middle East, with 76.6 percent of its total population (76 million) living in urban centers. Its level or urbanization was only 20 percent in 1950 and 43.9 percent in 1980. The number of cities having 10.000 or more inhabitants is 528, and those with 100.000 population is 138. There are seven cities with a population of one million and over. The distribution of cities among various city-size categories seems to be rather unbalanced, in the sense that more than three fourths of the urban population is concentrated in the size category of 100.000 and over. A similar inequality exists between the level of urbanization in different geographical regions. For instance, while the degree of urbanization is as high as 91 percent in the Marmara Region, with İstanbul at its center, and 83 percent in Central Anatolia, it is not higher than 55 percent in such regions as Eastern Anatolia and the Black Sea. There is no doubt that such inequalities reflect at the same time relative socio-economic underdevelopment of the regions concerned.

---

* International Forum on the Smart Cities and Public Contracting, University of Rosario, Bogota, Columbia, 11-13 April 2012.

On the other hand, the Constitution of Turkey requires the establishment of a territorial organization based on the principles of centralization and decentralization (Art.123). Decentralized institutions, in other words, local authorities are a) the departments, b) municipalities, and c) the village administrations (Art.127). Municipalities which are established in settlements with 5.000 and more inhabitants are in charge of meeting the common service needs of local communities. At present there are 2950 municipalities, 81 departments and nearly 36.000 village administrations in Turkey.

In view of the fact that Turkey is a developing economy with 12.500 US Dollars per capita GNP, local authorities have to possess necessary resources to finance the construction of urban infrastructure, major urban facilities and services, without increasing their dependency upon the central government funds. However, a certain amount of funds from the national budget is allocated to local authorities every year, in accordance with the constitutional principle requiring that they have to be provided with necessary financial means in proportion to their competencies. (Art.127).

The Structure and Features of Urban Governance

Even in a world of rapid globalization, the significance of localities and local communities continues to increase. Almost everywhere central and local authorities are in need to cooperate in order to meet the pressing needs of populations as well as to utilize local authorities as a means to strengthen participatory democracy. Turkey is a multipartite democracy where public services are carried out in accordance with the principles of centralization and decentralization within the integral unity of administration. All constitutions adopted since the establishment of the Turkish Republic in 1923 defined Turkey as a politically unitary state.

Three basic provisions of the constitution are important in this respect. The first is the Article 123 of the Constitution, as touched upon above, stipulates that the administration is an integrated whole, and the formation and functions of the administration are based on two complementary principles, namely centralization and decentralization.

The second is the Article 126, which regulates the organization of the central government and the structure of its field organization. National territory is divided into provinces (departments) on the basis of geographical conditions, and the requirements of the public services. The provinces are governmed according to the principle of *deconcentration*. Central administrative authorities comprising more than one province may be established to ensure efficiency and coordination in the provision of public services. For example, the Administration of Southeast Anatolian Regional Development Project comprising 9 provinces is in charge of helping the region to get rid of its relative underdevelopment.

The third Article (Art.127) is exclusively concerned with local authorities. Municipalities and departments, in other words, provincial local administrations are in charge of carrying out most of the urban public services. Power sharing between the State and local authorities has to be shaped in conformity with the principle of decentralization.

Local authorities in Turkey are simply administrative entities established to carry out public responsibilities conferred upon them by their respective legislation. Because the general system of local government in Turkey is not *political administration,* but *administrative decentralization.* Despite the fact that recent developments in the theory and practice of local democracy blurred this distinction to a certain extent, no provision in the Constitution allows territorial authorities to be regarded as law making entities sharing with the State the powers emanating from the national sovereignty.

Local councils are composed of members elected directly by people every five years. Although the executive bodies of local authorities do not need to be elected, the mayors are elected directly by the residents of cities. Historically, political and administrative system of Turkey does not recognize broad powers and extensive autonomy to territorial authorities. As a result of the unitary character of the State, the central government has the power to exercise a strict control over local authorities in the following circumstances: a) To ensure the performance of local services in conformity with the principle of the integral unity of Administration. b) To secure uniformity of the public services over the national territory. c) To safeguard the public interest. d) To meet the local needs in an appropriate manner. Central supervision is rather broad and may include the *expediency* of he acts and decisions of local authorities, depending upon the meaning to be attributed to concept of *public interest.* There is no indication in the Constitution that central control and supervision will be confined to *legality* of the acts and decisions of the councils. Municipalities are entitled to be provided with financial resources commensurate with their functions.

The Constitution allows municipalities to form unions among themselves to perform certain public services more

efficiently. In order to form unions or associations municipalities are required to get the permission of the Council
of Ministers. Although Turkey has abstentions on the Paragraphs 2 and 3 of the Article 10 of the European Charter of
Local Self-Government, concerning the rights of local authorities to associate, both the Constitution and the respective legislation do not possess any obstacle to either association or cooperation. One of the important provisions of
the Constitution is the one that makes possible the establishment of metropolitan municipalities in the largest urban
centers. There are 16 metropolitan municipalities in Turkey.
These metropolitan municipalities include the largest cities,
like İstanbul, Ankara, and İzmir. The special Law (No:5216)
concerning metropolitan municipalities created a two-tier
system in these cities, dividing the responsibilities of performing the public services of local nature between the up-
per-level and lower-level (district) municipalities.

In principle, the procedures dealing with objections to
the acquisition by elected organs of local authorities of their
status of their organ, and their loss of such status, must be
resolved by the judiciary. However one of the most problematic provisions of the Constitution is an exceptional rule
of this principle that empowers the Minister of the Interior
to suspend those elected organs of municipalities if an investigation or prosecution is initiated against them, on the
grounds of offences related to their duties, pending judg-
ment. A new Municipal Law (No:5395) limited the time
period in which such organs will remain suspended by requiring that such decisions of the Interior Minister be reviewed every two months. If continued suspension from

office is not considered in the public interest, the measure shall be lifted.

Turkey is a candidate country to the European Union. It is at the same time a member of the Council of Europe since 1949. Fundamental legal and political document of the Council of Europe, which serves as a guideline for the development of local democracy and local governance, is the European Charter of Local Self-Government that was put into force in 1988. This instrument was signed by Turkey in 1988 and ratified in 1993. The basic principles of the Charter include those regarding the meaning and scope of local self-government, the administrative supervision of local authorities, their financial resources, their right to co-operate, and finally the principles concerning the right to legal protection.

Turkey abstentiated from ratifying several articles of the Charter. Three of these abstentions are concerned with financial issues: 1) A sufficiently diversified and buoyant financial system to enable local authorities to keep pace as far as practically possible with the real evolution of the cost of carrying out their tasks (Art.9, Par.4). 2) The right to be consulted on the way in which redistributed resources are to be allocated to them (Art. 9, Par.6), 3) The principle that grants to local authorities shall not be earmarked to the financing of specific projects as far as possible. Also the condition that provision of grants shall not remove he basic freedom of local authorities to exercise policy discretion over their own jurisdiction (Art.9, Par.7).

Some other abstentions of Turkey include the powers of local authorities to determine their own internal administrative structures (Art.6, Par.1), their right to be consulted in the planning and decision-making processes in all matters which concern them directly (Art.4, Par.6), functions and activities which are deemed as incompatible with the holding of an elective Office (Art.7, Par.3), proportionality of the administrative supervision over local authorities with the importance of the interests to be protected (Art.8, Par.3), the right of local authorities to belong to a domestic or to an international association for the protection and promotion of their common interests (Art.10, Par.2), their right to cooperate with their counterparts in other countries (Art.10, Par.3), and finally, the right to recourse to a judicial remedy for the legal protection of their rights and freedoms (Art.11).

However both the EU and the Council of Europe are keenly interested in getting Turkey to lift the above mentioned abstentions on the Charter, which are regarded as important steps in ensuring the development of local democracy. Such criticisms and suggestions may be found in the Progress Reports prepared by the EU, Accession Partnership Document and in the reports of the monitoring missions of the Council of Europe.

The European Union asks Turkey to implement the articles of the Charter which it did not have an abstention and to revise its position vis-a-vis the articles over which Turkey has put an abstention. It is obvious that most of the articles of the Charter on which an abstention was put may easily be subject to ratification because the rights and freedoms that they aim to provide are already used extensively (and *de facto*) at present by Turkish municipalities.

Policies of Urban Development

Policies of urban development in Turkey have to be assessed from the point of view of the principle of *subsidiarity*. The Article 5 of the Amsterdam Treaty (Article 3/b of the Maastricht Treaty) defines the principle of subsidiarity as the following: "In areas which do not fall within its exclusive competence, the Community (EU) shall take action in accordance with the principle of subsidiarity, only if and insofar as the objectives of the proposed action cannot be sufficiently achieved by the member States and can therefore by reason of the *scale and effects* of the proposed action, be better achieved by the Community". The major aim is to bring the decision-making as near as possible to the level where citizens can influence it. The same principle is defined clearly in the Article 4, Paragraphs 2 and 3 of the European Charter of Local Self-Government in the following terms: "Local authorities shall have full discretion to exercise their initiative with regard to any matter *which is not excluded from their competences nor assigned to any other authority.* Besides, public responsibilities shall be exercised by the authorities *which are closest to the citizens.* Allocation of responsibility to another authority will be allowed only depending upon *the extent and nature of the task and the requirements of efficiency and economy.*

"Policies of urban and regional development are essentially formulated by the central government. The central government is assisted by the State Planning Organization in this endeavor. The main executive organ in charge of formulating urbanization, regional development and environmental policies is the Ministry of Environment and Urban Development. In principle, master plans of the cities are prepared and approved by the municipal councils with no approval at all by the central government. However, legal arrangements put into effect during the last several decades, especially during the last ten years, demonstrate that the operation of existing centralized system is completely incompatible with the principle of subsidiarity explained above.

The Law on Urban Development (No:3194) requires that cities with 10.000 or more inhabitants should work out master plans in order to ensure a balanced and healthy urbanization. Although, in principle, the city councils have the final power, in the plan preparation process, exceptionally, the Ministry of Environment and Urban Development and several other central government departments have been given the same power to be used in different circumstances. For example, The Ministry of Environment and Urban Development may prepare city master plans in the following cases: a) for metropolitan areas comprising more than one city. b) for those settlements that are prone to natural disasters. c) for settlements where large-scale social housing projects are implemented. d) for settlements where squatter houses constitute the most important planning problem, and finally, e) for the cities where there are ports, airports, and highways crossing from inside or surrounding the city boundaries. On the other hand, in addition to this Ministry, Ministry of Forests, Ministry of Culture and Tourism, Mass Housing Administration, and several other central government departments are empowered with working out city master plans. This means that the principle of subsidiarity will remain just on the paper, if all these central departments are going to use all the planning powers given to them by their respective legislation.

The major problem of urban development and management is to deal with expanding squatter settlements and to put into effect urban transformation projects. Especially from the end of the Second World War, in parallel with accelerated urbanization, the need for supply of urban land to meet growing demand for urban social housing increased enormously. This was the beginning of the formation of squatter settlements in Turkey. It is remarkable to note that the number of squatter houses (gecekondus) increased from 50.000 in 1955, to 2.5 million in 2010. It can be safely estimated that as much as 29 percent of the urban population, a total of 12.5 million people is actually living in 2.5 million gecekondus.

The Mass Housing Administration, in cooperation with municipalities play an important role in meeting the housing needs. The main target groups of the housing policy are socially underprivileged segments in the society which need financial and other kinds of assistance to resolve housing problems. The role of the housing cooperatives, as non-profit housing organizations is rather negligible at present. Their share in the total housing production increased up to 35 percent in the late 1980's, but witnessed a sharp decline to less than 10 percent in 2010, due to the mortgage policy of the Mass Housing Administration favoring private construction firms by loans.

Despite the fact that the Constitution provides, in its article concerning the right to property (Art.35), that this right shall not be used in contravention of the public interest, there is no real restriction upon the rent seeking efforts of the landowners which make the solution of the problems of homelessness almost impossible. Under these conditions, another provision of the Constitution regarding the right to housing is deemed to remain just on paper.

In the implementation stage of their master plans, cities benefit from the assistance of a central finance agency, which had been established during the first years of the Republic (1933), namely the Iller Bank (the Bank of Local Authorities) , which not only finances provision of the infrastructure needs of municipalities and other kinds of local authorities, but at the same time carries out some of these technical services through its divisions created for the purpose of simply performing such services as sewerage systems, mapping, dringing water, installation of heating systems. New Municipal Law put into effect in 2005 made it possible to establish an advisory civil society organization in municipalities, called "urban council", comprised of the representatives of major public and private institutions and all stakeholders to develop strategies for the future of the city in every field. The proposal of urban councils can only be put into effect upon their approval by the city council.

A final issue interesting urban administrations closely is the persisting regional disparities in Turkey. There are striking socio-economic disparities between the Western and Eastern regions in the country. Policies of regional development have not been much efficient so far. Despite all efforts of the State Planning Organization, it has not been possible to change the underdevelopment characteristics of the Eastern and Southeastern Anatolian Regions. Recently, upon the proposal of the European Union, 26 Regional Development Agencies have been established, in order to reduce regional disparities. However, while each of these agencies will essentially be dealing with their own development, it is difficult to guess to what extent the final objective of reducing overall regional inequalities could be reached through competition among regions.

Policies of Environmental Protection

Everyone has the right to live in a healthy and balanced urbanization according to the Article 56 of the Turkish Constitution. The Constitution emphasizes at the same time that it is the duty of the State and the citizens to improve the natural environment and to prevent environmental pollution. In addition to this, several other articles in the Constitution provide legal guarantees for the protection of natural and man-made environmental values. One of these prohibits the exercise of the right to property in contravention of the public interest (Art.35). Another puts the coastal areas under the sovereignty and at the disposal of the State, with the consequence that in the utilization of the sea coast, lake shores or river banks, and of the coastal strip along the sea and lakes, public interest is to be taken into consideration with priority (Art.43).

To prevent the loss of cultivable agricultural land is also the duty of the State (Art.44). Similarly, providing land to farmers with insufficient land could not lead to a fall in production or to the depletion of forests and other land and underground resources. The responsibility of the State to ensure the conservation of historical, cultural and natural assets and wealth is also underlined in the Constitution (Art.63). More specifically is charged with the duty to enact the necessary legislation and to take appropriate measures for the protection of forests and the enlargement of their areas. No amnesties or pardons to be granted for offences against forests shall be legislated. The restraining of forest boundaries is also prohibited by the Constitution (Art.169), except in respect of areas whose preservation as forests is considered technically and scientifically useless, but whose conversion into agricultural land is found definitely advantageous.

The Environment Law (No:2873) of 1983, amended in 2006 (by the Law No:5491), defines the concept of "environmental protection" as the activities for the preservation of ecological balance, prevention of degradation and pollution in the air, water and land, and for their improvement. According to the general principles of the Environment Law, it is the duty of the people to protect the environment, and to comply with the measures taken for that purpose. Health of all human beings is to be taken into account to protect and improve the environment. Sustainable environment and sustainable development are the fundamental concepts of the Environment Law guiding the formulation and implementation of environmental policies. In addition to the principle of *sustainable development,* Environment Law adopted several other guiding principles such as *participation, prevention,* and *polluter pays.* All economic enterprises and other *institutions* are required, in their decisions of land and resource use, and project evaluation, to strike a balance between the goals of environmental protection and development. They must choose the most appropriate methods and technology in order to achieve that end. An *environmental impact analysis* has to be made by all the entrepreneurs for their planned establishments, in order to avoid their adverse impact upon environmental values.

Those who damaged the environment are held responsible for their acts or neglect, even the negative impact is caused without their fault (*the principle of objective responsibility*). Citizens have the right to recourse to administrative authorities and to ask to stop any activities which degrade the environment whenever are informed or affected by them. A specific Law on the Right to Information (No: 4982) passed, in 2003, allows them to be informed about anything that affects the environment. In principle, tools available to public authorities for the protection of the environment are mainly market-based instruments such as taxes, charges, participation rates, financial incentives, carbon trade and the like. A final policy instrument which is no less important than the others is *education for environmental protection and increasing public awareness*. For this purpose, public radio and TV channels are required to broadcast at least two hours a month programmes on environmental protection.

In addition to the Environment Law, the Municipal Law and the Law on Public Health, numerous special legislation possess rules to be applied for the protection and preservation of environmental assets. The Law on the Protection and Cultural Values (No: 2863), the Law on the Protection of the Bosphorus (No:2960), the Law on the Protection of Coastal Areas (No:3830), Urban Development Law (No:3194), the Law on the Encouragement of Tourism (No:2634), the Forests Law (No: 6831), the Law on Water Products (no: 1380) , the Law on the Protection of Animals (No: 5199), and the Law on the Protection of Land (No: 5403) are a few of these legislations.

There are nearly 300 associations actively working in the fields of the protection of flora and fauna, biological diversity, and all natural assets and historical and architectural heritage. Although an actual, personal and legitimate interest in the issue at stake is a precondition for seeking the annulment of an administrative act or decision in the courts, the Procedural Law of Administrative Courts makes an important exception for those matters of public interest like city master plans, historical buildings and the protection of the environment.

In addition to the Ministry of Environment and Urban Development, the major components of the environmental management system are some other central ministries like Forests and Water Affairs, Culture and Tourism, Energy and Natural Resources, and local authorities and their unions.

Concluding Remarks

It is beyond any doubt that proper protection of the environment can only be ensured through the effective involvement of the citizens in decision-making processes regarding urban development and environmental issues. Channels for participation for associations, foundations, labor unions, cooperatives and professional organizations have to be widely open for the success of urbanization and environmental policies. Effective contribution depends upon the level of consciousness of the public as a whole towards the environmental values, complementarity of economic development and environment, in other worlds, sustainable development. So far, the public played an important role in influencing the legislative and executive bodies. Judiciary, has been playing, in its turn, an important function to ensure sustainable urbanization.

In addition to increasing public awareness, consciousness of decision-makers is of utmost important. Unless they are not well informed about the exact nature of such concepts as sustainable development, intergenerational equity, precautionary principle, common and differentiated responsibility, the principles of participation and the like, it would be practically impossible to carry out the suggestions laid down in the international declarations or conventions. Turkey is still witnessing indifference at least on the parts of some decision-maker to such issues of nuclear power plants, hydroelectric power installations, protection of historical and natural assets in general.

Turkey is either signatory or party to nearly 30 of the international conventions or treaties concerning the environment. Being a candidate for the full membership of the European Union, she needs to adjust her legislation and practices to the norms prevailing in the European Community in a relatively short time. She has the obligation to put into effect the legal norms of all ratified legal instruments, which charge Turkey, as full member states, to protect the environment not only for present, but also for future generations and the mankind as a whole.

A final point has to be made in general here which is no less than any other point mentioned above. Inadequate interest all over the world in planning at all levels (national, regional and local) is gradually attracting more attention of those who have deep concern for sustainable development. The anti-planning attitude observed in many countries up to now is being encouraged and supported by some by some international finance institutions.

The pre-judged and excessive emphasis upon almost use-lessness of the public sector and planning, including urban governments and planning authorities, and the increasing anti-planning attitude, may end up with leaving the shaping of urban environments completely to the free play of the market forces, which may be neither economically more efficient, nor acceptable from the standpoint of social justice. This seems to be absolutely contradictory with the principle of prevention as a rational component of the concept of sustainable development.

Short Bibliography

Keleş, Ruşen, *Kentleşme Politikası (Urbanization Policy)*, İmge Publishers, Ankara, 2012 (12th ed.).

Keleş, Ruşen, *Yerinden Yönetim ve Siyaset (decentralization and Politics)*, Cem Yay.,İstanbul, 2012 (8th ed.).

Keleş, Ruşen, Hamamcı, Can and Çoban, Aykut (eds.), *Çevre Politikası (Environmental Politics)*, İmge Publishers, Ankara, 2012 (7h ed.).

Keleş, Ruşen and Danielson, Michael, *The Politics of Rapid Urbanization: Government and Growth in Modern Turkey,* Holmes and Meier, New York, 1985.

Keleş, Ruşen, *Urban Poverty in the Third World: Theoretical Approaches and Policy Options,* Institute of Developing Economies, Tokyo, 1988.

Keleş, Ruşen, "Urban Development and Sustainable Management for the Mediterranean Towns", Paper submitted to the meeting of the Working Group for Urban Management, Mediterranean Commission for Sustainable Development, Split, Croatia, 1999.

Keleş, Ruşen, "Impact of Urbanization on Fertile Agricultural Land in Turkey", Driss Ben Ali, Antonio di Guliio, Mustapha Lasram et Marc Lavergne (sous la direction de.),*L'Urbanisation et l'Agriculture: Conflits et Complémentarités,* L'Harmattan, CİHEAM, Paris, 1996, pp.145-154.

Keleş, Ruşen, "Regional Cooperation for Environmental Protection"(with special reference to the Mediterranean Region), Erich Weiss and Tanja Zangger (eds.), *Functions of the Regions in the Realms of Spatial Planning, Landed Property, and Environmental Protection*, Peter Lang, Bern, 2002, pp.25-40.

Keleş, Ruşen, "National Protection: The Case of Protected Areas in Turkey", *Naturopa*, Council of Europe, No:85, 1997, pp.23-24.

Keleş, Ruşen, "The Sustainability of Sustainable Urbanization", Paper presented to the 30th International Symposium on Sustainable Spatial Development of the European Continent: Interdisciplinary Approaches, Willy Claus and Paul Trappe (eds.), *Nachhaltipe Raumliche Entwicklung auf dem Europaischen Kontinent Interdisziplinare*, Ansatza, Social Strategies, Vol.32, Peter Lang, Bern, 2000, pp.213-228.

Keleş, Ruşen, "Sustainable Urban Development under Unsustainable Condiitions", Derya Oktay (ed.), *Inquiry into Urban Environment: Issues Concerning Urban, Housing, and the Built Environment*, Eastern Mediterranean University, Famagusta, 2006, pp.27-38.

Keleş, Ruşen, "Territorial Governance in Turkey", Paper presented to the International Conference on Territorial Governance: Disintegrating States in an Integrating Europe? New and Old Challenges, European Studies Center, St.Antony College, University of Oxford, 28-30 November, 2006.

Keleş, Ruşen, "Urban Sprawl and its Implications for Sustainable Urban Development", Semra Atabay and Buket Ayşegül Özbakır (eds.), *New Perspectives in Eco-Technology and Eco-Economy*, Yıldız Technical University, Faculty of Architecture and Strategic Research Center, İstanbul, pp.13-16.

Keleş, Ruşen, "The Quality of Life and the Environment", Paper presented to Asia Pacific Conference on Environment-Behaviour Studies, Famagusta, North Cyprus, 7-9 December 2011.

The Relevance of the Delos Declarations for the Problems of Urbanization and Environment Facing the World Today*

Abstract

Twelve Delos Symposia have been held during 1963-1972, ten on board ship, and the last two in Athens and at the Apollonian in Porto Rafti. Two hundred twenty-four eminent planners, architects, philosophers, geographers, scientists have attended and made considerable contributions to the success of the meetings through Delos Declarations.

Worldwide problems of urbanization in developing and developed worlds, city growth and planning, urban identity, regional development, resource conservation, housing, transport and communications, local self-government, issues of human settlements have been dealt with an intensive interest in making human beings happier in their urban environments.

The United Nations Conferences on human settlements have been largely influenced by the opinions expressed and conclusions reached at the Delos Symposia, and these, in their turn influenced the progress of thinking concerning the Science of Human Settlements.

When examined carefully, one could easily notice how the emergence of numerous modern concepts used in planning, architecture and environmental sciences, such as sustainable development, the rights of future generations, ethical holism, cooperation among

---

* Book published in Greek in Honour of Constantinos A. Doxiadis, Founder of Ekistics, the Center of Science for Human Settlements, by the Association of Colleagues and Friends of Constantinos A. Doxiadis, Athens, 2009, pp. 156-159.

nations, citizen participation, and the public interest, are influenced by Delos Declarations. It is not difficult to find also great similarities between the thoughts developed during the UN conferences of Stockholm, Rio de Janeiro, İstanbul, Johannesburg, the Urban Charter of the Council of Europe, the EU Guiding Principles of Spatial Development, and the Delos Declarations.

Introduction

Despite the fact that some scholars emphasized in the past that the reason for the fact that Doxiadis is so little-known today was a real neglect, I think that the decision of the Association of Collaborators and Friends of C. A Doxiadis to organise the present meeting to discuss the activities and evolution of the ideas of Doxiadis and their local and international impact is crucially important both scientifically and ethically. This event will not only help filing the so called gap pointed out by some scholars, it will also provide an opportunity to look at the intellectual accumulation of thoughts centered around Ekistics in the light of relevance for the problems of urbanization and environment facing the world today.

Twelve Delos Symposia have been held during 1963-1975, ten on board ship, and the last two in Athens and the Apollonion, Porto Rafti. 224 eminent planners, architects, philosophers, geographers, scientists have attended and made considerable contributions to the successes of the meetings through Delos Declarations.

The leading role of Constantinos A. Doxiadis in the organization and intellectual formation of the symposia was undeniable and extremely important. The author of this paper had the privilege to attend one of the last meetings that was held in Athens in the early 1970's and had the honour to meet Doxiadis personally as one of the correspondents of the *Journal of Ekistics*. Worldwide problems of urbanization in developing and developed worlds, growth of cities and planning, urban identity, regional development, resource conservation, social housing, transport and communications, local self-government, a variety of issues concerning human settlements have been dealt with intensive concern for making human beings happier in their urban environments.

I believe that the United Nations Conferences on Human Settlements, both Vancouver (1976) and İstanbul (1996), have been largely influenced by the opinions expressed and conclusions reflected in the Delos Symposia; and these, in turn, influenced the progress of thinking concerning the Science of Human Settlements, both directly and indirectly.

When examined carefully, one could easily notice to what extent is the emergence of numerous modern concepts used widely in planning, architecture and environmental sciences, such as sustainable development, the rights of future generations for natural resources and environmental assets, ethical holism, cooperation among nations, citizen participation, and the public interest, influenced by Delos Declarations.

It is not difficult to find also close similarities between the thoughts developed during the UN environment conferences of Stockholm (1972) and Rio de Janeiro (1992) and the Delos Declarations. Similar influences can also be found in the Johannesburg (Rio+10) Declaration on Sustainable Development, the Urban Charter of the Council of Europe (1992 and 2004) and the Guiding Principles of Spatial Development prepared CEMAT, European Conference of Ministers Responsible for Regional Planning, under the umbrella of the Council of Europe.

Brief references will be made below to each of the documents mentioned earlier and an effort will be made to show to what extent were relevant the far-sighted analyses and prescriptions of the Delos Declarations for the contemporary problems of urbanization, housing, settlements and environment.

Urbanization

As noted in the Habitat Agenda in 1996, "Rapid urbanization, the concentration of urban population in large cities, the sprawl of cities into wider geographical areas and the rapid growth of mega-cities are among the most significant transformations of human settlements. During the course of history, urbanization has been associated with economic and social progress, the promotion of literacy and education, the improvement of the general state of health, greater access to social services, and cultural, political and religious participation... Cities and towns have been engines of growth and incubators of civilization and have facilitated the evolution of knowledge, culture and tradition, as well as industry and commerce".[1] As right noted by the First Delos Declaration, a universal feature of the worldwide revolution was the movement of people into urban settlements at an ever faster rate. World population increased by 2 percent a year, urban population by over 4 percent in two decades following the Second World War. During the latter half on the 20 th century there was a continuous transformation of the world's population into urban dwellers. The urban population has increased from less than 30 percent of the total in

---

1   United Nations, **Habitat Agenda**, Paragraphs: 99 and 7, 1996.

1950 to more than 47 percent at the beginning of the 21 st century. It is estimated by the United Nations that by the year 2006 more than half of humankind will begin to live in urban areas. It is also expected that figure to rise to 57 percent around 2020.[2] The rate of urbanization of the world total population was 2.37 percent during the 1990-2000 period while this figure was as high as 3.30 percent in developing countries for the same period.

Particularly the developing countries with least financial resources suffer considerably from the adverse consequences of excessive urbanization, manifested through enormous backlogs in shelter, infrastructure and services, increasingly overcrowded transportation systems, unsustainable consumption patterns, deteriorating sanitation and environmental pollution. All these are often associated with general conditions of urban poverty, insecure land tenure, unsatisfactory housing conditions, urban crime and homelessness.

As emphasized by the Declaration of Delos Twelve which was convened in July 1975 only two weeks after the death of Constantinos A. Doxiadis, the world has learned through these symposia that urbanization, if handled in an appropriate manner, can broaden the range of opportunity and favor equal rights. And that there was room for optimism since it was the speed of the process that created the crisis. Therefore, it was assumed that "the trend was not the destiny. Despite the many difficulties, we can look toward the future with optimism". Constant emphasis put on the need for planned intervention in the regulation of settlement issues is faced with a contradictory challenge as expressed by the practice and publications of the World Bank, which

2   United Nations, **Basic Facts on Urbanization**, UNCHS, Nairobi, 1996, pp. 1-2.

strongly oppose to any intervention in social and economic life.[3] There is no doubt that pressing problems of rapid urban growth, balanced regional development and adequate infrastructure for settlements will need the initiative of public authorities in both developing as well as developed nations for a long time to come. A *revived laissez-faire, laissez passer* approach was never found suitable for solving the problems of urbanization of contemporary world.

The Need for a Holistic Approach to Human Settlements and Institutional Matters

The main concern of the Delos Symposia has been to establish a *holistic* approach to the study of human settlements since the beginning in order:

a. to develop in its own right a new discipline of human settlements;

b. to initiate basic research of the most far-reaching kind;

c. to bring together specialists from other relevant disciplines to work together with an *interdisciplinary* approach on projects in this field,

d. to work out new methods of training the men who can assume leadership and responsibility in the sphere of action;

e. to attract some of the best young minds into this new area of research, development and practice.

It is on this understanding that Ekistics grid was developed as to include such sub- systems as anthropos (people as individuals), nature society, shells (buildings) and networks

---

3   World Bank, From Plan to Market: World Development Report, Washington D.C., 1997.

(roads, utilities, transportation, communications and administrative boundaries). *Holistic* approach to human settlements also included institutional components as its integral parts. It was clearly indicated that there was a clear need for the most far-reaching reform and reinforcement of existing institutions and procedures. The active participation of man, not only as parent and worker, but as learner and artist and citizen, was essential. The fact that the application of the basic sciences in the universities to human welfare had been fragmented was no longer acceptable. The Second Delos Declaration clearly emphasized that Ekistics endeavored to draw all aspects of human welfare such as health, nutrition, education, transportation and housing together within the framework of man-in-community. It was assumed that "it is only by looking at all aspects of these networks as part of a whole system of settlements that we can hope to rationalize and develop these networks so as to provide a framework for the future well-being of man".[4] These ideas had a far-reaching impact upon the development of such new concepts as comprehensive development and planning in the coming decades.

Three particular fields have drawn attention during the Second Symposion from the perspective of a holistic approach to human settlements: These were a) the content of a discipline of human settlements; b) the methods of training men and women to work in this new field of Ekistics; c) and some of the political and economic obstacles that are likely to impede the development of an integrated approach. Accordingly, the Declaration of Delos Seven underlined the need to short cut the kind of integration by a

4   **Delos Eight, Report of the Eight Symposion**, July 3-10, 1970.

multi-disciplinary approach that will enable us to treat our subject matter as a whole, rather than attempting to fit together its fragmented practioners.

It seems that there is a crucially important connection between some of the opinions expressed during the Second and Eleventh Delos Declarations and the concrete steps taken to reorganize the institutional set-up of the United Nations. More specifically, the participants insisted that such issues as shelter, settlement space, human development, human health, historic and natural areas, existing buildings, transport and service networks, education and governmental set-up, affecting all types of human settlements required:

1. "That human settlements be recognized within the United Nations as a separate sector of activity.

2. That appropriate organizational measures be taken within the framework of the United Nations to meet the needs of this new individual sector.

3. That the proper share of United Nations funds be allocated to the sector of human settlements and further financing be sought on a scale more adequate to the extent of urban crisis."

In addition to these proposals, signatories of the Twelfth Declaration, emphasized the critical need to establish a United Nations Agency or major programme for human settlements. The most appropriate opportunity was certainly the organization of the UN Vancouver Conference in 1976, which has given birth to the creation of the UN Center for Human Settlements (INCHS) In order to bring together fragmented faces of policy and to combine them in a genuine strategy in the field of human settlements. They openly called for the immediate creation of a UN organization for human settlements with adequate authority to:

1. Work with existing agencies to give priority to planning and development of human settlements.
2. Assist governments to devise methods of allocating a larger share of their income to the improvement of their settlements.
3. Give urgent attention to the training, education and research related to the planning, development and management of human settlements.
4. Invite countries to share internationally relevant information on their problems and their solutions for human settlements.
5. Urge governments to consult one another whenever human settlements plans in one country could have repercussions in neighboring countries.

The creation of the UNCHS also urged many international agencies with separate programmes covering part of the field of human settlements "to adopt the ekistic approach" in their own work and to collaborate closely with each other to produce integrated policies. At both conceptual and institutional levels, holism of the Ekistics helped considerably better understanding of development and planning of human settlements. This feature is highly clear in the following statement of the Istanbul Declaration adopted at the end of HABITAT II Conference of 1996: "Human settlements problems are of a multi-dimensional nature. It is recognized that adequate shelter for all and sustainable human settlements development are not isolated from the broader social and economic development of countries and that they can not be set apart from the need for favorable national and international frameworks for economic development, social development and environmental protection, which are indispensable and mutually reinforcing components of sustainable development ".[5]

One concrete proposal made during the Delos Ten Symposion suggesting that "local government must be brought closer to people" reminds us of the fashionable principle of subsidiarity incorporated into the *acquis communautaire* of the European Union.[6] According to this principle, all public services of local nature must be performed by local governments unless they could be performed better by higher - level public authorities or technical or economic considerations require their handling by other authorities.[7]

Guiding Principles for Sustainable Urban and Spatial Development

In Delos Declarations adopted in different symposia at different dates between 1963 and 1975, numerous principles to guide sustainable urban and spatial development have been debated and adopted. Particularly the Declarations of the Eleventh and Twelveth Symposia can be regarded as a complete collection of these principles. Adequate shelter for all, development to be regarded as a positive and dynamic concept, not merely of land use, but of the space above and below the land surface with a view to ensure the supremacy of public interest, preservation of human scale and dignity

---

5   United Nations, **The Istanbul Declaration and the Habitat Agenda,** 3-14 June, 1996, Istanbul, Turkey, p. 14.

6   Ruşen Keleş, "The Principle of Subsidiarity in Service of Sustainable Development", and **Delos Ten, Declaration of Delos Ten,** July 9-17, 1972.

7   Council of Europe, **European Charter of Local Self-Government,** Strasbourg, 1985, (Art. 4, Par. 3).

in urban settlements, optimal scale in order to preserve the mental and physical health of the community and each of its members, respect for historic and natural assets of the settlements as a part of the heritage of humanity, appropriate handling of the vast number of inadequate and substandard settlements and their building stocks, rational use of transport and service networks to serve rather than endanger life, emphasis at all levels of education on the knowledge of settlements in order to comprehend and manage human communities with dignity and freedom, and introduction of appropriate administrative, political and financial institutions to respond to their needs were among the issues debated and the suggestions made for the solution of pressing problems regarding them. Again and again, references have been made to equal rights and access to community facilities, community services and places of work. These were perceived as issues requiring intelligent planning, provision of dwellings and related facilities for the needs of all groups in the society.

The need was stressed to retain natural and historical areas within the settlement pattern. Housing and community buildings should not be allowed to deteriorate to the point of no return. In this context, the Ekisticians deplored the destruction of irreplaceable cultural values through careless stewardship, thus predicting the significance of the concept of *sustainable development* long before this concept was put in the agenda of the environmentalists.

It was remarkable to see that in the last Delos Declaration, attention was drawn to a highly important planning principle that "landownership can be more properly perceived as ownership of space". This is certainly considered as one of the rightest steps to be taken towards the elimination of land speculation and to ensure the resolution of the housing problems of low-income families. Similar suggestions had been made by French Philosopher Henri Lefebvre, in the 1970's, in his well-known book, *La Production de I 'Espace*.[8]

The document that is called *The Guiding Principles for Sustainable Development of the European Continent*, that was adopted in Hannover, in September 2000, by the European Ministers responsible for Regional Planning, reflects almost the same spirit as to the reconciliation of urban and spatial development and the concerns for the preservation of cultural and natural values.[9]

Impact of Globalization, Planning and Participation

One of the most important observations made during one of the Delos Symposia (Seventh, July 1969) was the attention drawn to some non-material consequences of the process of globalization. For instance, it was pointed out that there was not only a world-wide crisis urbanization but there was also "a basic distortion of values" in society's failure to allocate resources for the improvement of human settlements, the upgrading of the total environment, the strengthening, protection and education of young and the equalization and enlargement of individual opportunity.

---

8   Henri Lefebvre, **La Production de I' Espace (The Production of Space)**, Anthropos, Paris, 1974.

9   Council of Europe, European Conference of Ministers Responsible for Regional Planning (CEMA.T), Guiding Principles for Sustainable Development of the European Continent, adopted at the 12 th Session of the European Conference of Ministers Responsible for Regional Planning on 7-8 September 2000 in Hannover.

The vital point in starting a development strategy for cities was to propose a concrete plan and to reorder priorities in resource allocation. To ensure world order and prevent nuclear disaster, to meet the population explosion, to halt the contamination of air. water and land, to provide food, housing and basic amenities for the billions were recognized as the most pressing priority areas that are still waiting for satisfactory solutions nearly four decades after the Seventh Delos Symposion. According to Delos Declarations, planning is a suitable instrument that can introduce ideal concepts, concerning not how the city will be, but how it could and should be. A very harsh priority setting was recommended within the framework of an understanding that in many areas of the world, one man's gain should no longer be another man's loss, but that in other areas there was genuine scarcity.

Perhaps for the first time in planning history, a reference was made to the quality of the planning targets in the sense that, though specific, they should be *flexible* enough to be changed in the course of implementation by a continuous process of *trial and error*. Of course, a natural corollary was the need for a maximum involvement of the public in the planning process, which in the coming decades has come to be known as public participation in planning. As it was underlined in the text of the Delos Five Declaration, the achievement of the goals of public participation, required giving the citizens the chance of access to the widest possible range of free choice, that is called the freedom to be consulted about their choices. Here we find a fair and balanced reconciliation of planning with democratic values. As rightly pointed out in the text of the Ninth Declaration, "the settlements' pattern should not come to the citizen in a shape so fixed and predetermined by external authority that there can be no free play or creativity for development and change".[10] The Delos Nine participants went so far in this respect as to suggest that while the decisions about neighborhoods should be in the hands of local groups, "as far as possible, the design of housing would be determined by those who are to live in it".[11] A clearer expression of the need for participation was used by the Declaration of Delos Ten as following: "Citizen involvement in the solution of ekistical problems is indispensable".[12] This undoubtedly requires educational programmes for people of all ages and all degrees of specialization.

The same themes have been addressed again in Delos Seven in the most striking way, referring to the reduction of slavery, exploitation, poverty and second class citizenship for some portions of mankind, as the result of definite decisions taken in the past. As to the steps to be taken, Delos Seven had suggested that the representation based on geographical units was unsatisfactory, and therefore we needed also a representation of group interests, such as the poor, the miserable, the disadvantaged, and greater possibilities for individual choice, for quality of human contacts and multiple group relationships had to be created. Thirty years after the Delos Seven, the Habitat Agenda devoted a whole section to the needs and the role of the vulnerable groups and the people with special needs among its strategies (Paragraphs 93-98). Similarly, at the beginning of 1990's, the vital role

10   **Delos Nine, Declaration on the State of Emergency in Human Settlements**, July 12-19, 1971.

11   **Ibid.**

12   **Delos Ten, Declaration of Delos Symposion 1972**, July 9-17, 1972.

to be played by and participation of such groups as women, youth, indigenous people and underprivileged in environmental management and development has been underlined in the principles 20 through 22 of the Rio Declaration on Environment and Development (1992). The same value attributed to public participation and to the need for access of vulnerable groups and the underprivileged to the planning process has been emphasized in the respective sections of the European Urban Charter, a legal instrument of the Council of Europe that was adopted in 1992.[13]

Another point that has to be touched upon briefly is the emphasis of the Declaration Delos Ten upon the proposal to bring local government closer to the people and to ensure active participation in decision-making.[14] This suggestion has something to do with the principle of subsidiarity which was defined by the Maastricht (1993) and Amsterdam (1997) Treaties and the European Charter of Local Self-Government (1985) as the principle requiring that public responsibilities must be carried out, preferably, by the authorities as close as possible to the citizens. There is no doubt that the intellectual accumulation nourished by numerous Delos Symposia had a considerable impact on the transfer of this principle from theology to governmental practice.

Adequate Shelter as a Human Right

Even after the adoption of the Universal Declaration of Human Rights by the UN General Assembly in 1948, the use of the concept of right with regard to housing, was not

13   Conseil de l'Europe, **La Charte Urbaine Européenne**, Strasbourg, 1993, p. 63-66 and 87-91.
14   **Delos Ten, Op. Cit.**

popular. The Article 25 of the said Declaration stated that "everyone has the right to a level of life sufficient to guarantee his feeding, well-being, of himself and his family, particularly for nutrition, dressing, housing, health care and necessary social services...".[15] It is interesting to note that right before the First UN Conference on Human Settlements (1976) that was convened in Vancouver, Delos Eleven declared that a Charter for Human Settlements has to be formulated and three basic human rights have to be defined there. These were The Right to Shelter, The Right to Equality, and The Right to Dignity. The ultimate goal of the human right to shelter must be one person/ one room; and in the first stage, one family/one dwelling. Even after twenty years following the Vancouver Conference on Human Settlements, humanity had observed that it is far from having reached the targets set during the Conference. Therefore, during the Second UN Conference on Human Settlements (Habitat II), the heads of state or government and the official delegations have reaffirmed their commitment to "*the full and progressive realization of the right to adequate housing as provided for in international instruments*". To that end, they have committed themselves once again to seek the active participation of public, private and non-governmental partners at all levels to ensure legal security to tenure, protection from discrimination and equal access to affordable, adequate housing for all persons and their families.[16] One could easily see throughout the evolution of the concept of

---

15   Maguelonne Dejeant-Pont et Marc Pallemaetrs, Droits de l'Homme et Environnement, Ed, du Conseil de l'Europe, Strasbourg, 2002, p. 51.

16   United Nations, **The İstanbul Declaration and the Habitat Agenda**, Nairobi, 1997, p. 5 (par. 8).

the right to adequate housing the impact of the opinions developed during Delos Symposia during 1960's and 1970's.

In connection to meeting the housing needs of the poor, attention was drawn to the deteriorating role of "the unregulated urban land markets and inflated land values". There is no doubt that as a result of these phenomena, massive high rise building are designed as offices in such a way as to sterilize city life. As apartments, they break up local intimate relationships, imprison mothers and young families and impoverish the imaginative life of a whole generation of children.[17] Humanity is confronted today both in developed and the developing world with social, economic, cultural and even psychological consequences of the misuse or abuse of the right of ownership in land. We must underline the fact that, as it was touched upon briefly above, recent policies of some of the international finance institutions tend to discourage public intervention in order to regulate imperfections of the land markets.

Social Justice and the Need for International Cooperation

One of the themes that has occupied the minds of the Ekisticians was to assist the establishment of a public order based on social justice both domestically and at international level. With this concern in mind, the Delos Five Declaration underlined the need to address a fundamental political and moral issue concerning the relationship among citizen and the nations. It was suggested that inside the cities, wealthier citizens can pass on some of their surplus to

17   **Delos Nine, Declaration on the State of Emergency in Human Settlements,** July 12-19, 1971.

poorer neighborhoods through taxation and investment. Inside the country, poorer regions can be helped in the same way, inspired by solidarity considerations. Although the moral obligations of citizenship and the political and administrative structures for such transfers exist, they were not used at sufficient scale. One could assume that under the impact of globalization and further liberalization of world economy, intervention in social and economic life by governments will no longer be encouraged, and as a result, requirements of social justice will be left more and more to market forces. This shows us that the need emphasized by Delos Declarations some thirty years ago is more pressing at present than before.

Similarly, in a larger context, it was pointed out that since both the instruments and the obligations for a fruitful solidarity between wealthy nations and developing nations were largely lacking, the rich ones should fix their annual contribution to world development at the level of at least one percent of Gross National Product. Despite the fact that such a proposal had been made during the UN Conference on Trade and Development in 1964 and subsequently the UNCTAD was created, and the constant efforts of the former German Chancellor Willy Brandt, no concrete steps have been taken afterwards and the discrepancies continued to exist. However, there is still a need "to bring the tasks and opportunities of the urban revolution to the center of public policy and private interest, to develop strategies of creative change and to mobilize the resources to turn man's dream of a better urban life into a daily reality".[18] Suggestions made during the Delos Symposia have had their impact also on

18   **Delos Five, Report of the Fifth Symposion,** July 22-29, 1967.

the formulation of certain legal principles concerning the moral responsibilities of rich nations to the poor with respect to environmental protection and sustainable development. For example, Principle 7 among the proposed legal principles attached to the Brundtland Report declares that "States shall ensure that conservation is treated as an integral part of the planning and implementation of development activities and provide assistance to other States, especially to developing countries, in support of environmental protection and sustainable development".[19] Another requirement of such a cooperation between nations is that environmental policies of all the States should enhance and not adversely affect the present or future development, potential of developing countries, nor should they hamper the attainment of better living conditions for all.[20]

Regional Development

In a time where planning for regional development was almost unknown to decision-makers, Delos Three has drawn the attention of the mankind towards the need to tackle the problem of regional underdevelopment, by emphasizing that the problems of urban spread or mass migration to the cities could not be dealt with locally since they cut across most of the customary lines of authority. It was suggested that the emergence of regional agencies and systems for planning and administration was simply a symbol of striving to match new human environment with appropriate

---

19   United Nations, World Commission on Environment and Development, **Our Common Future (Report of the Brundtland Commission),** Oxford University Press, Oxford, 1986, p. 349.

20   **Declaration of The United Nations Conference on the Human Environment,** Stockholm, 1972 (Principle 11).

institutions in charge of controlling the area and regions necessary to achieve this purpose. Specific purposes of concrete examples in the field were mentioned as, for example, the redress of economic imbalances as in Mezzogiorno in Italy, the easing of migration by developing alternative growth poles as in Guayana Project in Venezuela, and the settlement of immigrants as in the Lakisch Project in Israel.[21] Timely warning have been made regarding the nature and functions of existing regional institutions and the lessons they hold for future regional development. As a result, density issues and regional development have been two specific issues debated in Delos Three. This was eleven years before the announcement of the Vancouver Declaration to the world public opinion, where due regard was given to the role to be played by regional planning in meeting the needs of human settlements.

Environmental Considerations and Natural Resources

Worldwide concern for environmental protection and the increased consciousness for more rational use of natural resources are developments that are halted by the efforts of the United Nations which are culminated in organizing the UN Stockholm Conference on Environment and Development in 1972. Similar concerns had been reflected into the Report of the Club of Rome *The Limits to Growth* that was published in the same year. It Is remarkable to note that Delos Three had made a reference to some consequences of population growth and technological progress which were not self-correcting and needed public intervention. These were visual monotony, lack of satisfaction of urban design,

21   **Delos Three, Report of the Third Symposion,** July 12-19, 1965.

pollution of air and water. These problems were among the basic elements which reduced man's pleasure and pride in his urban setting.[22] In the following year, participants of Delos Four concentrated their analyses on the quality of various aspects of the eco-system. The stress was on natural resources, wilderness areas for recreation, untouched natural habitats for biological research, water tables and circuits and unpolluted air, which all were, in varying degrees, in need of protection against the encroachments by human beings.

It was pointed out that "the land between and beyond the urban centers was suffering increasingly from the inadequate or exploitative methods of both agricultural and urban development. As the city advances, a fall-out of disorder, neglect and ugliness tends to spread with it"[23]. It was agreed that the present chaotic combination of overdensity and sprawl added to the production of an unacceptable urban landscape. According to the pessimistic diagnosis of the Delos Four participants, that was shared by the authors of *The Limits to Growth* nearly a decade later, mankind has not yet found the aesthetic means of understanding and ordering creatively the vast elements of complex and dynamic change which have overtaken the city.

The same pessimism continued to exist throughout the 1960's with regard to pressing problems of urbanization, settlement and environment as reflected in the Delos Six Declaration in 1968. There was a growing urgency with regard to such worldwide problems as the search for a world order to eliminate war, the need to check the population explosion, to provide food to prevent starvation, *to halt the*

---

22   **Delos Three, Report of the Third Symposion,** July 12-19, 1965.
23   **Delos Four, Report of the Fourth Symposion,** July 16-23, 1966.

contamination of the environment, and to deal with *the discrepancy between resources and expectations that exist in so many countries of the world.*[24] Similar ideas underlying the interconnectedness of peace, development and environment were incorporated into the text of the Rio Declaration on Environment and Development only one and a half decade after the Delos Six.[25] According to the concerned principle of the Rio Declaration, "Peace, development and environmental protection are interdependent and indivisible".

Repeatedly, attention was drawn into the fact that if we treat the living ecology of the planet as a seamless web, within which breaks are disastrous we can plan for the way in which man's construction of an artificial environment can complement and improve the natural environment of this planet. It is with this understanding that it was suggested that "Within this cosmological system, we will no longer seek to maximize isolated effects, one at the expense of another, but seek to optimize and integrate the factors involved for the benefit of man".[26]

Even an instrument as specific as recycling was in the agenda of Ekisticians during the Delos Eight. They have recognized that constituents of many products made by man for his use must be recycled [27], because the trend was towards use and re-use rather than ownership, and sequential multiple use rather than merely individual use in order to

24 **Delos Six, Delos Declaration 1968: Man and his Settlements,** July 6-13, 1968.

25 Principle 25 of the Rio Declaration on Environment and Development.

26 **Delos Seven, Report of the Seventh Symposion: Society and Human Settlements,** July 12-19, 1969.

27 **Delos Eight, Report of the Eight Symposion: Networks and Human Settlements: Policies for the Future,** July 3-10, 1970.

overcome the scarcity of non-renewable natural resources. One should not forget that the demands of our population are growing and our planetary resources are limited. It was further pointed out by the Declaration of the Eight Symposion that while recycling of some products will require largescale operations, closing the cycle of water and re-use of water several times had potentials even in small communities. This was an early announcement of the principle of *sustainable development* that was going to be used in international legal instruments as far as sixteen years later than Delos Eight.[28] This was related to a more substantial issue in environmental protection which concerned the right of future generations over the resources of the planet. Such concepts as "children yet unborn"[29] have been used in Delos declarations as early as in the 1960's; and the need was expressed for immediate change in environmental conditions and the nature of our society for the benefit even of infants still unborn.[30]

Delos Nine rightly emphasized the need to have a different approach to the understanding of environmental issues as conceptualised earlier and underlined the importance of stimulating new and creative forms of human settlements in which balanced human communities could be formed. In other words, the more traditional regulations covering basic biological needs such as water, sewage disposal,

28   United Nations, World Commission on Environment and Development, **Our Common Future (Report of the Brundtland Commission),** Oxford University Press, Oxford, 1986.

29   **Delos Six, Delos Declaration 1968: Man and his Settlements,** July-13, 1968.

30   **Delos Seven, Report of the Seventh Symposion: Society and Human Settlements,** July 12-19, 1969.

unpolluted environments, space and safety had to be taken together with basic policies for human settlements.[31] In addition, this new requirement should be not only written into legislation but accompanied by effective inspection, including automatic monitoring devices and by stringent penalties for infringement.

Conclusions

We have been living in a world that is considerably different from the one of the 1960's and 1970's. Revolutionary changes have taken place since then in communications technology and industrial development. Social, economic and political life have been deeply influenced by all these changes. Material and non-material conditions have been greatly influenced as a result of continuing globalization. The world is still struggling with the problems encountered in this process of transformation, and the nations as well as international organizations are trying to develop the necessary means to reduce social and economic costs to humanity while increasing profitability. One of the most important problems still waiting for solution is unsatisfactory living conditions all over the world, deteriorating environmental quality and the impact of irrational and contradictory settlement policies.

A number of selected and distinguished scholars, philosophers, authors, and practioners of planning, architecture and environmental sciences under the leadership of late Constantinos A. Doxiadis have greatly contributed to both theory and practice of the Science of Human Settlements

31   Delos Nine: Declaration on the State of Emergency in Human Settlements; July 12-19, 1971.

(Ekistics) during the Delos Symposia convened between 1963 and 1975. It is the sincerebelief of the present author that the intellectual caliber of the ideas developed during the debates in Delos Symposia is extremely high and relevant to the enlightenment of the most pressing problems facing the world today.

Thank to their visdom, expertise and prediction, decision-makers, teachers and planners of the 21st century will have no difficulty to find the most appropriate solutions to such contemporary problems as rapid urbanization, rational settlement pattern, regional underdevelopment, sustainable architecture and urban development, eradication of poverty within cities, deteriorating environmental conditions, housing for the poor and middle-income families, bringing local authorities as close as possible to the citizens, and the like.

I would suggest that the texts of the Delos Symposia Declarations be published under the title of Delos Principles and put into the use of concerned schools and departments of the universities.

Bibliography

Birnbacher, Dieter, La responsabilité envers les générations futures, Presses Universitaires de France, Paris 1994.

Conseil de l'Europe, La Charte Urbaine Europeenne, Strasbourg, 1993.

Council of Europe, European Charter of Local Self-Government, Strasbourg, 1985.

Council of Europe, European Conference of Ministers responsible for Regional Planning (CEMAT), Guiding Principles for Spatial Sustainable Development of the European Continent, adopted at the Twelveth Session of the European Conference of the Ministers responsible for Regional Planning, 7-8 September 2000, Hannover.

Declaration of the United Nations Conference on Human Environment, Stockholm, 1972.

Déjeant-Ponts, Maguelonne et Pallamaerts, Marc, Droits de l'Homme et l'Environnement, Ed. du Conseil de l'Europe, Strasbourg, 2002.

Delos Three, *Report of the Third Symposion,* July 12-19, 1965.

Delos Four, *Report of the Fourth Symposion,* July 16-23, 1966.

Delos Five, *Report of the Fifth Symposion: Strategy for Human Settlements,* July 22-29, 1967.

Delos Six, *Delos declaration 1968:"Man and His Settlements ",* July 6- 13, 1968.

Delos Seven, *Report of the Seventh Symposion: "Society and Human Settlements",* July 12-19, 1969.

Delos Eight, *Report of the Eight Symposion:"Networks and Human Settlements: Policies for the Future":* July 3-10, 1970.

Delos Nine, Declaration on the State of Emergency in Human Settlements, July 12-19, 1971.

Delos Ten, Declaration of Delos Symposion 1972, July 9-17, 1972.

Delos Eleven, Declaration of Delos Symposion Eleven: Action for Human Settlements, July 8-12, 1974.

Delos Twelve, Declaration of Delos Symposion 1975, July 13-18, 1975.

Keleş, Ruşen, "The Principle of Subsidiarity in Service of Sustainable Development", in D. Camarda and L. Grassini (eds.), Options Mediterraneennes, No:57, Local Resources and Global Trades: Environment and Agriculture in the Mediterranean Regions, CI-HEAM/ IAMB-EU-DG-XII, Bari, 2003, 99.109-115.

Lefebvre, Henri, La Production de l'Espace, Editions Anthropos, Paris, 1974.

United Nations, World Commission on Environment and Development, (Brundtland Commission), Our Common Future, Oxford University Press, Oxford, 1986.

United Nations, The Istanbul Declaration and Habitat Agenda, UNCHS, Nairobi, 1996.

United Nations, Rio Declaration on Environment and Development, Nairobi, 1992.

United Nations, Basic Facts on Urbanization, UNCHS, Nairobi, 1996.

United Nations, The Johannesburg Declaration on Sustainable Development, Nairobi, September 2002.

World Bank, From Plan to Market, World Development Report, 1997, Washington.

Urban Turkey in The Year 2000: A Pessimistic Scenario[*]

In a little more than decade, the world population will begin to live in the 21st century. It will reach 6.4 billion level with an increase of 2.4 billion in comparison to 1975. At the same time, for the first time in history, urban-rural balance of the world population will be changed in favor of the first. In terms of numbers, population growth will be faster in 2000 than today, with an annual addition of 100 million people compared to 75 million in 1975.

Almost 90 percent of the population increase will take place in less developed countries. By the year 2000, urban population of less developed countries will be around 2.1 billion, as compared to 1 billion of the more developed countries. While the economic growth rates of the less developed countries are expected to be higher than those of the industrialized nations, the GNP per capita in most poor countries remains low. Widening of the existing large gap between the rich and poor nations seems to be inescapable. Although the world food production was projected to increase 90 percent during the 30 year period between 1970 and 2000, the global per capita increase of food production will be no more than 15 percent over the same period.

[*] Turkish Political Science Association, Turkey in the Year 2000, Ankara, 1989, pp.199-232.

Furthermore, the bulk of the increase will be consumed by the countries that already have relatively high per capita food consumption and calorie intake.

According to the findings **the Global Report to the President**, if present trends continue, the world in 2000 will be more crowded, more polluted, less stable ecologically, and more vulnerable to disruption than the world we live in now. Services stresses involving population, resources, and environment are clearly visible ahead. Despite revolutionary advances in technology, life for hundreds of millions of desperately poor will be no better; and for many, it will be even worse. Unless the nations act decisively to change the current trends, humanity is expected to face a foreseeable crisis.

Not only great disparities among nations, but also those within countries are expected to continue. Former President of the World Bank, Mr. Mc. Namara had pointed or that every decade of delay in reaching replacement fertility, the world's ultimately stabilized population would be about 11 percent greater. And unless the fertility levels decline to replacement levels, environmental deterioration caused by large populations would create living conditions that make reductions in fertility difficult to achieve; and on the other hand, continuing population growth world increase further the pressures on the environmental and land. These pessimistic expectations, inspired by neo-Malthusian views promise nothing more than a much trouble world at the beginning of the 21st century.

Mediterranean Region

Let us have a brief look at the situation in the Mediterranean Region, although it is risky to make, scientifically uncertain forecasts in the field of demography, they are necessary for the establishment of scenarios for future developments. With this caution in mind, one must remember that by the year 2000, the total population of the Mediterranean Basin will be increased by about 100 million to a total population of 440 million inhabitants. According to the estimates of **the Blue Plan**, Italy and France with prectically stabilizing populations, will have been replaced by Turkey and Egypt, as the most populous nations in the region, with a population of 65 million and 63 million, respectively. Average annual growth rate during 1980-2000 will be 4.1 percent for Libya, 3.5 percent for Algeria, 3.4 percent for Syria, 2.4 percent for Morocco, 2.2 percent Tunisia, 2 percent for Egypt and 1.9 percent for Turkey. The same forecasts visualize Turkey and Egypt with 100 million inhabitants each, possibly more for Turkey, in the year 2025.

Turkey

It can be easily admitted that Turkey is not an exception to the foregoing demographic conditions.

Just as socio-economic characteristics of Turkey are influenced by the world-wide trends in demography and economic relations, present and future urban Turkey is and will be, to a great extent, and outcome of the changes in the socio-economic and political parameters that will prevail at the turn of the present century have to be taken into consideration in order to have a more or less realistic picture of urban Turkey by that time. However, it must be kept in mind also that urban Turkey in 2000 will not be simply a product of socio-economic dynamics of the years between 1987 and 2000, but a result of a long historical development process.

Population

Based on the assumption of various fertility decline rates, it is estimated that the total population will reach a level between 66.6 and 74.0 million. However, a moderate fertility decline alternative will make the population of Turkey grow up to 71.4 million by 2000. The main assumption behind these estimates is not only the fertility and mortality rates, but also is that the rates of internal and international migration will remain unchanged. For instance, it has been assumed by Tuncer that natural population increase per thousand will decline to 26.7 during 1985-1990, to 25.7 during 1990-1995 and to 24.6 during 1995-2000. Allowing for the minus 0.6 per migration rate during 1995-2000, it is expected that population increase per thousand in the same period will be no more than 24. It is also generally assumed that accelerated urbanization will reduce the reproduction rate though social change. But the reality is just the opposite and the findings of most survey changes or no change at all in urban fertility rates.

H. Cillow, using the findings of a research done by the U.N., predicts that even under the conditions of slow population growth, the population of Turkey is likely to reach 69.4 million by 2000. According to his estimates, Infant mortality is expected to decrease from 103 to 39 for females and from 110 to 48 for males during the same period 1995-2000.

Table 1: National Population Projections (000)

Years	B. Tuncer's Estimates			SPO	SIS
	V Variant	B Variant	C Variant		
1985	49,968	50,700	50,891	49,482	50,664
1990	55,770	57,217	57,929	55,008	56,941
1995	61,402	64,227	65,649	60,829	64,485
2000	66,605	71,351	74,005	66,455	73,029

A recent study carried cut by the General Directorate of Environment estimated that the population of Turkey will be somewhere between 69 and 72 million by the year 2000. According to the findings of this study that formulated various scenarios for the immediate future of Turkey, the rate of population growth will be less. than that of the countries of the Mediterranean Basin as a whole.

It is common to formulate scenarios for future developments under various assumptions. Most of the scenarios take as their starting points various estimates of population growth rates, growth of per capita income, unemployment international economic relations, etc. None of the population projections for Turkey is in favor of developing optimistic scenarios. Essentially, the effect of the determinants differs marginally from each other. As the most important determinant of development, population growth affects considerably the rate of economic growth. It is my belief that there will be no major structural change in the Turkish economy before the end of this century and therefore any positive impact upon the urban sector is unlikely to occur. It is mainly because of this conviction that I did not consider appropriate or useful to attempt to formulate different kinds of scenarios under various hypotheses. Consequently, an essentially pessimistic scenario has been designed with exceptional lights of optimism.

Urbanization

Turkey is one of the most rapidly urbanizing countries in the World. Although almost half of its population lives in urban centers (in places of 10.000 and more inhabitants), the annual rate of urbanization has been, throughout the last 25 years, around 6 percent. Only after 1970, a slight slowing in the annual rate of urbanization has been observed. As a matter of fact, the annual rate of urbanization declined from 7.2 percent during 1965-1970, to 6.3 percent during 1970-1975 and to 4.3 percent during 1975-1980. It increased again to 5.1 percent during 1980-1985. The slowing down prior to 1980 can be interpreted as a result of increasing inflation rates and threatening insecurity in the cities caused by political violence. Although it has slowed down somewhat, rapid urbanization is still continuing at a rapid pace as reflected in the absolute figures.

As a result of economic development and hopes to find better employment opportunities, the percentage of those living in urban centers rose dramatically during the last 35 years. If current trends in urban growth continue until the turn of the century, and it seems that there is no real indication that they will not, then an overwhelmingly large proportion of the population will be living in cities. It is estimated that this percentage will be increased from 50.3 percent in 1985 to 70 percent by 2000.

Table 2: Growth of Urban Population in Turkey (1960-2000)

Years	Urban Population	% of the Total
1960	6,999,025	25.2
1985	25,791,617	50.3
2000	45,000,000	70

It is generally accepted that the increase of urban population is caused mainly by two demographic factors. One is the natural growth and the second rural to urban migration. Both factors played a significant role for a long time in Turkish urbanization. However, the generally accepted hypothesis that declining birth rates in the cities make the migration component the most significant factor in urbanization, does not hold true for the case of Turkey where the birth rates are still considerably high even in the metropolitan centers.

The growth of urban population takes place in the larger size categories, namely in the cities of 100.000 and more inhabitants. As a matter of fact, their relative share in urban population increased from 45.3 percent in 1960 to 64.9 percent in 1985 and it is estimated that it will be 75 percent by 2000. During the 1960-1985 period, 18.5 million people began to live in cities, and it can be safely assumed that 20 million more will be living in urban areas by the year 2000. Out for this 20 million people, nearly 18 million will be settled in cities of 100.000 and more inhabitants.

As to the individual cities, it can be assumed that a few more cities, in addition to Istanbul (9 million), Ankara (5.5

million) and Izmir (4 million), will be added to the category of cities of one million and more inhabitants. These are Adana (2.5 million), Bursa (2 million), Gaziantep (1.3 million) and Konya (1 million). The population of the following 12 cities, namely Kayseri (900.000), Mersin (900.000), Sivas (800.000), Antalya (800.000), Elazığ (700.000), Eskişehir (650,000), Diyarbakır (650.000), Samsun (600,000), Kırıkkale (500.000), Erzurum (500.000), Zonguldak (500.000) and Şanlurfa (490.000), will have more than half a million population.[1] The total population of the largest 7 will be around 25 million, in other words, nearly 56 percent of Turkey's urban population. Only Istanbul will accommodate almost ten million inhabitants which will be roughly equal to the population of Greece.

Table 3: Cities by Size-Categories (1960-2000)

Size Categories	1960	1985	2000
I) 10.000-20.000			
Population	940.850	2.603.883	3.150.000
% of total urban	15.8	10.1	7.0
Number of cities	69	189	180
II) 20.000-50.000			
Population	1.447.966	3.493.409	2.250.000
% of total urban	21.9	13.6	5.0

---

1   In one of the SPO publications, slightly different estimates are mad efor the size of cities. First group cities: Istanbul (8.425.000), Ankara (4.930.000), İzmir (3.500.000), Adana (2.5000.000), Bursa (1.310.000), Gaziantep (1.3000.000); second group: Konya (950.000), Sivas (870.000), Kayseri (850.000), Elazığ (750.000), Antalya (702.000), Samsun (685.000), Eskişehir (660.000), Diyarbakır (625.000), Erzurum (530.000), Zonguldak (500.000). D.P.T., **Konut Sektör Raporu** (Housing Policy Working Paper), SPO 1870, SPD 365, Ek Tablolar: s.18, December 1982.

	Number of cities	51	111	150
III)	**50.000-100.000**			
	Population	1.222.719	2.952.218	5.850.000
	% of total urban	17.0	11.4	13.0
	Number of cities	18	45	55
IV)	**100.000 and more**			
	Population	3.387.490	16.739.380	33.750.000
	% of total urban	45.3	64.9	75.0
	Number of cities	9	35	65
	Total urban	6.999.025	25.788.890	45.000.000
	Total number of cities	147	380	450
	Average city size	47.612	67.866	108.889

Table 4: Number and Size of Large Cities by 2000

Size Categories	Number of Cities		
	1960	**1985**	**2000**
Over 1 million	1	3	7
500.000 – 1 million	2	2	11
100.000 – 500.000	6	3	47
Total	**9**	35	65

Urban Employment

Among the forces contributing to mass migration to urban centers, push factors are particularly important. They are the result of higher birth rates and relatively low level of productivity and income in the agricultural sector. This results in an excess of population in relation to cultivable land and tends to inhibit any improvement in rural living conditions. On the other hand, the pulling characteristics of major cities, strengthened by the improvements of the network of transportation communication throughout the country and the changes in the economic structure of cities are not negligible despite the fact that they are not as important as the push factors. Better employment opportunities and wage differentials in urban areas, as compared with the countryside, served to reinforce the existing tendencies to migrate to cities especially until the 1970's.

However, one has to be careful not to give a too optimistic impression about the employment structure of urban centers. Marginal sectors in major metropolitan cities is quite large and keeps expanding. The amount of surplus labor in the non-agricultural sector is considerably large not only in absolute figures, but also in percentages. The rate of unemployment, including disguised unemployed is around 15 percent, and the amount of non-agricultural (urban) surplus labor will be not less than 3 million by 1989.

In relation to the future increase of the per capita GNP, which is expected to be around 1.886 U.S. Dollars by 2000, lack of capital, inflation, unemployment and the declining prosperity are expected to become highly severe economic problems in the cities. In order to be able to employ the totality of the labor force in gainful occupations, achieving an annual growth rate of 10 percent is mandatory. Even the most optimistic estimates show that in the coming 15 years, the annual economic growth rate can not be higher than 6-7 percent. During the last 20 years, 1 million people have been added annually to the labor supply, and at present the absorptive capacity of the economy is only half of this figure.

There is not much reason to expect a radical improvement in the economic conditions compared to the past two decades. Estimates made by B. Tuncer show that by the year 2000, urban labor supply will reach well over 15 million and a considerable part of it which is not demanded by industry will be working sectors whose productivity levels are significantly lower than the productivity levels of the modern sectors including agriculture (Tuncer, 59 - 60).

Our rather pessimistic view on the urban employment structure is mainly inspired by the scenario developed in the first phase of the Blue Plan, which assumes that the past 20 years' trends will continue under more adverse conditions and economic conditions will gradually get more severe. These adverse conditions may take such forms as the continuation of import restrictions imposed by the developed countries of Europe, United States and Canada, inflation, oil crisis, and energy shortages. Under such adverse influences, assuming that the rate of growth during 1987-2000 will be 3.1 percent per year, and that population growth rate will be 2.4 percent per year, then the national income will not be more than 1.163 U.S. Dollars by the year 2000 (Blue Plan, 221). When the fact that the creation of employment in the industrial for one person costs about 35 million T.L. as 1987, (approximately 40.000 U.S. Dollars) is taken into consideration, one could easily agree that Turkey will be faced with a serious urban unemployment problem by the end of the century.

Urban Infrastructure

Housing and squatting problems as well as the inadequacy of urban public services together with lack of urban infrastructure are closely related with the general conditions of the economy. Perhaps the most important and severely felt needs of urban areas is drinking water. Inadequacy of sewerage systems should also be added to the infrastructure problems. Although the dwelling units with piped water increased greatly in number during the last two decades, there still exists great bottlenecks in the sewerage systems. The unsatisfied need is still alarming. Water needs are also growing at a rapid pace and it is estimated that it will double up by the year 2000. The most striking increase of need is for drinking water. There is a steady increase in the number of smaller municipalities having modern water installations.

However, only 20 percent of dwellings in urban areas have now connections to modern sewerage systems.

Rapid urbanization makes the service performance levels in metropolitan centers highly inadequate in relatively short periods. Water needs of cities of 100.000 and more population are met by the central government, namly by the State Water Works (DST). By 1990, only 80 percent of their needs will be met. The water installations of smaller municipalities, those between 3.000 and 100.000 inhabitants, are within the responsibility of the Bank of Provinces (İller Bankası). Again, according to the estimates made by the U.N. in connection with International Drinking Water Supply and Sanitation Decade, by 1990, 290 out of 949 such municipalities of (30.6 percent of the total) will be provided with sufficient water supply.

The share of the drinking water and sewerage investments in total investment figures increased from 4.5 percent in 1981 to 8.5 percent in 1986. However, the service performance is far from being satisfactory.

Despite the fact that in order to meet the needs for water and sewerage for the year 2000, a total investment of 2.251.395 million TL. at 1985 prices will have be made by DSI before the turn of the century.

Bank of the Provinces, ISKI (Istanbul Water and Sewerage Administration), DSI and the General Directorate of Rural Services will play their part in achieving the target mentioned above.

However, it is much doubtful that the need for such a huge investment could be met. It is primarily because of the inadequacy of these urban services that during 1977, 6882 people were identified suffering from typhoid, fever, paratyphoid, dysentery, bru cellosis and hepatitis, and 41 died from these diseases (Official Gazette No: 17813, September 15, 1982). Especially in the squatter settlements, lack of sewerage system creates a growing threat to the health of increasing number of urban poor. Unless the need for investment is immediately met, there will be every reason to be fearful for the material health of the urban masses.

Table 5: Water Needs of Turkish Municipalities
(Billion cubic meters)

Nature	Years	
	1985	2000
Drinking and use water	4.73	9.07
Irrigation	31.80	57.60
Industry	4.00	7.30
Total	40.53	73.97

Urban Public Transportation

As the working population in metropolitan areas increases, urban public transportation begins to face serious bottlenecks. Even at present, average journey to work is nearly 60 minutes in Istanbul Metropolitan Area. Lack of an efficient system of public transportation in major centers will tend in the near future to increase the time spent for daily trips to and from work places. It is expected that the average time necessary for journey to work increase from 60 to 90 minutes for Istanbul by the year 2000.

Rapid increase of population and that of the number of private cars make daily traffic in the streets much worse than at present and it will tend to aggravate the existing urban transportation problems. It is almost certain that there will be no restriction on the use of private cars because of the public demand and of the pressures of car manufacturers. Increasing share of the private cars in urban transportation is not only wasteful from the standpoint of the economy, but also it adds to the deterioration of traffic conditions.

It is also certain that it will be no longer possible to alleviate traffic congestion in metropolitan centers by trying to rearrange the road junctions. Unless the present attitudes of some planners to regard the transportation issue as an end itself without paying any attention to its relationships with the structure of the economy and society, and land use is altered, urban public transportation may be expected to continue as an urban problem more aggravated than at present.

As a result of further concentration of people and industrial activities in Istanbul and Marmara region, it might be necessary to have several more bridges on the Bosphorus, in addition to the one being presently constructed.

On the other hand, haphazard physical developments and unplanned decentralized pattern of the metropolitan area will make it mandatory the establishment of a rapid transit network immediately in order to make mass transportation possible. It is quite doubtful whether the conditions of Turkey's economy will be favorable to meeting the prohibitively high costs of such large investment projects without increasing further the foreign debt burden of the country.

Housing and Squatting

Housing is the number one problem in urban Turkey at present and it will undoubtedly be so by the end of the century. It is estimated that yearly housing needs will be around 300.000 units, but the number of dwellings actually constructed is as small as two thirds of the real need. The gap has. been filled up so far by increasing number of gecekondus. It is again estimated that during the 15 years that ends by the year 2000, there will be an additional need for 6.3 million units, in other words, an annual need of at least 315.000. If one adds the number of needed new units to meet the already accumulated needs, one reaches a yearly need figure of 425.000.

Until 2000, almost half (47 percent) of the annual need will be created in the largest five cities only. These are Istanbul, Ankara, Izmir, Adana and Bursa. Their shares will be 70.000, 50.000, 35.000, 25.000 and 20.000', respectively, taking into consideration their rate of urbanization, population growth and the change in the family size (KENT-KOOP Konut 81, 22-23). It goes without saying that major housing problems will be felt in the larger cities and they will certainly reach much larger dimensions as these cities continue to grow.

The above mentioned housing needs estimates are similar to the forecasts made by B, Tuncer in the middle of the 1970's, who found that total housing needs will be around 7.4 million units during 1985 - 2000, which represents an annual need of 490.000. This figure includes not only the demographic demand, but also the replacement demand and the demand stemming from other sources (such as demolitions, expropriations, earthquakes, fires, etc.) and they would require to increase considerably the capacity of the housing sector to build social dwellings. Urban housing stock of Turkey comprises a total of 7.064.742 units and it is now estimated that in the coming 15 years it has to be doubled up. The figure above also includes the unlicensed dwellings that are called "gecekondu". The extent of the need will certainly put the policy makers in a difficult position for the allocation of scarce resources to competing purposes.

Squatting is more than a housing problem but it is closely with it. Dual structure of large cities is well reflected in the contradictions between the planned neighborhoods on one hand, and illegally built gecekondu settlements, on the other. At present, 70 percent of the inhabitants of Ankara live in shanty towns. The figure is 50 percent for both Istanbul and Izmir. More than three quarters of all gecekondus are located in the largest five cities. The share of Ankara alone is 30 percent.

In 1960, there were 240.000 gecekondus in Turkey, 12 million people living in them, totaling to 16.4 percent of urban population, while in 1985, 7.5 million people, as many as 29.5 percent of urban population live in 1.5 million gecekondus. Unless the present trends in rapid urbanization, land speculation, an uneven income distribution pattern is reversed, one might expect a total of 12.5 million people, as many as 25.5 percent of urban population, living in 2.5 million gecekondus in major Turkish cities by the year 2000. The difference between the percentage of gecekondu inhabitants in urban population in 1985 and 2000 may be attributed partly to the efforts of the government to implement new social housing policies.

One should not overlook the fact that present schemes formulated by the government under its new developmentalism approach are primarily aimed at helping the middle and lower-middle income families, and they cannot remedy at all the chronic housing deficit in the sector comprising the lowest income groups. In other words, the new Mass Housing policies might undoubtedly contribute to reducing the rate of increase of housing deficit, but they cannot be regarded as a definite remedy for the solution of gecekondu problems. Since there seems to be not much chance to alter the present uneven income distribution pattern in the short run, the problems of "Ganz unten", in the words of Günter Wallraff, may be expected to continue and the semi-organized market for squatter housing will continue to function as before even beyond 2000.

It has been assumed so far that the process of squatting was a rational response of urban poor to the failure of the public and private housing markets to provide shelter for the poor. Squatting was regarded as an optimal solution to housing problem. It was optimal both for the employer and the employees for the reproduction of the labor force and for the maintaining of the capitalist system. However, K.

Kartal's researches came up with the finding that the gece-kondu building process was crucially expensive economically. On the other hand, a great number of gecekondus are already substandard and deprived of all major urban amenities. Moreover, gecekondu inhabitants get gradually unsatisfied with their shelters as they become more urbanized. As a result of the social depreciation of the gecekondu buildings, attempts to replace them cause repetitive investments. Demolition is sometimes required by new housing legislation. Demolition and replacement constitute a significant part of the housing need. It can be safely assumed that at least 10 percent of the present gecekondus will be demolished by the year 2000 and this will create additional demand for housing.

The concept of housing as a public service makes it mandatory for the government or municipalities to intervene in the urban land market to curp land speculation and to exercise a certain rent control for the benefit of low and middle-income families. At present, such policies are not implemented effectively. Contrarily, the laws pardoning the illegally built gecekondus and providing the squatters with the land titles encourage prospective gecekondu builders and reduce the amount of urban land that is available for social housing purposes. If present partisan considerations in the distribution of land titles to gecekondu inhabitants continue, the problem of urban land supply will take extremely severe dimensions before the end of the century.

It is also expected that the present rate of owner occupiers which is nearly 55 percent be declined to less than 50 percent in urban areas by 2000, and that of tenants which is about 36 percent be increased to more than 45 percent as a result of increasing urbanization. This seems inescapable despite the prevailing values of Turkish families and governmental efforts to favor owner occupied housing. Such an expectation renders the need for rent control in one form or another still more important.

Disparities Among Geographic Regions

Social and economic differences among geographic regions appear to be an enduring problem of settlement pattern of Turkey. They are, to a certain degree, an aspect of rural-urban differences. Regional inequalities are a function of economic, social and political structure and historical development of the country. Since only the existence of large urban centers can diffuse development upon their hinterlands through their spread effects, it is not difficult then to see why some regions like the East, South-East and the Black Sea lagged behind the relatively developed Western regions in terms of industrial and cultural development and the standards of living.

None of the 9 cities of 100,000 and more inhabitants existed in Turkey was in the above mentioned regions in 1960. The state of the Eastern regions were particularly striking with their semi-feudalistic production relations prevailing in part of it. In their careful study of Turkey's social and cultural structure during the early 1960's, George and Barbara Helling found alarming inequalities between regions and referred to "the existence of two different Turkeys within the national boundaries", thus drawing attention to regional and rural-urban disparities.

Although the achievements of the planned development period are impressive as far as the balanced distribution of public services among various regions are concerned, regional disparities are still standing.

The rate of urbanization during 1960 - 1985 increased from 16.1 percent to 39.9 percent in the South-Eastern region and from 13.4 percent to 31.1 percent in the East.

Table 6: Urbanization and Geographic Regions (1960-2000)

Regions	Years					
	1960		1985		2000	
	Urban Pop. (%)	No: of cities	Urban Pop. (%)	No: of cities	Urban Pop. (%)	No: of cities
Marmara	43.3	30	74.1	66	90	85
Aegean	30.3	21	54.8	44	58	50
Mediterranean	31.6	21	52.7	47	60	60
Central	24.8	26	53.3	84	64	95
East	13.4	11	31.1	36	38	45
South-East	16.1	9	39.9	31	50	40
Black Sea	25.2	27	29.2	72	34	80
Total		145		380		450
Urb. Pop.	25.1		50.3		70	

The rate of urbanization may be considered as a composite index of all social, economic and cultural development indicators. The role of the priorities given to backward regions in the planned development period (1963 on) for the distribution of the investments of health, education and urban infrastructure is not negligible in the increase of the rate of urbanization of the less developed regions. However still exists remarkable inequalities among regions. And of course, neither the private nor the public sector could ignore the importance of the availability of urban infrastructure in their investment decisions. Regional development policies adopted by the Development Plans have not been as much effective as it was hoped to be simply because of the propensity of the entrepreneurs to prefer as industrial location already developed regions and metropolitan centers.

For the year 2000, a slightly different picture may be expected. Because, even today, 13 out of 35 cities with a population of 100.000 and more are in the regions of Eastern and South-Eastern Anatolia and in the Black Sea. In the coming 15 years, 30 more cities will be added to this category and 20 more them will be situated in the regions which are regarded as less developed at present. This is perhaps one of the few optimistic expectations one can have for the near future of Turkey, no matter how will be the internal structure of those centers.

The reason is not only the existence of several relatively large and rapidly growing cities but also the promise of the multi-purpose Southern Anatolian Development Project. This project will include 15 dams of various sizes, 18 hydroelectric power plants and provides the opportunity to increase not only the energy production but also the total amount of territory that can be irrigated. The region of Southeastern Anatolia is an underdeveloped region with rich but untapped resources. It comprises 6 provinces, namely Adıyaman, Diyarbakır, Gaziantep, Mardin, Siirt and Şanlıurfa in part or in total.

Although the area overs about one tenth of the total land surface of the country and 1/11 of the total population, it possesses the totality of petroleum and phosphate resources and reserves of the country, and one fourth of the cultivable land, underground waters and hydroelectric energy. At present, only 2 percent of the irrigation opportunities and 0.2 percent of the energy resources are used. The construction of most of the components of the project will be terminated before 2000 and the project as a whole will bring dramatic changes, in the production capacity of the region. It is estimated, for instance, that, 22 billion Kwh/year power, will be produced. This will be equal to the total energy production of Turkey in 1981. As far as the irrigation is concerned, a territory of 300.000 hectares larger than the irrigated land by public authorities during 1923 - 1987 will be irrigated. Only the Atatürk Dam will produce more than sone third of the regional energy output and it will increase the amount of agricultural product 10 to 60 times.

All these may change the socio-economic structure of the Southeastern region radically. Out-migration will slow down to a large extent and the growth rate of cities like Şanlıurfa, Diyarbakır, Gaziantep, Batman and Siirt and a dozen of medium-sized cities will be increased. Absorption of surplus population by the increased demand for labor of new employment opportunities in the urban centers in the region will further contribute to the replacement of the decentralized pattern of settlement by a centralized one through checking internal migration. This is why the rate of urbanization of the Southeast Region is estimated to be around 50 percent by 2000. Change in the economic structure of the region in parallel to urbanization will also have far reaching effects upon all social development indicators such as literacy, communication exposure, religion, world outlook, and the like.

Whether the conflict stemming from the ethnical characteristics of the region will be intensified or not will depend upon the changes to take place in the relationships of the productive forces. In other words, unless the semi-feudal production relations are reversed through a radical land reform and through systematic efforts to employ the idle labor in industries suitable for the needs and potentials of the region, outside forces determined to exploit the geo-political position of the region as well as dissidents within the national boundaries will not hesitate to make the maximum profit out of the backwardness of the region. Therefore, the Southeastern Anatolian Development Project has to be supported with socioeconomic policies aimed at creating structural changes in the regions if it is going to eradicate poverty and check the separatist tendencies in the area.

Environment

Public concern for the protection of environmental values is rather new in Turkey and it has developed after major natural and historical environmental assets have been partly or totally damaged as a result of urbanization during 1950-1985. Taking the factor of environment into consideration within the course of industrialization, modernization of agriculture and urbanization was adopted as a principle only after the Third 5 Year Development Plan (1973 - 1978) and the official view adopted in the plans maintained that development policies do not contradict at all environmental policies. On contrary, they reinforce each other. However, certain crucial bottlenecks exist. One of the most significant bottlenecks is concerned with the utilization of water, land, air and energy resources. The problems concerning the level of per capita national income, housing, land erosion, natural disasters, protection of forests and coastal areas, balanced nutrition, etc., are all related to environment. The role of education, technology and resource allocation is not less important.

It was estimated by the Blue Plan authors that according to the most optimistic guesses, not more than 1 percent of the GNP may be allocated to the purposes of environmental protection. Although this amount is a little more than the previous figures it will still be insufficient for the achievement of the goal, and a considerable improvement in environmental conditions can not be expected with such a negligible increase of financial resources to be devoted to environment.

It is suffice to simply mention that only in Istanbul 200 motor cars per day begin to operate in the streets to aggravate the air pollution. Another dimension of environmental problems is the rapid concentration of population and increased construction activities in coastal areas of the Marmara, Aegean and the Mediterranean regions. It may be assumed that social change accelerated by rapid urbanization will increase the demand for touristic and recreative opportunities, and consequently the need for protection of coastal areas will be much greater by 2000 than at present.

We assume that urbanization and industrialization will affect environment adversely in several ways: first, by increasing the conversion of valuable agricultural land into urban uses and by concentrating increasing population in coastal areas; secondly, by increasing indirectly demand for more touristic establishments and for more infrastructure investments in touristic regions. Finally, it may be assumed that positively, citizens' concern for the protection and development of environmental values will be increased as urbanization proceeds. Increasing public concern is apparent in in the results of several surveys carried out on various socio-economic groups (S. Özdemir, **Sosyal Değişme ve Çevre,** Ankara, 1987). Efforts of the same groups to create a political party are the indicators of utilizing this potential for political purposes. One can assume that by the year 2000, there will be at least one political party based on the principle of the protection of ecological values. Proponents of other opposition groups looking for alternative life styles may also join the ecologists.

A final note may be necessary for the need for international cooperation in the 2000's for the protection of environment. When the fact that most of the problems of environment stems from negative externalities between neighboring countries, the importance of international cooperation in this field becomes greater. Radiation threat created by Chernobyl accident and the problems of acid rain in Western European countries are two examples. There will be a clear need for Turkey to take all necessary measures to anticipate and solve international legal and economic problems. For the Mediterranean, it has been demonstrated, for instance, that the Mediterranean coast is being polluted less by lateral countries than by other countries of Europe. Turkey, as a likely member of the European Community must be ready by 2000 to face many more environmental issues. This and similar questions will of course increase the need for international cooperation in the field of environment.

Local Authorities and Local Democracy

Administration of local affairs is entrusted with democratically elected local bodies according to Turkish Constitution (art. 127). They are governed by elected organs. Out of three kinds of local government, municipalities are the most important and popular ones, not only in terms of the functions they perform, but also in their relative share in total population. The share of total population living within municipal boundaries steadily increased during the last 50 years. It increased from 25.4 percent in 1935 to 28.2 percent in 1945, to 37.9 percent in 1955, to 47.5 percent in 1965, to 57.7 percent in 1975, and to 60.3 percent in 1985. The figure is expected to rise to 63.2 percent in 1989 and to 77.0 percent in the year 2000. Almost 20 percent of the municipalities are settlements with a population of 10.000 or less, which means that they can not be regarded "urban centers" by the generally accepted criterion.

Traditionally, Turkish local authorities have been weak both politically and financially, as a result of the centralized nature of the administrative system. However, even after the World War II, in other words, during the multi-party system, municipalities were barely more than the branches of the central government despite the lip service given to the democratic character of these grass roots institutions. It was mainly because of the central tutelage powers over their decisions and actions and the concentration of all financial powers at the center.

During the military and semi military interventions of 1960 and 1980, central controls over municipalities were largely expanded. In more liberal periods like 1973 - 1974 and 1977 - 1979, search for more democratic and participatory local authority concept was supported by the political parties in power. Especially after the 1983 parliamentary elections, certain concrete steps have been taken towards real decentralization. Several examples may suffice to clarify this point. The first was the attempt to increase the local revenues and the allocation of a certain percentage of the national revenues to municipalities. Second is the establishment of a two-tier administrative mechanism in the metropolitan areas like Istanbul, Ankara, Izmir, and Adana. Finally, by modifying certain laws, some of the central controls over municipalities, such as the approval of city development plans, were either loosened or lifted up altogether.

However, a great majority of Turkish municipalities are weak in technical staff and therefore it is doubtful whether the increased powers will be utilized by them appropriately or not, in accordance with law and in favor of the public interest. Perhaps a distinction between the metropolitan and other large cities and the smaller and weaker ones has to be made, and a system of technical and administrative assistance, in addition to the financial one, has to be established to protect the municipalities from the misuse or abuse of their powers. In doing this, a particular attention has to be paid not to violate the principle of local autonomy and to exercise necessary central controls in a didactic way.

To assume that in the coming 15 years, the present tendency to increase the autonomy of local authorities will discontinue and the central government will attempt to exercise gradually increasing controlling powers over municipalities, is not irrealistic. Such an anticipation also includes reducing the municipal shares allocated from the national budget. The reason is that by the year 2000, the demand for capital of the central government will not be favorable to supporting local authorities as generously as during the period 1980 - 1987.

Increased financial autonomy of municipalities in the last several years has induced them to act more independently without much control by the agents of the central government. This resulted in wasteful use of resources, as in the case of the import of work machines to be used in municipal affairs. No control is exercised upon the types, prices, exchange requirements and the quality of these machines which could have been imported by the Local Government Bank as an official coordinator on behalf of the municipalities.

As in all other fields, there seems to exist an increasing interest on the part of the policy makers in privatization of public services, in other words, in expanding the scope of the private enterprise and private ownership in the performance of local public services. Privatization has of course its own merits particularly in the performance of certain local services. However, in countries like Turkey, where serious imbalances in income distribution exists taking over the whole responsibility of such services as housing, public transportation, garbage and the like, may endanger the optimal use of these services by large segments of the society.

We can assume that social and economic conditions of Turkey at the beginning of the 21st century will not allow increasing privatization of local services. Moreover, development of the concept of local democracy would consider the expansion of privatization in local services entirely incompatible with the very existence of local government.

Politically motivated increases in the number of municipalities has always a hot issue. Their number increased from 492 in 1930 to 628 in 1950, to 1.303 in 1970 and to 1.728 in 1980. With recent additions of small municipalities, the number of municipalities became 1.900 in Turkey.

Most of the politicians regard the mushrooming of municipalities as a proof of their respect for local democracy. Almost 80 percent of all municipalities are very small settlement units with a population of less than 10.000. Changing the status of tiny villages into municipalities has only a symbolic meaning. One can expect no change in the attitude of national political leaders in this respect in the immediate future and the number of municipalities would reach 2.000 by the year 2000.

Three-year experience with a new kind of administrative system in metropolitan centers showed that there are several inconveniences stemming from its administrative and political characteristics. Tensions between the upper level governments and the district municipalities, conflicts originating from the unbalanced sharing of powers and functions and the criteria used for the allocation of resources to the municipalities at different levels may cause further inefficiencies in metropolitan areas in the coming years.

At present, the common belief of the district mayors is that the district municipalities are no more than the branches of the metropolitan municipality. They are treated so de facto and de jure. Almost all important functions are left to upper level councils. Now it seems certain that the coming 15 years will provide policy makers the opportunity to revise the system of metropolitan administration in the light of past experiences. In such a revision, care must be taken to incorporate some guarantees into the system to make it operational under different political climates. More clearly, the system should work when the councils at both levels are controlled by different political parties and when district mayors and the metropolitan mayor are not the members of the same political party. Unless the system is modified in that direction, a further intensification of conflicts in metropolitan municipalities and a consequent inefficiency in local services may be inescapable.

A final remark concerning the future of local government is needed in order to assess the likelihood of giving more powers to regions. It is generally accepted that local authorities are democratically constituted channels for the expression of regional diversities within the national union. Response of the central governments to the pressures from the periphery for more autonomy sometimes leads to the creation of regional corporate bodies like regional councils even in non-federal states as in France. It seems to me that the pressing need of better economic and cultural integration of some less developed regions in Turkey will not end up with a rearrangement of the politico-administrative structure of the state in that direction in the near future. More clearly, in the coming 15 years, Turkey will not attempt to modify its constitution to have regionally elected councils or elected governors in the provinces. This guess is based on the widespread belief that traditionally political decentralization is not favored in this country since it is situated in a much sensitive geopolitical location. Therefore, it can be safely assumed that any attempt to set up autonomous or semi-autonomous local councils in various regions will not be tolerated.

Socio-Political Consequences of Orderless Urbanization

Inhabitants of squatter settlements reflect almost all aspects of social change and development quite well. It is generally agreed upon that slum dwellers are no longer villagers in their world outlook, value systems socio-psychological attitudes and political behavior, although the great majority are of rural origin. The slum dweller is a new type of man, even though he is not urbanized in the broadest sense of the word. He can be regarded as being in the middle of rural-urban continuum. The idea that rural to urban migration that results in slum formation also ruralizes urban centers is not shared by many.

People living in squatter settlements neither choose to protest against government, nor participated in street demonstrations until the late 1970's. Their role in political life consisted of actively participating in the elections, and passively of being handled by various political forces. However, some studies revealed that during the years of political instability that resulted in 1980 military intervention, unemployed masses living in the squatter settlements were mobilized by the militants of the right and the left. Political fractions on both sides attempted to divide and to establish their control over them. Thus, they were able to form the so called "liberated quarters" in metropolitan areas. Slum dwellers were manipulated to participate, even sometimes reluctantly, in political violence. It is very doubtful that they would play a role in destabilizing the political structure in Turkey, unless they faced a grave problem of hunger.

The article 23 of the new Constitution concerns restricting the individual freedom of residence for the purpose of "ensuring sound and orderly urban growth" through law. One can assume that no government would attempt to restrict that freedom because of the peoples' attachment to urban life. However, official attitudes often constitute an aggravating factor as in the case of Squatting Pardoning Law of 1984 (Law No: 2981). This and similar legislation tend to give the squatter the hope that slum dwellers will ultimately be given the titles to the land on which their shacks are built. Since there is an absolute limit to the amount of urban land available for distribution to poor, it is most likely that future governments will have to change this legislation and will have to stop land distribution in squatter settlements. Such a change is likely to cause discontent and perhaps direct or indirect protest movements by the poor urban masses.

Marginal character of slum dwellers was more striking in the late 1940's than at present. Contrastingly, they acquired a non-marginal character during the period 1950 - 1980. In a third phase which covered 1960 - 1970, they became gradually a consuming group under the impact of urbanization. During the last phase which began in the early 1970's, most of them felt themselves free to make profit out of the land speculation. In other words, they became small-scale land speculators.

Marginal productivity of great majority of slum dwellers is much lower than their marginal propensity to consume. At present, it is more appropriate to regard the informal sector, as a sector not helping the formal sectors of the economy, but as one that shares many economic functions with it. It operates especially in the fields where formally organized entrepreneurs seem to be unwilling to enter. Employers utilize this [reserved army of slum dwellers] to control the demands for higher wages by their own organized labor. This sector creates and fosters increasing consumption habits which are no less important for the development of capitalism. However, it is a unanimously held view that the present day conspicuous consumption tendencies inflated by urbanization may have significant impact upon gradual erosion of moral value systems of the people in the near future.

Any prediction concerning the future of the squatter settlements will necessarily depend upon the future growth and structural change of the national economy. If we assume that slums are a product of underdevelopment and uneven income distribution, preconditions of its gradual shrinking will, of course, be the elimination of the poverty in general. On the other hand, in case they are normally regarded as an aspect of the housing shortage, that would mean that Turkey will face, for a long time to come, a critically serious low cost housing problem. Both of these approaches are closely related to the future of the economy. It is obvious that a great majority of the population will still be under the absolute poverty line, by 2000, which is not only an indicator of the low income level, but also, of ignorance, malnutrition, diseases and inadequate housing conditions and urban public services.

Finally, the new type of man created by urbanization and industrialization is someone who is rather difficult to satisfy not only in terms of the quality of public services, but also of the requirements of participatory democracy. If the tensions of the urban poor, motivated and nourished by their relative deprivation, can not be cured, then the vanguards of any political crisis will not have much difficulty in finding devoted allies among them.

Reducing rural-urban differences, regional disparities and intracity tensions born out of the dual structure of metropolises require the formulation of wise and long-range economic and social development plans. Since the effects of wisely implemented plans are felt only in the long run, even in the case of using less liberal and more interventionist contemporary policies, one can safely assume that present trends will continue to prevail by the beginning of the 21st century.

References

Ankara Üniversitesi Ziraat Fakültesi, Tübitak, T.C. Ziraat Bankası, **Güneydoğu Anadolu Projesi,** Tarımsal Kalkınma Sempozyumu, 18-21 Kasım 1986.

Barney, Gerald O. (ed.), **The Global 2000 Report to the President of the United States**, Vol. 1, Pergamon Press, N.Y., 1980.

Brown, Lester and Jodi L. Jacobson, **The Future of Urbanization: Facing the Ecological and Economic Constraints**, Worldwatch Paper, No: 77, May, 1987.

Cillov, Halûk, "Türkiye Nüfusu Bünyesindeki Gelişmeler", **Prof. Fadıl Hakkı Sur'un Anısına Armağan**, SBF, Ankara, 1983.

Danielson, Michael N. and Ruşen Keleş, **The Politics of Rapid Urbanization**, Holmes and Meier, N.Y., 1985.

DPY, **V. Beş Yıllık Kalkınma Planı Nüfus Tahminleri,** SPD, Ankara, Şubat, 1983.

Eisenstadt, S.N. and A. Shachar, **Society, Culture, and Urbanization**, Sage, Beverly Hills, 1987.

Göymen, Korel et al. (eds.) **Local Administration: Democracy versus Efficiency?, Analysen**, No:103-104, Freiedrich-Ebert Stiftung, Bonn, 1982.

Heper, Metin, (ed.), **Democracy and Local Government: Istanbul in the 1980's**, The Eothen Press, North Humberside, 1987.

Heper, Metin, (ed.), **Dilemmas of Decentralization: Municipal Government in Turkey, Analysen**, No: 123-124, Friedrich-Ebert Stiftung, Bonn. 1986.

İmar ve İskan Bakanlığı, Bölge Planlama Dairesi, **Türkiye'de Kentsel Gelişmeyi Etkileyen Faktörler, Ankara, 1962.**

Keleş, Ruşen, "Urbanization, Population and the Environment", **Population and Environment Conference**, Environmental Problems Foundation of Turkey, Ankara, 1982.

Keleş, Ruşen, "Population Structure of Turkey", in **Türkei**, ed. by Klaus Detlev Grothusen, Südosteuropa-Handbuch, Band IV, Vandenboeck and Ruprecht, Göttingen, 1985.

Keleş, Ruşen, "The Effects of External Migration on Regional Development in Turkey", in **Uneven Development in Southern Europe**, ed. by Ray Hudson and Jim Lewis, Methuen, London, 1985.

Keleş, Ruşen, "Over-all Impact of Slums and Slum Dwellers on the Societal Structure in Turkey", Institute of Developing Economies, Tokyo, February, 1983.

Keleş, Ruşen, "Kentleşme ve Kamu Yönetimi Sorunları", **Hızlı Kentleşmenin Yarattığı Ekonomik ve Sosyal Sorunlar**, Sİ-SAV, İstanbul, 1986.

Keleş, Ruşen, **Kentleşme ve Konut Politikası**, SBF, Ankara, 1984.

Keleş, Ruşen, Artun, Ünsal, **Kent ve Siyasal Şiddet**, SPr, Ankara, 1982.

Keleş, Ruşen, Fehmi Yavuz, **Yerel Yönetimler**, Turan, Ankara, 1983.

Keleş, Ruşen, Fehmi Yavuz, **Çevre Sorunları**, SBF, Ankara, 1983.

Keleş, Ruşen, Hiromasa Kano, **Economic Development and Social Consciousness: Turkey under Developmentalism**, Institute of Developing Economies, Tokyo, 1986.

KENT-KOOP, **Konut 81**, Ankara, 1982.

Mediterranean Action Plan, Blue Plan, 1st Phase, **Overview of the Mediterranean Basin: Development and Environment**, Paris 1987.

Newland, Kathleen, **City Limits: Emerging Constraints in Urban Growth**, Worldwatch Paper No: 38, April 1980.

Ornauer, H, et al. (eds.), **Images of the World in the Year 2000**, Mouton, The Hague, 1976.

Paddison, Ronan, **The Fragmented State: Political Geography of Power**, St. Martin's Press, London, 1983.

Shorter, Frederick C. and' M. Macura, **Trends in Fertility and in Mortality in Turkey: 1935-1975**, Committee on Population and Demography, Washington D.C., Report No; 8, 1982.

SPO, **New Emphasis on Structural Change in the Urban Sector**, UN Commission on Human Settlement, 9th Session, Istanbul, 1986.

Şeker, Murat, **Güneydoğu Anadolu Projesi**, V Yayınları, Ankara, 1987.

Tuncer, Baran, **Turkey's Population and Economy in the Future**, The Development Foundation of Turkey, October 1977, Ankara.

Türkiye Çevre Sorunları Vakfı, **2000 Yılına Doğru Türkiye**, Ankara, 1987.

Tekeli, İlhan, Murat Güvenç, "Ankara Nüfusundaki Gelişmeler ve Nüfus Artışının Bileşenleri", **Ankara: 1985'ten 2025'e** (to be published by EGO).

The World Commission on Environment and Development, **Our Common Future**, Oxford University Press, Oxford, 1987.

World Bank, **Turkey: Urban Sector Review**, October, 1983.

The Periphery in The Center: Some Political Features of Turkish Urbanization[*]

"It seems that realities of social and economic structure, including the characteristics and patterns of urbanization, deeply affect political development. In countries where rapid, unbalanced and disorderly urbanization tends to concentrate population in major urban centers, unemployment, feelings of relative deprivation and the manipulation of formally and informally organized political groups exert a certain impact upon rural migrants to keep away from center parties. As a result, social, economic and political factors tend to nourish the growth of extremist or fundamentalist movements in society."

Introduction

The center and the periphery have long been key concepts in Turkish politics and also in the analysis of the political dimensions of urbanization.[1] They have had both a spatial

---

[*]   Ekistics, Vol. 420 (May-June 2003) and Vol.421 (July-August 2003), pp.211-217.

[1]   Şerif Mardin, "Center- Periphery Relations: A Key to Turkish Politics?" Political Participation in Turkey, ed. By Engin Akarlı and Gabriel Ben-Dor (Istanbul, Boğaziçi Univeristy Publications, 1975); Metin Heper, "Center and Periphery in the Ottoman Empire", International Political Science Review,

and a socio-cultural content. There is no doubt that both meanings of the concept were closely interrelated and their interaction intensified as the communication system in the country progressed considerably during the post-war years. Major urban centers represented the center while the rural areas have been identified as the periphery in this context. Similarly, squatter settlements and their residents that constituted almost 35 percent of urban population were regarded as the periphery as opposed to the planned sections of the major cities which were considered as the center in the true sense of the concept.

Population growth, urbanization and industrial development contribute to the creation of broad opportunities for all the countries in the world, but at the same time, they create numerous socio-economic and physical problems that cannot be resolved easily and inexpensively. Although such problems that are either created by urbanization itself or aggravated by increasing rate of urbanization concern every nation, it is the developing countries that are affected most by these processes. Turkey is no exception to this observation. Nearly two thirds (65 percent in the 2000 Census) of her population live in urban centers. The absolute number of urban residents has increased from 7 to 44 million during the last four decades. The average rate of increase of rural, total and urban populations during the same period has been 1 percent, 2.5 percent and 6 percent, respectively. The number of cities, defined as urban settlements

Vol.1, No:1, 1980, pp.81-105; see also Edward Shils, "Center and Periphery", in The Logic of Personal Knowledge: Essays Presented to Michael Polanyi on his 70th Birthday (New York, Free Press, 1967), and Jean Gottmann (ed.), Center and the Periphery: Spatail Variations in Politcs (Chichester, Wiley, 1980).

of 10,000 or more population, has also increased from 147 in 1960 to 320 in 1980 and to 475 in 2000 (fig.1).[2] More than two thirds of the urban population live in urban centers with more than 100.000 population.

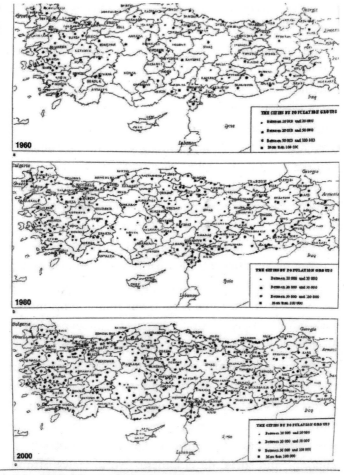

Fig. 1: Turkey – Distribution of urban centers in 1960 (a), 1980 (b) and 2000 (c).

2   Ruşen Keleş, Kentleşme Politikası (Urbanization Policy), 7th ed. (Ankara 2002), p.59.

Not all the geographical regions urbanize at the same pace mainly due to economic, social, geographical and political factors. The degree or urbanization of the Western region of Marmara is nearly 80 percent while the same rate for the regions of the East and the Black Sea is less than 50 percent (fig.1a, 1b,1c).

Perhaps a more striking feature of Turkish urbanization patterns is that there are deep contrasts in the internal structures of major metropolitan centers as appeared between illegally built-up squatter settlements and regularly constructed residential areas. This is an expression of the uneven income distribution in society. The percentages of the urban population living in squatter settlements in major cities such as Istanbul, Ankara and Izmir are 65 percent, 70 percent and 60 percent, respectively. Under these conditions, squatter settlements in Turkish cites can no longer be regarded as "marginal" because it is the planned sections of many major cities that can justify such characterization. Employment opportunities in rapidly urbanizing cities have not increased at the same pace as out-migration from rural areas and the hopes of rural migrants to find expanding job opportunities in those centers are seldom met.[3]

Uncontrolled urbanization tends to increase the unemployment and underemployment rates in metropolitan centers. A migratory movement, a kind of social and economic erosion, transferring poverty from villages to urban centers, can hardly be considered as a reel contribution to economic and social development. World views, attitudes and behavior of migrants are considerably influenced by

---

3   Ruşen Keleş, "City, urbanization and informal sector," in Tuncer Bulutay
     (ed.), Informal Sector (Ankara, State Institute of Statics, 2001).

poverty conditions, which also tend to have far reaching implications for public order.

How do politics and urbanization affect each other?

First of all, politics play a certain role in controlling and shaping urbanization. There is no doubt that to find rational solutions to the economic, social and physical problems created by urbanization requires either to take up and to try to remedy all of these issues one by one or to formulate and implement general policies that might have a chance to change the settlement pattern in the country in the country in the long run, though which each of the above-mentioned individual problems can also be solved spontaneously. Urbanization policy aims to influence the shape, pace and geographical distribution of migratory movements in order to foster national development.

Even in liberal economies such interventions in socio-economic life are regarded as necessary steps for saving the future of cities. Since urbanization in Turkey following the emergence of the first squatter settlements in metropolitan centers accelerated after the Second World War, it was not before the beginnings of the 1960s that serious public policies to deal with it were formulated. The attitudes of both politicians and bureaucrats were in favor of unauthorized building activities of the squatters during the decades following the Second World War. Perhaps it was difficult to opt for an alternative policy of discouragement in a democratic and parliamentary political regime respectful of individual freedoms. As a result, even the socio-economic models aiming at keeping the farmer in his village and improving his living and working conditions in place did not attract much attention.

An amendment made to the Constitution of 1982 (Art.23) provides that freedom of settlement can be restricted by an Act of Parliament with the aim of ensuring orderly urbanization. As in any other multi-party parliamentarian democracy it is almost impossible to restrict this freedom even to attain the abovementioned goal. Starting from the First Five Year Development Plans, the State regarded urbanization as one of the requirements for development and encouraged a growth pole policy for a more balanced population distribution among major cities and regions. The major tools of such a policy were not repressive measures but essentially the policies of investment, tax, credit and personnel. The growth of medium-sized cities, not the giant metropolises, was going to be encouraged.

The policy of squatter settlements during the last 50 years aimed to regularize their physical layout and legal positions, to integrate them with the larger society and to meet their infrastructure needs by taking measures for the prevention of further squatting. These are the main characteristics of the policies or urbanization and squatting shaped by politicians.

But in practice, there was a false impression, as if migration from rural to urban areas was going to be encouraged. No real control was exercised over the distribution of population and economic activities within the framework of regional plans. This increased the regional inequalities and the cities faced enormous infrastructure problems. Despite the fact that all laws on squatting enacted between 1948 and 1966 banned illegal building, the number of squatter houses actually built increased from 240,000 in 1960 to 2.2 million in 2002. And the number of people living in these settlements increased from 1.2 million to 11 million. Therefore, it can be safely assumed that mainly political party interest induced decision makers to be tolerant towards squatting and this fact aggravated further the issue of unplanned urbanization. Short-range political interest have also made it difficult to protect fertile agricultural lands, forests, coastal areas and the natural values of touristic regions.[4] In other words, the supremacy of public interest over private interests in the process of urbanization was not ensured.

As to the impact of urbanization on politics, it is in order to remember some of the preliminary theoretical analyses. The first was formulated by political scientist Karl W. Deutsch. According to Deutsch, the concept of social mobilization comprising such factors as urbanization, exposure to mass media, increasing literacy, the ratio of non-agricultural occupations and per capita national income is precondition of political participation. As a result, political behavior is affected by social change or mobilization. This causes a differentiation in voting behavior in rural and urban areas. It is assumed that urban residents are more eager for participation in elections than villagers. This theory suggests that the higher the rate of urbanization, the higher the rate of participation in election in urban centers. Of course, the direction of participation is as important as the density of participation. In other words, a more important question is to know for whom the urban residents will be voting. There are different views in this respect:

---

4   Turkey, National Report on Sustainable Development 2002, World Summit Sustainable Development, Johannesburg 2002.

- Some scholars believe that the residents of squatter settlements, in other words those living in unauthorized settlements, will have more reason to vote for essentially conservative political parties encouraging them to migrate, simply because they are better off in the city as compared with village life and they have to be on good terms with existing decision makers in power in order to ensure that their shack house should not be demolished and continue to be a sort of guarantee of their social security in the future.

- A second view assumes that urbanization favors political parties with left-of-center ideologies, because rural migrants faced with numerous hardships in the cities are gradually alienated from the rest of society. Most of them become unemployed or underemployed, and the conditions of relative deprivation that they experience and the inadequacies in living conditions push them to the left of the spectrum. Thus, it is quite normal that these masses with unsatisfied needs support political parties that aim to change the status quo.

- According to the views of those in a third category of scholars, a shift to the left in the spectrum and becoming more radical occurs not immediately but from the second generation on. Because, as the new generations become more conscious about their differences with prosperous segments of the city and their own relative deprivation, it becomes more difficult to prevent them from being radicalized. Certainly, the process of radicalization takes time. They from explosive political groups that may be manipulated by radical group in society. Such radical elements can approach them easily for the exploitation of their anger to throw out even democratically formed governments as experienced in some Latin America countries. Finding of some survey carried out in Turkish cities in the late 1970s and early 1980s provide ample evidence in this respect.[5]

Deterioration of the values systems under the influence of worldwide globalization as reflected in the expansion of the rent economy, development of the underground economy, decrease in respect for natural and environmental values, is no less important than the characteristics or urbanization as it affects political behavior.

Despite the fact that in theory it is generally accepted that urbanization fosters participation, the experience with elections throughout the multiparty regime in Turkey since 1946 indicates that this is not the case. In other words, rates of participation in parliamentary elections have been much higher in rural areas than in urban centers. On the other hand, voting data on past elections in squatter settlements, that can be viewed as the best indicators of urbanization, show that newly urbanized residents did not vote mostly for the left-of-center parties. It would be safer to underline that the trend does not seem straight in this respect during the last several decades. For example, in the 1973 and 1977 municipal elections, what the theory predicts was more or less confirmed in cities with relatively high urbanization rates where labor population was also high. In fact,

---

5   Ruşen Keleş and Artun Ünsal, Kent ve Siyasal Şiddet (City and Urban Violence), (Ankara, Faculty of Political Science, 1982).

candidates of the parties won the mayoralties in those cities. But paradoxically, in the 1984 local elections, even in a city like Istanbul which is in the center of the most urbanized region of the country, conservative political parties were the major winners.[6] A few years later, the following municipal elections in Istanbul revealed that once again the center left Republic Party was the leading political party in both Istanbul metropolitan municipality and its lower-level district municipalities.

In the light of these conditions, it would be a safer assumption to accept that urbanization is only one of numerous factors affecting voting behavior and there may be many other independent variables that might affect the patterning of political structure and behavior. For example, political violence witnessed in such squatter settlements in Istanbul as Ümraniye, Gaziosmanpaşa, Kadıköy, during the 1970s and 1990s, has been definitely nourished by the unplanned and disorderly character of urbanization as well as other socio-cultural and economic features of society.

What have we learned from the recent past?

Contrary to the prevailing assumption of the theories, it seems that urbanization does not affect political behavior in the predicted direction. In other words, by increasing degree and rate of urbanization, electors are not inclined to vote heavily for the leftist parties. In this sense, the political and administrative influence of the periphery on major cities continues to increase. Such a trend gives the impression that the periphery plays an increasing role in the center. In the rest of this paper, we will be dealing with the

6   Ruşen Keleş, Kentleşme Sürecinde Türkiye, p.12.

analysis of the data on national and local elections during the 1980s and 1990s.

A comparison of the 1989 and 1994 local elections reveals that the most successful political party in these elections was the Welfare Party, a radical islamist fundamentalist party, which received its strength mainly from the squatter settlements surrounding central Istanbul. In table 1 a comparison can be found of the successes of the Welfare Party (RP) and the Social Democratic Republican Party (SHP) in the abovementioned elections.

It is remarkable to observe that the majority of the right and right-of-center parties won the mayoralties in metropolitan centers and in the headquarters of the provinces and sub provinces in 1994, while the left-of-center party (SHP) gained mainly mayoral elections in relatively smaller settlements. There is striking shift in the votes cast for the SHP in 1989 to the RP in 1994.[7] A great many factors such as the distortion imposed upon the political structure by the 12 September 1980 military intervention, general economic and socio-cultural features of the nation, differences among the technique of organization, operation and information works of the political parties, the ways in which their candidates are chosen, inequalities in the distribution of the benefits created by disorderly urbanization and concrete difficulties faced by the residents of different types of settlement played a considerable role in changing the voting patterns. In additions to the above-mentioned factors, the fact that physical, social and cultural factors did not keep pace with rapid population concentration in cities created unsatisfactory living conditions in major metropolitan ar-

7   Erol Tuncer, op. cit.

eas. Reflections of the negative consequences of unhealthy urbanization in cities even encouraged some observers to argue that "Turkey was going to be rightest in general" and the RP, an islamist fundamentalist political party was going to be essentially "an urban-based political party."[8] In fact, the same political party won the elections not only in rapidly growing cities, such as Diyarbakır, Elazıg, Erzurum, Kayseri, Malatya, Sakarya, Trabzon, Konya, Sivas, Kahramanmaras, Sanlıurfa and Van, but in the largest metropolises like Istanbul and Ankara as well.

Table 1
Mayoral offices gained by the Welfare Party (RP) and the Social Democratic Republican Party (SHP) in the Municipal Elections of 1989 and 1994 (number of mayors)

Municipality	Welfare Party (RP)		Social Democratic Republican Party (SHP)	
	1989	Gains in 1994	1989	Losses in 1994
All municipalities	71	256	662	226
Metropolitan municipalities	1	5	6	4
Provincial municipalities	4	18	36	28
District municipalities	19	76	290	155
Rural municipalities	57	157	390	39

(Source: Erol Tuncer, 27 Mart 1994 Yerel Seçimleri, Sayısal ve Siyasal Değerlendirme (Local Elections of 27 March 1994. A Statistical and Political Assessment). (Ankara, Tesav, 1994), pp. 15-16).

Table 2
Election results in Turkey and in Istanbul, 1950-1995 (in percent)

Year	Turkey			Istanbul		
	Center Right	Center Left	Others	Center Right	Center Left	Others
1950	53.3	39.9	7.8	52.7	24.3	23.0
1954	56.6	34.8	8.6	61.9	26.3	11.8
1957	47.3	40.6	12.1	52.7	40.5	6.8
1961	34.8	36.7	28.5	41.8	38.2	20.0
1965	52.9	28.7	18.4	53.2	29.7	17.1
1969	46.5	27.4	25.1	47.8	33.8	18.4
1973	29.8	33.3	36.0	48.9	28.5	23.6
1977	36.9	41.4	21.7	58.2	28.4	13.4
1987	45.4	33.3	21.3	51.6	39.9	9.5
1991	51.0	31.6	17.4	46.3	36.5	17.2
1995	38.9	25.4	35.7	41.3	32.6	26.1

(Source: Mustafa Sönmez, İstanbul'un İki Yüzü (Two faces of Istanbul) (İstanbul, Arkadaş, 1996), p. 107).

A feature of the political history of Istanbul, as the capital city of Turkey, indicates that throughout the second half of the 20th century, center-left and center-right political

---

8   Ruşen Çakır, Ne Şeriat, Ne Demokrasi: Refah Partisini Anlamak (Neither Sharia, nor Democracy: Understanding the Welfare Party), (İstanbul, Metis, 1994), pp. 222-227.

parties keep losing, while parties with extreme and rather radical world views are constantly gaining strength. However, when the trend in voting patterns in Istanbul is compared with that of Turkey in general, one can conclude that the same trend is much more sensible in Turkey than in Istanbul. In table 2, one can find the figures pertaining to both Turkey and Istanbul.

The most striking feature of table 2 is that the vote received by extremist parties increased from 9.5 percent in 1987 to 17.2 percent in 1991 and to 26.1 in 1995. This figure was still around 15 percent in the 1999 national elections.[9] There is a corresponding decrease throughout the election years in the votes of the center parties either on the right or on the left. Empirical research carried out in Istanbul and its immediate surroundings reveals that differentiation in the religious and ethnic backgrounds of the inhabitants played a considerable role in pushing the electors to the extreme. It was also argued that industrial centers seemed attractive to the migrant urban poor which strived for more security in the city.[10] The fear of the migrants concerning likely clashes between their traditional value system and the changes brought about by urbanization put a certain pressure upon the newly urbanized population to rely more on religiously oriented political parties.[11] One should keep in mind that general economic and social conditions, uneven income distribution, development policies that ne-

9   Ş. Ilgü Özler, "Politics of the Gecekondu in Turkey: The political choices of urban squatters in national elections," Turkish Studies, vol. 1, no. 2 (Autumn 2000), p.52.

10   N. Narlı, S. Dirik and M. A. Gizer, "Türkiye'nin Siyasal Haritası" ("Political map of Turkey"), Milliyet, 29 April-7 May, 1996, pp. 4 and 9.

11   Ibid., p. 9.

glected welfare aspects of development and finally dis- orderly and unplanned urbanization have all exerted a certain influence upon the voting behavior of the urban poor. The level of development of settlements has an undeniable impact upon voting behavior. In fact, when we classify the districts of Istanbul into various categories of socio-economic development, we clearly see how the shares of the votes received by different political parties vary from one district to another. For example, the district of Istanbul can be grouped into three different categories in this respect:

- In the first group are the least developed or the poorest inhabitants. Such districts as Sultanbeyli (70.3 percent), Esenler (46.1 percent), Bağcılar (46.1 percent), Ümraniye (45 percent), Gaziosmanpaşa (41.1 percent), Kağıthane (40.6 percent), Eminönü (40.2 percent), Pendik (39. 1 percent), Beyoğlu (37.2 percent), Kartal (36.3 percent) are the poorest settlements. The vote of the Welfare Party received from the residents of these settlements is higher than both in other parts of Istanbul and in the rest of Turkey. The majority of the population living in these districts are of rural origin and they constitute nearly one third (32.9 percent) of the city's total population.[12]

- The second category includes the most developed districts like Şişli, Kadikoy, Adalar, Beşiktaş and Bakırköy where the percentage of the votes received by the Welfare Party is the smallest. These figures for these districts are 20.6, 20.0, 15.1, 14.3 and 12.0 percent, respectively. The population of these districts

12   Mustafa Sönmez, Istanbul'un İki Yüzü (Two Faces of Istanbul), pp. 109-110.

is approximately 23 percent of the total population of the city.

- Finally, at the intermediate level, we find those districts that can be regarded as relatively developed, such as Tuzla, Güngören, Bayrampaşa, Eyüp, Fatih, Bahçelievler Üsküdar, Beykoz, Büyük Çekmece, Zeytinburnu, Küçük Çekmece and Maltepe; 44.1 percent of the electors live in these districts. The total vote that the Welfare Party received in these quarters varies between 28 percent and 35.6 percent.

All this evidence suggests that the squatters' support for the Welfare Party is not necessarily indicative of an increase in support for radical Islam. Rather, it is the latest in a series of rational realignments on the part of urban squatters in an attempt to best serve their social, economic and service needs.[13] What is also true is that there is a noticeable shift in voting patterns from the center parties towards those that are far beyond the center, particularly in those cities where the great majority of the population are recent rural migrants and live in conditions of relative poverty. Therefore we can conclude that changes in voting behavior can not be taken up independently from the pace and patterns of urbanization. Several recent scholarly studies on the class structure of the Istanbul metropolitan area shed adequate light on the above mentioned differentiation in voting behavior.[14]

---

13 Ş. İlgü Özler, "Politics of the Gecekondu...," Turkish Studies, op. cit, p. 54.

14 See: Korkut Boratav, İstanbul ve Anadolu'nun Sınıf Profilleri (Class Profiles of Istanbul and Anatolia), (Istanbul, Tarih Vakfı Yurt Yayınları, 1995); Oğuz Işık ve Melih Pınarcıoğlu, Nöbetleşe Yoksulluk (Poverty by Turns), (İstanbul, iletişim, 2001); Murat Güvenç and Oğuz Işık, "İstanbul'u okumak: Statü-Mülkiyet Farklılaşmasına İlişkin bir Çözümleme Denemesi"

What can be expected in the near future?

Policy sciences teach us that structural problems of an economic and social character facing a nation can not be remedied in the short run through legal and partial interventions. It is obvious that such problems have been created as a result of a long process of accumulation of a great many economic, social and political factors and therefore their solutions may take a relatively long time.

Uneven income distribution is one of these factors. Although squatting appears to be a consequence of rapid urbanization, the latter is more like one of the accelerating factors than the main reason responsible for the squatting process. The basic source of the squatting problem should be sought in unbalanced income distribution and in the inadequacy of the related development policies. It is an obvious fact that disorderly and unhealthy urbanization is more an outcome of working and living conditions prevailing in the rural sector than the attractiveness of the employment opportunities offered by the urban centers. Both official and unofficial estimates indicate that these poverty conditions will persist in the near future and the present rate of population growth will not be stabilized before 2025.

Both developmental features and demographic trends in the country can be controlled effectively through planning. Yet, urbanization and squatting process seem to be entirely

("Reading Istanbul: An analytical essay concerning differentiations on the Basis of Status and Ownership"), Toplum ve Bilim (Society and Science), 1996, pp. 6.60; Murat Güvenç, "İstanbul'u Haritalamak: 1990 Sayımından İstanbul Manzaraları" (Mapping Istanbul: Profiles of the City Reflected in the 1990 Population Census), Istanbul, no. 35, 1996; Sema Erder, Kentsel Gerilim (Urban Tension), Um-Ag, Ankara, 1997; Sema Erder, Ümraniye (Istanbul, İletişim, 1996).

out of public control at present. In some of the squatter settlements in Istanbul, the criminal sector known as the "land and squatting mafia" has even succeeded in replacing the authority of the public institutions to guide urban development and settlement in metropolitan areas.[15] Almost all of the political party leaders, by their encouraging statements and attitudes, have contributed, in their turn, to the persistence of the issue, in both national and local elections, in order to get the votes of the those who represent the periphery in the center.

Migration from rural to urban centers, from eastern to western regions continues and it adds to increasing regional inequalities. Unless the Southeastern Anatolian Development Project achieves its goals, the size of the periphery in major metropolitan areas may not have a chance to be minimized in the foreseeable future. Therefore, efforts to expand the scope of the regional development projects to cover the whole territory of the nation may provide some hope, because the distribution of population and economic activities between regions, metropolitan areas, cities, small towns, villages are aspects of the same phenomena and they cannot be separated from each other.

Rural migrants continue to live in cities as villagers without being adequately urbanized. They maintain their rural value systems and behavioral patterns for a long time in the city. The identity crisis they face pushes them often to radical mass actions, movements and political parties.[16] Those

15   TBMM, İstanbul İlinin Sorunları, Meclis Araştırma Komisyonu Raporu, (Report of the Parliamentary Investigation Commission on the Problems of the Province of Istanbul), (Ankara, 1992), p.30.

16   Nur Alkış, "Siyasete Gecekondu Damgası" ("Squatting stamp on politics"), Cumhuriyet (Daily Cumhuriyet), 22-27 January, 1995, p. 6.

who look at the future with feelings of confidence are few.
In the 1994 local elections, according to the public opinion
polls, nearly 41 percent of the voters thought that none of
the political parties participating in the elections was powerful enough to solve their economic, social and political
problems; 36.6 percent of the voters believed that there was
such a party and this was the Welfare Party (the religiously
oriented radical party).[17]

The weak identity impression of local and central authorities plays a significant role in political instability. Increasing cleavages between center-left and center-right parties since the early 1980s, with no real difference of political
ideology in their programs, pushed the hopeless rural migrants to the extremist political party that bases its relative
strength on religious beliefs. Worldwide revival of Islamic
fundamentalism in some regions of the world especially
during the 1980s and 1990s has also influenced extremist
elements largely manipulated from outside in this country.
infiltration occurred more easily in the outskirts of Istanbul and other large cities as the conditions of the periphery
in the center were considerably suitable to such endeavors.

There is no doubt that the increase of the vote potential
of an extreme rightest party from the youth, women and
workers living in squatter settlements or from other parts
of the cities can be regarded as normal in a democratic system with legally recognized political parties. However, as
witnessed during social political movements occurring in
such settlements of Istanbul as Gaziosmanpaşa, Ümraniye
and Kadiköy, they easily become uncontrollable in joining
the illegal militants protesting against the constitutional

17   Ibid., p.6.

order of the state. Therefore, the limits of the freedom of the parties that seem to be sympathetic towards extremist movements are the constitutional principles that guarantee law and order in society.

Concluding remarks

It seems that realities of social and economic structure, including the characteristics and patterns of urbanization, deeply affect political development. In countries where rapid, unbalanced and disorderly urbanization tends to concentrate population in major urban centers, unemployment, feelings of relative deprivation and the manipulation of formally and informally organized political groups exert a certain impact upon rural migrants to keep away from center parties. As a result, social, economic and political factors tend to nourish the growth of extremist or fundamentalist movements in society. In order to stabilize political structure, those who have migrated from rural areas into urban centers, in other words the periphery in the center, must be integrated with the whole of society by concerted economic and social action with appropriate instruments.

References

ALKIŞ, Nur (1995), "Siyasete Gecekondu Damgası" ("Squatting stamp on politics"), Daily Cumhuriyet (22-27 January).

BORATAV, Korkut (1995), Istanbul ve Anadolu'nun Sınıf Profilleri (Class Profiles of Istanbul and Anatolia), (Istanbul, Tarih Vakfı Yurt Yayınları).

ÇAKIR, Ruşen (1994), Ne Şeriat, Ne Demokrasi: Refah Partisini Anlamak (Neither Sharia, nor Democracy: Understanding the Welfare Party), (Istanbul, Metis).

ERDER, Sema (1997), Kentsel Gerilim (Urban Tension), (Ankara, um-ag.).

(1996), Ümraniye (Istanbul, iletişim).

GOTTMANN, Jean (ed.) (1980), Center and the Periphery: Spatail Variations in Politcs (Chichester, Wiley).

GÜVENÇ, Murat (1996), "İstanbul'u Haritalamak: 1990 Sayımından İstanbul Manzaraları" (Mapping Istanbul: Profiles of the City Reflected in the 1990 Population Census), Istanbul, no. 35.

(2000), "Introduction to urban poverty", in Halis Akder and Murat Güvenç, Yoksulluk (Istanbul, TESEV). and Oğuz Işık (1996), "İstanbul'u okumak: Statü-Mülkiyet Farklılaşmasına İlişkin bir Çözümleme Denemesi" ("Reading Istanbul: An analytical essay concerning differentiation on the basis of status and ownership"), Toplum ve Bilim (Society and Science).

HEPER, Metin (1980), "Center and Periphery in the Ottoman Empire", International Political Science Review, vol.1, no:1, pp. 81-105.

IŞIK, Oğuz and Melih PINARCIOĞLU (2001), Nöbetleşe Yoksulluk (Poverty by Turns), (Istanbul, İletişim).

KELEŞ, Ruşen (1996), Kentleşme Sürecinde Türkiye (Turkey in the Process of Urbanization), (Izmit, Kosiad).

(2001), "City, urbanization and informal sector," in Tuncer Bulutay (ed.), Informal Sector (Ankara, State Institute of Statics).

(2002), Kentleşme Politikası (Policy of Urbanization), (7th ed.), (Ankara, İmge).

and ARTUN ÜNSAL (1982), Kent ve Siyasal Şiddet (City and Urban Violence), (Ankara Faculty of Political Science, Ankara University).

MARDİN, Şerif (1975), "Center-periphery relations: A key to Turkish politics," in Engin Akarlı and Gabriel Ben-Dor (eds.), Political Participation in Turkey (Istanbul, Boğaziçi University Publications).

NARLI, N., S. DIRLIK and M. A. GIZER (1996), "Türkiye'nin Siyasal Haritası" ("Political map of Turkey"), Daily Milliyet (29 April-7 May).

ÖZLER, S. İlgü (2000), "Politics of the Gecekondu in Turkey: The political choices of urban squatters in national elections," Turkish Studies, vol. 1, no. 2 (Autumn).

SHILS, Edward (1967), "Center and Periphery", in The Logic of Personal Knowledge: Essays Presented to Michael Polanyi on his 70th Birthday (New York, Free Press).

SÖNMEZ, Mustafa (1996), Istanbul'un İki Yüzü (Two Faces of Istanbul), (Istanbul, Arkadai).

TBMM (1992), İstanbul İlinin Sorunları, Meclis Araştırma Komisyonu Raporu, (Report of the Parliamentary Investigation Commission on the Problems of the Province of Istanbul), (Ankara).

TUNCER, Erol (1994), 27 Mart 1994 Seçikleri: Sayısal ve Siyasal Değerlendirme (Local Elections of 27 March 1994: A Statistical and Political Assessment), (Ankara, TESAV).

TURKISH REPUBLIC (2002), National Report 2002, Submitted to the World Summit on Sustainable Development, Johannesburg, 2002 (Ankara).

Policy Implications of Sustainable Urbanization in Case-Study of Turkey*

Abstract

If sustainable urbanization is defined as the maximization of economic efficiency in the use or resources including air, water and soil, maintaining natural resource stocks at or above their present level, ensuring social equity I the distribution of development benefits and costs and avoidance of unnecessary foreclosure of future development options, urban development management in Turkey cannot be considered as meeting these requirements. Present characteristics of urbanization would not allow meeting the needs of the present generations without compromising the ability of the future generations to meet their own needs.

Urban development is considerably influenced qualitatively and qualitatively by rapid urbanization. It has been rapid, but also one-directional, unbalanced and unplanned. It operates to increase the rate of unemployment and underemployment in major cities and to inflate the informal sector. Rapid urbanization has also been characterized since 1950 by a rapid increase in the number of squatter dwellings that surrounded the major cities.

National economy could not cope adequately with the task of providing employment technical and social infrastructure such as

*   D. Camarda and L. Grassini (eds.), *Interdependency between Agriculture and Urbanization: Conflicts on Sustainable use of Soil and Water*, CIHEAM-IAMB, Politecnico di Bari, Tunis, April 3-6, 2000, pp.113-128.

housing, transportation, communications, sewerage, public health, educational and cultural service needed. Policies of urbanization, migration, housing, urban land as squatter settlements have not succeeded in realizing the kind of urban development that might be regarded as the outcome of a sustainable urban management. Related to this issue is the inadequacy of the planning techniques in use. The traditional comprehensive master planning techniques that have been in use during the last four decades failed in attaining the aims for such resources as water and fossil fuels, in promoting public transport and enhancing energy savings in building design and layouts.

Carrying out sustainability assessments of spatial plans, development programmes and projects and incorporating analysis and measures of rational sustainability in city planning through regional resource inventories, liaisons among local authorities involved in regional resource management and the development of renewable resource strategies have not been the tools used in urban development.

The concern for maximizing the private rather than the public interest in using the urban land dominated the practice of urban planning. National and local politicians did not hesitate, at times, to co-operate with the major actors who had vital interest in land speculation. Under these conditions, the constitutional provisions concerning the protection of natural resource such as land, water, forestry, historical, cultural, and architectural assets could not be implemented appropriately.

The paper will concern the implications of non-integrating the considerations of sustainable urban development and management in the city master plans.

Résumé

Si l'urbanisation durable est définie comme une maximisation de l'utilisation des ressources, y compris l'air, l'eau at le sol, tout en maintenant les réserves des ressources naturelles au même niveau ou à un niveau supérieur à celui actuel, en assurant l'équité sociale dans la répartition des bénéfices et en évitant la forclusion des couts de la forclusion inutile des options de développement futur, la gestion du développement urbain en Turquie ne satisfait pas ces besoins. Les caractéristiques actuelles de l'urbanisation ne pourront permettre de satisfaire les besoins des générations actuelles sans compromettre la capacité des générations futures de satisfaire leurs besoins.

L'étendue et la qualité du développement urbain sont considérablement influencées par l'urbanisation rapide. Elle a été rapide, mais aussi unidirectionnelle non équilibre et non planifiée. Elle engendre un accroissement du taux de chômage et du sous-emploi dans les principales villes et le gonflement du secteur informel. Depuis 1950, l'urbanisation rapide est aussi caractérisée par un accroissement également rapide du nombre d'habitations squatter qui entouraient les principales villes.

L'économie nationale n'a pas réussi à assurer d'une manière adéquate l'emploi, les infrastructures techniques at sociales tels que le logement, le transport, les communications, les systèmes d'égout, les services de santé publique, d'instruction et culturels. Les politiques de l'urbanisation, de la migration, du logement, du terrain urbain et dés établissements illégaux n'ont pas réussi à réalise le type de développement urbain qui pourrait découler d'une gestion urbaine durable. Il s'ajoute l'adoption de techniques de planification inadéquates. Les techniques traditionnelles de planification globale qui ont été utilisées ces quatre derniéres décennies n'ont pas réussi à atteindre les objectifs liés aux ressources telles que l'eau et les combustibles fossiles, à promouvoir le transport public et améliorer les économies d'énergie dans la conception des bâtiments.

L'évaluation de la durabilité des plans spatiaux, des programmes et des projets de développement et l'analyse et les mesures d'une durabilité rationnelle dans la planification des villes, à travers les inventaires des ressources régionales, les liaisons entre les autorités locales s'occupant de la gestion des ressources régionales et du développement des stratégies des ressources renouvelables, n'ont pas été utilisées en tant qu'outil pour le développement urbain.

La planification urbaine a été dominée par le souci de maximiser l'intérêt privé plutôt que l'intérêt public dans l'utilisation des terres urbaines. Les politiciens au niveau national et local n'ont pas hésité, parfois, à coopérer avec les principaux acteurs qui avaient des intérêts vitaux dans la spéculation des terres. Dans ces conditions, les dispositions constitutionnelles concernant la protection des ressources naturelles telles que la terre, l'eau, les forêts, les biens historiques, culturels et architecturaux ne pourraient pas être mises en application d'une manière appropriée. Ce travail portera sur les implications de la non-intégration du concept de développement et de gestion urbaine durable dans la réalisation des plans directeurs des villes.

Sommario

Se per urbanizzazione s'intende la massimizzazione dell'efficienza economica nell'uso delle risorse quali aria, acqua e suolo, mantenendo le riserve delle risorse naturali al livello attuale o superiore, assicurando l'equità sociale nella distribuzione dei benefici e dei costi dello sviluppo ed evitando superflue preclusioni alle future possibilità di sviluppo, la gestione dello sviluppo urbano in Turchia non soddisfa questi requisiti. Le attuali caratteristiche dell'urbanizzazione non permetterebbero di soddisfare i fabbisogni delle generazioni presenti senza compromettere la capacità delle generazioni future di soddisfare i propri fabbisogni.

L'entità e la qualità dello sviluppo urbano sono fortemente influenzate da un'urbanizzazione rapida ma anche unidirezionale, squilibrata e non pianificata. Essa favorisce la disoccupazione e la sotto-occupazione nelle principali città e alimenta il settore informale. Dal 1950, la rapida urbanizzazione è anche caratterizzata da un altrettanto rapido aumento del numero d'alloggi abusivi intorno alle principali città.

L'economia nazionale non ha potuto svolgere adeguatamente il compito di fornire lavoro, infrastrutture tecniche e sociali quali alloggi, trasporti, comunicazioni, sistema fognario, servizi sanitari, educativi e culturali. Le politiche d'urbanizzazione, di migrazione, degli alloggi, delle terre urbane per insediamenti abusivi non sono riuscite a realizzare un tipo di sviluppo urbano che scaturirebbe da una gestione urbana sostenibile. A questo problema si aggiunge l 'inadeguatezza delle tecniche di pianificazione utilizzate. Le tecniche tradizionali dei piani generali urbani usate negli ultimi quarant'anni-non sono riuscite a raggiungere gli scopi legati alle risorse quali l'acqua e i combustibili fossili, a promuovere il trasporto pubblico e migliorare il risparmio energetico nella progettazione delle costruzioni.

La massimizzazione dell'interesse privato piuttosto che di quello pubblico nell'uso delle terre urbane, ha dominato la pratica pianificatoria urbana. A livello locale e nazionale, i politici non hanno esitato, a volte, a collaborare con i principali attori coinvolti nella speculazione dei terreni. In queste condizioni, le misure istituzionali sulla protezione delle risorse naturali quali il suolo, le acque, le foreste, i beni storici, culturali e architettonici non si sono potuti attuare in misura adeguata. Il presente lavoro tratterà principalmente delle implicazioni della non-integrazione delle considerazioni di sviluppo e gestione urbana sostenibile nei piani generali delle città.

Introduction

Urbanization may be defined as the movement of population from rural to urban areas, the growth of cities in number and size and the increase of the share of urban population in total population. Such a definition should not overlook the fact that urbanization entails at the same time a transformation in the structure of the economy and proceeds in parallel with a certain change in human behavior at least in theory. The reason why I felt the need to express the words "at least in theory" is that urbanization as defined above does not fake place all the time and everywhere in the same way. Especially, the characteristics of urbanization in developing economies differ widely from those in already developed and industrialized nations.

Sustainability adds new dimensions to urbanization. Conversely, urbanization, depending upon its pace, nature and patterns, may create numerous problems or opportunities that will need special treatment. Because sustainable urbanization is the maximization of economic efficiency in the use of resources including air, water and soil, maintaining natural resource stocks at or above their present level, ensuring social equity in the distribution of development benefits and costs, and avoidance of unnecessary foreclosure of future development options. Our aim in this paper is to see whether urban development management meets these requirements in Turkey. At first glance, one gets the impression that present characteristics of urbanization in Turkey would not allow meeting the needs of the present generation without compromising the ability of future generations to meet their own needs, using the definition of the Brundtland Report.

Since the publication of the Report called *Our Common Future* in 1987, it was expected that the nations of the world would have revised their development and urbanization policies in such a way to allow all biotic and non-biotic elements of the eco-system to sustain their vitality forever. The Rio Declaration, Agenda 21, other official Rio documents and numerous international legal environmental instruments are full of repetitions of the concept. When applied to the field of urban development, it is assumed that sustainable urbanization can be secured only when master planning is directed to minimize travel needs, promote public transportation, conserve fertile agricultural lands, avoid wasting other sensitive and non-renewable ecological resources and enhance energy savings in building designs and layouts. This would certainly require carrying out sustainability programs and projects and incorporating

analysis and measures of regional sustainability in city planning practices through regional resource inventories, vertical and horizontal coordination among all public authorities
and private entities involved in regional resource management and the development of renewable resource strategies.

Most of the countries in the Mediterranean basin were
not able to realize the principles formulated in the Agenda
21, particularly with respect to sustainable urbanization. Turkey is not an exception to such an observation. Urban development is considerably influenced qualitatively and quantitatively by rapid urbanization. Urbanization has been not
only rapid, but also one-directional, unbalanced and disorderly. It operates to increase the rate of unemployment and
underemployment in major cities and to inflate the informal sector. Rapid urbanization has also been characterized,
since 1950, by a rapid increase in the number of squatter
dwellings in major cities.

National economy could not cope adequately with the
task of providing employment, technical and social infrastructures such as housing, transportation, communications,
sewerage, public health, educational and cultural services
to meet the needs of rapidly urbanizing populations. Policies for managing urbanization, migration, housing, urban
land and squatter settlements have not succeeded in realizing the kind of urban development that might be regarded
as the outcome of a sustainable urban management. Related
to this issue is the inadequacy of the planning techniques
used. The traditional comprehensive master planning techniques that have been in use during the last four decades
have failed in achieving the aims of resource conservation
and rational management.

The concern for maximizing the private rather than the public interest in using urban land dominated the practice of urban planning. National and local politicians did not hesitate, at times, to cooperate with major actors who had significant interests in land speculation. Under these conditions, the constitutional provisions concerning the protection of natural resources such as land, water, forestry, historical, cultural and architectural assets could not be implemented appropriately.

Patterns of Urbanization

Turkey's economic and social parameters will determine the country's population growth rate in the first quarter of the 21st century. The results of the Population Census taken at the end of 1997 showed that Turkey's population in that year was 64 million. it can be assumed that by the beginning of the 21st century, this figure exceeded 67 million. Regardless of the kind of social change that takes place, even if rapid urbanization is expected to pull down the birth rate, several studies carried out in the squatter settlements of the major cities indicate that these areas will continue to exhibit a high fertility rate.

Today, regardless of the fact that 64.6 % of the country's population live in cities (communities of 10,000 or more inhabitants), over the past four decades, the annual average rate of urbanization has been around 6%. Nevertheless, the growth rate of the total population and that of the rural population were far below this figure during the same period.

It is estimated that the urban population ratio will increase even more rapidly in the years ahead, rising from 64.6% in 1997 to 75 percent by the year 2010. Although nearly 40 million people live at present in cities, this figure is expected to reach 55 million by 2010. Furthermore, urban population continues to exhibit a tendency to be concentrated in the very large cities, which are at the same time the main sources of all sorts of urban and environmental problems. While the ratio of urban population in cities of 100,000 and upwards was 45% in 1990, it rose to 69.7% by the year 1997. It is expected to go as high as 75% by the year 2010. This will bring in the already existing overcrowded urban centers more than 10 million people during the first decade of the 21st century. The number of cities will be around 500, those with 100,000 or more inhabitants will be around 100, and those having over one million inhabitants will be around 15.

We assume that the pace and patterns of urbanization is one of the most important independent variables for environmental degradation. We also use the word environment in its largest sense as encompassing social and economic characteristics of the population such as poverty, unbalanced income distribution, unemployment, and inadequacy of such public services like health and education. All this in addition to the conventional indicators for the quality of living environment expressed commonly in terms of the various kinds of pollution.

The squatter settlements constitute one of the most important indicators of unsustainable urbanization. In fact, illegal housing and squatting rank at the top of the list of environmental problems caused by haphazard and disorderly urbanization. They dominate the appearance of the largest cities. Only one third of the yearly need of 500,000 social housing spaces is met at present by regular market mechanisms. The rest is being met by squatter houses Nearly 30%

of Turkey's urban population live in these informal and illegal settlements which reflect a fragmented social structure in which numerous adverse socio-cultural, psychological and political consequences flourish together with the
waste of scarce resources.

The ratio of those living in these shack dwellings is as
high as 7 percent in Ankara, 60% in Istanbul and 50% in
Izmir. This is essentially a reflection of the uneven income
distribution and poverty, not simply a problem of housing.

The number of these houses increased from 240,000 ac-
commodating 1.2 million people (16.4% of the urban population) in 1960 to 3.5 million units housing 17.5 million
people, nearly 40% of the urban population in 1997. Squatter settlements developed in an unplanned manner and in
complete violation of the urban land use plans. They cause
distortions of the planning principles and render the article of the Constitution guaranteeing land ownership (art.
35) to remain only on paper.

It has been estimated that approximately 150,000 hectares of the best quality of agricultural land were converted
into non-agricultural uses in these areas from 1975-1995.
Turkey's experiences show that squatting was an activity of
both genuine self-help and mutual help from 1945-1965,
while a partial commercialization appeared in the process
of squatter house production in the following 15 years. Beginning from the 1980's, a complete commercialization of
this sector drew attention. Squatter dwelling is no longer
an output of self-help and mutual help initiatives because
the labor of the homeless and their family members is entirely left outside the production process. The provision of
the building lot, the design and actual construction of the
dwellings are assumed by commercially organized firms,

and sometimes, by the underground forces that are called the "Mafia of land and squatting", which are often able to substitute public authority.

The use value is completely replaced by the exchange value of the commodity in this sector. The meaning of the informal sector within the context of urbanization and town planning has come to be equated with disorder, waste and irregularity. In other words, the informality became formalized.

According to some research findings, the number of the illegal land subdivisions in Istanbul increased from between l 50,000-200,000 in 1975 to nearly 3 million in the late I 990's. In this city alone, a total of 10,000 hectares of urban land and semi-urban land, including forest, has been subjected to informal subdivision. As a result of the population increase that will be caused by the settlement in informally subdivided land deprived of basic urban infrastructure, approximately 10 million people are expected to be added to the existing inhabitants of Istanbul (which is presently 11 million) in the first decade of the new millennium.

Under these conditions, it would be no exaggeration to state that the squatting process is an important social and economic phenomenon operating to prevent sustainable urbanization. The waste of urban land belonging to present and future generations is not compatible with the very concept of sustainable development.

Agriculture and Sustainable Urban Development

Urban development that does not care for the principles of sustainable development and the protection of natural resources paves the way f or the destruction of fertile agricultural lands, green areas and all kinds of open spaces. Especially in rapidly industrializing regions, agricultural land is often expropriated for industry with no regard at all to the levels of productivity. An agriculturally valuable belt of land surrounding the Mersin and Adana-Osmaniye agglomerations located in the Mediterranean Region has been totally appropriated for urban development and industrial purposes even though it would have been possible to establish these installations on less fertile agricultural lands and still operate them productively.

The most fertile agricultural land is being increasingly occupied by industry, which is causing problems in the rational use of limited resources. Waste of valuable agricultural land is particularly visible along the coasts of Çukurova, Mediterranean, Aegean and Marmara Regions.

In these regions, even the fertile land which has been developed for agricultural use by the allocation of considerable funds from the State budget is gradually being sacrificed as a result of public indifference. Grasslands and forests also began to be cleared for farming and constructing residential buildings as a result of population growth and the mechanization of agriculture.

Table 1: Land Assets of Turkey and Their Use

Categories of use	Amount (ha)	Percent of total (%)
Agricultural land	27,699,004	35.6
Pastures	21,745,690	28.0
Forests	23,468,463	30.2
Settlements	569,400	0.7
Other lands	3,212,175	4.1
Water surfaces	1,102,396	1.4
Total	77,797,127	100.0

Source: Necmi Sönmez (1992), "Çevre Toprak ve Insan », in Keles R. (1997) (Ed.), *Insan, Çevre, Toplum* İmge, Ankara, p.69.

Table 2: Categories of Lands According to Their Quality

Qualifications	Amount (ha)	Percent of total (%)
ARABLE LANDS		
1st class	5,012,537	6.4
2nd class	6,758,702	8.7
3rd class	7,574,330	9.7
4th class	7,201,016	9.3
Total	26,546,585	34.1
NON-ARABLE LANDS		
5th class	165,547	0.2
6th class	10,238,533	13.2
7th class	36,288,553	46.6
Total	46,692,633	60.0
LANDS UNSUITABLE FOR CULTIVATION (8th class)	4,557,909	5.9
TOTAL	77,797,127	100.0

Source: Turkey's Environmental Problems Foundation (1991), *Türkiye'nin Çevre Sorunları*, 1991, (Environmental Problems of Turkey, 1991), Ankara.

Although the amount of high quality land is extremely limited, there Is an ongoing waste even of the land irrigated by enormous State. A great majority of the land irrigated as a result of public investments was occupied by urban uses during the 1970's and 1980's. If the 4,778,399 hectares under cultivation are subtracted from the total of 5,012,537 hectares of first class land in Turkey, one can conclude that the remaining 234,138 hectares of land is devoted to the following uses: grasslands (69,061 hectares), pastures (108,499 hectares), forests (5,824 hectares) and a variety of urban uses such as factories, roads, airports, and other forms of inappropriate downright destruction.

In order to shed more light on the extent of the damage to agricultural land, two phenomena closely related to rural and urban migration and to the behavioral consequences of urbanization may be used as examples. One is the land occupied by industrial establishments, and the second is the impact of tourism and secondary houses in coastal areas. The 15 biggest cities, with few exemptions, are at the same time, the most developed and industrialized centers of the country where organized industrial districts and small industry zones constitute the major sources of economic activity.

The location of industrial establishments also constitutes a serious threat to the sustainability of the valuable agricultural land. Table 3 below clearly shows how the encroachment of industry destroys the most valuable lands in those cities. It is interesting to note that the number of cities where only less than ten percent of the land occupied by industrial establishments on significantly fertile agricultural land is few. It is no more than 5 out of a total of 67.

Although the areas converted to urban, industrial or service uses constitute only 5% of the total area of Turkey; this figure tends to give quite a misleading impression about the reality. The land simply taken away by these activities is usually of prime quality, especially in the coastal zones. Industrial establishments preferring to locate along the coastline may not have an extensive coverage as far as the coastal area is concerned. However, they are usually important sources of soil, air, marine as well as visual pollution.

The paper mill near Taşucu, İskenderun Iron and Steel Mill, Botat and Aliada refineries are a few examples of non-agricultural uses with profound negative environmental impact. Construction of free trade zones in several coastal centers, like Adana-Yumurtalık, Izmir-Gaziemir, Antalya and Mersin, has the potential of creating immense adverse effects on the environment, both in the sense of extra roads and increased traffic and pollution on the existing roads.

**Table 3: Land Occupied by Industrial
District in Major Cities of Turkey**

Cities	(a)	(b)	(b) / (a)
Adana	1400	280	20%
Ankara	556	138	25
Antalya	292	234	80
Bursa	610	519	85
Diyarbakır	270	162	60
Erzurum	100	90	90
Eskişehir	420	420	100
Gaziantep	735	662	90
Mersin	400	400	100
Istanbul	400	320	80
Izmir	742	223	30
Kayseri	650	585	90
İzmit	300	150	50
Konya	520	416	80
Samsun	274	247	90

(a) Land occupied by the industry (hectares).

(b) Portion of the land that is agriculturally valuable (hectares).

Source: Özdemir Özbay, "Ülkemizde Su ve Toprak Kaynaklarının Kullanımı ve Korunmasında Yasal Durum, Tarımda Su Yönetimi ve Çiftçi Katılımı Sempozyumu", TMMOB, Ziraat Mühendisleri Odası, Ankara, 1995, p.49.

The spread of residential areas upon prime land is a common phenomenon. Particularly, secondary housing built in touristic and coastal areas deserves special attention. Construction of secondary housing increased considerably during the last three decades. They are owned and mostly used by middle and higher-income segments of the residents of the largest cities. Although they provide certain opportunities from the owners' point of view, they create several adverse effects in some other respects. The latter can be summarized as follows: a) loss of agricultural land, forests, etc. to secondary homes in Kutadasy, Davutlar (Aydın), between 1975 and 1985, a coastal strip of al least 30 kilometers by 750 meters was totally covered by secondary housing on fertile land; b) displacement of local population due to local employment; c) increasing prices due to higher purchasing power of new residents; d) excessive seasonal strain on infrastructure and considerable investments that will be fully used only in the peak season; e) excessive strain on the health, police, and other public services as a result of the population increase caused by seasonal attractions.

Similar problems are observed in the Bursa metropolitan area, 300 kilometers south of Istanbul. Turkey's booming world famous textile industries and Renault car manufacturing plants are situated in this area. Lack of planning and illegal subdividing and leasing of public lands have played an important role in the disappearance of arable land. As a result of booming industrial and residential developments which have been situated on the once arable and fertile lands, the Bursa plain looks more red than green with its tiled rooftops. The process of transformation from agriculture to non-agriculture was enhanced by the establishment of the first organized industrial district in Bursa in the early 1960's. Due to its proximity to the city of Bursa, flatter areas previously used for cultivation were preferred by businesses for further investments and a competition for the best quality land soon started between enterprises of different sizes. Towns and settlement areas sprung up around factories and service facilities engulfing arable land during this process. Industrialization is particularly fast on the Mudanya-Bursa road. In addition, illegal settlements have been created in surrounding settlements such as Demirtat Kestel, Gürsu, Samanlı, Vakıfköy and Balıklı. Big firms building factories have invaded the whole area polluting the air, water and soil.

Nearly 85% of the total territory of Turkey is subject to soil erosion of various intensities. 54% of the land is affected by severe erosion, and 20% by a less violent erosion. Three fourths of the cultivated agricultural land are under the impact of erosion. In other words, only 5 million hectares of agricultural land can be regarded as erosion-free.

Major reasons of using the most fertile agricultural land are human settlements, industry, transportation, tourism, infrastructure and similar investments as in the case of Thrace. In making such choices, the fact that the agricultural output of the highest economic value can be achieved only on the best quality lands is usually forgotten. Although only 15% of Turkey's land resources is sufficiently fertile, most of the productive agricultural land is being wasted simply on the grounds that "alternative land was not available".

The main responsibility can be attributed to the lack of appropriate legislation, technical inefficiencies, political pressures and central and local authorities. Continuous efforts of those seeking to maximize their own profits tend to undermine the role of agriculture in the economy and to disregard the importance of agricultural land as a non-reproducible national asset.

Simply because the route of the national highways was designed unconsciously in Thrace, 46,000 hectares of agricultural land began to be used for non-agricultural purposes. Several years ago the value of the loss in produce (wheat) was estimated to be around 13 trillion TL (one US dollar is presently 560 TL). Land lost as a result of misuse amounted to 324,000 hectares in the provinces of Edirne, Tekirdağ and Kırklareli. The increase in the amount of the misused land was 216% from 1985-1991 and 727% from 1985-1998. At present, 1700 factories are being operated in Thrace which has been designated, under normal conditions, as an "agricultural site" because of its topographical qualities, structure of land and irrigation opportunities. Within the triangle of Çorlu-Çerkezköy-Lüleburgaz, settlements that are 200 kilometers away from Istanbul, 499 factories are established on the most fertile agricultural land.

In the country as a whole, misuse of land and the use of agricultural lands tor non-agricultural purposes increased tremendously during the last two decades (1978-1996) at an unprecedented pace (333%) and amounted to 25 millions of hectares. Out of these lands, 573,000 hectares are of agricultural nature. State Water Works reported that the lands; open to irrigation realized through considerable investments, deteriorated into concrete buildings from 1985-1993 particularly in such cities as Ankara (16%), Erzurum (9%) and Eskisehir (8%).

Legal and Institutional Aspects

A major guarantee is article 168 of the Constitution, requiring that natural wealth and resources belong to the State. The protection of fertile agricultural land is an extremely important matter for a country that derives its economic potentials from the agricultural sector and the amount of its high quality lands is limited. According to article 56, everyone has the right to live in a healthy and balanced environment. It is the duty of the State and citizens to improve the natural environment and to prevent environmental pollution. The Constitution also provides some other legal guarantees for the protection of natural and man-made environmental values.

For instance, article 35 prohibits anyone to exercise the right to property in contravention of public interest. Article 43 puts the coastal areas under the sovereignty and at the disposal of the State, with the consequence that in the utilization of the sea coast, lakes shores and river banks, and the coastal strip along the seas and lakes, public interest has to be taken into consideration as the primary guide. Of course, constitutional stipulations exist that are directly concerned with the protection of lands. Prevention of the loss of agricultural land is mentioned as the duty of the State in article 44 of the Constitution. Similarly, providing land to farmers with insufficient acreage could not lead to a fall in production or to the depletion of forests and other land and underground resources. The responsibility of the State to ensure the conservation of historical and natural assets and wealth is also underlined in the Constitution (art. 63).

More specifically, the State is charged with the duty of enacting the necessary legislation and taking appropriate measures for the protection of forests and increasing the forestry areas. No amenities or pardons to be granted for offenses against forests can be legislated. The restraining of forest boundaries is also prohibited by the Constitution (art. 169), except in respect to areas whose preservation as forests is considered "technically and scientifically useless". Although the Constitution does not allow, in principle, reducing the amount of forestries, it permits it in exceptional cases, depending upon the discretion of the executive power. These exceptions are so large that they make it possible to ignore altogether the effective implementation of the principle itself. More concretely, in addition to the above-mentioned exceptional case, restriction is allowed in those forests that have completely lost their quality as a forest since 1981 and are presently used as orchards, farms and olive groves, and in areas where compact settlements composed of urban or rural buildings exist.

On the other hand, the Environment Law of 1983 (No. 2873) defines the concept of "environmental protection" as the activities for the preservation of ecological balance, prevention of degradation and pollution in the air, water and land, and for their improvement. According to the general principles of the Environment Law, it is the duty of the people to protect the environment and to comply with the measures taken for that purpose. Health of all living beings is to be taken into account with priority as a factor in all measures taken to protect and improve the environment. The law seems to have accepted the principle of "sustainable development" by stating that all kinds of regulations and measures to be adopted with a view to protect and improve the environment must be in compliance with the goals of improve the environment must be in compliance with the goals of economic and social development: All economic enterprises and other institutions are required, in their decisions of land and resource use and project evaluation, to strike a balance between the goals of environmental protection and development. They must choose the most appropriate methods and technology in order to achieve that end.

An environmental impact analysis has to be made by all public and private entrepreneurs for their planned establishments, in order to avoid their adverse impact upon environmental values. Such a requirement is also an implication of integrating the principle of environmental impact analysis, enshrined in the documents of the Rio Summit and other international legal documents, into domestic legislation. However, the mere existence of such a principle in the legislation is not sufficient to ensure and guarantee its effective use in practice. There are numerous examples where both public authorities and private sector institutions begin their actual investments with no regard at all to this requirement and consequently are faced by judicial sanctions.

In addition to the Environmental Law, the Municipal Law (1930) and the Law on Public Health (1930), numerous special legislation possess rules to be applied for the protection and preservation of environmental assets. The Law on the Protection of Cultural and Natural Values (1983) (No. 2863), The Law on the Protection of the Bosphorus (1983) (No. 2960), the Law on the Protection of Coastal

Areas (1992) (No. 3830), Urban Development Law (1985) (No. 3194), The Law on the Encouragement of Tourism (1982) (No. 2634), the Law on Forests (1956) (No. 6831), the Law on Water Products (1971) (No. 1380) are a few of these legislations.

In order to protect the values of historical and natural importance of cities and towns, and to ensure sustainable urbanization, the above-mentioned laws empower the central authorities or the provincial agents of the central government to intervene in, and in certain cases, take over the planning powers of local authorities. This frequently gives way to tensions between the center and the cities and towns in the periphery.

Urban development legislation openly prohibits the decrease of the amount of land allocated for open spaces in master plans by modifying plans themselves. This is regarded as not being of public interest. Similarly, the legislation on the protection of agricultural land is not favorable to the utilization of highly productive agricultural land for non-agricultural purposes as required by the growth of urban population and rapid urbanization. As touched upon earlier, although a special by-law prohibits the utilization of the 1st to 4th category of productive agricultural land for urban development needs, in many parts of the country, particularly in the south, west and Marmara regions, de facto occupations of these kind as a result of the pressures on land created by rapid urban growth, large-scale cooperative housing schemes and even public and private industrial establishments, make the implementation of these legal provisions almost impossible.

A law passed in 1973 (No. 1757) which was called the Law on Land and Agriculture Reform possessed provisions preventing the use of agricultural lands for non-agricultural purposes. Even the use of land unsuitable f or cultivation was prohibited by that law. But a subsequent law enacted in 1984 entitled as the Law on Agricultural Reform concerning Land Management in Irrigation Areas (No. 3083) paved the way for allowing the use of agricultural land for non-agricultural purposes "in necessary conditions". There is no doubt that this expression is rather indefinite and vague and needs to be defined in every case by the executive power. Therefore, a by-law was issued in 1989 to shed light onto the implementation of the rule and its exceptions. It aims to arrange the use for non-agricultural ends of all agricultural lands belonging to the Treasury and the lands owned by both public institutions and private people. It provides the executive with the power to make necessary arrangements not only for the areas within the municipal boundaries, but also in rural areas. For the first time, agricultural lands in Turkey have been classified into eight quality groups by this by-law on the basis of their basic characteristics. The first four categories comprise the most fertile agricultural lands. Article 4 of this by-law has made the allocation of all kinds of lands within the boundaries of urban development, partial development and implementation plans, and in the already settled areas for non-agricultural end, subject to the permission of the Ministry of Village Affairs (General Directorate of Rural Services). For this purpose, the principle was to begin the allocation of agricultural lands from the 8th category, in other words the least fertile lands. A particular emphasis in the by -law is that the lands opened to irrigation as a result of public investments could not be appropriated for non-agricultural purposes. Allocations to purposes such as housing, education, industrial districts, health, commercial centers investments could be made only by starting from lands of dry farming.

A modification made in this by-law within one year from being put into force (February 1990) has allowed exceptional practices that might endanger the sustainability of land resources in this country. According to this exceptional rule, even the irrigated lands of 1st, 2nd, 3rd and 4th categories could be allocated for non-agricultural ends provided that "more appropriate lands were not available for companies and cooperatives with more than 1,000 shareholders and the share of each shareholder does not exceed 1 percent of its capital, and for the establishment of industry and trade centers to be created with H view to produce and to market for export".

A new modification took place in the by-law later on (October 1991) and the above mentioned exceptional rule has been further expanded against public interest. According to this new change, in addition to the above mentioned economic activities, those who are holders of investment incentives obtained from the government for integrated industrial investments for aircraft, vessels and cars which are deemed to be particularly important for the economy will also benefit for the allocations of best quality agricultural lands.

Upon this change that has taken place, according to rumors, in order to realize an important investment project (a Toyota car factory in the Sakurada plain belonging to an influential businessman close to the Prime Minister and his party) the Chamber of Agricultural Engineers has filed a suit at the respective administrative court against the Ministry of Village Affairs which had prepared the by-law for its annulment. A similar change was effectuated in 1990 in order to enable a politician close to the Prime Minister to establish or expend his textile factory in the city of Bursa. The main reason for this application Was that the change made to the by-law with respect to the expansion of the exceptional rule was not in compliance with the public interest.

The Council of State (Danıştay), the highest administrative court in this country, has annulled in 1993 the above-mentioned by-law and its modified provisions (June 30, 1993; Subj.: 1991/4431; Decision: 1993/2779).

It was argued by the mentioned Chamber of Agricultural Engineers that changes made in the by-law constituted a sharp deviation from the main goals of the by-law. Such a change was in contradiction of national needs and scientific facts aimed primarily towards such goals so as to maximize the short term interest of the investor instead of increasing the common and long-term benefits of the society. According to the interpretation of the issue by the Council of State, "article 45 of the Constitution was not favorable to the destruction of agricultural lands, pastures and meadows". The "power of the public authority issuing and changing the by-law was not used in the public interest in this case". "It is clearly stated in the respective laws that lands irrigated with special means by public authorities could not be appropriated for non-agricultural purposes. This is the rule and the exceptions to the rule are specified there".

The Council of State, referring to the 6th Five Year Development Plan also underlined the fact that to modernize production methods, reduce the dependency of agriculture on climatic conditions, or meet the nutritional needs of the population and develop the export of agricultural products were among the targets of the Plan and therefore the most rational use of land and water resources was essential to achieve these ends. Based mainly on such legal and political assessments, the Highest Court maintained that such fertile lands could not be sacrificed to industrial investment needs merely on the grounds of the non-availability of alternative sites, which is a highly indefinite expression.

The government prepared a new by-law concerning the use of agricultural lands for other purposes in 1998. Since it contained similar provisions that might produce adverse consequences for the sustainability of each element of the eco-system, particularly for the rational use of cultivable land resources, the Chamber of Agricultural Engineers again applied to the Council of State for its abolishment. The main arguments of the Chamber are relevant for the concept of sustainable development under discussion:

- The exceptions are so broad that they can not be compatible with common and long-term interests of the society. In the practice, they can not be reconciled with the principle of sustainable development repeated in the 7th Five-Year development Plan.

- The title of the by-law contradicts its goals, which must consist of the regulation of the use of agricultural lands in the public interest. In its present wording, it gives the impression that it tends to encourage the waste of agricultural lands.

- In the previous formulation of the scope of the protected agricultural lands the only exception was the forest areas, while the new by-law was expanded to also include pastures, meadows, summer pastures on high ground and winter quarters for animals. Reducing the area to be protected is in contradiction with the public interest.

- There is a difference between the definitions of irrigated lands made by the former and new by-laws. The new by-law added to the category of irrigated lands those lands that might be irrigated through existing water resources without requiring additional establishments. Such wording has of course narrowed down the of irrigated lands worth being protected. As a result, even the smallest initiative to irrigate agricultural land will prevent naming it as irrigated agricultural land.

Another additional effort to enlarge the scope of exceptions is to include among them high tech investments made in the hopes of increasing exports and backed by foreign capital. In the original wording, only industrial districts and commercial centers were cited.

The main argument of the Chamber of Agricultural Engineers is that all these changes made to the by-law are related to private and specific interests and therefore can be regarded as measures taken in the public or general interest. In a preliminary decision, the Council of State supported this view, but the final verdict is to be given in the following months.

Another debate that has recently taken place within this framework is between TEMA (TEMA is an NGO established for the protection of soil against erosion) and the Confederation of Employers' Unions (TISK) with regard to measures taken to protect agricultural land. The latter aligned itself with the official position of the government by arguing that location of industry is quite important for economic development and welfare and those opposing it might cause irreparable harm to industrial development. This point of view reminds one of the theses maintained by the signatories of the Heidelberg Appeal that was adopted on the eve of the Rio Summit in 1992. They focused what environmentalists do as "an irrational ideology" that had the potential of slowing down social and economic development. ("Appel de Heidelberg du 14 avril 1992 aux chefs d'Etats et de gouvermements Éthique, L'écologie: humanisme ou naturalisme? No. 13 1994/3, pp. 110-117).

On the other hand, TEMA argued that article 166 of the Constitution was concerned with planning as a tool for development and a certain balance was required to be established between industry on one hand and agriculture on the other in order to achieve a balanced development. Yet, the existing by-law was an obstacle in achieving such a goal. What was done by the changes in the by-law signified "Industry imports, but the agriculture does not". Formulation of policies for the protection of the environment, prevention of all kinds of pollution, and improvement of the quality of the environment are entrusted with the Ministry of Environment establish in 1991. Of course, in addition to the coordinating powers of this Ministry, the Ministries of Agriculture and Village Affairs, Natural Resources and Energy, Public Works and Settlements, Public Health, and the Interior Ministry have their respective duties, among others, to contribute to ensure sustainable urbanization as defined at the beginning. The Ministry of Environment also has local organizations set up in the provinces. Moreover, in about a dozen areas of natural and historical interest, "special protection areas" have been established since 1988 in order to protect these areas sensitive to pollution and degradation. Special planning and building principles and guidelines are implemented in these regions by the Special Protection Agency that is attached to the Ministry of Environment. Planning and building control powers of the municipalities that are situated in these areas are transferred to the cited central institutions. Similarly, in Southeast Anatolia, a special de-concentrated authority is in charge of the implementation of a large-scale integrated regional development project, which includes sections dealing with the preservation of land and water resources and at the same time environmental values.

Concluding Remarks

Beyond any doubt, proper protection of the environment can only be ensured by the effective involvement of the citizen in decision processes regarding environmental issues. Participation channels associations, foundations, labor unions, cooperatives and professional organizations are largely open. But an effective contribution depends upon the level of public consciousness as a whole toward the environmental values, complementarily of economic development and environment, in other words sustainable development. So far, the public has played an important role in influencing the legislative and executive bodies. Judiciary has been playing an important function to ensure sustainable urbanization.

Although an actual, personal and legitimate interest in the issue at stake is a precondition for seeking the annulment of an administrative act or decision in the courts, the Law on Administrative Procedures makes an important exception for those matters of public interest such as city master plans, historical buildings and the protection of the environment. in other words, citizens sensitive to environmental issues have the opportunity to apply to the courts for the administrative of decision concerned, no matter if their rights are violated or not. They also have recourse to administrative authorities to stop any public or private undertaking that harms the environment. Citizens and civic society organizations play an important and increasing role, by using this right provided by the Environment Law (art.30) in the protection of environment in the country.

This is certainly not enough. In addition to increasing public awareness, consciousness of decision-makers is of utmost importance. Unless they are not well informed about the exact meaning of concepts. Such as sustainable development, intergenerational equity, precautionary principle, common and differentiated responsibility, principle of participation and similar, it would be practically impossible to carry out the suggestions of intonational conferences. Turkey is witnessing a still persisting indifference on the part of some decision-makers to issues of nuclear power plants, protection of natural and historical assets and natural resources in general. There are examples of university campuses established on the forestland in contravention to the principle of the rule of law, but with ceremonies in the presence of even the President of the Republic. Car factories and similar plants are almost free to settle on the most fertile farmland with no due regard to conditions of sustainability. These and similar problems require intense educational efforts to train everyone concerned.

Finally, Turkey is either signatory or part of most of the international conventions concerning the environment. Being a candidate for the membership of the European Union, it needs to adjust its legislation and practices to the norms prevailing within the European community in a relativity short time. Even today Turkey is part of more than 30 international treaties and conventions, which aim at the protection of the environment. It has the obligation to put into effect the legal norms of all these legal documents, which charge Turkey, as other member states, to protect the environment not only for present, but also for future generations and mankind.

A final point has to be made in general which is no less important than an other point mentioned so far. Inadequate interest in the world in planning at all levels (national, regional and local) is gradually attracting more attention of all observes. This anti-planning attitude observed in many countries up to now is being encouraged nowadays and supported by international finance and economics institutions. It has to be remembered that the title of the IBRD's World Development Report was named From Plan to Market a few years ago. The report for the year 2000 also adopted an approach almost hostile to planning.

It seems that this excessive and pre-judged emphasis upon almost the uselessness of the public sector, including urban governments and planning authorities, and the following anti-planning stand, end up with leaving the shaping of urban environments to the free play of the market forces which may be neither economically more efficient, nor acceptable from the standpoint of social justice. This seems to be, at the same time, contradictory with the principle of prevention as a rational component of the concept of sustainable development. It is really to understand the position of some international organizations while insisting on the concept of sustainability on one hand; they constantly recommend anti-planning policies to developing nations on the other. The following sentences from the recently published World Development Report 2000, which is called Entering the 21st Century, is highly illustrative of the decreasing role of public and planning authorities in the world. This will of course create numerous obstacles for ensuring sustainable urbanization in the developing world: "Since the 1950's, the common model of urban management has charged the public sector with planning and delivering basic services. But this model has failed to yield satisfactory outcomes in low-income countries. One argument is that governments should withdraw as primary service providers and assume the role of the enabler, relying increasingly on the private sector to deliver basic services".

References

Barnier V, Tucoulet C. (1999), "Villes et environnement: de l'ecologie urbaine a la ville durable", *La documentation française*, 829, Paris.

Cangır C. (1991), "Amaç Dışı Arazi Kullanımı" (Misuse of Land), TMMOB Ziraat Mühendisleri Odası, Toprak, Insan, Çevre Sempozyumu (Symposium on Lan Man and Environment), June 3-4, 1991, Ankara.

Ceran T. (1996), "Kırsal Kesim, Göç ve Kentleşme" (Rural Sector, Migration and

Urbanization), *HABITAT II*, Istanbul.

Ceran T. Ten N. (1999), "Türkiye'de Tarımsal Yapı ve Kentleşme" (The Structure of Agriculture and Urbanization in Turkey), Ankara.

Ecologie Politique, les villes durables, Printemps, Paris, 13, 1995.

Ethique: I 'Ecologie, Humanisme ou Naturalisme?, Appel de Heidelberg aux chefs d'Etats et de gouvemements, 13, 1994/13.

Haktanır K., (1997), "Doğal Kaynak Olarak Toprak" (Land as a Natural Resource) in Keles R., Insan, Çevre, Toplum (Man, Environment and Society), Imge, Ankara, pp. 226-229.

Keles R. (1996), " Impact of Urbanization on Fertile Agricultural Land in Turkey", in Ben Ali D., Di Guilio A., Lasram M., Lavergne M. (Eds.), *Urbanisation et Agriculture en Mediterrannee: Conflits et Complementarites,* L'Hannattan, CIHEAM, Paris, pp. 145-154.

Keles R. (1997), "The Impact of Urbanization on Urban and Rural Environment in Turkey", Paper presented at the International Conference "The Urban Environment in the Mediterranean. The Population Flow from Rural to Urban Areas: Problems and Implications", Malta, October 5-7, 1997.

Keles R. (1999), "Urban Development and Sustainable Management for the Mediterranean Towns (Turkey)", Paper prepared for the meeting of Working Group for Urban Management, Mediterranean Commission for Sustainable Development, Split, April 26-2, 1999.

Keles R. (199 7), "National Protection: The Case of Protected Areas in Turkey", *Naturopa,* Council of Europe, 85, pp. 23-24.

Knight R.V. (1993), "Sustainable Development-Sustainable Cities", *International Social Science Journal,* 45, pp. 35-54.

Sönmez N., (199 7), "Çevre, Toprak ve lnsan" (Environment, Land and Man), in Keles R. (Ed.), *Man, Environment and Society,* lmge, Ankara, pp. 68-71.

International Cooperation for Sustainable Urban Development in the Mediterranean Region[*]

Cooperation for Environmental Protection

Starting from the post-war years, cooperation among nations has become one of the major tools recommended for conflict resolution and fruitful cooperation to enhance social, economic and environmental development. The Charter of the United Nations, declarations and action plans of habitat I (1976) and II (1996), the Stockholm (1972) and Rio Declarations and Action Plans (1992) are few examples where the importance of international cooperation is emphasized.

The Principle 22 of the Stockholm Declaration recommended that the States *cooperate* to develop further the International Law regarding liability and compensation for the victims of pollution and other environmental damage caused by activities within the jurisdiction or control of such states to areas beyond their jurisdiction. According to the Principle 24 of the UN Conference on Human Environment (Stockholm), international matters concerning the

[*] The author thanks Mrs. Silvia Laria, Dr. Nesrin Algan, Mr. Franco La Torre and Mr. Mohamed Boussraoui for their valuable suggestions.
Paper presented to the Workshop on Urban Management and Sustainable Development in the Mediterranean, Barcelona, Spain, 5-7 July, 2001.

protection and improvement of the environment should be handled in a *cooperative spirit* by all countries on equal footing. *Cooperation* through multilateral or bilateral arrangements or other appropriate means is essential to effectively control, prevent, reduce and eliminate adverse environmental effects resulting from activities conducted in all spheres, in such a way that due account is taken of the sovereignty, and in the interests of all states.

In the World Charter of Nature (UN General Assembly, Res.37/7, 1982), a certain mandate is provided for all parties concerned (States, other public authorities, international organizations, individuals, groups and corporations) *to cooperate* in the task of conserving nature through common activities and other relevant actions, including information exchange and consultations.

In addition to the reference in its preamble to the "creation of new levels of *cooperation among States*", the Rio Declaration (Principle 7) underlines the need for States "*to cooperate* in a spirit of *global partnership* to conserve, protect and restore the health and integrity of the Earth's eco-system. In view of the different contributions to global environmental degradation, States have common but differentiated responsibilities. The developed countries acknowledge the responsibility that they bear in the international pursuit of sustainable development in view of the pressures their societies place on the global environment and the technologies and financial resources they command".

The Principle 12 of the Rio Declaration also refers to the requirement for the States *to cooperate* to promote a supportive and open international economic system that would lead to economic growth and sustainable development in all countries, to better address the problems of environmental degradation. And international consensus is advised as a suitable ground on which environmental measures addressing transboundary or global environmental problems could be based. Finally, within the spirit of the principle 14 of the same Declaration, States are invited *to effectively cooperate* to discourage or prevent the relocation and transfer to other States of any activities or substances that cause severe environmental degradation or are found to be harmful to human health. It would be safe to assume that *cooperation* is conceived in International Environmental law more as a procedural instrument than as a substantial issue that is made related to almost all substantial matters concerning global environmental degradation.

Upon an enabling act of The General Assembly of the United Nations (Resolution 2997/XXVII), The UN Environment Programme decided that the main functions of Governing Council of this Organization should include *the promotion of international cooperation* in the field of environmental protection. It was of course much earlier than this that the UN General Assembly had adopted a Declaration on Principles of International Law Concerning Friendly Relations and Cooperation Among States in Accordance with the Charter of the UN in 24 October 1970, making ground for further cooperation in more specific fields.

The Agenda 21 goes further to insert a sentence among its specific objectives as "to strengthen *cooperation and coordination* on environment and development in the UN system and other intergovernmental and non-governmental sub-regional, regional and global institutions and non-governmental organizations in the field of environment and development". It is within such a spirit that the Commission on Sustainable Development had been created in 1993. Its role is to act as a forum for *international dialogue on sustainable development,* to monitor progress on the implementation of Agenda 21 and activities related to the integration of environmental and developmental goals".

The Agenda 21 has a particularly important sub-section dealing with its regional and sub-regional cooperation and implementation. It suggests that regional and sub-regional cooperation will be an important part of the Conference (Rio) outcome. The UN Regional Economic Commissions, regional development banks and regional economic cooperation organizations, within their respective agreed mandates, can contribute to this process by a) promoting regional and sub-regional capacity building; b) promoting the integration of environmental concerns in regional and sub-regional development policies; c) promoting regional and sub-regional *cooperation*, where appropriate, regarding transboundary issues related to sustainable development.

It was also pointed out that there was a need for closer *cooperation* between UNEP and UNDP, together with other relevant institutions. The Agenda 21 further underlined the need for "an effective link between substantive action and financial support "and consequently pointed out that a close and effective *cooperation* was required between the UN bodies and multilateral financial organizations".[1]

Brundtland Report had defined sustainable development as the kind of economic and social development that meets the needs of the present without compromising the ability of the future generations to meet their own needs. Core ideals and themes within sustainable development have been summarized elsewhere as requiring 1) economy-environment

1   UNEP, *Handbook of Environmental Law*, UNEP, Nairobi, 1992, pp.32-33.

integration, 2) intergenerational obligations, 3) a human right to environment, 4) protection of the non-human world, 5) promoting the quality of life, and 6) participation.[2] The concept of "common concern of mankind" adds a new dimension to the need for the protection of planetary resources in the sense that it requires the involvement of all countries, all societies and all classes of people within countries and societies in achieving the ideal of sustainable development, taking into consideration long-term temporal dimension of the right to environment.[3] Such an understanding would of course require having some sort of ethical responsibility to share the burdens of environmental protection, in other words, a social duty for cooperation.

Sustainable Urban Development

Cities play an important role in meeting the goals of sustainable development. As it is known, the great majority of the world population will be living soon in cities and towns and the Mediterranean Region is not an exception to this observation. Worldwide, city-based producers and consumers already account for most of the renewable and non-renewable resource consumption and waste generation as noted in the Brundtland Report.[4] Meeting the current needs of urban populations should not acquire the dimensions to constitute a threat to sustainability of the develop-

2   J. Connelley and Graham Smith, *Politics and the Environment: From Theory to Practice,* Routledge, London, p.3.

3   R.S. Pathak, "The Human Rights System as a Conceptual Framework for Environmental Law", in Edith Brown Weiss (ed.), *Environmental Change and International Law,* The UN University Press, Tokyo, 1992, p. 228.

4   World Commission on Environment and Development, *Our Common Future,* Oxford University Press, Oxford, 1987, p.8.

ment. Therefore, the priority actions have to be centred on reducing both excessive consumption of natural resources and the burden of wastes on the global environment. Such initiatives may include reducing fossil fuel consumption through energy conservation, more efficient transportation systems, and reducing the amount of waste through pollution prevention.[5] There is no doubt that these longer-term ecological concerns are relevant particularly to the Mediterranean cities in the way of development, for as they grow and prosper, their consumption of resources and generation of wastes will rise accordingly unless action is taken now to promote the efficient use of resources and the minimization of waste.

Sustainable urban development, sustainable urbanization and sustainable cities have become the concepts used frequently in the literature especially during the 1990's. It is assumed that sustainable urban development can be realized only when master planning is directed to minimize travel needs, to promote public transportation, to conserve fertile agricultural lands, to avoid wasting other sensitive and non-renewable ecological resources and to enhance energy savings in building designs and layouts. This would require certainly carrying out sustainability programmes and projects and incorporating analysis and measures of regional sustainability in city planning practices through regional resource inventories, vertical and horizontal coordination among all public authorities and private entities involved in regional resource management and the development of

5   The World Resources Institute et al., *The Urban Environment: World Resources, a Guide to the Global Environment*, HABITAT II, June 1996, a special reprint from *World Resources*, 1996-1997, p.145.

renewable resource strategies. In other words, sustainable urban development may be understood as the maximization of efficiency in the use of resources, maintaining natural resource stocks at or above their present level, social equity in the distribution of development costs and benefits and the avoidance of unnecessary foreclosure of future development options.

According to a definition of the European Economic Commission, the ideal sustainable community is characterized by such factors as environmental integrity, economic vitality and the social well-being.[6] Urban sprawl, congestion, increasingly poor air quality, and shortage of land for affordable housing are some of the symptoms of unsustainable urban development. Trends in population growth, physical expansion of the city compounded by the ideology of economic growth and increasing level of consumption are some of the factors further intensifying these symptoms.[7] The Earth's non-renewable resources are being depleted, mountains of solid, liquid and toxic wastes pollute the air, water and soil and threaten local and regional habitat. As these current trends persist, it is becoming clearer that solutions to seemingly isolated environmental, economic and social concerns are linked and require more holistic solutions. That is why environmental, economic and social policies have to be integrated in order to ensure the compatibility of all these elements.

It is beyond any doubt that the realization of a sustainable and liveable city requires an integrated decision-making

---

6   Economic Commission for Europe, *Guidelines on Sustainable Human Settlements, Planning and Management,* New York and Geneva, 1996, p.25.

7   *Ibid,* p.25.

framework and a fundamental shift in traditional approaches. Therefore, there is a need to be a change in focus from curative measures such as pollution reduction and remediation towards measures based on anticipation and prevention, from consumption to conservation, and from managing the environment to managing rising demands on the environment.

The urban physical environment is a complex mix of *natural elements* such as the air, water, land, climate, flora and fauna, and *built environment* such as buildings, infrastructures and urban open spaces constructed or modified for human habitation and activities, aesthetic and historical heritage. While social values, behaviours, laws and traditions influence physical environment, the environment also influences human behaviour and social relations.

Two characteristics of urban areas give way to consequences that may be detrimental for sustainable development: First, inhabitants and enterprises depend on natural resources to live and on natural processes for breaking down or diluting their wastes. Second, urban areas can concentrate a large range of environmental hazards, such as biological pathogens in the air, water and soil, chemical pollutants and physical hazards.[8] In other words, city- related environmental problems abound as rapid urban growth proceeds.

Attempts to create legislative frameworks must respect for general environmental limits set at global and national levels. Through the official planning process and a series of regional and local plans, it is necessary to provide a

---

8   OECD, Development Assistance Committee, Working Party on Development Cooperation and Environment, 21st Meeting, Paris, 13-14, June 2000, *The Urban Environment and Development Cooperation; a Resource Book,* Paris, 2000.

framework for guiding the spatial development of human settlements. Implementation of these policies is a shared responsibility of different levels of government, particularly the local authorities, the private sector, the business community and the local people. Main policies targeted at ensuring sustainable urban development may be summarized in the following categories.[9]

Conserve, protect and enhance natural areas and life forms and processes they support and define the capacity of areas and boundaries which limit further development.

Promote compact community policies. This may entail intensification, redevelopment of existing neighbourhoods and residential areas, enhancement of streetscapes, rural landscapes and unique architectural features.

Optimise the density potential of the existing urban areas through intensification and rehabilitation in order to make the most efficient and effective use of public investment infrastructure, and conserve natural resources and agricultural land.

Balance the location of the labour force with employment opportunities.

Limit the use of the car through the maximization of the use of transport alternatives, including public transport, commuter rail, bicycles and walking. Promote better logistics in order to limit the need for the transport of goods.

Promote a sense of community, create opportunities for social interaction.

Preserve coherence of the landscape and take action to develop green structures as an important element of the

9   Economic Commission for Europe, *Guidelines...*, op.cit., p.26-27.

urban infrastructure in order to preserve nature and biological diversity.

Ensure that environmental considerations and the "precautionary principle" become an integral part of plans, policies, programmes and projects in both the public and private sector.

Integrate the concept of "net environmental gain" in assessing development.

Recognize choice and diversity in lifestyles.

Maintain options to facilitate the meeting of the community's future needs.

Encourage the development of medium-sized cities as a network of complementary urban settlements to big cities, in order to develop a more balanced hierarchy of human settlements, which will be sustainable. However, initiatives to reduce environmental hazards in cities should not imply increased ecological disruption in surrounding areas.

Encourage the utilization of already built-up areas so as to limit urban sprawl, utilize infrastructure, while safeguarding the cultural and historical heritage.

Similarly, the principle characteristics of a sustainable city are underlined elsewhere as comprising the following: a functionally and socially mixed structure, controlled and reduced mobility, a participative democracy, economic management, eco-systemic management, a patrimonial and recyclable city, an adaptable and flexible city and finally a more compact city[10]. According to the same author, sustainable

10   Olivier Godard, "La ville durable: une tentative de réponse", *Ville et Environnement: de l'Ecologie Urbaine à la Ville Durable,* par Véronique Barnier et Carole Tucoulet, La Documentation Française, No: 829, 29 octobre 1999, p.47.

cities or sustainable urban development must involve, first of all, reducing the consumption of energy, space and natural resources of the city. Secondly, new spatial units of planning and management of urban space have to be defined. Thirdly, a new urban landscape, abolishing the contradiction between a city of exclusive construction and a countryside that serves no more than the nature must be searched for. Fourthly, an ecological reasoning has to be applied to urban populations and to the organization of the built environment. And finally, the concept of the built environment has to be conceived within a long-term perspective.[11] There are close similarities between the characteristics of sustainable urban development just mentioned and the guiding principles for sustainable spatial development of the European Continent adopted during the European Conference of Ministers Responsible for Regional Planning in Hannover in September 2000.[12]

It is a surprising coincidence that the European Urban Charter adopted by a Resolution (No: 234) of the Council of Europe during 17-19 March 1992 encompasses, in each of its chapters dealing with different urban rights, principles of sustainable urban development that originate from the main philosophy of sustainable development defined in the 1992 Rio documents.[13] The rights connected with the transport and mobility, environment and nature in towns,

---

11 Olivier Godard, *Ibid, pp.*45-47.

12 Council of Europe, European Conference of Ministers Responsible for Regional Planning (CEMAT), *Guiding Principles for Sustainable Development of the European Continent, Hanover, September 7 and 8, 2000, Strasbourg, 17 March 2000, MAT-12-HF 35.*

13 Council of Europe, Standing Conference of Local and Regional Authorities, *The European Urban Charter*, Resolution 234, 27th Session, Strasbourg, 17-19 March 1992, 30 March 1992.

the physical forms of cities, the urban architectural heritage, housing, urban security and crime prevention, disadvantaged and disabled persons in towns, sports and leisure in urban areas, culture and health in towns, citizen participation, urban management and urban planning, economic development of cities are all regulated there with due regard to the principles of sustainability. Particularly the role of local authorities in ensuring sustainable development is carefully emphasized in the following terms: a) Local authorities should adopt policies to prevent pollution. b) Local authorities have a responsibility to protect nature and green spaces c) City centres must be safeguarded as important symbols of the European cultural and historic heritage. d) The provision and management of open space in the city are integral parts of urban development. e) It is essential that the volume of travel, particularly by private car, be reduced. And the street must be recovered as a social arena. f) Multiculturalism and non-discrimination are fundamental aspects of urban policies. g) Citizen participation in local political life must be safeguarded through the right to elect representatives, freely and democratically.

It is in order now to address the questions how all these requirements can be met, what international and regional agreements and financial opportunities exist to make these principles applicable in the Mediterranean Region. International Environmental Law, Environmental Politics, Urban Environmental Management, Local Government are the major disciplines that constitute the general framework in which sustainable urban development questions in the Mediterranean can be analysed and resolved.

The Case for Mediterranean Countries

A Mediterranean tradition, a fragmented area with major urban centres dispersed, a very fragile environment, a sharp division between the coastal and inland areas and a growing population characterize the whole Mediterranean region. The entire region is fragmented by mountains and sea and both the level and pattern of development vary significantly between different parts of the region. Arable land capable of cultivation is particularly limited and scattered. Highly dynamic and prosperous areas, areas experiencing rapid de-industrialization, slowly industrializing and rural areas and finally the inland form its prevailing economic fabric. Differences between sub-regions are accompanied by broader disparities between coastal areas, which are heavily populated and attract most of the industry and services, and inland areas where population is sparse and ageing and agriculture is dominant.[14] Generally, an increasing proportion of people live in towns and cities, many large cities appear to have grown relative to smaller towns and cities both in terms of population and employment, and there is a marked tendency for population to increase in areas where large cities are located, but at the same time for both to become more dispersed across the region as people move out of city centres to the suburbs, or to towns close by or to coastal areas. The total population increased from 285 millions in 1970 to 427 millions in 2000, and it is expected to be around 523 millions by 2020. The degree of urbanization is to be risen from 64 percent in 2000 to 72

---

14   European Commission. *Europe 2000+: Cooperation for European Territorial Development*, EC Regional Policies, Brussels, 1994, p.197.

percent in 2025, bringing an additional 100 million people into the urban centres.[15]

The Mediterranean region is dominated by a few isolated, large urban conurbations, which have failed to stimulate development in neighbouring areas. Although there are a great many small and medium-sized towns, they are in general poorly equipped with few facilities. As revealed by the report of the national questionnaire prepared by PAP/RAC in January 2001, 71 percent of the big cities and 57 percent of the medium-sized cities in the South had complaints from environmental pollution. These percentages were 50 percent and 30 percent respectively in Northern countries of the Mediterranean region.

Inadequate public transportation (70 percent of the big cities in the North, 57 percent of the big cities of the South) and illegal spontaneous building (57 percent in the Southern big cities) and the lack of infrastructure (43 percent in all cities in the South) were the main urban problems mentioned most frequently. The responses of the city authorities to the survey carried out for the MCSD indicated a considerable dissatisfaction with the quality of life in general and with its major components that are at the same time generally agreed upon indicators of sustainable development.[16]

Pollution of the sea is a real problem throughout the area, 70 percent of municipal wastewater and a large amount of

15 *Cities and sustainable development in the Mediterranean.* Working paper prepared by the Blue Plan for the Mediterranean Commission on Sustainable Development, July 2000; UNEP. *The Mediterranean Action Plan (MAP).* Athens, 2000.

16 MCSD, *Report on the National Questionnaire,* prepared by PAP/RAC, Sophia Antipolis, January 2001 and *Report on the Questionnaire for City Authorities,* by PAP/RAC, Sophia Antipolis, January 2001.

industrial waste water being discharged without any treatment. The prospective developments in the region touched
upon above tend to exacerbate several planning and environmental problems that might threat the conditions of sustainability especially in the southern and eastern parts of
the region. The first is the growth of metropolises, such as
Cairo, İstanbul, Casablanca, Tunis, Alexandria and İzmir,
that is leading to problems of urban planning, water supply, drainage, waste disposal and urban transport.[17] Secondly, so far as the transport across the Mediterranean is
concerned, air and sea services are infrequent and in need
of modernisation, while port and airport facilities need to
be improved and expanded. Thirdly, Mediterranean countries are not only producers of energy, but also large consumers. As a result, most of the oil producing Mediterranean countries, with the exception of Libya, could see both
their proven and potential reserves exhausted sometime between 2000 and 2025, according to the estimates of the Blue
Plan. The environment represents the fourth major concern,
particularly as regards pollution of the Mediterranean. The
amount of wastewater discharged into the sea is increasing
significantly not only from agriculture and tourism but also
from cities and industry. Finally, the availability of water re-

17 Population in Istanbul conurbation is increasing by between 300 thousand
    and 500 thousand every year and in all the countries, population is highly
    concentrated in a few big cities. In 1990, 23 percent of the urban population
    in Algeria lived in cities over 1 million, 35 percent in Turkey (and 24 per-
    cent in Istanbul alone), 36 percent in Morocco (26 percent in Casablanca),
    36 percent in Jordan (all in Amman), 37 percent in Tunisia, 45 percent in
    Israel, 52 percent in Egypt (39 percent in Cairo) and 66 percent in Syria (33
    percent in Damascus). The density of population in such places is often
    extremely high, as in Cairo, where there were nearly 30 000 inhabitants per
    square kilometre, as against 20 000 in Paris and 17 500 in Barcelona.

serves raises questions about large hydraulic projects, irrigation and the desalination of sea water.[18]

Environmental Cooperation Among the Mediterranean Countries

The Mediterranean countries have already taken action through a policy of cooperation: 17 Mediterranean countries signed in 1976 the Barcelona Convention for the implementation of a Mediterranean Action Plan (MAP), under the auspices of the United Nations Environment Programme. In addition, and since 1990, the World Bank and the European Investment Bank have combined their efforts in the Mediterranean under the METAP (Mediterranean Environmental Technical Assistance Programme).

Cooperation between the countries in the region had been emphasized by the Blue Plan[19] as a means of managing the coast (protected areas and water treatment plants), urban areas (water disposal, reducing air pollution and traffic), water reserves and the sea (combating pollution from shipping, managing fish stocks); of preserving and extending forests and preventing forest fires; and of minimizing the risks of erosion, earthquakes, accidents at sea and toxic waste. Another important resource to be protected is certainly the heritage of cultural treasures.

As a UNEP supported initiative, the Mediterranean Action Plan is an action-oriented cooperative effort involving

18 European Commission, *Europe 2000+: Cooperation for European Territorial Development*, EC Regional Policies, Brussels, 1994, p.244.

19 *Mavi Plan: Akdeniz Havzasinin Gelecegi (The Blue Plan. Futures for the Mediterranean Basin)*, edited by Michel Grenon and Michel Batisse. Ankara, Turkish Ministry of Environment, 1993.

today 20 countries bordering the Mediterranean Sea as well as the European Union. Within the framework of this cooperative endeavour, the Mediterranean countries are determined to meet the challenges of environmental degradation in the sea, coastal areas and inland and to link sustainable resource management with development, in order to protect the Mediterranean region. As parts of their responsibilities with respect to the protection of the environment deriving from international instruments, Mediterranean countries have to pay particular attention to the protection of the sea and the coastal areas.[20] Main international agreements are: the Ramsar Convention (Ramsar, 1971), the UN Human Environment Declaration (Stockholm, 1972), the Convention for the Protection of the World Cultural and Natural Heritage (Paris, 1972); the IMO International Convention for the Prevention of Pollution from Ships, as modified by the Protocol of 1978 (MARPOL 1973/1978), the UN Declaration on Environment and Development and Agenda 21 (Rio, 1992), the Convention on Biological Diversity (Rio, 1992) and the Jakarta Mandate (1995) adopted by the Second Conference of the parties to the Convention on Biological Diversity.

The 1976 Barcelona Convention for the Protection of the Marine Environment and the Coastal regions in the Mediterranean (as amended in 1995) constitutes a whole with its subsequent six protocols:

20   Nesrin Algan, "Common International Commitments of Turkey and Greece on the Protection of the Aegean Sea with Special Reference to the Mediterranean Action Plan", *The Agean Sea 2000*, edited by Bayram Öztürk, Proceedings of the International Symposium on the Aegean Sea, 5-7 May 2000, Bodrum, pp.237-240.

Dumping Protocol: Protocol for the Prevention and Elimination of Pollution in the Mediterranean Sea by Dumping from Ships and Aircraft or Incineration at Sea, (1976),

Emergency Protocol: Protocol Concerning Cooperation in Combating Pollution of the Mediterranean Sea by Oil and other Harmful Substances in Cases of Emergency, (1976),

LBS Protocol: Protocol for the Protection of the Mediterranean Sea against Pollution from Land-Based Sources and Activities (1980),

SPA Protocol: Protocol Concerning Specially Protected Areas and Biological Diversity in the Mediterranean (1995),

Offshore Protocol: Protocol for the Protection of the Mediterranean Sea against Pollution resulting from Exploration and Exploitation of the Continental Shelf and the Seabed and its Subsoil (1994),

Hazardous Wastes Protocol: Protocol on the Prevention of Pollution of the Mediterranean Sea by Transboundary Movements of Hazardous Wastes and their Disposal (1996).

All these Protocols, together with *the Barcelona Convention* itself, constitute the so-called Barcelona System which aims at curbing the pollution, protecting the natural and cultural heritage, ensuring the sustainable management of coastal zones and integrating the environment and development. Rational land use policies to be implemented within a well-defined urban environmental management system are also an integral part of the general operational framework.[21]

The Barcelona Convention and the MAP Protocols take account of recent developments in International Environmental Law, in the light of which, the Mediterranean

---

21   UNEP, *The Mediterranean Action Plan (MAP)*, Athens, 2000, p.6.

states are expected to comply with main principles such as *the Polluter-Pays principle, the Precautionary principle, that of Public participation and access to information, Environmental impact assessment, sustainable development, integration, cooperation, common but differentiated responsibility.*

Once all the legal instruments are signed and ratified by the member states, then their task is to take appropriate steps to implement all necessary measures to comply with the Barcelona system. This is certainly a matter of more funding and enforcement than mere concern.

All Mediterranean countries cooperating within this system are the Contracting Parties to the Barcelona Convention. The Mediterranean Trust Fund to which all MAP Contracting Parties contribute, together with voluntary contributions, the European Union, UN agencies and the Global Environment Facility are its primary sources of finance. A number of Mediterranean NGOs and some international assistance programmes such as METAP (Mediterranean Environmental Technical Assistance Programme) support MAP's activities.

The Mediterranean Commission on Sustainable Development, established in 1996, is in charge of serving as an advisory body to MAP on such issues as sustainable management of coastal zones, water demand management, sustainable development indicators, eco-tourism, information, awareness and public participation, free trade and environment, industry and sustainable development, and urban management.[22]

MAP is regarded as a working model for regional environmental cooperation. Its country-driven approach and

---

22   Nesrin Algan, "Common International Commitments...", *op.cit.*, p. 244.

the sense of ownership of the programme among Mediterranean States at different stages of development are the basic factors in its success.

It has been pointed out that the success of international
cooperation within the Med Plan system is limited. Because
the environmental impacts of "improvements" resulting from
all of this international cooperation remain small, few in
number, and controversial. It is obvious that states, international organizations, NGO's and expert communities can respond to environmental challenges at the international level.
In some member states like France, Greece, Italy and Spain,
environmental policy development was guided and pushed
by EC/EU environmental policy, rather than the MAP regime. Some countries in the region lack sufficient state environmental policy capacity to comply or implement MAP
commitments and only pilot programmes and projects with
international funds appear to be influenced significantly by
internationally agreed upon environmental standards. Even
if financial assistance of the international funding institutions were adequately provided, the amount of such assistance relative to domestic and foreign investment is quite
small. Without functioning state organizations, there exists
no location for embedding of transnational principles and
norms for environmental policy.[23]

It is therefore clear that state capacity and the availability
of financial and administrative resources remain centrally

23   Stacy D. VanDeveer, "Capacity Building Efforts and International Environ-
     mental Cooperation in the Baltic and Mediterranean Regions", in Stacy D.
     VanDeveer and Geoffrey D. Dabelko (eds.), *Protecting Regional Seas: Devel-
     oping Capacity and Fostering Environmental Cooperation in Europe* (Con-
     ference Proceedings: "Saving the Seas: Developing Capacity and Fostering
     Environmental Cooperation in Europe), 14 May 1999, The Woodrow Wil-
     son International Centre for Scholars, pp.24-29.

important for national level adoption of regime principles and policy norms and the implementation of international commitments. Particularly in the Southern Mediterranean region, organizational capacity of the state is a primary factor limiting the influence of transnational normative force. It seems that a lack of a centralized regime and limited state administrative capacity have limited MAP's abilities to push state compliance with the international commitments and the EU actors and standards will have a chance to play an increasingly role in this respect.[24]

Mediterranean Cooperation for Sustainable Urban Development

As touched upon above, Mediterranean countries represented nearly half a billion-resident population in the year 2000 and the urban population is estimated to rise by around 38 percent in the coming two decades. Especially along the urbanized coastal line, the quality of urban environment is deteriorating rapidly. Not only the overcrowding and economically declining urban centres, but also urban air and noise pollution caused by excessive car use badly affect the quality of urban life. The number of cars in the region contributing to the extreme traffic congestion is expected to increase three times over the next three decades. Inland populations gravitating towards the coastal urban areas aggravate further the problems of urban sprawl including unsatisfactory infrastructure conditions and uncontrolled levels of energy and water consumption.

Within the framework of the Mediterranean Action Plan, the Ninth Meeting of the Contracting Parties (Barcelona,

---

24   Stacy D. VanDeveer, "Capacity Building.", *op.cit*, pp. 30-32.

1995) approved certain priority fields of activities for the environment and development in the Mediterranean Basin to cover the period 1996-2005 that might have a close bearing on sustainable development in the region. Among the priority fields of activities appear such sectors as integrated management of natural resources, integrated management of coastal areas, waste management, agriculture, industry and energy, transport, tourism, conservation of nature, landscape and sites that might influence sustainable urban development in the region directly or indirectly.

Particularly the section on Urban Development and the Environment contains the main principle of such a development approach. It aims a) to encourage town decision-makers to apply sustainable development policies in compliance with Agenda 21 and keeping in mind the United Nations Conference Habitat II. b) to promote active urban policies for energy control, non-polluting transport, waste management, sustainable use of water, and the creation of urban amenities, paying greater attention to underprivileged districts. And c) to develop and implement programmes for the rehabilitation of zones affected by hostilities.[25]

Although all of these tasks require the involvement of local, regional, national, international actors as well as the active commitment and support of NGO's and labour and business organizations, local authorities as the level of government closest to the people, have a unique responsibility in this field if one keeps in mind the principle "Think globally, act locally."

---

25   UNEP, *Mediterranean Action Plan and Convention for the Protection of the Marine Environment and the Coastal Region of the Mediterranean and its Protocols,* (Informal document, revised), Athens, 1997, p.37.

The Role of Cities in Sustainable Development
Local Agenda 21 Initiatives

The Agenda 21, Action Programme agreed to by 179 states at the Earth Summit in Rio in 1992 reflects a global consensus towards integrated policy-making concerning environment and development. In Chapter 28 of Agenda 21, local authorities in each country are called upon to undertake consultative processes with their populations in order to achieve a consensus on a Local Agenda 21 for and with their communities. Key partners in Local Agenda 21 processes include different layers of government, as well as civil society organizations and the private sector, with local authority in the driving seat. Indeed, local authorities are a strategic entry point for the initiatives aimed at resolving conflicts between urban development and the natural environment. Therefore, the participation of local authorities is a primary determining factor in fulfilling the activities in Agenda 21 at local level. It is remarkable to note that since 1992, in about 2000 local authorities in more than 70 countries, Local Agenda 21 campaigns have been started.[26]

Habitat's Experience in Urban
Environmental Management

The Istanbul Declaration (1996) adopted the strategy and principles of partnership and participation as the most democratic and effective approach for the realization of the commitments made during the Habitat II Conference. The Heads

26 Raf Tuts and Eleanor Cody, "HABITAT's Experience in Local Agenda 21 Worldwide over the Last Ten Years: Approaches and Lessons Learned", *Industry and Environment (Urban Environmental Management)*, Vol.23, No: 1-2, (January-June 2000), p.12.

of State or Government have recognized local authorities as their closest partners and essential in the implementation of the Habitat Agenda. They have decided to promote decentralization through democratic local authorities and to work to strengthen their financial and institutional capacities in accordance with the conditions of countries, while ensuring their *transparency, accountability and responsiveness* to the needs of people.[27]

The paragraph 180 of the Habitat Agenda deals with decentralization and strengthening of local authorities and their associations as a part of the Section devoted to capacity building and institutional development.

To increase local autonomy and participation in decision-making, implementation, and resource mobilization and use, to develop education in citizenship,

To emphasize the role of individuals as actors in their communities,

To support local authorities to acquire revenue-generating mechanisms,

To facilitate the exchange of technology, experience and management expertise vertically and horizontally between government and local authorities in the delivery of public services, expenditure control, resource mobilization,

To enhance the performance of local authorities,

To encourage institutionalisation of broad-based participation, including consultative mechanisms, in decision-making and management processes at the local level,

---

27   UNCHS, *The Istanbul Declaration and the Habitat Agenda,* UN Conference on Human Settlements (HABITAT II), Istanbul, Turkey, 3-14 June 1996, pp.5-6.

To establish public-private citizen's partnerships, within the framework of governance, for urban innovation, and,

To enable local authorities and their associations/networks to take initiatives in national and international cooperation and, in particular to share good practices and innovative approaches to sustainable human settlements management, are among the major recommendations made in the Habitat Agenda to enable local authorities to play an increasing role in sustainable urban development. Their role is also underlined in the chapter devoted to the implementation and follow-up of the Habitat Agenda the UN Supported Urban Environment Activities. The principal Habitat programmes promoting Local Agenda 21 initiatives are *Sustainable Cities Programme* and the *Localizing Agenda 21 Programme*.

The Sustainable Cities Programme (SCP)

The Sustainable Cities Programme (SCP) is a joint UNCHS/UNEP programme for the development of a sustainable urban environment, founded in 1990 on broad-based and meaningful public participation on environment-development issues. Its demonstration operations include two Mediterranean countries, namely Egypt and Tunisia. The programme is active in more than 40 cities. It aims to build capacities in urban environmental planning and management at the local, regional and national levels, providing a forum in which every voice can be heard and through which diverse local resources can be mobilized. City demonstrations are used to apply the concept and approach of the programme and these are over time institutionalised at the municipal level. Demonstrations are then replicated nationally and regionally. At the global level, the programme facilitates the exchange of experience, creating environmental planning and know-how. It captures lessons of experience and disseminates information. It also helps to mobilize technical and financial resources.

The EU has also launched in 1993 a Sustainable Cities Project whose main aims were to promote new ideas on sustainability, foster a wide exchange of experiences, disseminate good practices on sustainability at the urban level and to formulate recommendations for the EU institutions, national, regional and local authorities to assist the implementation of the EU's environmental action programmes.

Localizing Agenda 21's

Habitat's Localizing Agenda 21 offers a multi-year support system for selected medium-sized cities in Kenya, Morocco and Vietnam to develop their Local Agenda 21's. These cities are typically provincial headquarters with between 50 000 and 500.000 inhabitants. Localizing Agenda 21 Programme supports the development and implementation of broad-based environmental action plans that focus on context-specific aspects of municipal planning and management. The programme enhances the capability of local authorities to integrate these action plans into a strategic structure plan and fulfils the local authority's pivotal role between all public and private local development actors.

The programme works together with partners at the local level towards a long-term shared vision on the desirable development and structure of the city. Throughout the process, actors at every level are involved in the planning and decision-making process. Disputes are resolved between different levels of civic society. Multi-disciplinary Local Teams based at the municipal council level serve as the focal point for information exchange, studies and projects concerned with local sustainable development. An increasing number of local, national and international actors are reorienting and integrating their activities into these Local Agenda 21 processes.[28]

Lessons learned from this experience suggest that information sharing is a prerequisite for participatory decision-making, city consultations contribute to city-wide ownership and lead to firm commitments, the demonstration projects have a significant strategic value in the sense that they give visible evidence of "something happening", they can test and refine methodologies of participatory, bottom-up approach and they can rise the morale of those involved in the projects. Another important lesson to be learned in this respect is that the priority projects must be adopted by the relevant local government authorities, which should be encouraged to participate in their financing as a precondition for seeking external resources. It has been noted that vision building, implementing concrete actions and promoting communication between stakeholders is no less important and there should be a balance between these three components. In other words, vision without action does not produce immediate tangible results and action without vision does not address strategic long-term conditions, which ensure that essential resources for a qualitative urban life are available for future generations.[29]

---

28   Raf Tuts and Eleanor Cody, "Habitat's Experience…", *op.cit., pp. 12-13*.
29   Raf Tuts and Eleanor Cody, *Ibid*, p.14-15.

A final observation on localizing experiences of the Agenda 21 is that those projects concentrating on building capacity in medium-sized cities are more likely to achieve sustainable impact than in larger cities. As urban environment problems in these cities are often in their early stages, much can still be accomplished in terms of prevention through choosing pathways of sustainable development. In medium-sized cities there are fewer external factors interfering with urban development as compared to larger cities. Therefore, it is easier to isolate causes and effects related to improved environmental planning and management and the quality of the living environment.

The Urban Management Programme (UMP)

Another urban environment programme governed and supported by the UN is the Urban Management Programme (UMP), which is funded jointly by the United Nations Development Programme (UNDP) and a number of bilateral agencies. It is executed by the UNCHS (habitat) with the World Bank as an associate agency. The programme focuses on the following areas: urban land management, the provision and maintenance of urban infrastructure, municipal finance, the alleviation of urban poverty and the protection of the urban environment. Since 1990, the UMP helped cities define broad environmental strategies and build the capacity to manage urban problems.

Partnerships for Istanbul+5

As a result of continuous efforts towards partnership, the United Nations, local authorities, the World Bank and some non-governmental organization achieved significant progress particularly since the Habitat II Conference. One of these is the role played by the World Federation of United Cities (formerly UTO, namely the United Towns Organization) in *sustainable urban development*. All the above-mentioned organizations plus IULA (International Union of Local Authorities) and the WACLAC (World Association of Cities and Local Authorities Coordination) are presently cooperating to play an active role in the preparatory stages of İstanbul+5 meeting that will convene in June 2001. With a view to promote the principle of local autonomy and to improve and perpetuate sustainable development, UTO which represent 1 500 local authorities and IULA are trying to create a unified world organization of local authorities. UTO's proposal to work on the financing of urban development in this framework seems quite realistic and relevant to sustainable development. It also serves as the secretariat of a new initiative that is called *The Mediterranean Platform of Associations of Local Authorities and national Committees* that will be in charge of carrying out reflection on local development and the central role of elected representatives, both at political and technical level.

The Chances of Medium-Sized Cities

It is worthwhile to search for the possibilities to promote medium-sized cities as sustainable settlements as against giant metropolises. The fact is that despite the many local, regional, national, European and international environmental charters, Action Programmes, Declarations, Protocols, Plans and Policies, the environmental conditions and urban sustainability are still deteriorating in the majority of small and medium-sized cities in the Mediterranean. Is it because economic, financial, political and managerial capabilities of these cities are unsatisfactory or mainly because the limitations set by external factors that medium-size cities are losing their sustainable characteristics? Or both of the above-mentioned factors contribute to their ineffectiveness in sustainable development?

Four major factors can be held responsible for the present situation[30]: First of all, the urban sustainability of the medium-sized cities depends to a large extent on the sustainability policies and the achievements of the large cities. Their financial, industrial, political and social influences are more powerful than the medium-sized cities. For example, the energy choice of a country, favouring nuclear power plants of solar energy, is very often determined by the assessment of the estimated needs of large city populations. Once the choice is made, it is rather difficult for medium-sized cities to take steps in different directions. They have the same experience with super, mega and hypermarkets that are the choices of the big cities. This does not mean that medium-sized towns have no options at all in the way towards sustainable development. They may enter into many forms of cooperation and coalition among themselves in order to create the critical size in terms of local initiative capability, market dimensions, etc.

30 Riccardo Petrella, "Is It Possible to Promote "Intermediary" Cities' Sustainability within the Present Context of Triumphant Global Market Competitive Capitalism?", in *Intermediate Cities in Search of Sustainability*, The Research and the Attica Workshop, Lavrion, 4-6 October 1995 European Foundation for the Improvement of Living and Working Conditions, Luxembourg, 1996, pp.8-13.

A second point is that there can be no urban sustainability in the absence of social sustainability. Social sustainability may be understood as the development of a society that ensures and reconciles social justice, economic efficiency, democratic participation, cultural diversity and environmental governance. Sustainability is a holistic concept, like total quality, and its success depend upon people's behaviour, value systems, transparency and accountability in both public and private decision-making.

A third factor affecting the chances of medium-sized cities to sustain has something to do with some principles and consequences of globalisation. In other words, sustainable urban development depends on the normal functioning of the political economy in the public interest. Today, we witness a regression phenomenon in this respect. The public sphere is shrinking and the space reserved for the private interest and the market forces is expanding. Competitiveness, technological innovation, liberalization, deregulation and privatisation have become the new commandments of our times and the sustainability of the medium-sized cities has no chance to get the support of European and other international finance institutions in case they tend to resist them. As a result, they chances may be bound to be reduced considerably.

A final bottleneck is that urban sustainability cannot be left to market forces alone, because the market pretends to govern within a short- term perspective whereas sustainability is a matter of long-term concern. In this framework, only large cities have significant political power to play with and to pursue their own global metropolitan strategies, entering into alliances with global firms and competing with each other to be the most effective location for global firms. As a result, the free application of market principles and mechanisms make the medium-sized cities quasi-impotent to govern the ongoing process in the direction towards sustainability.

Even as they are surrounded by these constraints, medium-sized cities can give priority to structural forms of cooperation with other cities within the country and across countries. They may increase their capacity of autonomous vision and goals for the future by concentrating on research and development for technological innovation that are relevant for sustainable urbanization.These may include new telecommunications, water, energy and health infrastructures, land use, education and social services, leisure, sport and entertainment activities. Then it may be easier to ensure the minimum level of financial resources necessary and small and medium-size enterprises will have a chance to enhance their entrepreneurial capabilities[31]. This requires first of all the adoption of the principle by the states of giving priority to intermediate cities in their overall policies. That is dictated by the social justice as well. Because there is nothing more unequal than the equal treatment of unequal.[32]

Enabling Autonomous Local Authorities in Europe

Although most of the urban development strategies are designed by central governments, local authorities will have an increasing role in ensuring sustainable development depending upon the degree of devolution enjoyed in each

31   Riccardo Petrella, *op.cit.*, p. 13.
32   Voula Mega, "Background Paper", *Intermediate Cities in Search of Sustainability, op.cit.*, pp. 19-57.

country. As noted by the Brundtland Report, the institutional and legal structures of local governments in most developing nations, including the great majority of Mediterranean countries, are inadequate. The lack of political access to an adequate financial base and a growing centralization make local governments weak institutions that do not gain the expertise, authority and credibility needed to deal with local problems[33]. In order to be able to address the problems of urban development, city governments need enhanced political, institutional and financial capacity, notably access to more of the wealth generated in the city.

The European Charter of Local Self-Government

The Council of Europe is making a serious effort during the last half century to strengthen autonomous and powerful local authorities as one of the most solid foundation stones of the future united and integrated Europe. Through its Congress of Local and Regional Authorities, it was successful to promote local autonomy, which is a common and democratic value all over Europe. The Congress is also concerned with all questions of policy, which affect local and regional authorities, the most important ones being restructuring local and regional self-government, rural and urban development, and protection of the environment, education, culture, social services and the public health.

The European Charter of Local Self-Government that was adopted by the Committee of Ministers of the Council of Europe in June 1985 is now signed by 38 members and ratified by 34 states (Belgium, France and Switzerland are

33   The World Commission on Environment and Development, *Our Common Future*, Oxford University Press, Oxford, 1987, pp.247-248.

some of the non-ratifying states) out of the total 43 member states. It sets out the fundamental principles of local autonomy. The basic philosophy of the Charter rests on the belief that the degree of local autonomy enjoyed by local authorities may be regarded as a yardstick for a genuine democracy. It aims to guarantee the political, administrative and financial independence of local authorities and it tends to commit the states that ratified the Charter to comply with its principles.

Local self-government, according to the Charter, denotes the right and the ability of local authorities to regulate and manage a substantial share of public affairs under their own responsibility and in the interests of the local population. They have to exercise this right through the decision-making bodies freely elected. In addition to the existence of elected local councils, recourse to direct citizen participation, such as having assemblies of citizen, local referenda, etc., has to be open to citizen.

Although not literally mentioned in the text of the Charter, the principle of *subsidiarity* is defined in the following terms: Local authorities shall have full discretion to exercise their initiative with regard to any matter which is not excluded from their competence nor assigned to any other authority. And, *public responsibilities shall be exercised by those authorities, which are closest to the citizen. Allocation of responsibility to another authority will be allowed only depending upon the extent and nature of the task and the requirements of efficiency and economy.* The same principle is enshrined in the Article 3/B of the Maastricht Treaty in the following terms: *"In areas which do not fall within its exclusive competence, the Community shall take action in accordance with the principle of subsidiarity, only if and in so far as the objectives of the proposed action can not be sufficiently achieved by the member states and can therefore by reason of the scale or effects of those actions be better achieved by the Community".*

Consultation is another element of local autonomy which requires that local authorities be consulted in due time and in an appropriate way, in the planning and decision-making processes for all matters which concern them directly.

The central control and supervision (tutelage) over local authorities is limited to the control of compliance with the law and with constitutional principles (le contrôle de légalité). A state supervision with regard to expediency (le contrôle d'opportunité) is not allowed in principle. In order to be regarded as genuinely autonomous public entities, local authorities have to be provided with financial resources, which are commensurate with their responsibilities. The provisions of the Charter concerning their own financial resources, equalization procedures and the safeguards for their political independence all tend to strengthen local authorities in such a way to carry out their functions in an appropriate way.

A final component of the concept of local autonomy as defined in the Charter, which is considerably important from the standpoint of international cooperation for sustainable development, is the provision entitling local authorities to form consortia and to have the right to belong to a national or international association for the protection and promotion of their common interests.

In accordance with a recommendation made by Habitat II Conference in Istanbul in 1996, an Experts Group

Meeting was held in Nairobi in 1998, under the auspices
of the UNCHS, to prepare a Draft World Charter of Local
Self-Government in order to ensure worldwide application
of the principles of local autonomy. The text of the European
Charter of Local Self Government was taken as a starting
point and further refinements and additions were made. It
is expected that the final text be submitted to the UN General Assembly by June 2001. There is no doubt that the more
the number of states ratifying the Charter, the more will be
the chances of cities to live up with their responsibilities in
the field of sustainable development.

European Cities and Towns Towards Sustainability: The Aalborg Charter

The First European Conference on Sustainable Cities and
Towns took place in Aalborg, Denmark, in 1994. It gave
birth to one of the most important documents on sustainable development at local level. This is the Aalborg Charter. Nearly five hundred local authorities signed up to the
Charter coming from 35 European countries representing
more than 100 million European citizens. By signing up to
this Charter, a signatory local authority makes a strong commitment to sustainable development and Local Agenda 21.
The Aalborg Charter gives a clear message that economic
development, social welfare and protection of the environment cannot be achieved separately from each other.[34]

The Charter maintains that the city or town is both *the
largest unit* capable of initially addressing the many urban
architectural, social, economic, political, natural resource

---

34 Anthony Payne and Peter Löffler, "The Aalborg Charter: Cities and Towns
    on the Move Towards Sustainability", *Naturopa, No: 89, 1999, p.4.*

and environmental imbalances damaging our modern world and *the smallest scale* at which problems can be meaningfully resolved in an integrated, holistic and sustainable fashion. Therefore, it is suggested that the principles of sustainability be integrated into all policies (art.1.3). Thematic issues dealt with in the individual sections of the Aalborg Charter cover a wide range of spectrum from *urban economy* and *social equity* to *land use patterns, urban mobility, responsibility for the global climate, prevention of ecosystems toxification, local self-governance.* Signatory local authorities engage themselves to develop sustainable ways of living and to design and manage the cities towards sustainability. In order to rise to this challenge, the representatives of cities and towns claim the rights to self-governance, according to the principle of subsidiarity. Providing local authorities with a solid financial base is mentioned in the Charter as one of the preconditions of urban sustainability. Perceiving citizens as key actors and the involvement of the community in ensuring sustainability in addition to the political, technical, administrative and economic tools and instruments for urban management towards sustainability characterize the basic philosophy of the Aalborg Charter.

The European Sustainable Cities and Towns Campaign that was also initiated by the adoption of the Charter aims at the same time to engage all interested parties in the Local Agenda 21 processes. This campaign is built around a partnership of the following five networks and associations of local authorities: Eurocities, CEMR (The Council of European Municipalities and Regions), ICLEI (The International Council for Local Environmental Initiatives), UTO

(United Towns Organization) and WHO (World Health Organization).

The Aarhus Convention

An international convention adopted by the United Nations Economic Commission for Europe is highly relevant to international cooperation for urban sustainable development in the Mediterranean. The Convention that was adopted and opened to signatures in 1998 is called *the Convention on the Access to Information, Public Participation in Decision-Making and Access to Justice in Environmental Matters*. In the article one, its objective is stated as the following: (Art.1). "In order to contribute to the protection of the right of every person of present and future generations to live in an environment adequate to his or her health and well-being, each party shall guarantee the rights of access to information, public participation in decision-making, and access to justice in environmental matters in accordance with the provisions of this Convention".

Parties to the Aarhus Convention engage themselves in taking proper enforcement measures, in establishing and maintaining a clear, transparent and consistent framework to implement the provisions of the Convention. They have to ensure that officials and authorities provide guidance to the public in the implementation of its principles. An appropriate recognition of, and support to associations, organizations or groups promoting environmental protection have to be ensured by the signatory states. The Convention suggests (Ar.7) that the States parties to it make appropriate practical provisions for the public to participate during *the preparation of plans and programmes relating to the environment, within a transparent and fair framework.*

It is beyond any doubt that a proper implementation of the Aarhus Convention will provide a unique opportunity to all concerned with the environmental protection to contribute to the realization of sustainable urban development. Mediterranean countries have to be encouraged to ratify this Convention in order to make it sure that Mediterranean citizens enjoy the right to live in an environment adequate for his or her health and well-being appropriately.

Transboundary Cooperation Between Cities

Local authorities in Europe are encouraged by a Convention adopted by the Council of Europe to establish transboundary relationships in economic, social, cultural, environmental matters. This is *the European Outline Convention on Transfrontier Cooperation between Territorial Communities and Authorities* (Madrid, 21.5.1980).[35] The Outline Convention has been strengthened by two subsequent protocols in 1995 and 1998, respectively[36]. The matters to be dealt with within the framework of transboundary cooperation are urban and regional development, energy, nature and water conservation, protection of the atmosphere, mutual assistance in disaster relief and the like. There is room for European territorial communities or authorities to enhance their cooperation for sustainable development by ensuring flexibility in administrative procedures, to lift the legal objections before fruitful cooperation and to equip territorial communities or authorities with necessary finan-

35 Council of Europe, *European Treaty Series: 106*, Strasbourg, 1999.
36 Council of Europe, *European Treaty Series: 159 and 169*, Strasbourg, 1999.

cial and other means. Some of the Turkish local authorities in eastern and western regions of the country already attempted to develop closer ties with their counterparts in Georgia, Azerbaijan, Ukraine and Armenia in the East and North, and in Greece and Bulgaria in the West during the last several years. Symposia that were held in Trabzon, Turkey (1997), Sochi, Georgia (1996), Edirne (Turkey and Svelingrad, Bulgaria (1998) Temasvar, Romania (1999), Edirne, Turkey (2000) are remarkable examples of such attempts.

Similar experiences among the member states of the European Union are encouraged and supported during the last several decades. A great number of projects of cooperation such as *Interreg A, Phare, Tacis, Lace, Eures, Recite, Urban, Terra, Meda, Phare Democratie, Phare Partenariat, etc.* are co-financed by the European Union and other international institutions [37]. A number of funds and programmes are available for transfrontier, interregional and transnational cooperation within the EU as in the case of FEDER (Fonds Européen de Développement Régional), which is the most appropriate instrument for international cooperation. However, the actions supported by the European Union are limited by some factors such as the lack of funds for the least developed regions, lack of cooperation tradition, lack of administrative and legal framework and the exclusion of certain actors.[38]

---

37 Parlement Européen, Direction Générale des Etudes, Document de Travail, Série Politique Régionale, W-19, *La Coopération Transfrontalière et Interrégionale au Sein de l'Union Européenne*, Luxembourg, 1996.

38 *Ibid.*, p.67; see also: Charles Rico, *Les Régions Frontalières et l'Intégration Européenne, Livre Blanc de l'Assemblée des Régions d'Europe*, Centre d'Observation Européen des Régions (COEUR) et Diputacion General de Aragon, Zaragoza, 1992, pp-57-68.

Various other programmes have been implemented within the EU in order to support environmental policies and integrated approaches. Key elements of the main approach are the principles of *integration* and the concept of *shared responsibility*. Integration includes both *internal integration* between the various environmental issues and *external integration* of environmental objectives into other EU policies like industry, transport, energy, agriculture and tourism. The second requires sharing the responsibility for the environment between the EU and the member states, along with other relevant partners, including territorial authorities. Since more than 80 percent of the population of EU lives in cities and towns, urban areas are the places where the problems of the environment touch most the quality of everyday life of citizens. As a result, there is a strong urban dimension to many of the EU's environmental actions.[39]

Among the numerous EU initiatives, the LIFE Third Countries programme specifically encourages the implementation of environmental policies and activities in non-member countries.

Technical and Financial Assistance in the Mediterranean

Technical and financial assistance is the key factor of success for any programme designed for sustainable urban development. The Habitat II Agenda has reminded the target of 0.15 percent of the GNP of developed countries, suggested by the Paris Declaration of 1990, for assistance to the least developed countries as soon as possible and the need to

---

39   European Union, *Towards Sustainable Human Settlements*, UN HABITAT II Conference, 3-14 June 1996.

increase the share of funding for the programmes of sustainable human settlements to achieve the objectives and goals of the Habitat Agenda.[40] Heads of State and Government signing up the habitat II Agenda and Istanbul Declaration committed themselves to raise that amount to 0.7 percent of the GNP's of the developed countries.[41] Although there exists numerous programmes of technical and financial assistance that might be used for sustainable urban development in the region, their extent is far from being at a satisfactory level.

The Mediterranean Environmental Assistance Programme (METAP)

Mediterranean Environmental Technical Assistance Programme is devoted to promoting regional activities and primarily concerns the capacity building and the launching of new concepts and innovative approaches. METAP was created during the early 1990's, following a joint report (Environmental Programme for the Mediterranean) of the World Bank and the European Investment Bank (EIB), drawing the attention to ending urgently the pollution in the region and adopting a permanent strategy for sustainable solutions.[42] Born as a joint initiative of the two banks (WB and EIB), the METAP is also financed by the European Union, UNDP, and other bilateral donors as in the case of Canada, Japan, and Switzerland, that have been associated later. Although

---

40   UNCHS, *The Istanbul Declaration and the Habitat Agenda,* Nairobi, 1997, p.119.

41   *Ibid.,* p.31.

42   Banque Européenne d'Investissement, *Pour un Euro-Partenariat en Méditerranée: Le rôle de la Banque Européenne d'Investissement,* 1997, p.4.

it is not a European programme, the EU has contributed considerably to it.

METAP realized concrete programmes during the last ten years. During its Phase I (1990-1992) an inventory was made on the environmental situation in the Mediterranean. In the Phase II (1992-1995), it contributed to the creation of some ad hoc institutional structures and to the realization of feasibility studies for specific investment projects. Such studies have been realized, during the last years, in such countries as Algiers, Cyprus, Egypt, Israel, Jordan, Lebanon, Malta, Morocco, Syria, Tunisia and Turkey. METAP assisted financing 121 technical assistance projects during the same period. A number of investment projects, such as the one concerning Tripoli sewerage system, have also been realized with funds from the World Bank and the European Investment Bank. The third Phase (1996-2000) of METAP has concentrated on the priority themes in conformity with the strategic priorities of the region which are a) the capacity building and participation, b) stopping and preventing of the pollution in critical zones, and c) the integrated management of water and coastal resources.[43] METAP Phase IV (2000-2005) will follow almost the same lines followed so far.

The MedCities Network

The METAP established the *Med-Cities Network* in 1991 to support local environmental planning and capacity building in order to facilitate the sustainable development in urban areas. It offers the possibility to establish and to reinforce the cooperation between Mediterranean cities in the fields of environmental protection and resource management.

---

43   Banque Européenne d'Investissement, *Ibid.*

Med-Cities is a regional network of mayors and senior local officials representing 27 Mediterranean coastal cities. It
has two sources of funding: The European Commission and
METAP. Some of its projects are directly financed by bilateral cooperation (France, Spain), the World Bank (Sousse,
Tripoli, Tangiers, Oran) and the European Investment Bank
(Limassol).[44] For 1998-1999, the Medcities Network has received new financial support from the European Commission (Life Programme) to carry out new activities in its
member towns. It followed the support granted by the same
programme between 1995 and 1997 and which made it possible to carry out environmental audits, awareness-raising
and training activities and action to strengthen the institutional capacities of municipalities.

The European Investment Bank

Favouring the protection of the Mediterranean environment,
reinforcing the regional ties and developing the private sector as well as the promotion of the principles of integration
and cohesion of the EU are among the general objectives of
the European Investment Bank. For this purpose, its spending between 1992 and 1997 amounted to Euro 3.521.8 million. Financial support of the European Investment Bank
takes place actually within the framework of Euro-Mediterranean Partnership that was started in 1995 by the European Union and twelve Mediterranean partner countries
during the Barcelona Conference.

The protection of the environment and ensuring sustainable development is among the priority goals of the EIB for

44   Mohamed Boussraoui, "Medcities: A blueprint for progress", *Naturopa*, No:
      89, 1999, p.24.

a long time. It provides 3 percent interest reduction for the infrastructure investments aiming at environmental protection. Particularly because of this incentive that the demands for loans in the sector of water supply increased considerably. In other words, the annual volume of the loans of the Bank multiplied eight times as a result of this bonus as compared to the previous years. Between 1997 and 1999, the Bank supported 18 projects of environmental protection realized in 8 Mediterranean countries with a global amount of Euro 623 million.[45] No fixed amount of loan is provided for any country and within the context of Euro-Mediterranean partnership the so-called interest bonus is applicable to all environment projects without exception. Ensuring the economic viability of the investment projects is not regarded as a sufficient precondition for their acceptance unless an environmental impact assessment guarantees that they will not produce harmful consequences for the environment. In principle, the European Investment Bank does not cover more than 50 percent of a financing plan. Generally, the share is much smaller and varies between 30 and 40 percent. The Bank expects that the initiator of the project contribute a substantial amount of its cost and its own role remains just as the one of a catalyst. This is an essential rule in the EU's cooperation policies with third countries, which requires close involvement of the beneficiary populations. According to this rule of *decentralized cooperation,* the involvement of the civil society of the beneficiary countries is required in the definition of the priorities and implementation of the EU aid programmes so as

45   *Ibid.,* p.5.

to meet more adequately and effectively the needs of the beneficiary populations.

The Euro-Mediterranean Partnership

The Euro-Mediterranean Partnership was established at the level of foreign ministers of the European Union member states and 12 Mediterranean Partner countries in 1995 (Barcelona Conference). It aims to promote the long-term growth and stability in the concerned countries, and to ensure 1) a political and security partnership, 2) an economic and financial partnership, and 3) a partnership in social, cultural and human affairs, including the environment. It is expected that the creation of a free trade zone during the period 2000-2010 between the European Union and its Mediterranean partners would constitute a basis for a closer economic integration. It will provide Euro 6,425 million during 2000-2006 basically for the projects of infrastructure and large-scale industrial establishments.[46]

In order to meet the objectives, Euromed Conferences were held in the following cities: Malta (1997), Palermo (1999), Valencia (1999), Stuttgart (1999), Lisbon (2000) and Marseilles (2000). In the meantime association agreements have been adopted with PLO (1997), Tunisia (1998), Morocco (2000) and Israel (2000).[47]

The MEDA (Mediterranean Development Assistance) programme which encompasses the 27 Euromed partners,

---

46 Banque Européenne d'Investissement, *L'Action de la BEI en partenariat avec les pays méditerranéens (Algérie, Chypre, Egypte, Gaza/Cisjordanie, Israël, Jordanie, Liban, Malte, Syrie, Tunisie, Turquie,* Oct.2000, p.3.

47 European Commission, Euro-Mediterranean Partnership, *The Barcelona Process: Five Years On (1995-2000),* p.7.

provides a financial assistance through the intermediary of the European Union to promote the creation of lasting ties in all the fields of common interest such as politics, security, economic and financial issues, social, cultural and human questions. Some of the countries cooperating within this programme are at the same time candidates for full EU membership.

The concerned ministers commended the action by the European Investment Bank over the period 1995 to 1999 EUR 4.6 billion and its provision as very long-term funding to the Mediterranean countries. The same ministers attending the Fourth Euro-Mediterranean Conference in Marseilles Nov.2000) found satisfactory the indicative figure adopted by the Council of the European Union, for MEDA II, the allocation of EUR 5,350 billion for the period 2000 to 2006. They have noted that the EIB would establish the main strands of its action (*infrastructure, sustainable development, the private sector and reconstruction in the Eastern Mediterranean*) within the framework of indicative multiannual sectoral programming for the entire Mediterranean region. They accepted the EIB's offer (over and above its mandate from the EU (Euro 6.4 billion for the period 2000 to 2007) to contribute a further Euro 1 billion from its own resources over the same period. That additional amount is expected to contribute to the implementation of projects of regional interest and to projects of common interest between the European Union and the Mediterranean partner countries.

All Euromed priorities for regional economic cooperation, namely industry, water, information society, energy and transport, concern sustainable urban development directly or indirectly. The environment occupies a separate place among these priorities. It has to be underlined, in this connection, that one of the sectoral Euro-Mediterranean Ministerial Conferences had been held exclusively on *environment*, in Helsinki in 1997, in which the SMAP was established. The SMAP, namely, Short and Medium Term Environmental Action Programme, includes as main priority fields of action: *integrated water management, waste management, Hot Spots, integrated coastal zone management, combating desertification.* The first two are mainly urban-based issues while the remaining three may concern urban centres indirectly.

Since the beginning, the Barcelona process drew the attention to the need of cooperation for the environment. Assessing environmental problems in the Mediterranean region, defining the initiatives to be taken, establishing a short and medium-term priority environmental action programme for intervention coordinated by the European Commission, and strengthening coordination with the Mediterranean Action Plan, continuously appeared to be among the priorities and recommendations of the Barcelona process. In the same documents, municipalities and regional authorities have been constantly invited to be closely involved in the operation of the Euro-Mediterranean Partnership. This need was particularly emphasized in the ministerial conferences.

Regional cooperation of MEDA suffers from the difficulties encountered by the programmes called *decentralized cooperation*, which had been launched within the framework of the *Renovated Mediterranean Policy.* According to this policy, local authorities (*Med-urbs*), universities (*Med-campus*) and media professionals (*Med-media*), were encouraged and supported to cooperate among themselves.

These programmes have been stopped in 1996, following a report of the European Court of Accounts. Although it was expected that they start again within the framework of MEDA, none of them operates effectively at present.[48] The principal obstacles to the success of the programmes entitled *decentralized cooperation* concern the identification of the levels of cooperation, namely the role of local and regional authorities and monitoring and evaluation of the projects of decentralized cooperation that requires human and financial resources of which the Commission, in charge of MEDA, does not dispose.[49]

Accompanying Euro-Mediterranean Foreign Ministers' meetings, Euromed Civil Forums were held in Barcelona, Malta, Stuttgart and Marseilles by those involved in non-governmental cooperation in order to present their demands and to express their vision of the Partnership. These Civil Forums bring together NGO's (trade unions, business and other associations, chambers of commerce) and local authorities from EU Member States and Mediterranean Partners. During the Euromed Civil Forum 2000 (Marseilles, November 2000), it has been decided to create a permanent forum of Euro-Mediterranean local authorities that will meet every year, alternatively in a country of the European Union and a Mediterranean Partner country. It was emphasized in the same meeting that local authorities had a crucial role to play in sustainable urban development and their projects had to be eligible to bilateral and regional programmes and finally, within the framework of decentralized

48   Institut de la Méditerranée, "MEDA. Etat des lieux du processus de Barcelone, 1995-2000", Marseille, sept.2000.
49   Institut de la Méditerranée, "MEDA: Etat des lieux de processus de Barcelone, 1995-2000", Marseille, sept. 2000, p.44.

cooperation, relationships between different levels of local authorities, those between local authorities and states and those between local authorities and civil society had to be strengthened. The utility and the significance of these co-operative experiments for sustainable urban development are beyond any doubt.

Finally, the Euromed Heritage II is another EU programme of which activities are relevant to sustainable development. Both its general and specific objectives are concerned with Mediterranean countries. Generally, the cultural heritage is both an essential factor in the identity of each country and a means of facilitating comprehension between the various countries and cultures of the region. The cultural heritage of the Mediterranean reflects the powerful links that unite Europe and the Southern shores of the Mediterranean. The ultimate objective of the programme is to establish the idea of a common Euro-Mediterranean heritage that incorporates different customs and traditions. Specifically, it aims to increase the capacity of the Mediterranean countries to manage and develop their cultural heritage. The Euromed Heritage II offers financial resources, channels for disseminating knowledge, frameworks for exchanges of experiences, parameters for the identification of new components and dimensions of the cultural heritage and finally new perspectives for the development of the cultural heritage.

The World Bank

The World Bank remains as the largest donor institution in the urban assistance field and a leader in urban policy innovation within the donor community. Its annual lending for urban projects averaged US Dollars 1.5 billion in the late 1980's and it was expected to more than double in the early 1990's[50] Over 150 explicitly urban projects were to be funded during the 1990's, representing nearly 9 percent of its total lending. Since about 40 percent of the World Bank's loans may be of direct benefit to urban residents, the significance of its contribution to sustainable urban development in general becomes obvious.

In the 1950's and 1960's, before the formation of the Bank's Urban Department in 1969, loans were made mostly for infrastructure, which included some urban project. Starting from the beginnings of the 1970's, the World Bank's urban activities focused on individual projects for the most part concerned with the elimination of poverty. In the 1980's, the focus shifted to economic issues and citywide management issues, particularly the strengthening of the capacity to deliver urban public services. During the 1990's, the productivity of urban economics, employment issues, improved infrastructure and services, controlling the deterioration of the urban environment, achieving better understanding of urban problems occupied the agenda basically.[51] All developing countries, including those in the Southern and Eastern Mediterranean have at times benefited from the loans of the Bank, depending upon their degree of eligibility.

The World Bank has also cooperated with the UNDP on the Water and Sanitation Programme, which has become increasingly active in urban and peri-urban areas to meet the challenges of the International Drinking Water Supply and Sanitation Decade. Most of the Bank's loans in urban areas

---

50   Richard Gilbert, Don Stevenson, Herbert Girardet and Richard Stren, *Making Cities Work: The Role of Local Authorities in the Urban Environment*, Earthscan Pub. Ltd., London, 1996, p.75.

51   *Ibid.*, p. 75.

reflected an evolution from a sectoral approach to an emphasis on building capacity in local governments. A Vice-Presidency for Sustainable Development has been established as a result of the recognition of the growing importance of urban environmental issues, especially those related to air and water pollution, waste management and sanitation.

The most important point concerning the World Bank is to remember that its financial support is a reflection of a world view that the Bank is trying to make it prevail on a worldwide basis. This is an economic development model that is based on economic liberalism, globalisation, trade liberalization and privatisation. The city, according to this philosophy, has a unique role to play in enhancing these ideals.[52] New lending policy of the World Bank regarding urban sustainable development is primarily based on the idea that in order to attract the investments of the private sector to the city, it is necessary not only to improve urban infrastructure, but also to increase the management capacity of local authorities. This enabling policy requires certainly the improvement of technical qualifications of municipal officials and an effective coordination between local and national authorities.[53] The reason for pronouncing of the term *decentralization* in the works of the Bank so frequently is the likely contribution that cities could make to the enhancement of globalisation. This was also the reason why the Bank changed its strategy from physical planning and related subsidies towards an enforced engagement in urban management[54] that became the dominant theme in

---

52   Annik Osmont, *La Banque Mondiale et les Villes, Ed. Karthala,* Paris, 1995, p.19.

53   *Ibid.*, p. 145.

54   *Ibid.*, p. 147.

its operations. Therefore, attempt to assess the operations of the World Bank simply from a financial point of view would miss the essential point that consists of its ideological position.[55] However, liberal policies of the Bank stroke particularly the poor simply because of the diminution or disappearance of the subsidies as a result of privatisation.[56]

Concluding Observations and Suggestions

1. Urban settlements are clearly central to meeting the goals of sustainable development. Most of the principles of sustainable development as formulated in the relevant articles of Stockholm and Rio Declarations can be used for ensuring sustainable urban development. The majority of the population of Mediterranean countries will soon be living in cities and towns. City-based producers and consumers already account for most of the renewable and non-renewable resource consumption and waste generation. The expectation that in the near future while more than 60 percent of the population will be living in cities and a very large share residing in coastal areas, makes the whole Mediterranean region highly vulnerable to the effects of unsustainable developments. The multiplication and further growth of cities and uncontrolled spread of settlements and building activity increase the cost of sensitive ecosystems adversely and aggravate the situation further.

The principle of sustainable urban development means that in urban settlements, not only the way in which people live, but also the settlements themselves and the ecosystems

---

55   H. Bretaudeau, *La Banque mondiale, P.U.F.,* Paris, *1986, p.5.*
56   Annik Osmont, *op.cit.,* p.162.

that support them must be sustainable. In order to achieve sustainability in the Mediterranean region and to meet the needs of rapid urbanization and of increased building activities in coastal regions, *international cooperation in technical and financial fields is vitally important*. However, a brief review of the international funding arrangement for cooperation open to the Mediterranean peoples reveals that *the number of such programmes is too many. And they present a wide variety in their nature and landing conditions*, which tend to decrease their efficiency to a large extent. *It seems that a unique Mediterranean cooperation agency has to be established, integrating the financial and other functions of major international funding institutions interested in sustainable urban development in the region. Particular economic conditions of each country in the region have to be taken into account in appraising the proposed projects. Calling for an international conference to discuss various aspects of financial issues and the terms of funding operations would be useful.*

With respect to the institutional context for urban cooperation, the capacity and orientations of urban governments have to be changed. The major weaknesses of local governments consist of the lack of financial resources, inadequacy of powers and professional staff to mobilize necessary funding. Particularly, the degree to which national governments allow development cooperation agencies to work directly with their territorial authorities needs to be improved without jeopardizing the homogeneity of the operations. The capacity of local governments to invest in basic infrastructure without funding from higher levels of government is extremely limited. Despite this fact, they must look for ways to mobilize local funds first before applying for external assistance. In other words, the main target within the institutional context has to be decentralization, enabling local authorities as the basic units to deal with urban sustainability, to become more democratic, efficient, accountable, transparent and responsive. The provisions of statutes of some European institutions concerning the principle of subsidiarity, which calls for the devolution of policy-making powers to the lowest appropriate tier of government may form a useful framework in this respect.

Local governments are not only responsible for urban policies and environmental management, bur also they act as facilitators and enablers of action by all interests in society.[57] Therefore, local authorities must be encouraged to participate fully in the works of the Council of Europe (CLRAE) and the European Union (The Committee of the Regions) in order to be able to act as genuinely autonomous entities and to work more efficiently towards the goal of sustainable urban development. *The principles of the European Charter of Local Self-Government have to be put into practice by all Mediterranean States regardless of being a member of the Council of Europe or a non-member. The Framework Convention for Transboundary Cooperation provides broad opportunities for regional cooperation towards sustainable urban development. Therefore, States should remove all kinds of obstacles before the neighbouring territorial authorities to develop transboundary and transfrontier cooperation. An international symposium may be organized in cooperation with the Council of Europe's relevant departments (Congress of Local and Regional Authorities of Europe) and*

---

57   Jaime Ravinet, "Local Authorities: Crucial Partners in the Implementation of the Habitat Agenda", *Habitat Debate*, Vol.3, No:1, March 1997, p.19.

the European Union on the principles of the Charter concerning subsidiarity, local finance, central supervision and international cooperation.

In addition to local authorities, the NGO's have a solid place in urban environmental management and planning. They can bring valuable technical and financial assistance, mobilize local expertise and develop local legitimacy for urban development projects by supplying knowledge of local conditions, needs and priorities as in the case of the activities of Local Agenda 21's.[58] *The potential role and contributions of the NGO's in matters relevant to sustainable urban development may be evaluated in an international conference with the participation of the representatives of major Local Agenda 21's from the countries of the region.*

Certainly, there are reasons why should international donors invest in urban environment. First of all, population and poverty concentrate in urban regions. Secondly, improved urban environmental management can not only contribute much to reducing poverty, but also can limit the transfer of environmental costs to rural areas and to future generations. Finally, urban centres provide economies of scale and opportunities for cost recovery in environmental interventions and well-managed urban systems have the potential to contribute further to regional and national economic programmes.

From a macro-economic perspective and contrary to the prevailing tendency of the World Bank and other donor institution, *it may be more rational to blend market reforms with regulatory mechanisms in order to help developing*

---

58   OECD, *The Urban Environment and Development Cooperation: A Resource Book,* 2000, p. 70.

nations to achieve sustainable urban development. In this respect, the World Bank's persistent approach to *market supremacy* as expressed clearly in the title of its 1996 World Development Report, namely *From Plan to Market*, (as in the case of the 1999-2000 World Development Report, entitled *Entering the 21st Century*), does not seem compatible with the requirements of sustainable urban development as suggested in Rio, nor with the basic needs of developing countries. Regulatory controls need to encompass such questions as who get access to services and under what conditions, how to promote a shift towards full cost recovery without penalizing the poor excessively, and to introduce systems which link charges accurately to the levels of service or pollution, and finally to set appropriate minimum standards of service to protect the environment.

Privatisation provides certain benefits as improved investment and sensitivity to customer demands, plus a reduced draw on public spending. However, it is no panacea. If poorly regulated, it can have negative impacts, raising service costs beyond the reach of the poor, reducing cross-subsidies between rich and poor, and reducing the extent of service provision.[59] Therefore, although it seems that there is a need for regulation of deregulation, it is not an easy task to be realized by recipient countries. However, one should keep in mind that no economic project is likely to succeed unless minimum conditions imposed by funding institutions were met.[60] From this perspective, it would be advisable and more realistic for the states and territorial authorities in the

---

59 OECD, *The Urban Environment and Development Cooperation...op.cit.*, p.82).

60 Cynthia Hewitt de Alcantra, "Uses and Abuses of the Concept of Governance", *International Social Science Journal*, No: 155, March 1998, p. 106.

region to make an effort to respect the rules imposed by funding institutions in the short run.

How addressing sustainable urban development requires an integrated and multi-disciplinary approach, combining aspects of participatory land-use planning[61], pollution control, transport planning, environmental impact assessment, economic instruments, administrative reform and public education. Appropriate land-use planning can provide substantial environmental benefits ranging from better living environments to lower greenhouse gas emissions. In case land-use planning fails to achieve its objectives, it often pushes low-income households to the periphery and to land still poorly controlled by owners or regulators. This may result in untimely and unnecessary conversion of agricultural land into urban uses that can be detrimental for unsustainable development.

In addition to those mentioned in the Subsection of this paper dealing with Sustainable Urban Development (pp.4-8), some practical rules for the realization of sustainable urban development may be proposed for especially rapidly urbanizing countries of the region, related to the founding and extension of urban settlements.[62] First of all, *the founding of new settlements anywhere by private initiatives (partnerships or private individuals) should be banned unless existing urban settlements have become saturated. The consumption of natural capital that takes place when land profiteering motivates the creation of new urban settlements should be regarded*

61   Susan Owens, "Interpreting Sustainable Development: The Case of Land Use Planning", in Michael Jacobs (ed.), *Greening the Millennium: The New Politics of the Environment,* Blackwell, Oxford, 1997, pp. 87-97.

62   European Commission. *The Law of Sustainable Development: General Principles,* Michael Decleris, Brussels, 2000, pp.116-120.

as unnecessary, wasteful or even destructive. Secondly, in no case, creation of urban settlements within fragile ecosystems is permitted. And finally, the founding or extension of settlements should not be permitted haphazardly, nor should they be left to the initiative of land development enterprises.

These and similar conditions must be accepted by international financial institutions and be used as required rules for lending for urban development and sustainable urban management purposes. But, care must be taken to the fact that measures resulting in curbing urban development for any reason whatsoever may not be reconciled with the established practices and more recent liberal policies of the World Bank to utilize urban centres as focal points of free trade, globalisation, deregulation and privatisation.

The urban sustainability of medium-sized cities depends to a large extent on the sustainability policies and achievements of large cities, because their financial, political, social influence are more powerful than the medium-sized cities. There are several special factors that make the task of medium-sized cities more difficult. First, those that are not situated within easy reach of a large city need to be of a minimum size in order to be able to provide the range of services. Secondly, towns which are neither of the required size nor in a convenient location might be able to compensate for this by being part of a network of towns or by developing links with a large city, with which the communication links are relatively efficient. Finally, the towns below a critical size face serious problems, irrespective of their links with other cities and towns. They need to specialize in a particular activity and develop the infrastructure and services that go with it.

Generally, regional and international programmes addressing the development needs of medium-sized cities do not exist. There is a real possibility that a large number of medium-sized towns will suffer decline of population and employment in the future and this would produce serious adverse effect on environmental conditions.[63] There seems to be nothing to do else than trying to develop their necessary infrastructure and services and strengthening the local capacity for the planning and implementation of urban development strategies. Then, *it would be worthwhile to suggest that their problems and potentials be discussed and the ways to improve their situation be looked for in a region-wide international conference.*

The overall objective is to ensure that critical urban environmental problems are resolved as a part of a long-term commitment to see that urban development contributes to the achievement of the goals of sustainable development. This means that environmental aspects need to be considered in all urban development interventions. This could maximize the urban contribution to sustainable development provided that a culture of sustainability is also developed. The meaning of this suggestion is a clear shift in human consciousness to change human, corporate and institutional behaviour towards the practice of sustainability.

In order to carry out properly the principles of international agreements (treaties, conventions, protocols, etc.) and the guidelines (declarations) adopted in international conferences, the States must be invited to take formal and informal steps to implement their legal obligations. They have to develop, adapt and modify their relevant national

---

63   European Commission, *Europe 2000+, op.cit.,* pp. 109-110.

legislation, following the ratification of the above-mentioned legal instruments. There is also a need to give effect to national policies, programmes and strategies, in other words, regulatory measures. The States should designate competent national authorities or a focal point, where necessary, for international liaison purposes. Particularly the States which have not become yet parties to the European Charter of Local Self-Government and other international legal instruments concerning either local autonomy or sustainable development have to be urged to do so at their earliest convenience.

The European Union as a Contracting Party to the Barcelona Convention should set up a unit to deal with matters of urban sustainable development. And territorial authorities have to be supported in their activities targeted to encourage sustainable development. Bilateral and multilateral cooperation between the EU member states and non-member states also have to be supported with sufficient fund.

Bibliography

Algan, Nesrin, "Common International Commitments of Turkey and Greece on the Protection of the Aegean Sea with Special Reference to the Mediterranean Action Plan", in Bayram Öztürk (ed.), The Aegean Sea 2000: Proceedings of the International Symposium on the Aegean Sea. Bodrum, Turkey, 5-7 May 2000, pp. 237-248.

Banque Européenne d'Investissement, Pour un Euro-Partenariat en Méditerranée: Le rôle de la Banque Européenne d'Investissement, 1997.

Banque Européenne d'Investissement, L'Action de la BEI en Partenariat avec les pays méditerranéens, octobre 2000.

Barnier, V et C.Tucoulet, Villes et Environnement: de l'écologie urbaine à la ville durable, La Documentation Française, No: 829, octobre 1999.

Boussraoui, Mohamed, "Medcities: a blueprint for progress", Naturopa, No: 89, 1999, p.24.

Bretaudeau, H., La Banque Mondiale, P.U.F., Paris, 1986.

CEMAT, (European Conference of Ministers Responsible for Regional Planning), Guiding Principles for Sustainable Development of the European Continent. Hanover, September 7-8 March 2000.

Conneley, James and Graham Smith, Politics and the Environment, Routledge, London, 1999.

Council of Europe, European Treaty Series: No: 106, Strasbourg, 1999.

Council of Europe, European Treaty Series: No: 159 and 169, Strasbourg, 1999.

Council of Europe, Standing Conference of Local and Regional Authorities, The European Urban Charter, Resolution 234, 27th Session. Strasbourg, 17-19 March 1992, (30 March 1992).

European Commission, Europe 2000+: Cooperation for European Territorial Development, EC Regional Policies, Brussels, 1994.

European Commission, Euro-Mediterranean Partnership, The Barcelona Process: Five Years On: (1995-2000), 2000.

European Commission, The Law of Sustainable Development: General Principles, by Michael Decleris, Brussels, 2000.

European Foundation for the Improvement of Living and Working Conditions, Intermediate Cities in Search of Sustainability, The Research and the Attica Workshop, Lavrion, 4-6 October 1996.

European Union, Towards Sustainable Human Settlements, UN Habitat II Conference, 3-14 June 1996.

De Alcantra, Cynthia Hewitt, "Uses and Abuses of the Concept of Governance", International Social Science Journal, No: 155, March 1998.

Gilbert, Tichard, Don Stevenson, Herert Girardet and Richard Stren, Making Cities Work: The Role of Local Authorities in the Urban Environment, Earthscan, 1996.

Godard, Olivier, "La ville durable : une tentative de réponse", Ville et Environnement : de l'Ecologie urbaine à la ville durable, par Véronique Barnier et Carole Tucoulet, La Documentation Française, No: 829, Paris, octobre 1999.

Hanf, Kenneth and Alf-Inge Jansen (ed.) Governance and Environment in Western Europe: Politics, Policy and Administration, Longman, Essex, 1998.

Höll, Otmar (ed.) Environmental Cooperation in Europe: The Political Dimension, Westview Press, Boulder, 1994.

Inoguchi, T, E.Newman and G. Poolette (eds.) Cities and the Environment: New Approaches for Eco-Societies, UN University Press, Tokyo, 1999.

Institut de la Méditerranée, "Meda: Etat des lieux de processus de Barcelone (1995-2000), Marseille, septembre 2000.

Lafferty, W.M. (ed.) Implementing LA 21 in Europe: Mew Initiatives for Sustainable Communities, European Commission and ProSus, Oslo, 1999.

Low, N. et al (eds.) Consuming Cities: The Urban Environment in the Global Economy after the Rio Declaration, Routledge, London, 2000.

Mavi Plan: Akdeniz Havzasinin Gelecegi (The Blue Plan. Futures for the Mediterranean Basin), edited by Michel Grenon and Michel Batisse. Ankara, Turkish Ministry of Environment, 1993.

Mediterranean Commission on Sustainable Development. Working group on urban management. Cities and sustainable development in the Mediterranean. Working paper prepared by the Blue Plan, July 2000.

Mediterranean Commission on Sustainable Development. Working group on urban management. Report on the National Questionnaire and Report on the Questionnaire for City Authorities, prepared by PAP/RAC, Sophia Antipolis, 2001.

Mega, Voula, "Background Paper: The European Urban Environment Agenda and the Intermediate Cities", in European Foundation Intermediate Cities in Search of Sustainability, 1996.

OECD, Development Assistance Committee, The Urban Environment and Development Cooperation: A Resource Book, Development Cooperation Directorate, Working Party on Development Cooperation and Environment, 21st Meeting, Paris 13-14 June 2000.

Osmont, Annik, La Banque Mondiale et les Villes, (ed.) Karthala, Paris, 1995.

Owens, Susan, "Interpreting Sustainable Development: The Case of Land Use Planning", in Michael Jacobs (Ed.) Greening the Millenium? The New Politics of the Environment, The Political Quarterly, Blackwell, London, 1997.

Özturk, Bayram (ed.) The Aegean Sea 2000, Proceedings of the International Symposium on the Aegean Sea. Bodrum, Turkey, 5-7 May 2000.

Parlement européen, Direction Générale des Etudes, Document de Travail, Série Politique Régionale, W-19, La Cooperation Transfrontalière et l'Intégration européenne, Luxemburg, 1996.

Pathak, R.S., "The Human Rights System as a Conceptual Framework for Environmental Law", in Edith Brown Weiss (ed.) Environmental Change and International Law, The UN University Press, Tokyo, 1992, pp. 205-243.

Payne, Anthony and Peter Löffler, "The Aalborg Charter: Cities and Towns on the Towards Sustainability", Naturopa, No: 89, 1999.

Petrella, Ricardo, "Is it Possible to Promote Intermediate Cities, Sustainability within the Present Context of Triumphant Global Market Competitive Capitalism?", Intermediate Cities in Search of Sustainability, European Foundation for the Improvement of Living and Working Conditions, The Research and the Attica Workshop, Lavrion, 4-6 October 1995, Luxembourg, 1996, pp.8-13.

Ravinet, Jaime, "Local Authorities: Crucial Partners in the Implementation of the Habitat Agenda", Habitat Debate, Vol.3, No: 1. March 1997, pp.19.

Rico, Charles, Les Régions Frontalières et l'Intégration Européenne, Livre Blanc de l'Assemblée des Régions d'Europe, Centre d'Observation Européen des Régions et Diputacion General de Aragon, Saragosse, 1992.

Tuts, Raf and Eleanor Cody, "Habitat's Experience in Local Agenda 21 Worldwide over the Last Ten Years: Approaches and Lessons Learned", Industry and Environment (Urban Environmental Management), Vol.23, No: 1-2, January-June 2000.

UN Economic Commission of Europe, Guidelines on Sustainable Human Settlements Planning and Management, New York, 1996.

UNCHS, The Istanbul Declaration and the Habitat Agenda, Nairobi - 1998.

UNEP, Handbook of Environmental Law, Nairobi - 1992.

UNEP, Mediterranean Action Plan and Convention for the Protection of the Marine Environment and the Coastal Regions of the Mediterranean and its Protocols, (Informal document, revised), Athens, 1997.

UNEP, The Mediterranean Action Plan (MAP), Athens, 2000.

Van Deveer, Stacey and Geoffrey D. Dabelko (eds.) Protecting Regional Seas: Developing Capacity and Fostering Environmental Cooperation in Europe, Conference Proceedings: Saving the Seas: Developing Capacity and fostering Environmental Cooperation in Europe. The Woodrow Wilson International centre for Scholars, Washington DC, 14 May 1999.

Weiss, Edith Brown (ed.) Environmental Change and International Law, The UN University Press, Tokyo, 1992.

The World Resources Institute, World Resources: A Guide to Global Environment, Habitat II, Istanbul, a Special Reprint from World Resources, 1996-1997.

The World Commission on Environment and Development, Our
    Common Future, Oxford University Press, Oxford, 1987.

The World Bank, World Development Report, 1996, From Plan to
    Market, Washington D.C., 1996.

The World Bank, World Development Report, 1999-2000, Entering
    the 21st Century.

The Principle of Subsidiarity in Service of Sustainable Development*

Introduction

The Mediterranean region as a whole is being rapidly urbanised, and the amount and the quality of the soil and water resources are greatly influenced by the rapid increase of urban populations, industrial development and the influx of population into tourist centres along coastal regions. Therefore, it can be assumed that the market solutions alone may not be effective for better protection of natural resources, and some sort of regulatory action by local public authorities and the NGO's be utilised at the same time. Public-private partnership in handling issues of resource conservation and an increasing role by local authorities seems to be essential.

Strengthening local authorities to enable them to cope with the environment and natural resources would not only ensure discouragement of wasteful exploitation of resources but also would stimulate democratic public participation and consultation. In order to enable local authorities to play an increasing role, constant efforts are being made by major European institutions, like the European Union and the Council of Europe. The United Nations Organisation, in

* D. Camarda, L. Grassini (eds.), Local Resources and Global Trades: Environments and Agriculture in the Mediterranean Region, Bari, CIHEAM, Options Méditerranéennes, No:57, 2003, pp.109-115.

its turn, through its specialised agencies and international conferences, supports the efforts to make both the principles of subsidiarity and sustainable development to prevail in the relationships between the administrative levels closest to the citizens and the higher administrative echelons.

The principle of subsidiarity, for example, is one of the most frequently pronounced concepts within this context. Since 7 out of 11 countries that co-operate within the present research project are members of the European Union, and 9 out of 11, members of the Council of Europe, this principle that concerns more than one set of linkages, namely those between local and central governments, those between the members of a federation and the federation itself, and between national and international regulatory agencies, gain particular significance.

Thinking on the Concepts
Sustainable Development

The idea suggesting that the concern to meet the current needs of urban populations should not acquire an extent and nature to constitute a threat to the sustainability of resources and development.[1] Therefore, priority actions have to be centred on reducing all kinds of wastes on the global environment. Such initiatives may include reducing fossil fuel consumption through energy conservation, more efficient transportation systems, and reducing the amount of waste through pollution prevention.[2] There is no doubt that

1   World Commission on Environment and Development, *Our Common Future*, Oxford University Press, 1987, p.6.
2   The World Resources Institute et al., *The Urban Environment*, World Resources. A Guide to the Global Environment, Document II, June 1996. A special report from World Resources Inc., 1996-1997, p.14.

these longer term ecological concerns are relevant to both urban and rural areas. However, cities in the way of rapid development will face enormous increases in resource consumption and generation of wastes as they grow and prosper unless action is taken now to promote the efficient use of resources and the minimisation of wastes.

Sustainability can be regarded as the successor of the earlier demand for quality of life. It is generally accepted that sustainable development should not be left to market forces but must be a responsibility of the state. Another principle of sustainable development requires that all public policies to be harmonised and prohibits any degradation of natural, cultural and social capital. Respect for the carrying capacity of both man-made systems and ecosystems, restoration of disturbed ecosystems, the protection of bio-diversity, restrained development in fragile ecosystems, qualitative development and the satisfaction of man's aesthetic needs and a sound system of values and environmental awareness in people are other elements of a viable concept of sustainable development.[3]

As stressed in the European Union's report to the UN Habitat II Conference, sustainable development is identified as a much broader concept than environmental protection. It has economic, social and cultural as well as environmental dimensions and embraces notions of equity between the people in the present, and between generations. It implies that further development should only take place as long as it is within the carrying capacity of natural and man-made

---

3   Michael Decleris, *The Law of Sustainable Development: General Principles*, Environment Directorate-General, European Union, Luxembourg, 2000, p.19.

systems.[4] It is assumed that sustainable development can be realised only when master planning, in the urban context, is directed to minimise total needs, to promote public transportation instead of private one, to conserve fertile agricultural land, to avoid wasting other sensitive ecological resources, and to enhance energy saving in building design and layouts. This would require carrying out sustainability in city planning processes, vertical and horizontal co-ordination among public authorities and private institutions involved in regional resource management and development of renewable resource strategies. In other words, sustainable urban development may be understood as the maximisation of the efficiency in the use of resources, maintaining natural resource stocks at or above their present level, ensuring social equity in the distribution of development costs and benefits and the avoidance of unnecessary foreclosure of future development options.

According to a definition of the Economic Commission of Europe (ECE) of the United Nations, the ideal sustainable community is characterised by such factors as environmental integrity, economic vitality and social well-being.[5] Urban sprawl, congestion, increasingly poor air quality, and the shortage of land for affordable housing are some of the symptoms of unsustainable but not sustainable development. The Earth's non-renewable resources are being depleted, mountains of solid, liquid and toxic wastes pollute the air, water and soil, and threaten local and regional habitat. As these current trends persist, it becomes clearer

4   European Union, *Toward Sustainable Human Settlements,* UN Habitat II Conference, İstanbul, 3-14 June 1996, p.17.
5   Economic Commission for Europe, *Guidelines on Sustainable Human Settlements, Planning and Management,* Geneva, 1996, p.25.

that solutions to seemingly environmental, economic and social concerns are linked and require more holistic solutions. This is the reason why environmental, economic and social policies have to be integrated in order to ensure the compatibility of all these elements.

Two characteristics of urban areas give way to consequences that may be detrimental for sustainable development: First, inhabitants and enterprises depend on natural resources to live and on natural processes for breaking down or diluting their wastes. Second, urban areas can concentrate a large range of environmental hazards, such as biological pathogens in the air, water and soil, chemical pollutants and physical hazards.[6] Therefore, through an official planning process, it is necessary to provide a framework for guiding the spatial development of human settlements in such a way as to minimise the environmental costs. Implementation of such policies is a shared responsibility of different levels of government, particularly the local authorities, the business community and the local people, in an understanding of partnership approach.

Main policies targeted at ensuring at ensuring sustainable development may be summarised in the following categories[7]:

1. Conservation, protection and enhancing natural areas and life forms.

2. Promotion of compact community policies.

6   OECD, Development Assistance Committee, Working Party on Development Co-operation and Environment, 21st Meeting, Paris, June 2000, *The Urban Environment and Development Co-operation,* A Resource Book, Paris 2000.

7   ECE, *Guidelines,* op.cit. pp.26-27.

3. Encouragement of the utilisation of already built-up areas so as to limit urban sprawl.

4. Optimisation of density potential of existing urban areas.

5. Limitation of the use of the private car through the maximisation of the use of public transport alternatives, including commuter rail, buses, bicycles and walking.

6. Promotion of a sense of community, and creation of opportunities for social interaction.

7. Ensuring that environmental considerations and the precautionary principle become an integral part of the plans, programmes and projects.

8. Integration of the "net environmental gain" in assessing development.

9. Preservation of the coherence of the landscape.

10. Encouragement of the development of medium-sized cities as a network of complementary urban settlements to big cities, in order to develop a more balanced hierarchy of human settlements.

It is a surprising coincidence that the European Urban Charter (1992) encompasses, in each of its chapters dealing with urban rights, principles of sustainable urban development that originate from the main philosophy of sustainable urban development. The rights with connected with the transport and mobility, environment and nature in towns, the physical form of cities, urban architectural heritage, housing, urban security and crime prevention, disadvantaged and disabled persons in towns, sports and leisure in towns, citizen participation, urban management and urban planning, economic development of cities are all regulated there with due regard to the principle of sustainability.

Particularly, the role of local authorities in ensuring sustainable development is emphasised in the following terms: 1. Local authorities should adopt policies to prevent pollution. 2. Local authorities have a responsibility to protect nature and green spaces. 3. City centres must be safeguarded as important symbols of identity, and of the European culture and historical heritage. 4. The provision and management of open space in the city are integral parts of urban development. 5. It is essential that the volume of travel, particularly the private car, be reduced. 6. Multiculturlisme and non-discrimination are fundamental aspects of urban policies. 7. Citizen participation in political life must be safeguarded through the right to elect representatives, freely and democratically.

An institutional mechanism that was created in 1996 and called the Mediterranean Commission on Sustainable Development is acting since then as an advisory body to the Mediterranean Action Plan (MAP) on such issues as sustainable management of coastal zones, water demand management, sustainable development indicators, eco-tourism, information, awareness and public participation, free trade and environment, industry and sustainable development, and urban management.[8]

---

8   Nesrin Algan, "Common International Commitments of Turkey and Greece for the Protection of the Aegean Sea with Special Reference to the Mediterranean Action Plan", *The Aegean Sea 2000* ed.by Bayram Öztürk. Proceedings of the International Symposium on the Aegean Sea, 5-7 May 2000, Bodrum, pp.237-240.

Subsidiarity

Subsidiarity that is being used frequently in the European institutions means that decisions should be taken as closely as possible to the citizen. It has been introduced by the preamble of the Maastricht Treaty in 1992 in order to regulate the relationships between the European Union and the member states. Since Amsterdam, paragraph 2 of the Article A has read: "This Treaty marks a new stage in the process of creating an ever closer union among the peoples of Europe, in which decisions are taken are taken as openly as possible and as closely as possible to the citizen". According to the new Article 5 of the Maastricht Treaty, "In areas which do not fall within its exclusive competence, the Community shall take action in accordance with the principle of subsidiarity, only if and in so far as the objectives of the proposed action can not be sufficiently achieved by the member states and can therefore by reason of the scale or effects of those action be better achieved by the Community".

Subsidiarity is a principle of organisation in both social, economic, environmental and political fields. It means that where possible, decisions should be taken by the individual or the family, not by society at large; by the local community, not by the state; and by the member states of a federation, not by the federation itself; by the member states of the European Union, not by Brussels". It is argued that the subsidiarity principle can be found in three different sources: Firstly, it is said that it was developed by catholic social philosophy and in that sense the old philosophical idea of personal autonomy is behind this principle. It is transferred from this source into social and political organisation. Its second source is political and constitutional theory. According the latter, the principle of democracy requires decisions to be taken close to the citizen and with citizen participation. Thirdly, it is argued that decision-making on a smaller scale is more efficient than decision-making in larger units. As such, it has become an element of argumentation in controversies about centralisation versus decentralisation in political systems. As briefly mentioned above, it is used to defend local autonomy against state power, or member states of a federal state against the centre.[9]

Elsewhere, the basic sources of the principle of subsidiarity were shown as Althusius (liberty), American Confederalists (liberty), Economic Federalism (efficiency), Catholic Personalism (justice) and a liberal contractualist case for subsidiarity.[10]

The concept dates back to ancient history but its current meaning bears the traces of the Catholic social theory of the 19th and 20th centuries. It is highly debatable whether this principle also applies to the relationships between the European Union and the subdivisions of its member states.[11] It is also questionable whether this Maastricht principle can

9   Michael Bothe, "The Subsidiarity Principle", *in* Edward Dommen (ed.) *Fair Principles for Sustainable Development*, Edward Elgar, Aldershot, 1993, p.123.

10 Andreas Follesdal, "Subsidiarity and Democratic Deliberation", in Erik Oddvar Eriksen and John Erik Fosum (eds.) *Democracy in the European Union: Integration Through Deliberation*, Routledge, London, 2000, pp.88-90.

11 Heinrich A.Hoffschulte, "The Subsidiarity Principle: The Basis of Local and Regional Sel-Government in the European Unioné, International Conference on the Council of Europe Charters f Local and Regional self-Government: Subsidiarity in Action. Responsibilities and Finances of Local and Regional Authorities" Council of Europe, CLRAE, Ancona, Italy, 14-16 October 1999, p.4. Also: Scaefer's overview cited in the same source: Die deutsche kommunale Selbsverwaltung in der Europaeischen Union", p.285.

be used as a yardstick to apportion public responsibilities and financial resources between the central governments and their sub-national authorities. Because the principle of subsidiarity is a criterion for allocating tasks between the European Union and the Member states, not for deciding whether tasks should be assigned to a level below central government.[12] Opinions expressed elsewhere suggesting that the European Commission acknowledged that it regarded itself as bound by this principle also to respect local and regional authorities as parts of the member states both in its work and when presenting regulations and directives relating to local and regional authorities.[13]

In addition to the new Article 5 (formerly 3/b) of the Maastricht Treaty, European Union expressed openly its intention with regard to the discretionary competence of the member states in environmental matters on various occasions. It was generally accepted that environmental standards adopted by the EC were only the lowest common denominators and should thus not prevent Member states from taking more stringent measures to protect their environment. As a result, certain provisions to protect the Member states' interest in taking more severe and strict environmental measures have been inserted into the EC Treaty when it was amended in order to introduce environmental protection as a field of Community policy.

Article 100a (par.4) and Article 130r (par.1) contain different opportunities for more stringent national environmental protection rules. According to the latter, "Community

---

12   European Commission, *Regional and Local Government in the European Union: Responsibilities and Resources,* Luxembourg, 2001, p.23.

13   Ibid., p.5.

shall take action relating to the environment to the extent to which the objectives (in this field) can be attained better at Community level than at the level of the individual Member states...". Certainly, this apportionment of the competencies between the European Union and the Member states can be utilised in order to enable local and regional authorities to take the most appropriate measures to ensure sustainable development.

One of the basic premises on which the principle of local autonomy is based on the principle of subsidiarity that is implicit in the Preamble of the European Charter of Local Self-Government, which refers to " local authorities with real responsibilities as an administration both effective and *close to the citizen*, without using the word of subsidiarity. The principle of subsidiarity is explicitly mentioned in the Article 4 (paragraphs 2 and 3), but still without using the word of subsidiarity. In its form conceptualised by the European Charter of Local Self-Government, the principle of subsidiarity means that "Local authorities shall ...have full discretion to exercise their initiative with regard to any matter which is not excluded from their competence nor assigned to any other authority...Public responsibilities shall be exercised by those *authorities which are closest to the citizen.* Allocation of responsibility to another authority will be allowed only depending upon the extent and nature of the task and the requirements of efficiency and economy". This is an explicit preference of a decentralised pattern of decision-making to a centralised form of decision-taking and action.[14]

---

14 Rusen Keles, "European Standards for Local Democracy", Conference on the Institutional Dialogue between the State and Local Authorities, Baku,

Contributions of Subsidiarity to Sustainable Development

As mentioned by the Declaration of Ancona on Subsidiarity in Action: The Council of Europe Charters of Local and Regional Self-Government[15], the excessive accumulation of responsibilities due to the development of the welfare state and the centralisation of power required by government in order better to meet the demands of a complex and increasingly diversified society have gradually reduced the effectiveness of public action and created an impression of growing distance between the centralised public authorities and the citizen. Such a development can not be defended on the grounds of neither democracy, nor economy and efficiency. The principle of subsidiarity is a criterion which can guarantee both respect for democracy and the effective exercise of public powers.

Although numerous UN supported programmes existed to realise sustainable development, it was first at the end of the Habitat II Conference (1996) that the İstanbul Declaration adopted a strategy and principles of partnership and participation as the most democratic and effective approach for the realisation of the commitments made in the Conference. Participant nations have decided to promote decentralisation through democratic local authorities and to work to strengthen their financial and institutional capacities in accordance with the conditions of countries, while ensuring their transparency, accountability and responsiveness

Azerbaijan, 5-6 December 2001.

15 Council of Europe, CLRAE, International Conference on the Council of Europe Charters of Local and Regional Self-Government: Subsidiarity in Action, Ancona 16 October 1999, CONF/ANC (99) 5.

to the needs of people.[16] The paragraph 180 of the Habitat Agenda deals with decentralisation and strengthening of local authorities and their associations as a part of the section devoted to capacity building and institutional development. The Sustainable Cities Programme, the Local Agenda 21's, the Urban management Programme, the Mediterranean Platform of Association of Local Authorities are all making serious efforts to increase the capacity of local authorities. In addition to these and many other similar programmes, several multilateral conventions adopted at the European level offer vast opportunities for enabling local authorities to play a more efficient role in ensuring sustainable development. Below, in a short review of these instruments, an effort will be made to see what could be their likely contributions to the sustainability of natural resources and environmental values.

The European Charter of Local Self-Government

This document was adopted by the Council of Europe in 1985. It is nor signed by 39 members and ratified 34 states (Belgium, France and Switzerland are some of the non-ratifying states) out of the total 43 member states. The Charter sets out the fundamental principles of local autonomy. The basic philosophy of the Charter rests on the belief that the degree of local autonomy enjoyed by local authorities may be regarded as a yardstick for a genuine democracy. It aims to guarantee the political, administrative and financial independence of local authorities and it tends to commit the states that ratified the Charter to comply with its principles.

16   UNCHS, *The İstanbul Declaration and the Habitat Agenda,* UN Conference on Human Settlements (Habitat II), İstanbul, Turkey, 3-14 Ju1996, p.5-6.

Local self-government, according to the Charter, denotes the right and ability of local authorities to regulate and manage a substantial share of public affairs under their own responsibility and in the interests of local population. They have to exercise this right through the decision-making bodies freely elected. In addition to the existence of elected local councils, recourse to direct citizen participation, such as having assemblies of citizen, local referenda, etc., has to be open to citizen. The principle of subsidiarity is defined in the Charter in the following terms: "Local authorities shall have full discretion to exercise their initiative with regard to any matter which is not excluded from their competence nor assigned to any other authority. And, public responsibilities shall be exercised by those authorities, which are closest to the citizen. Allocation of responsibility to another authority will be allowed only depending upon the extent and the nature of the task and the requirements of the efficiency and economy." Almost the same principle is enshrined, as noted above, in the Article 5 of the Maastricht Treaty.

The central control and supervision of local authorities is limited to the control of compliance with the law and with constitutional principles (legality control). A state supervision with regard to expediency is not allowed in principle. In order to be regarded as genuinely autonomous public entities, local authorities have to be provided with financial resources, which are commensurate with their responsibilities. The provision s of the Charter concerning their financial resources, equalisation procedures and safeguards for their political independence all tend to strengthen local authorities in such a way to carry out their functions in an appropriate way.

Consultation is another element of local autonomy which requires that local authorities be consulted in due time and in an appropriate way, in the planning and decision-making processes for all matters which concern them directly. A final component of the concept of local autonomy, which is considerably important from the point of international co-operation for sustainable development, is the provision entitling local authorities to form consortia and to have the right to belong to a national or international association for the protection and promotion of their common interests.

The Aalborg Charter

The Aalborg Charter is the second international document according to which nations can co-operate for the protection of the environment. The First European Conference on Sustainable Cities and Towns gave birth in 1994 to one of the most important documents on sustainable development at local level. Nearly five-hundred representatives of local authorities coming from 35 European countries and representing more than 100 million European citizens had signed up the Charter. The Charter maintains that city or town is both the largest unit capable of addressing the many urban architectural, social, economic, political, natural resource and environmental imbalances damaging our modern world and the smallest scale at which problems can be meaningfully resolved in an integrated, holistic and sustainable fashion. Therefore, it suggested that the principles of sustainability be integrated into all policies

Thematic issues dealt with in the individual sections of the Aalborg Charter cover a wide range of spectrum from urban economy and social equity to land use patterns, urban mobility, responsibility for the global climate, prevention of ecosystems toxification and local self-governance. The Charter gives a clear message that economic development, social welfare and protection of the environment cannot be achieved separately from each other.[17] Perceiving citizens as key actors and the involvement of the community in ensuring sustainability in addition to political, technical, administrative and economic tools and instruments for urban management towards sustainability characterise the basic philosophy of the Aalborg Charter.

The Aarhus Convention

The Aarhus Convention is an important international legal instrument adopted by the UN Economic Commission for Europe that is relevant to international co-operation for sustainable development in the Mediterranean Region. The Convention that was adopted in 1998 is called the Convention on the Access to Information, Public Participation in Decision-Making and Access to Justice in Environmental Matters. Parties to the Aarhus Convention engage themselves in taking proper enforcement measures, is establishing and maintaining a clear, transparent and consistent framework to implement the provisions of the Convention. They have to ensure that officials and authorities provide guidance to the public in the implementation of its principles. An appropriate recognition of, and support to associations,

---

17   Anthony Payne and Peter Löffler, "The Aalborg Charter. Cities and Towns on the Move Towards Sustainability", *Naturopa*, No:89, 1999, p.4.

organisations or groups promoting environmental protection have to be ensured by the signatory states. The Convention suggests (Art.7) that the States parties to it make appropriate practical provisions for the public to participate during the preparations of plans and programmes relating to the environment, within a transparent and fair framework.

It is beyond any doubt that a proper implementation of the Aarhus Convention would provide a unique opportunity to all concerned with the environmental protection to contribute to the realisation of sustainable development. Therefore, Mediterranean countries have to be encouraged to ratify this Convention in order to make it sure that Mediterranean citizens enjoy the right to live in an environment adequate for his or for her health and well-being appropriately.

Trans-frontier Co-operation

Local authorities in Europe are also encouraged by another Convention adopted by the Council of Europe to establish Trans-boundary relationships in economic, social, cultural, environmental matters (Madrid, 21 May 1980). This is the European Outline Convention on Trans-frontier Co-operation Between Territorial Communities and Authorities.[18] The Outline Convention has been strengthened by two subsequent protocols in 1995 and 1998, respectively.[19] The matters to be dealt with within the framework of Trans-boundary co-operation are urban and regional development, energy, nature and water conservation, protection of the atmosphere, mutual assistance in disaster relief

18   Council of Europe: European Treaties Series: 106, Strasbourg, 1999.
19   Council of Europe: European Treaties Series: 159 and 169, Strasbourg, 1999.

and the like. There is ample room for European territorial communities or authorities to enhance their co-operation for sustainable development by ensuring flexibility in administrative procedures, to lift the legal objections before fruitful co-operation and to equip territorial communities or authorities with necessary financial and other means.

Similar experiences among the member states of the European Union are encouraged and supported during the last several decades. A great number of projects of co-operation under various titles are now co-financed by the European Union and other international institutions.[20] Among numerous EU initiatives, the LIFE Third Countries programme specifically encourages the implementation of environmental policies and activities in non-member countries.

Concluding Remarks

The principle of sustainable development means that in urban settlements, not only the way in which live, but also the settlements themselves and the Eco-systems that support them must be sustainable. In order to achieve sustainability in the Mediterranean Region and to meet the needs of rapid urbanisation and of increased building activities in coastal regions, international co-operation in technical and financial fields. Use of international legal instruments of which some have been briefly reviewed above may considerably contribute to the achievement of the goals. However, with respect to the institutional context for urban co-operation, the capacity and orientations of urban governments have to be changed. The major weaknesses of local

---

20   Parlament Européen: Direction Générale des Etudes, Document de Travail, Série Politique Rérionale, W-1996.

governments consist of the lack of financial resources, inadequacy of powers and professional staff to mobilise necessary funding. The capacity of local governments to invest in basic infrastructure without funding from higher levels of government is extremely limited. Particularly, the degree to which national governments allow development co-operation agencies to work directly with their territorial authorities needs to be improved without jeopardising the homogeneity of the operations. Local governments are not only responsible for urban policies and environmental management, but also they act as facilitators and enablers of action by all interests in society.[21]

How addressing sustainable development requires an integrated and multi-disciplinary approach, combining aspects of participatory land-use planning[22], pollution control, transport planning, environmental impact assessment, economic instruments, administrative reform and public education. In case land-use planning fails to achieve its objectives, it often pushes low-income households to the periphery and to land still poorly controlled by owners and regulators. This may result in untimely and unnecessarily conversion of agricultural land that can be detrimental for sustainable development. The overall objective is to ensure that critical environmental problems are resolved as a part of a long-term commitment to see that urban development contributes to the achievement of the goals of sustainable development.

---

21 Jaime Ravinet, "Local Authorities: Crucial Partners in the Implementation of the Habitat Agenda", *Habitat Debate*, Vol.3, No:1, March 1997, p.19.

22 Susan Owens, "Interpreting Sustainable development: The Case of Land-Use Planning" in Michael Jacobs (ed.), *Greening the Millennium: The New Politics of the* Environment, Blackwell, Oxford, 1997, pp.87-97.

Bibliography

ALGAN, Nesrin, "Common International Commitments of Turkey and Greece for the Protection of the Aegean Sea with Special Reference to the Mediterranean Action Plan", *The Aegean Sea 2000* ed.by Bayram Öztürk. Proceedings of the International Symposium on the Aegean Sea, 5-7 May 2000, Bodrum.

BOTHE, Michael, "The Subsidiarity Principle", in Edward Dommen (ed.) *Fair Principles for Sustainable Development,* Edward Elgar, Aldershot, 1993.

Council of Europe, European Treaties Series: 106, Strasbourg, 1999.

Council of Europe, European Treaties Series: 159 and 169, Strasbourg, 1999.

Council of Europe, CLRAE, International Conference on the Council of Europe Charters of Local and Regional Self-Government: Subsidiarity in Action, Ancona 16 October 1999, CONF/ANC(99)5.

DECLERIS, Michael, *The Law of Sustainable Development: General Principles,* Environment Directorate-General, European Union, Luxembourg, 2000.

Development Co-operation and Environment, 21st Meeting, Paris, June 2000, *The Urban Environment and Development Cooperation,* A Resource Book, Paris 2000.

Economic Commission for Europe, *Guidelines on Sustainable Human Settlements, Planning and Management,* Geneva, 1996.

European Commission, *Regional and Local Government in the European Union: Responsibilities and Resources,* Luxembourg, 2001.,.

European Union, Toward *Sustainable Human Settlements,* UN Habitat II Conference, İstanbul, 3-14 June 1996.

FOLLESDAL, Andreas Follesdal, "Subsidiarity and Democratic Deliberation", in Erik Oddvar Eriksen and John Erik Fosum (eds.) *Democracy in the European Union: Integration Through Deliberation,* Routledge, London, 2000.

HOFFSCHULTE, Heinrich A.Hoffschulte, "The Subsidiarity Principle: The Basis of Local and Regional Self-Government in the

European Unioné, International Conference on the Council of Europe Charters f Local and Regional Self-Government: Subsidiarity in Action. Responsibilities and Finances of Local and Regional Authorities" Council of Europe, CLRAE, Ancona, Italy, 14-16 October 1999, p.4. Also: Scaefer's overview cited in the same source: Die deutsche kommunale Selbsverwaltung in der Europaeischen Union".

KELEŞ, Ruşen, "European Standards for Local Democracy", Conference on the Institutional Dialogue between the State and Local Authorities, Baku, Azerbaijan, 5-6 December 2001.

OECD, Development Assistance Committee, Working Party on The World Resources Institute et al., *The Urban Environment*, World Resources. A Guide to the Global Environment, Document II, June 1996. A special report from World Resources Inc., 1996-1997.

OWENS, Susan, "Interpreting Sustainable development: The Case of Land-Use Planning" in Michael Jacobs (ed.), *Greening the Millennium: The New Politics of the* Environment, Blackwell, Oxford, 1997.1.

Parlament Européen, Direction Générale des Etudes, Document de Travail, Série Politique Rérionale, W-1996.

PAYNE, Anthony and Peter Löffler, "The Aalborg Charter. Cities and Towns on the Move Towards Sustainability", *Naturopa*, No:89, 1999.

RAVINET, Jaime, "Local Authorities: Crucial Partners in the Implementation of the Habitat Agenda", *Habitat Debate*, Vol.3, No:1, March 1997.

UNCHS, *The İstanbul Declaration and the Habitat Agenda*, UN Conference on Human Settlements (Habitat II), İstanbul, Turkey, 3-14 Ju1996.

WCED, World Commission on Environment and Development, *Our Common Future*, Oxford University Press, 1987.